Women with Vision

Women with Vision

The Presentation Sisters of South Dakota, 1880–1985

Susan Carol Peterson
and
Courtney Ann Vaughn-Roberson

University of Illinois Press
Urbana and Chicago

*Publication of this work was supported in part by
a grant from the Andrew W. Mellon Foundation.*

This book is printed on acid-free paper.

Library of Congress Cataloging-in-Publication Data

Peterson, Susan Carol, 1946–
    Women with vision : the Presentation Sisters of South Dakota,
1880–1985 / Susan Carol Peterson and Courtney Ann Vaughn-Roberson.
        p.   cm.
    Bibliography: p.
    Includes index.
    ISBN 0-252-01493-6 (alk. paper)
    1. Sisters of the Presentation of the Blessed Virgin Mary—South
Dakota—History. 2. South Dakota—Church History. I. Vaughn
-Roberson, Courtney Ann, 1949– II. Title.
BX4511.Z6S656 1988   271'.977'0783—dc19   87-20451
                                                                    CIP

To Greg and Glen, for their humor, love, and patience.

Contents

Preface

Despite pejorative social and theological depictions of females as corruptible and evil, during the sixteenth century select women religious began emphasizing the positive, alternative view that women's biblical history and unique talents destined them for a vocational mission as teachers, nurses, and public servants. In 1776, Irish educator Nano Nagle continued the tradition, founding what later in 1805 became the Sisters of the Presentation of the Blessed Virgin Mary. Throughout the nineteenth century many of her spiritual scions located themselves in parts of the United States. Our historical study concerns the branch that immigrated to Dakota Territory in 1880 and now is rooted in South Dakota. Combining perspectives from women's studies and professionalization literature, we contend that the ideological inspiration from Mary, Mother of Christ, and from foundress Nagle have been the linchpins of the sisters' historical drive to professionalize. Despite intermittent conflicts, such inspiration sustained their spiritual and teaching community during the late nineteenth century, and by the early 1900s it spurred the nuns to begin striving for ever higher levels of academic preparation, to make important apostolic decisions, to maintain a strong service ideal, and to practice a distinct code of ethics related primarily to education and health care, an apostolate that the Presentations added in 1901. In so doing, the sisters became part of a national drive in both the secular and religious worlds to professionalize the occupations of which they were a part.

Attempting never to lose sight of their ideals, during the 1960s and 70s the nuns experienced a reawakening of their almost two-hundred-year-old professional ideology, as they struggled to deinstitutionalize their congregational structure. Although South Dakota Presentations, women religious throughout the world, and other traditionally motivated female professionals have been successful, their future is tenuous. In many respects it lies with their ability, as a sisterhood, to resolve recurrent ironies embedded within and conflicts arising over their ideological mission. Moreover, the sisters' fate will continue to be greatly affected by the Catholic Church and its willingness to support their ever-evolving ideology, which once proclaimed their separate but unequal, but now proclaims their separate but equal, mandate to serve.

Most of the primary sources from which we build our narrative derive from the South Dakota Oral History Center in Vermillion, the Archives of the Diocese of Sioux Falls, and the Presentation Archives in Aberdeen, South Dakota. Our project would not have been possible if the sisters had not possessed a keen interest in preserving their past and a willingness to allow outsiders to look at their files. Special thanks go to Sister Helen Freimuth and Sister Alicia Dunphy; to Herbert Hoover and Bruce Milne of the University of South Dakota; and to Joseph Stout of Oklahoma State University for their encouragement and confidence. We also owe our gratitude to Lois Broady, Robert Lamm, Carol Taylor, Greta Mohon, Liz Smith, Shirley Hodges, Patti Kroenke, Sylvia Starr, Renée Heath, Lola Aagaard, Mary Oldham, Tammy Higdon, Brenda Stevens Hill, and Robbie Hackler. Valuable monetary assistance also derived from the University of North Dakota Faculty Research Committee, the University of North Dakota Women's Equity Committee, the South Dakota Committee on the Humanities, the University of Oklahoma Research Council, and the Associate Distinguished Lectureship Fund at the University of Oklahoma.

1. Professionalization: Revised and Revisited

□

Late in the nineteenth century, as the frontier period in American history faded into the industrial age, historian Frederick Jackson Turner lamented the waning of free open land, which in his mind had been the source of American democracy. Since Turner's era many historians and sociologists have observed that professions and their collective associations have replaced nineteenth-century communities and land ownership as many peoples' source of personal identity. In an attempt to identify and understand these powerful new occupational groups, twentieth-century sociologists have established distinguishing professional criteria to measure professionalism. Generally, the now traditional taxonomy that emerged states that a given career field must claim a distinct body of academic knowledge obtained only through a number of years in higher education, have a dedication to self-policing, be collegial, maintain an ethical code, hold a service orientation, and wield the power to make autonomous professional decisions.[1]

During the past twenty to thirty years, interpretivist or revisionist scholars have attempted to push the study of professions beyond the original approach and toward an alternative paradigm. Synthesizing and commending a number of these works, sociologist Douglas Klegon claims that professional recognition has not simply been a product of scoring high in one or all of the traditional categories, which in themselves may be meaningless. Instead, Klegon maintains that the real key to gaining this coveted status lies in the dynamics within any group and in its members' ability to identify external support for their goals. Although the subjects of our professionalization study, the South Dakota Sisters of the Presentation of the Blessed Virgin Mary, generally have strived for goals that resemble the ones numerated in the classic professional taxonomy,

1

Klegon's paradigm still provides an excellent framework within which to recount and analyze the nuns' occupational history; for through his frame of reference we can document and understand the history of the Presentations' emergent professional community in the nineteenth century and evaluate their efforts to professionalize during the decades that followed.[2]

The Presentation Sisters have taken their name from a feast celebrating the legendary consecration of the Virgin Mary, as a child, to the will of God. As they have inherited the role of Mary to teach, nurse, and succor God's children through occupational extensions of woman's traditional domestic duties, the nuns have insured their order's solidarity and advanced various members' professional goals. As did many other nuns, before 1968 each South Dakota Presentation took "Mary" as part of her personal religious name. Along with other nuns throughout the nation, over the years the South Dakota holy women pursued academic degrees, earnestly involved themselves with state and national professional associations, strived for autonomy in many religious and professional matters, and maintained high ethical standards, always an outgrowth of their ideological focus.[3]

Thus, while during the nineteenth century lawyers and other predominantly male occupational groups began forming associations, solidifying members, and identifying or mobilizing social support systems for their work, nuns and Protestant women did the same thing. Spurred on by their own woman-centered religious mission, the Presentations and other apostolic nuns found the courage to stay together and identify secular and religious approval: outwardly acquiescing to some Church edicts and societal prejudices but all the while quietly molding their neighbors' attitudes toward them and forcing changes in the official papal doctrine that governed them. Commenting on the kind of commitment that characterized the international Presentation order, Australian Sister M. Raphael Consedine observed in 1983 that during more than two hundred years of Presentation history, "When the . . . inconveniences and difficulties and sheer hard work of the schools weighed heavily, there was strength to be drawn from the companionship of like-minded women, from the ideals of sacrifice for the cause of Christ and of response to the needs of the Church. There was a sense of being part of a struggle for justice in which [education] had a major role."[4]

For the South Dakota Presentations and other more contemporary religious communities, the longevity of this dedication stems from its deep historical roots. After the death of Christ, early Christian sisterhoods planted the ideological seeds for what would lie dormant but ultimately would grow into an apostolic and, by the twentieth century, a professional commitment. Scholar Jo Ann McNamara explains that the first women who formed Christian cloisters exhibited a thirst for independence and personal expression beyond the homemaker role. During the centuries that followed in the Western world, the convent provided a refuge for many well-to-do women who left husbands or refused marriage, seeking instead a more spiritual or even intellectual life. Often nuns were versed in Latin and Greek; they reproduced beautifully written manuscripts and were poets, playwrights, and musicians. Extending beyond these personal accomplishments, some nuns put their own knowledge to work educating girls, primarily from affluent families, while others uplifted the poor and nursed the infirm.[5]

Although all of this activity may have had feminist implications, it was intended to glorify God through the cultivation of particularly female traits such as kindness, generosity, or selflessness, which were acquired in spite of women's alleged corrupt and inferior nature. During the tenth century, the nun Hrothsvith from Gandersheim, a Saxon convent, studied classical literature but only to master the technique for writing plays that embodied "the moral ideals of Christian teaching."[6] Moreover, although twelfth-century German nuns St. Hildegard of Bingin and St. Elisabeth of Schnau claimed to have the power of prophecy and subsequently wielded a great deal of influence over Church clerics and popes, they never claimed personal accomplishment. As Hildegard wrote, "I kept [my gift] hidden by silence until God and His grace willed to have it made manifest."[7] Similarly Mechthild, a thirteenth-century mystic residing in Helfta, another Saxon convent, also stated that her ability came solely from God. Assessing religious women's abilities in light of such self-effacement, scholars have produced contradictory analyses that either view religious ideology as a precedent for more contemporary female accomplishments or as one of the seeds of female oppression throughout much of the history of Western civilization. Regardless of who may be right, by the eleventh century the convents were used to sequester young women against their wills, and eventually the level of spirituality and learning began to decline in many of them.[8] Scholar Eileen Power writes, "in the course of its history monasticism produced many learned nuns, and from time to time certain convents acquired fame for their scholarship. But in England in the later Middle Ages the standard of education was low and learning was on the wane." Power continues that by the fourteenth century, bishops were writing nuns in French because so many of the women could not understand Latin, and during the following century still fewer nuns attained mastery of French. Such illiteracy produced "nuns and abbesses [who] could not read their own foundation charters," Power notes. Thus, increasingly nuns seemed to take the cloistered life less seriously, failing to attend prayers, retaining secular dress, and even holding dances.[9]

The prevailing social and Church attitudes toward women did not discriminate in favor of nuns or any other women with varying personal or religious philosophies. A body of misogynistic scientific and religious assumptions justified the need to guard all females closely. Reflecting the common perception of women's inferiority, physicians maintained that the female contributed nothing but incubation to the life of the unborn, a total product of the male sperm, and theologians proclaimed that women were weak and easily corrupted. If not married, they required the discipline of rigid religious indoctrination and the structurally regulated environment of what contemporary sociologists call a total institution. Thus, in 1298 Pope Boniface VIII imposed absolute enclosure on all religious, requiring that for official Church recognition they were to proclaim lifetime solemn (rather than dispensable simple) vows of poverty, chastity, and obedience and to focus their lives around praying, keeping silent as much as possible, and to living or working only within a restricted area. Although the pope reiterated that seclusion from the material world offered the best environment in which to seek a truly spiritual existence, the Church leader also attempted to position nuns within the direct hierarchical reach of male Church leaders and made sure that those women whose parents forced them into confinement would be unable to claim any of their family money.[10]

Despite papal rulings, the power of religious conviction was nurtured by communal living with like-minded females and often produced women who were willing to defy Church authority, believing that Mary's spiritual legacy destined them for an active, not

4

a reclusive, social role. Beguine sisterhoods had existed as early as the twelfth century and spread slowly throughout France, Belgium, Northern Germany, and Switzerland. They consisted of women who were willing to sacrifice official Church recognition and endure disapproval to spend much of their working lives outside the cloister performing acts of charity. Reformation and Counter-Reformation eras in Europe engendered similarly motivated communities in Italy. In 1537, Angela Merici founded the Ursuline order, an unenclosed association devoted to comforting the afflicted and educating the ignorant. After Merici died in 1540, the sisterhood spread to other countries, but congregations of various houses eventually accepted enclosure. For example, the Paris group made the transition in 1612. In accepting the necessary stipulation to obtain Church recognition, the women henceforth lived exclusively behind cloister walls, though they continued to educate pupils within the various Ursuline compounds.[11]

Other communities of Catholic women pursued an apostolic life, shunning confinement. Early in the 1630s, a French churchman, Vincent de Paul, assisted by Louise de Marillac le Gras, established the Daughters of Charity, a nursing sisterhood that avoided seclusion and sent participants everywhere they were needed. Thus for some Catholic women, the call to serve was greater than the desire to be fully recognized nuns. That heartfelt sentiment unified their efforts and, in the wake of Reformation spirit, won initial Church toleration and eventually found such high praise from officials that Merici and de Paul were declared saints.[12]

Even so, the Vatican's approval of unenclosed groups evolved slowly, and the Church tolerated brothers more readily than it did nuns. The Council of Trent (1545–63) restated cloistral regulations, and in 1566 Pope Pius V issued a bull *Circa Pastoralis* that reiterated the necessity for solemn vows and enclosure to obtain formal Church recognition. However, in 1749, after some policy vacillations, in *Quamvis Justo* Pope Benedict XIV offered tacit acceptance of, although no complete approval for, congregations or single religious communities unwilling to meet the criteria for full status. As a result, such groups usually labored not under the direct jurisdiction of the Holy Father in Rome, but under priests or local bishops who may or may not have sympathized with nuns' efforts to improve their credentials as teachers or nurses.[13]

Although apostolic sisters held questionable status for some time, by the eighteenth century they had written their stories into Catholic Church history, and their examples were available to other young women, such as Ireland's Nano Nagle, who would do the same. Educated in France, during the 1740s she soon began teaching Catholic children who were suffering from poverty and British persecution. In so doing, she founded, in 1776, what would become the Presentation Sisters. Resembling Merici or le Gras, she believed that one walked the path toward salvation through good works such as teaching, ministering, praying, and self-sacrificing. Thus Nagle avoided a cloistered existence that would have prevented her from visiting the indigent and allowed her to educate only those children who came to her. In 1784, the educator died. Following the pattern of the other well-known apostolic communities, her spiritual progeny continued their educational work but longed for official Church approval. Lacking the founder's intense spiritual commitment, the Presentations were better able to sustain each woman's personal drive, the order's internal cohesion, and its external support by seeking the pope's fullest blessing.[14]

Even before Nagle died, however, the social frontiers of the Americas and other colonial lands were requiring changes of other religious communities. Although many of the nun-immigrants were part of enclosed orders, the adaptations they would make eventually forced alterations in official papal policy. Even on the local level, recalcitrant Church officials were often moved to accept American-based sisters' dealings with the secular world because some of these New World nuns wielded tremendous social power and influence. Scholar Asunción Lavrin writes that women religious in seventeenth- and eighteenth-century colonial Mexico owned real estate and extended business loans, making "them as important as some of the most powerful . . . masculine orders, and an element of great economic significance in the life of the colonial city."[15] In 1727, the Ursulines located a convent and school in New Orleans, thereby becoming the first nuns to settle in a region that would later become part of the United States. By 1900, forty thousand nuns were part of this country's Catholic Church. Most of these communities were apostolic because they originated to provide education, health, and child care, or spiritual guidance for thousands of Catholic immigrants.[16]

Generally, the nineteenth-century nuns were European immigrants, and historian Mary Ewens explains that their adjustments to a New World life-style were often very stressful. Many sisters set aside the enclosure rule, went on begging tours, made habit alterations, and rescheduled or shortened the prayers such as matins and lauds (from the Latin breviary, a collection of psalms, hymns, and prayers typically offered at specific times during each day), all to survive and better serve their clients' needs. Susan Peterson's study on the Sisters of St. Francis mission teachers in South Dakota from 1885 to 1910 strengthens Ewens's conclusion. Peterson explains how taking simple vows and avoiding enclosure gave her subjects the freedom and mobility to form close associations with Indian families, thereby becoming successful teachers of Indian children. Similarly, in a study of the Order of St. Benedict in Minnesota and North Dakota, Sister Grace McDonald illustrates how pioneer conditions forced modifications of the Old World Benedictine convent. After reaching Minnesota in 1857, the New World women eventually gave up severe corporal penances, an inflexible schedule of prayers, and their traditional habit. As teachers, nurses, and hospital directors, they disagreed with male authority figures when necessary, worked with secular officials, and even taught adult males who attended one of their schools. Sister Mary Veronica McEntee's book on the Sisters of Mercy in Harrisburg indicates that McEntee responded to parishoners' needs and taught working boys who attended a night school conducted especially for them in Danville, Pennsylvania; while S. M. Johnston's work on the Ursulines in Galveston explains that the women tabled their enclosure restriction in order to teach in neighboring parochial schools.[17]

Biographical studies of other nuns record additional examples of determined apostolic efforts. In 1897, Sister Julia McGroarty founded Trinity College in Washington, D.C., to offer a higher-education alternative to Catholic women who, because of their gender, were continually denied admittance to the District's Catholic University of America (established in 1889).[18] Mother Mary Aloysia Hardey, who after 1847 headquartered in Manhattanville, New York, was another educational leader. A member of the Society of the Sacred Heart, she founded several teaching convents before and after the Civil War. In describing the source of Mother Hardey's capability to unify and motivate a congregation of sisters, her biographer concludes that an "inner humility . . . [derived from the matriarch's] own constant spiritual striving, [and] the insight quick to sense a troubled spirit, whether of pupil, novice, or parish neighbor, inspired a common effort for excellence."[19]

Similar changes were occurring for Presentations throughout the United States and the world, but change did not come swiftly. During the 1840s, Presentations in Madras, India, attended daily Mass in a cathedral at a distance from their convent; however, Presentation attempts to establish mid-nineteenth-century missions in Ireland at Kenmare and Granard failed because at Kenmare the nuns could not schedule school hours to accommodate their rule, and at Granard they refused a pastor's request to visit parishioners' homes. Moreover, Irish Presentations, who in 1854 had first settled in the United States at San Francisco, received papal approval eleven years later to modify their enclosure rule, but they hesitated to drop the timeworn practice.[20] Although the superior, M. Teresa Comerford, "believed enclosure was a mistaken practice for Presentation Sisters, keeping them at a distance from the poor they sought to serve, she felt bound to support the accustomed ways," one Presentation historian explained.[21] A more progressive attitude prevailed among the Presentations who in 1880 immigrated to Dakota Territory. In 1882, the newcomers established motherhouses at Fargo, North Dakota, and in 1886 at Aberdeen, South Dakota. Although the South Dakota sisters had experienced tremendous physical and emotional strife, as with Nagle in Ireland the trials strengthened their ideological commitment, camaraderie, and determination. Reaching outside their community during the few years of the nineteenth century that they lived on the Great Plains, the nuns had identified pupils and families who welcomed their "civilizing" influence. Moreover, supported by Bishops Martin Marty and Thomas O'Gorman, they had abandoned enclosure to perform their educational work and beg for money. Both South Dakota and North Dakota Presentations, and many of their other American colleagues, became part of the mounting international pressure that eventually would win full papal approval for unenclosed sisterhoods in which members took simple vows.[22]

Ewens concludes that numerous American bishops were part of the modernizing force, encouraging nuns' professional activities throughout the nineteenth century. Setting the standard, John Carroll, the first bishop appointed in the United States, maintained that

Catholics must assimilate culturally and that nuns' apostolic efforts in education were essential to the process. Bishop Carroll worked closely with women such as Mother Elizabeth Seton, who in 1809 founded the first indigenous American Catholic teaching sisterhood, the Emmitsburg Sisters of Charity.[23]

Of Irish descent and a neighbor to the South Dakota Presentations, Bishop John Ireland also promoted the Americanization of Catholics through the professional activities of women religious. Sister Helen Angela Hurley writes that John Ireland, while serving as Bishop of St. Paul from 1875 to 1888 and then archbishop until his death in 1918, encouraged the apostolic goals of religious such as Mother Seraphine Ireland, his biological sister and provincial superior of the Sisters of St. Joseph, headquartered in St. Paul.[24] "In 1896, ten sisters and six lay women were graduated from [the nun's] St. Joseph's Hospital Training School." Moreover, many of the sister-teachers were taking correspondence courses or actually attending classes at the University of Minnesota during the late nineteenth century. Bishop Ireland articulated the spirit with this enjoinder: "In your [own] institutions, let there be no routine, no deadening conservatism."[25] Living his principles, the churchman encouraged the order to found a college for women, St. Catherine's, which opened in 1911. Although the archbishop's judgment was couched in nineteenth-century perceptions of women's sphere, his vision was progressive. He once intoned: "I am a firm believer in the higher education of women: I covet for the daughters of the people, for so many of them, at least, as circumstances and position permit to aspire so high, the opportunities of receiving under the protecting hand of religion the fullest intellectual equipment of which woman is capable."[26]

A testament to other churchmen's outreaching sentiments, in 1864 the Congregation of Bishops and Regulars decreed that although five American Visitandine convents could take solemn vows, all other sisters in America must take simple ones. Moreover, the Third Plenary Council of the United States met in 1884, concluding that the quality and number of Catholic schools should be improved and that all nun-educators should receive some specialized training for their work.[27] A key figure at that conference, Bishop John Lancaster Spalding, supported what became known as "Americanism," maintaining, in one biographer's words, "that the church should, with dignity rather than in a combative spirit, enter into the living controversies of the age; should demonstrate that it was not opposed to culture and learning or the new developments in science; and that it should contribute to the literature and culture of the United States."[28] Also considering himself a realist, Ireland reached similar conclusions.

Despite these efforts, the training of nun-educators continued to reflect the varying levels of academic preparation among public school teachers and remained inconsistent among and even within orders; however, many nuns did strive to create good schools and become competent professionals. Some even worked in and with public school systems, helping to turn virulent anti-Catholicism into admiration of many religious. Considering the magnitude of the task, this feat was commendable. In St. Cloud, Minnesota, Benedictine Sisters convinced stubborn German-Catholic immigrants of the efficacy of Catholic-run schools, while the Sisters of St. Joseph in that same region dealt with German-versus-Irish squabbles over parochial school policy.[29]

Even though a relaxation in the traditional monastic life facilitated these successes, in 1869 Pope Pius IX issued *Apostolicae Sedes,* the last statement on enclosure before the codification of canon law in 1918. In a sense, many apostolic nuns were battling domination by international churchmen, who were involved in their own attempts to maintain authority within the Church and thereby present a professional image. *Apostolicae Sedes* "reaffirmed the regulations of Pope Boniface VIII and the Council of Trent regarding enclosure for those with solemn vows" and recalled that only the pope could give permission for cloistered sisters to receive pupils. Moreover, "in 1889 Rome added the requirements of living in common and wearing a habit to the conditions which had to be met before a group could obtain official recognition as a religious community."[30] Attempting to prevent the inevitable liberalization of these timeworn expectations, ten years later the pope condemned Americanism, which in his mind alleged "that vows taken by members of religious orders narrow the limits of human liberty and interfere with Christian perfection and the good of human society...."[31]

Thus the battle for modernization was hard fought, and some foreign-born and American nuns would not sacrifice the spiritual and practical security offered by the ultimate papal blessing. As one nun put it, she did not enter religious life just to "risk losing her soul."[32] In 1845, even the Emmitsburg Sisters of Charity sought affiliation with the pontifically approved French Daughters of Charity. As in the case of the Irish Presentations, the death of the Emmitsburg Sister of Charity founder Mother Seton seemed to drain the group of its distinctive fervor, in Klegon's assessment so necessary to solidarity.[33] Complying with the pope's ultimatum seemed to be the best way of reviving the community. As one Sister of Charity superior later explained, "We can never be sufficiently grateful for this favor." It is ultimately gratifying "to know that we are under the direct protection of Christ's Vicar on earth, and that our Constitution was approved by our dear Holy Father."[34] Yet once that act of union was consummated, the Emmitsburg Sisters' new charter forbade them from caring for infant boys. In so stating it reflected a belief held by numerous theologians that the purest religious woman completely disassociate herself with anyone or anything that could accentuate the Eve in her—her corruptible side. Although Mother Seton had been a widow with five children, two of whom had been boys, and although by the mid-nineteenth century her community ran most of the Catholic orphanages in the United States, the nuns handed over these homes to Mercy Sisters, Josephites, and Christian Brothers.[35]

Vocational opportunities for nuns were tempered by other European traditions. Several histories of religious houses in the United States record the distinction between choir sisters and lay sisters. The former performed the more professional duties, whereas the latter often functioned as housekeepers.[36] Mother Mary Caroline Friess, a nineteenth-century superior of the School Sisters of Notre Dame in Milwaukee, Wisconsin, was one of several administrators who had to deal with conflict resulting from this practice. Emphasizing that each nun could not function without all the others, she once chided an arrogant choir sister, "in this convent we are all servants of the same rank."[37]

The South Dakota Presentations and other Presentations throughout the world operated under this dual-status system until the 1960s, when the sisters began selecting their own vocations and sharing the housework. At least for the South Dakota sisters, their commonly held belief until this time that they were all working to continue Mary's mission seemed to minimize the conflict that arose between the two occupational groups.[38]

Despite accommodations to Old World values, the overriding trend throughout the United States and other emergent countries was still toward adjustment to individualism and the demands of a rugged climate. In 1900 and 1901, the Church was finally moved to alter its policy toward apostolic religious. The pope then offered official sanction to orders of nuns with simple vows; however, he still required that sisterhoods maintain an enclosed area within the cloister and discouraged nuns from teaching older boys, taking maternity cases, and caring for babies.[39] Evidence of such restrictions in the international Presentation Order surfaced in 1928. Although the South Indian Congregation's Constitutions called for nurses' training, the cardinal protector who was assigned to the sisters refused to allow them to work the maternity ward. When Mother M. Xavier Murphy petitioned to change the ruling, the churchman tore up the petition. It was not until 1936 that the Indian Presentations were authorized to train in midwifery.[40] Thus professionally bound women religious entered the twentieth century with both gain and concessions.

Although often from an unsympathetic distance, Protestant women had been and would be a part of these nuns' professional struggle. Like that of the Catholic sisters, Protestant-American heritage extended from the colonial period when self-assured Quaker and Puritan women used biblical passages to warrant their spiritual equality with men and their worth to society as nurturers. Their argument eventually evolved into the contention that, at least morally, women were men's equals or even superiors. Thus, as the apostolic nun found the strength from her ideology and from her earthly community to redefine tradition, so too did many Protestant women. One Puritan minister explained that by being confined for centuries in the home, away from the corruption of the world and in contact primarily with other homemakers, women had developed high ethical standards.[41]

Philosophically, then, the groundwork had been done. An ideology of separate gender spheres clearly maintained that women's distinctively different biological history had determined their appropriate roles in the family and in the remainder of the world. Thus during the American Revolutionary era male and female patriots contended that women should be formally educated for their roles as mothers. After all, as women they would be in charge of preparing their children for citizenship. Ironically this belief in women's domestic-yet-social worth would soon thrust many of them outside the home. The era of the Second Great Awakening, roughly occurring from 1795 to 1830, witnessed women proselytizers; and throughout the late eighteenth and nineteenth centuries females founded and ran fledgling frontier communities or rebuilt war-torn towns and cities. To accomplish their goals of erecting moral institutions, many of these women defied male authority figures, although a reciprocal element of social support was always crucial to their success.[42]

According to author Ann Douglas, sentimentalist female writers such as Harriet Beecher Stowe and other proponents of women's special social and religious roles put their brand on American cultural thought and consequently dictated the content of ministers' sermons. In a more direct manner, male physicians relied on some of this same nurturing spirit of reform to help them alter public apathy toward abortion during the antebellum years into outrage by the late 1880s. Remarking on similar changes in nineteenth-century America, historian Robert Griswold maintains that, particularly in the West, women who promoted an ideology of separate spheres not only molded the social environment of which they were a part, but also determined the content of acceptable familial behavior for men and women.[43]

Although Protestant laywomen were in the forefront of American reform efforts, Protestant religious did arise in England and the United States.[44] During the mid-nineteenth century in England, Anglican contemplative and apostolic orders of women were formed. The Community of St. Mary, originated in 1865, was the first indigenous sisterhood in the American Episcopal Church. Members pledged to remain, "secluded as far as may be from the world, [but in so doing] . . . to draw our thoughts and efforts toward the care of the poor and the instruction of the young; and by united prayer, and mutual sympathy and counsel, to comfort and support one another in our holy and blessed work."[45] In 1888, several years before the national drive to professionalize gathered momentum, the devout Methodist Lucy Rider Meyer established the Methodist deaconesses, who also generated a philosophically grounded camaraderie that fostered professionalism within the typically female fields of nursing, teaching, and social work.[46]

Thus, a variety of nineteenth-century women gained a sense of purpose from an ideology of motherhood perpetuated by an atmosphere of sisterhood. Commenting on the differences between various forms of domestic ideology common to women working in the nurturing fields, Mary Agnes Dougherty argues that formally organized religious groups such as deaconesses and Protestant or Catholic religious stressed the "sisterhood" over the "world mother" ideal common among social workers such as Jane Addams or suffragists like Carrie Chapman Catt.[47] However, a motherhood model has always existed for several orders of nuns, as well as for laywomen. Widowed mothers chartered Catholic orders such as the Emmitsburg Sisters of Charity. A Swiss woman, Mother Maria Anna Brunner, founded the Sisters of the Congregation of the the Precious Blood in 1884, and it is precisely her motherly characteristics that her spiritual descendants praise and attempt to emulate. Even before establishing her society, Mother Brunner fed and clothed many needy children, her biographer writes. Bruner was "called 'Mother,' not only by her own devoted six, but by the people of the neighborhood."[48] Of course the more pervasive example of Mary as a role model to congregations such as the Presentations indicates that many nuns were motivated by an ideal to give aid and comfort as a mother would do. Moreover, studies of nurses, social workers, and teachers indicate that, like women religious, many Protestant women developed sisterhood relationships as they lived in settlement houses and teachers' lodgings ("teacherages"). At least until the early twentieth century, it seems that religious and secular women involved in traditional female fields embraced some type of motherhood philosophy. The esprit de corps generated within different types of sisterhoods simultaneously held these communities of societal mothers together. Describing the process, a pioneer Presentation nun from Mount St. Michael's Orphanage in New York wrote: "We were few and we worked hard, but we were all united in one big family."[49]

Presentations and other nuns throughout the country helped shape an American culture that provided them with the essential external support necessary for professionalization in the twentieth century. By 1900, nuns and other women who would have been apprentice trained a few years earlier were receiving specialized academic education in the feminized fields. Especially during the nation's Progressive Era, predominantly single women formed professional associations to work for nationally recognized professionalization goals. Sister McEntee records that Harrisburg Sisters of Mercy in Harrisburg, Pennsylvania, formed the Educational Association of the Sisters of Mercy in 1908. Sometimes nuns and other women belonged to the same organizations, which pushed their members to strive for academic training and in other ways to work toward the accepted standards of professionalism.[50]

Definitely a part of this momentum, Sisters of St. Joseph in Minnesota and Benedictine nuns in Wisconsin seemed to ignore papal foreboding concerning nuns' involvement in health care early in the twentieth century. In 1900, Sisters of Charity of Leavenworth, Kansas, established a training school at their St. Joseph's hospital in Denver; there they offered courses in obstetrical nursing. The South Dakota Presentations joined this health care movement when they assisted physicians in a diphtheria epidemic that broke out early in the twentieth century. As a result, many of them began nurses' training, and the order owned and operated four hospitals by 1911. This innovation opened a new professional field in hospital administration for those nuns who had the interest in and talent for leadership in the health care field.[51]

Another sign of changing times came in 1911 when Catholic University first opened its doors to women, and again in 1918, when, in order to meet state and regional certification requirements in education and health care fields, American nuns began full-scale attendance at colleges and universities all over the country. What had begun centuries earlier as women's separate and limited sphere had evolved into a vehicle for professionalization—although only for women's stereotypical work. As those career areas became more and more available to women, their opportunities in male-oriented fields such as medicine, higher education, and law became increasingly limited.[52]

Eventually, therefore, a number of post-World War II feminists resurrected a nineteenth-century call for religious and social equality leading to the interchange, not separation, of male and female roles. This plea caused many professional nuns and laywomen great consternation because it directly attacked their linchpin—a female-centered ideology. At the same time, secular women were losing the power to mobilize because of the growing acceptability of married women being employed as teachers. Thus, the spirit of sisterhood generated in settlement houses and teacherages where single women had lived and worked became part of the past.[53]

Because she was a woman far ahead of her time, nineteenth-century feminist Elizabeth Cady Stanton had laid the groundwork for the attack, particularly against a religious ideology of separate spheres. Traditionally reared, she believed in God but as time wore on and she became more experienced, she could not accept the gender inequalities of mainstream Protestantism. In 1895, she and a handful of other women published *The Women's Bible*, a reinterpretation of the Bible intended to give all women a new, egalitarian ideology.[54] Twentieth-century feminist scholars continued the attack, arguing that binary religious thought is un-Christian. One such author, Sara Maitland, wrote, "For . . . Jewish Christians the Incarnation of Jesus, fully human, fully divine, reasserted that matter was good; that life of the community was not antithetical to individual liberty, and that all contributions and talents were of equal value to the whole. Dualism asserts the opposite—as soon as one begins to believe that certain qualities (nature, body, weakness, disability) are bad and opposed to God there is the desire to project them outwards, away from oneself."[55]

Building on a similar idea, Mary Daly warned women not to emulate the "idols of patriarchal religion" that might prevent them from experiencing "transcendence [to] . . . a new and more genuine spiritual consciousness" than ever before realized.[56] Although Daly discussed the importance of sisterhood in the liberation of women from religious sexism, she used the concept in a nontraditional, ideological context, claiming that it contained the power to eliminate the "Other" status of women, who like Mary, Mother of God, lived and were defined through their relationships to men. Daly's vision of female solidarity was, "revolutionary and revelatory. By refusing, together, to be objects—to accept the role of 'the Other'—women are beginning to break down the credibility of sex-role stereotyping and bring about a genuine psychic revolution in the direction of what I have called 'the sisterhood of man'—that is, in the direction of an androgynous society."[57] Forceful as Daly's arguments were and are, the debate over whether women should continue to function within a patriarchal religious system or create a new woman-centered spiritual ideology continues and is represented in the works of Elisabeth Schüssler Fiorenza and Rosemary Radford Ruether, respectively.[58]

The international Presentation Order has attempted to avoid ideological sectarian divisions. For example, in 1971, Presentations in Derby, England, began inviting Methodists and Anglicans into their convent to participate in group prayers and informal discussions. In return, the Presentations were asked to address other denominational meetings.[59] Rejoicing over this ecumenical movement, one Presentation wrote, "Alone, here in England, we are almost powerless against the organized Christlessness around us, so we multiply our strength by uniting with others and pray and study and act together."[60]

In addition to the Presentations, other apostolic religious have struggled with their attempts to modernize and yet preserve the traditional commitment that has provided communities with stability and unity. By the mid-twentieth century, some superiors had called students back to convents for periods of retreat and renewal. Summing up a prevalent view, Sister of Charity Mother Mary Francesca wrote, "I hope superiors are seeing to it that Sisters do not have to omit their prayers because of the stress of work. . . . We need our spiritual exercises now more than ever."[61] The Sister Formation Movement, spotlighted at the 1952 convention of the Catholic Education Association (founded in 1904), was a nation-wide Church effort to keep nuns professionally active and yet spiritually sound at the same time.[62]

Although woman's appropriate social and religious roles are barely mentioned in the documents of the Second Vatican Council (held from 1962 to 1965), the body's mandate that religious become more active in the secular world inadvertantly threatened further to erode the ideological commitment that many orders were struggling to maintain. Long tired of a separate and unequal existence compared with male clerics, feminist religious tied the new movement called "renewal" to their bid for equal rights. Acting on this principle, a few Catholic orders of nuns broke with the past and adopted a similar point of view. Tired of dealing with a recalcitrant bishop, in 1967 the Los Angeles-based Sisters of the Immaculate Heart of Mary sacrificed their official Church blessing by taking in men and married couples alike.[63]

Throughout chapter debates concerning habit alterations and occupational choices, the South Dakota Presentations entertained opposing points of view, but in the final analysis refused to interpret renewal as a catalyst for a new philosophical mission. Instead they reaffirmed Nagle's intentions reflected in both old and new apostolic directions. For instance, by the 1960s most sister hospital administrators believed that years of dealing with bureaucratic concerns had robbed them of their sense of spiritual purpose. To remedy the problem, they retained their policymaking function but reshaped their medical careers into positions that involved more personal contact with patients. Moreover, many other sisters' professional options were enriched and expanded to include ministries all over the country and in foreign lands as well. Truly, the once separate but unequal role of women had, for many Presentation professionals, remained separate but was now equal to that of men. In so doing, the Presentations have protected their community and its historic sense of purpose and yet continued to identify a needy clientele.[64]

The decision of these and many other religious and secular women teachers, nuns, and social workers to retain their separate ideology has prompted some researchers to label them as semiprofessional, unable to grasp the full meaning of professionalization. Exemplifying what one observer calls the "predominant gender hypothesis," Robert Habenstein and Edwin Christ contend that, unlike these "traditionalizers," the "professionalizer . . . is not motivated by any blanket dedication to an ideal."[65] She dedicates herself to practicing the science of an occupation. When contrasted with the professionalization successes of so-called "traditionalizers" like the Presentations, proponents of the "predominant gender hypothesis" appear biased against stereotypical female traits, especially when displayed by women because revisionist scholars have attacked physicians for concentrating too much on the long-associated male attribute of autonomy and for failing to care for their patients.[66]

Our study by no means totally refutes the semiprofessional label or the ironies involved in using an ideology of separate spheres to argue for all women's professional role outside the convent or home. It does, however, suggest that in the name of service to God and humankind many nuns have turned the potential suffocation of segregation into the potency of separatism. In the process, these women have endured the things they could not or would not change about their secular and religious environments but constantly pushed alterations in policy that would give them the necessary support for their work. The South Dakota Presentations have accomplished this task, enduring the conflicts among themselves, withstanding external criticism, and remaining in contact with Nano Nagle's Marian-like qualities. In so doing, the Presentations have professionalized, even though some scholars would call the nuns semiprofessional. It remains to be seen whether the sisters' historically evolving ideology can continue to empower their career-bound members and muster support for them from outside the community as well. Unreconcilable conflicts may arise. It is still to the nuns' credit that in the name of self-sacrifice a group of women has triumphed within an American environment that generally emphasizes materialism, personhood, and individualism.[67]

NOTES

1. Frederick Jackson Turner, "Statements of the Frontier Thesis" and "Later Explanations and Developments," in *The Frontier Thesis: Valid Interpretation of American History?*, ed. Ray Allen Billington (New York: Holt, Rinehart, and Winston, 1966), 9–30; Howard M. Vollmer and Donald L. Mills, *Professionalization* (Englewood Cliffs, N.J.: Prentice-Hall, 1966), 46–71; Robert H. Wiebe, *The Search for Order, 1877–1920* (New York: Hill and Wang, 1967), 64–65, 101–4, 152, 165–70, 182, 255–64, 245–49; David B. Tyack, *The One Best System: A History of American Urban Education* (Cambridge, Mass.: Harvard University Press, 1974), 112, 117–30; Thomas L. Haskell, *The Emergence of Professional Social Science: The American Social Science Association and the Nineteenth-Century Crisis of Authority* (Urbana: University of Illinois Press, 1976); Burton J. Bledstein, *The Culture of Professionalism: The Middle Class and the Development of Higher Education in America* (New York: W. W. Norton, 1976). In Merle Curti, *The Social Ideas of American Educators* (Totawa, N.J.: Littlefield, Adams, 1978), 328–29, the author notes that educator William T. Harris believed that displaced industrial workers could obtain education and enter one of the many emergent professions during the late nineteenth and early twentieth centuries. According to George Ritzer's "Professionalization, Bureaucratization, and Rationalization: The Views of Max Weber," *Social Forces* 53 (June 1975): 627–34, Weber did not perceive an inevitable conflict between professionalization and bureaucracy. Other studies conclude differently and depict aspiring professionals at odds with institutional managers. For examples, see W. Richard Scott, "Professionals in Organization—Areas of Conflict," in *Professionalization*, ed. Vollmer and Miller, 265–86; Ronald

G. Corwin, *Militant Professionalism: A Study of Organizational Conflict in High Schools* (New York: Appleton-Century-Crofts, 1970), 3–15, 243–79; Martin Haberman and T. M. Stinnett, *Teacher Education and the New Profession of Teaching* (Berkeley: McCutchan Publishing, 1974), 1–14; James E. Sorensen and Thomas L. Sorensen, "The Conflict of Professionals in Bureaucratic Organizations," *Administrative Science Quarterly* 19 (March 1974): 98–106; Richard H. Hall, "Professionalization and Bureaucratization," *American Sociological Review* 33 (Feb. 1968): 92–104; Elizabeth Morrissey and David F. Gillespie, "Technology and the Conflict of Professionals in Bureaucratic Organizations," *The Sociological Quarterly* 16 (Summer 1975): 319–32; Gloria V. Engel, "The Effect of Bureaucracy on the Professional Authority of Physicians," *Journal of Health and Social Behavior* 10 (March 1969): 30–41; Paul D. Montagna, "Professionalization and Bureaucratization in Large Professional Organizations," *American Journal of Sociology* 74 (Sept. 1968): 138–45; Erwin O. Smigel, *Wall Street Lawyer: Professional Organization Man?* (New York: Free Press, 1964); Harold L. Wilensky, "The Professionalization of Everyone?" *The American Journal of Sociology* 70 (Sept. 1964): 137–58; Stanley H. Udy, Jr., "Technical and Institutional Factors in Production Organizations: A Preliminary Model," *American Journal of Sociology* 67 (Nov. 1961): 247–54 and "Administrative Rationality, Social Setting, and Organizational Development," *American Journal of Sociology* 68 (Nov. 1962): 299–308. A few sources that enumerate the various categories are William J. Goode, "Community within a Community: The Professions," *American Sociological Review* 22 (Feb. 1957): 194–200; Ernest Greenwood, "Attributes of a Profession," *Social Work* 2 (July 1957): 45–55; Robert Perrucci, "Engineering, Professional Servant of Power," *American Behavioral Scientist* 14 (March/April 1971): 492–506. A somewhat opposite viewpoint is expressed in Robert A. Rothman, "Deprofessionalization: The Case of Law in America," *Work and Occupations* 11 (May 1984): 183–206. For an early but thorough bibliographic essay on professionalism see Morris L. Cogan, "Toward a Definition of Profession," *The Harvard Educational Review* 23 (Jan./Dec. 1953): 33–50. A more recent summary can be found in George Ritzer, *Man and his Work: Conflict and Change* (New York: Appleton-Century-Crofts, 1972), 350–62. Many professionalization studies of educators emphasize the taxonomic definition. For examples see Wayne K. Hoy and Cecil G. Miskel, *Educational Administration: Theory, Research, and Practice* (New York: Random House, 1982), 110–12; Johanna Lemlech and Merle B. Marks, *The American Teacher: 1776–1976* (Bloomington, Ind.: Phi Delta Kappa Educational Foundation, 1976); Paul G. Bulger, "Education as a Profession," (Washington, D.C.: ERIC Clearinghouse on Teacher Education, 1972). Some scholars disagree on whether teachers' union-oriented activities are evidence of professionalization. For a positive interpretation see Al Lowenthal and Robert Nielsen, "Unionism and Professionalism: Siblings?" (Washington, D.C.: American Federation of Teachers, 1977). For an opposing view, see Wayne J. Urban, "Organized Teachers and Educational Reform During the Progressive Era,

1890–1920," *History of Education Quarterly* 16 (Spring 1976): 35–52 and *Why Teachers Organized* (Detroit: Wayne State University Press, 1982).

2. Critics of the traditional taxonomy disagree with many of the above scholars. For examples, see Magali Sarfatti Larson, *The Rise of Professionalism: A Sociological Analysis* (Berkeley: University of California Press, 1977); Gabriel Gyarmati K., "The Doctrine of the Professions: Basis of a Power Structure," *International Social Science Journal* 27 (Winter 1975): 629–54; Douglas Klegon, "The Sociology of Professions: An Emerging Perspective," *Sociology of Work and Occupations* 5 (Aug. 1978): 259–83. For a classic portrayal of the unified professional community, see Goode, "Community within a Community" and "The Protection of the Inept," *American Sociological Review* 32 (Feb. 1967): 5–19. Although other authors have focused on the segmentation and diversity within the professions, the implication of their work is that some sort of leadership or unity within each group, whether democratic or authoritarian, is necessary for professional growth. For an example, see Haskell, *The Emergence of Professional Social Science*; Peter Jarvis, "A Profession in Process: A Theoretical Model for the Ministry," *The Sociological Review* 24 (May 1976): 351–64.

3. R. Rouillard, "Marian Feasts," *New Catholic Encyclopedia*, vol. 9 (New York: McGraw-Hill, 1967), 212; Sister Alicia Dunphy to the authors, Jan. 6, 1981.

4. M. Raphael Consedine P.V.V.M., *Listening Journey: A Study of the Spirit and Ideals of Nano Nagle and the Presentation Sisters* (Victoria, Australia: Congregation of the Presentation of the Blessed Virgin Mary, 1983), 318.

5. Jo Ann McNamara, "A New Song: Celibate Women in the First Three Christian Centuries," in *Women and History* 6/7 (Summer/Fall 1983): 1–154; Lina Eckenstein, *Woman under Monasticism* (New York: Russell and Russell, 1963); Eileen Power, *Medieval Women* (London: Cambridge University Press, 1975), 76–99; Joan M. Ferrante, "The Education of Women in the Middle Ages in Theory, Fact, and Fantasy," in *Beyond Their Sex: Learned Women of the European Past*, ed. Patricia H. Labalme (New York: New York University Press, 1980), 9–42; Natalie Zemon Davis, "Gender and Genre: Women as Historical Writers, 1400–1820," in *Beyond Their Sex*, 153–82.

6. Eckenstein, *Women under Monasticism*, 179.

7. Ibid., 264.

8. Ibid., 328–36. To some degree sources cited above indicate that the convent produced accomplished women. For an example, see Power, *Medieval Women*, 89–99. Other works rule out that an ideology of separate spheres has ultimately assisted women's professional efforts. For an example, see Barbara J. Harris, *Beyond Her Sphere: Women and the Professions in American History* (Westport, Conn.: Greenwood Press, 1978), 6–8.

9. Power, *Medieval Women*, 96–99.

10. Mary Ewens, O. P., *The Role of the Nun in Nineteenth-Century America: Variations on the International Theme* (New York: Arno Press,

1976, repr., Salem, N.H.: Ayer Publishers, 1984), 14–18; Sara Maitland, *A Map of the New Country: Women and Christianity* (London: Routledge and Kegan Paul, 1983), 11; Loretta Koley Jancoski, "Religion and Commitment: A Psycho-historical Study of Creative Women in Catholic Religious Communities," (Ph.D. diss., University of Chicago, 1976), 5; Ann Elizabeth Kelley, "Catholic Women in Campus Ministry: An Emerging Ministry for Women in the Catholic Church" (Ph.D. diss., Boston University Graduate School, 1976), 15. For a good discussion of total institution "inmates," see Erving Goffman, *Asylums: Essays on the Social Situation of Mental Patients and Other Inmates* (Hawthorne, N.Y.: Aldine Publishing, 1961), 1–124.

11. John Malcolm Ludlow, *Woman's Work in the Church: Historical Notes on Deaconesses and Sisterhoods* (London: Alexander Strachan, 1866, repr., Washington, D.C.: Zenger Publishing, 1978), 117–23, 156–58; Jancoski, "Religion and Commitment," 9–10; Phyllis Stock, *Better than Rubies: A History of Women's Education* (New York: Putnam, 1978), 90–100.

12. Ewens, *The Role of the Nun in Nineteenth-Century America*, 45; Elizabeth M. Jamieson, Mary F. Sewall, and Eleanor B. Suhrie, *Trends in Nursing History: Their Social, International, and Ethical Relationships* (Philadelphia: W. B. Saunders, 1966), 176–78; Vern L. Bullough and Bonnie Bullough, *The Emergence of Modern Nursing* (London: Macmillan, 1969), 70–73.

13. Jancoski, "Religion and Commitment," 9–10; Ewens, *The Role of the Nun in Nineteenth-Century America*, 18–20, and "The Leadership of Nuns in Immigrant Catholicism," in *Women and Religion in America*, vol. 1: *The Nineteenth Century: A Documentary History*, ed. Rosemary Radford Ruether and Rosemary Skinner Keller (New York: Harper and Row, 1981), 101–49.

14. For details on Nano Nagle's life, see chapter 2 of this volume.

15. Asunción Lavrin, "Women in Convents: Their Economic and Social Role in Colonial Mexico," in *Liberating Women's History: Theoretical and Critical Essays*, ed. Berenice A. Carroll (Urbana: University of Illinois Press, 1976), 270.

16. Ewens, *The Role of the Nun in Nineteenth-Century America*, 22, and "The Leadership of Nuns in Immigrant Catholicism," 101–49.

17. Ibid.; The Poor Clares of Reparation and Adoration, *Religious Communities in the American Episcopal Church and in the Anglican Church of Canada* (West Park, N.Y.: Holy Cross Press, 1956), 143; Susan Peterson, "Challenges to the Stereotypes: The Adaptation of the Sisters of St. Francis to South Dakota Missions, 1885–1910," *Upper Midwest History* 84 (1984): 1–9; Sister M. Grace McDonald, O.S.B., *With Lamps Burning* (Saint Joseph, Minn.: Saint Benedict's Piory Press, 1957); Sister Mary Veronica McEntee, R.S.M., *The Sisters of Mercy of Harrisburg: 1869–1939* (Philadelphia: Dolphin Press, 1939), 86; S. M. Johnston, *Builders by the Sea* (Jericho, N.Y.: Exposition Press, 1971). For a review of the literature and suggestions for further research on nuns, see Sister Elizabeth Kolmer, A.S.C., "Catholic Women Religious and Women's History: A Survey of the Literature," *Amer-*

ican Quarterly 30 (Winter 1978): 639–51. Other interpretive works on nuns include Marta Helen Danylewycz, "Taking the Veil in Montreal, 1840–1920: An Alternative to Motherhood and Spinsterhood" (Ph.D. diss., The Univeristy of Toronto, 1982); Susan Peterson, "Religious Communities of Women in the West: The Presentation Sisters' Adaptation to the Northern Plains Frontier," *Journal of the West* 21 (April 1982): 65–70; "'Holy Women' and Housekeepers: Women Teachers on South Dakota Reservations, 1885–1910," *South Dakota History* 13 (Fall 1983): 245–60; "Doing 'Women's' Work: The Grey Nuns of Fort Totten Indian Reservation, 1874–1900," *North Dakota History* 52 (Spring 1985): 18–25; and "A Widening Horizon: Catholic Sisterhoods on the Northern Plains, 1874–1910," *Great Plains Quarterly* 5 (Spring 1985): 125–32. Other more descriptive accounts are A Sister of the Precious Blood, *Not with Silver or Gold: A History of the Sisters of the Congregation of the Precious Blood, Salem Heights, Dayton, Ohio: 1834–1944* (Dayton: Sisters of the Precious Blood, 1945); Sister Helen Angela Hurley, *On Good Ground: The Story of the Sisters of St. Joseph in St. Paul* (Minneapolis: University of Minnesota Press, 1951); Sister Julia Gilmore, S.C.L., *We Came North: Centennial Story of the Sisters of Charity of Leavenworth* (St. Meinrad, Ind.: Abbey Press, 1961); Anna Blanche McGill, *The Sisters of Charity of Nazareth Kentucky* (New York: Encyclopedia Press, 1917); Louise Callan, *The Society of The Sacred Heart in North America* (New York: Longmans, Green, 1937); Sister Mary Agnes McCann, *The History of Mother Seton's Daughters: The Sisters of Charity of Cincinnati, Ohio: 1809–1917*, vols. 1, 2, and 3 (New York: Longmans, Green, 1917); Sister Marie De Lourdes Walsh, *The Sisters of Charity of New York: 1809–1959*, vols. 1 and 2 (New York: Fordham University Press, 1960); Sister M. Evangeline Thomas, *Footprints on the Frontier: A History of the Sisters of Saint Joseph: Concordia, Kansas* (Westminster, Md.: Newman Press, 1948); Sister M. Francis Borgia, O.S.F., *He Sent Two: The Story of the Beginning of the School Sisters of St. Francis* (Milwaukee: Bruce Publishing, 1965); Katherine Burton, *Bells on Two Rivers: The History of the Sisters of the Visitation of Rock Island, Illinois* (Milwaukee: Bruce Publishing, 1965).

18. Sister Joan Bland, S.N.D., "Sister Julia McGroarty," in *Notable American Women: A Biographical Dictionary*, vol. 2, ed. Edward T. James (Cambridge, Mass.: Belknap Press, 1971), 466–68.

19. Mother M. Williams, "Mother Mary Aloysia Hardey," in *Notable American Women*, ed. James, 131. For other biographical works on nuns, see Lucile McDonald, "Mother Joseph," in *The Women Who Made the West*, ed. The Western Writers of America (Garden City, N.Y.: Doubleday, 1980), 120–29; Thomas Richter, ed., "Sister Catherine Mallon's Journal: Part 1," *New Mexico Historical Review* 52 (Spring 1977): 135–55 and "Sister Catherine Mallon's Journal: Part 2," *New Mexico Historical Review* 51 (Summer 1977): 237–50; Sister Blandina Segale, *At the End of the Santa Fe Trail* (Milwaukee: Bruce Publishing, 1948); Covelle Newcomb, *Running Waters* (New York: Dodd, Mead, 1947); A School Sister of Notre Dame, *Mother Caroline and the School Sisters of Notre Dame in North America*, vols. 1

and 2 (St. Louis: Woodward and Tiernan, 1928); Annabelle M. Melville, *Elizabeth Bayley Seton: 1774–1821* (New York: Charles Scribner's Sons, 1951); Louise Callan, R.S.C.J., *Philippine Duchesne: Frontier Missionary of the Sacred Heart: 1769–1852* (Westminster, Md.: Newman Press, 1957); Sister Patricia Jean, S.L., *Only One Heart: The Story of a Pioneer Nun in America* (Garden City, N.Y.: Doubleday, 1963); James J. Walsh, *Mother Alphonsa: Rose Hawthorne Lathrop* (New York: Macmillan, 1930).

20. Consedine, *Listening Journey*, 268, 279, 283, 304.

21. Ibid., 304.

22. Ibid., 305. See chapter 3 of this volume.

23. Ewens, "The Leadership of Nuns in Immigrant Catholicism," 105–6; Melville, *Elizabeth Bayley Seton*, 154, 162–64, 179, 193–94.

24. Hurley, *On Good Ground*, 157, 192–93, 200, 212–13, 216–17, 226–27, 264.

25. Ibid., 220–21, 233; Bishop John Ireland quoted on 243.

26. Bishop John Ireland, quoted in Ibid., 226–27.

27. Ewens, *The Role of the Nun in Nineteenth-Century America*, 202, 253.

28. Bishop John Lancaster Spalding, quoted in Merle Curti, *The Social Ideas of American Educators* (Totowa, N.J.: Littlefield, Adams, 1978), 353.

29. McDonald, *With Lamps Burning*, 53; Hurley, *On Good Ground*, 84, 152. Examples of nuns' ability to overcome these obstacles are in references from notes 13 through 15.

30. Ewens, *The Role of the Nun in Nineteenth-Century America*, 203, 253.

31. Pope Leo XIII, paraphrased in Ibid., 254.

32. Anonymous nun, paraphrased in Ibid., 207.

33. Ibid., 126–27; Klegon, "The Sociology of Professions."

34. Mother Mary Berchmans, quoted in Sister Gilmore, *We Came North*, 241.

35. Melville, *Elizabeth Bayley Seton*, 253–78; Ewens, *The Role of the Nun in Nineteenth-Century America*, 126–27.

36. Ewens, *The Role of the Nun in Nineteenth-Century America*, 279–80. Several other references to choir-sisters and lay-sisters exist. For one, see Danylewycz, "Taking the Veil in Montreal." Another study of Wellesley College professors (contemporaries of the early South Dakota Presentations) notes that many faculty members succeeded because they lived with women who performed household chores. For details, see Patricia A. Palmieri, "Here Was Fellowship: A Social Portrait of Academic Women at Wellesley College, 1895–1920," *History of Education Quarterly* 23 (Summer 1983): 195–214. For a reference to internal occupational conflict, see M. Calvert, *The Mechanical Engineer in America, 1830–1910: Professional Cultures in Conflict* (Baltimore, Md.: Johns Hopkins University Press, 1957).

37. Mother Mary Caroline, paraphrased in Newcomb, *Running Waters*, 232.

38. See chapter 9 of this volume.

39. Ewens, *The Role of the Nun in Nineteenth-Century America*, 203, 252–57. See chapter 9 of this volume.

40. Consedine, *Listening Journey*, 323.

41. For references to colonial Protestant women's bid for spiritual equality with men, see Mary Maples Dunn, "Saints and Sisters: Congregational and Quaker Women in the Early Colonial Period," in *Women in American Religion*, ed. Janet Wilson James (Philadelphia: University of Pennsylvania Press, 1976), 27–46; Laurel Thatcher Ulrich, "Vertuous Women Found: New England Ministerial Literature, 1668–1735," in Ibid., 67–87; Lyle Koehler, "The Case of the American Jezebels: Anne Hutchinson and Female Agitation During the Years of Antinomian Turmoil, 1636–1640," in *Our American Sisters: Women in American Life and Thought*, ed. Jean F. Friedman and William G. Shade (Lexington, Mass.: D. C. Heath, 1982), 17–40; Mary Maples Dunn, "Women of Light," in *Women of America: A History*, ed. Carol Ruth Berkin and Mary Beth Norton (Boston: Houghton Mifflin, 1979), 114–36. For a specific reference to women's isolated state producing a morally superior human being, see Gerald F. Moran, "Sisters in Christ: Women and the Church in Seventeenth-Century New England," in *Women in American Religion*, ed. James, 47–65.

42. Key sources identifying Protestant women's new social role to rear moral, literate children for the new republic include Linda Kerber, *Women of the Republic: Intellect and Ideology in Revolutionary America* (Chapel Hill: University of North Carolina Press, 1980); Mary Beth Norton, *Liberty's Daughters: The Revolutionary Experience of American Women, 1750–1800* (Boston: Little, Brown, 1980); Glenda Gates Riley, "Origins of the Argument for Improved Female Education," *History of Education Quarterly* 9 (Winter 1969): 455–70. Other works emphasizing nineteenth-century Protestant women's evolving importance in religion include Barbara Welter, *Dimity Convictions: The American Woman in the Nineteenth Century* (Athens: Ohio University Press, 1976), 83–102; Nancy F. Cott, "Young Women in the Second Great Awakening," *Feminist Studies* 3 (Fall 1975): 15–29 and *The Bonds of Womanhood: "Woman's Sphere" in New England, 1780–1835* (New Haven: Yale University Press, 1977); Donald G. Mathews, *Religion in the Old South* (Chicago: University of Chicago Press, 1977), 111–20; Mary P. Ryan, "A Women's Awakening: Evangelical Religion and the Families of Utica, New York, 1800–1840," in *Women in American Religion*, ed. James, 89–110 and *Cradle of the Middle Class: The Family in Oneida County, New York, 1780–1865* (New York: Cambridge University Press, 1981), 105–44; Anne C. Loveland, "Domesticity and Religion in the Antebellum Period: The Career of Phoebe Palmer," *The Historian* 39 (May 1977): 455–71. A classic early study attributing to women the character of the American people is Alexis de Tocqueville, *Democracy in America* (New York: Alfred A. Knopf, 1945), 214. Other sources on women's social influence and/or important religious role include Martha Tomhave Blauvelt, "Women and Revivalism," in *Women and Religion in America*, ed. Reuther, 1–45; Rosemary Radford Ruether, "Women in Utopian Movements," in Ibid., 46–

100; Barbara Brown Zikmund, "The Struggle for the Right to Preach," in Ibid., 193–241; Carolyn De Swarte Gifford, "Women in Social Reform Movements," in Ibid., 294–340; Dorothy Bass Fraser, "The Feminine Mystique: 1890–1910," *Union Seminary Quarterly Review* 27 (Summer 1972): 225–39; Sandra L. Myers, *Westering Women and the Frontier Experience, 1800–1915* (Albuquerque: University of New Mexico Press, 1982); Julie Roy Jeffrey, *Frontier Women: The Trans-Mississippi West, 1840–1880* (New York: Hill and Wang, 1979).

43. Ann Douglas, *The Feminization of American Culture* (New York: Alfred A. Knopf, 1978); James C. Mohr, *Abortion in America: The Origins and Evolution of National Policy* (Oxford: Oxford University Press, 1978); Robert L. Griswold, "Domesticity and Western Women" (unpublished manuscript in the authors' possession) and *Family and Divorce in California, 1850–1890: Victorian Illusions and Everyday Realities* (Albany: State University of New York Press, 1982). Other historians' works, largely on women in the process of migrating westward, stand in contrast to Griswold's work. For examples, see Lillian Schlissel, *Women's Diaries of the Westward Journey* (New York: Schocken Books, 1982); John Mack Faragher, *Women and Men on the Overland Trail* (New Haven: Yale University Press, 1979); Marion G. Goldman, *Gold Diggers and Silver Miners: Prostitution and Social Life on the Comstock Lode* (Ann Arbor: University of Michigan Press, 1981).

44. Peter F. Anson, *The Call of the Cloister: Religious Communities and Kindred Bodies in the Anglican Communion* (London: S.P.C.K., 1955); Anna Brownell Murphy Jameson, *Sisters of Charity, Catholic and Protestant* (London: Longman, Brown, Green and Longmans, 1855); Sister Mary Theodora, C.S.M., "The Foundation of the Sisterhood of St. Mary," *Historical Magazine of the Protestant Episcopal Church* (March 1945): 38–52; T. J. Williams, "The Beginnings of Anglican Sisterhoods," *Historical Magazine of the Protestant Episcopal Church* (Dec. 1947): 362–68.

45. The Community of St. Mary, quoted in The Poor Clares, *Religious Communities in the American Episcopal Church*, 104. Also see 103.

46. Mary Agnes Dougherty, "The Methodist Deaconess: A Case of Religious Feminism," *Methodist History* 21 (Jan. 1983): 90–98. Other works on modern deaconesses include Charles W. Deweese, "Deaconesses in Baptist History: A Preliminary Study," *Baptist History and Heritage* 12 (Jan. 1977): 52–57.

47. Dougherty, "The Methodist Deaconess," 90–98.

48. A Sister of the Precious Blood, *Not with Silver or Gold*, 13.

49. Anonymous Presentation nun, quoted in Consedine, *Listening Journey*, 285.

50. Sister McEntee, *The Sisters of Mercy*, 224–29; Sister Gilmore, *We Came North*, 210. For the use of domestic ideology and/or religion as a base for emergent "women's" professions in the nineteenth century see Kathryn Kish Sklar, *Catharine Beecher: A Study in American Domesticity* (New Haven: Yale University Press, 1973); Dee Garrison, "The Tender Techni-

cians: The Feminization of Public Librarianship, 1876–1905," *Journal of Social History* 6 (Winter 1972–73): 131–59; Polly Welts Kaufman, *Women Teachers on the Frontier* (New Haven: Yale University Press, 1984); Keith E. Melder, "Woman's High Calling: The Teaching Profession in America, 1830–1860," *American Studies* 13 (Fall 1972): 19–47; Nancy Hoffman, *Woman's "True" Profession: Voices from the History of Teaching* (Old Westbury, N.Y.: Feminist Press, 1981); Jacqueline Jones, "Women Who Were More than Men: Sex and Status in Freedmen's Teaching," *History of Education Quarterly* 19 (Spring 1979): 47–60. For a reference to the professionalization of the traditional female sphere, see Susan Strasser, *Never Done: A History of American Housework* (New York: Pantheon Books, 1982), 180–223. For uses and expressions of sisterhood and women's separate existence see Estelle Freedman, "Separatism as Strategy: Female Institution Building and American Feminism, 1870–1930," *Feminist Studies* 5 (Fall 1979): 512–29; Blanche Wiesen Cook, "Female Support Networks and Political Activism: Lillian Wald, Crystal Eastman, Emma Goldman," in *A Heritage of Her Own: Toward a New Social History of American Women*, ed. Nancy F. Cott and Elizabeth Pleck (New York: Simon and Schuster, 1979), 412–41; Joan N. Burstyn, "Historical Perspectives on Women in Educational Leadership," in *Women and Educational Leadership*, ed. Sari Knopp Bicklen and Marilyn B. Brannigan (Lexington, Mass.: D. C. Heath, 1980), 65–75; Karen J. Blair, *The Clubwoman as Feminist: True Womanhood Redefined, 1868–1914* (New York: Holmes and Meier, 1980). For a discussion of the depth of women's intimacy and support for each other during the nineteenth century see Carroll Smith-Rosenberg, "The Female World of Love and Ritual: Relations Between Women in Nineteenth-Century America," in *A Heritage of Her Own*, ed. Cott and Pleck, 311–42.

51. Sister Gilmore, *We Came North*, 134–35. See chapters 6 and 7 of this volume.

52. A Sister of The Precious Blood, *Not with Silver or Gold*, 324; Meyers, "Sister Formation Movement," *New Catholic Encyclopedia*, vol. 13, 261–62; Harris, *Beyond Her Sphere*, 108–26; Rosalind Rosenberg, *Beyond Separate Spheres: Intellectual Roots of Modern Feminism* (New Haven: Yale University Press, 1982), 238–46.

53. Carl N. Degler, *At Odds: Women and the Family in America from the Revolution to the Present* (New York: Oxford University Press, 1980), 414; Gene P. Agre and Barbara Finkelstein, "Feminism and School Reform: The Last Fifteen Years," *Teachers College Record* 80 (Dec. 1978): 307–15. Also see chapter 9 of this volume.

54. For examples of the expansion and eventual dissolution of an ideology of separate spheres see Anne Firor Scott, "The Ever Widening Circle: The Diffusion of Feminist Values from the Troy Female Seminary, 1822–1872," *History of Education Quarterly* 19 (Spring 1979): 3–25; Cott, "Young Women in the Second Great Awakening," 15–29; Degler, *At Odds*, 360–61; Glenda Gates Riley, "The Subtle Subversion: Changes in the Traditionalist Image of the American Woman," *The Historian* 32 (Feb. 1970):

210–27. For reference to pragmatic feminism as a step away from traditionalism and toward feminism in the twentieth century, see June Sochen, *Movers and Shakers: American Women Thinkers and Activists 1900–1970* (New York: Quadrangle/The New York Times Book Company, 1973). For Sochen's model applied to teachers, see Marguerite Renner, "Teachers' Motivations in the Debate to Find the Perfect Teacher: Competing Ideologies in Late Nineteenth-Century American Schools," presented at the Western Social Science meeting, Fort Worth, Texas, April 1985. In Ryan, "A Women's Awakening," 89–110, female proselytizers are viewed as determined and forceful, but for the purpose of saving, not overthrowing, tradition. For an interpretation that claims these and other women's nineteenth-century religious and reform efforts led to moral influence but not real "power," see Barbara Leslie Epstein, *The Politics of Domesticity: Women, Evangelism, and Temperance in Nineteenth-Century America* (Middletown, Conn.: Wesleyan University Press, 1981). Works by or on Stanton include Elizabeth Cady Stanton, *The Woman's Bible: Parts I and II* (New York: European Publishing, 1895, repr., New York: Arno Press, 1972); James H. Smylie, "*The Woman's Bible:* And the Spiritual Crisis," *Soundings* 59 (Fall 1976): 305–28; Alma Lutz, "Elizabeth Cady Stanton," in *Notable American Women*, vol. 3 (1971), 342–47.

55. Maitland, *A Map of the New Country*, 19.

56. Mary Daly, "Theology after the Demise of God the Father: A Call for the Castration of Sexist Religion," in *Sexist Religion and Women in the Church*, ed. Alice L. Hageman (New York: Association Press, 1974), 126.

57. Daly, "Theology after the Demise."

58. Rosemary Radford Ruether, *Womanguides: Readings toward a Feminist Theology* (Boston: Beacon Press, 1985); Elisabeth Schussler Fiorenza, *Bread Not Stone: The Challenge of Feminist Biblical Interpretation* (Boston: Beacon Press, 1984).

59. Consedine, *Listening Journey*, 375.

60. Anonymous Presentation nun, quoted in Ibid., 375.

61. Mother Mary Francesca, quoted in Sister Gilmore, *We Came North*, 410.

62. "Sister Formation Movement"; Harold A. Buetow, *Of Singular Benefit: The Story of Catholic Education in the United States* (London: Macmillan, 1970), 180–81.

63. Sara Bentley Doely, *Women's Liberation and the Church: The New Demand for Freedom in the Life of the Christian Church* (New York: Association Press, 1970), 70–76. See chapter 9 of this volume.

64. See chapter 9 of this volume.

65. Robert W. Habenstein and Edwin A. Christ, *Professionalizer, Traditionalizer and Utilizer: An Interpretative Study of the Work of the General Duty Nurse in Non-Metropolitan Central Missouri General Hospitals* (Columbia: University of Missouri Press, 1963), 45–46. For portrayals of traditional career women as victims particularly of a male ideology of separate spheres, see Jo Ann Ashley, *Hospitals, Paternalism, and the Role of the*

Nurse (New York: Teachers College Press, 1976). Historical works that in some manner document the failure of domestic ideology to provide women with real professional choices or to promote a true professional equality between men and women include Jill Conway, "Perspectives on the History of Women's Education in the United States," *History of Education Quarterly* 14 (Spring 1974): 1–12; Keith E. Melder, "Mask of Oppression: The Female Seminary Movement in the United States," *New York History* 55 (July 1974): 261–79; Richard M. Bernard and Maris A. Vinovskis, "The Female School Teacher in Ante-Bellum Massachusetts," *Journal of Social History* 10 (March 1977): 332–45; David F. Allmendinger, Jr., "Mount Holyoke Students Encounter the Need for Life-Planning, 1847–1850," *History of Education Quarterly* 19 (Spring 1979): 27–46; Phillida Bunkle, "Sentimental Womanhood and Domestic Education, 1830–1870," *History of Education Quarterly* 14 (Spring 1974): 13–30; Roberta Wein, "Women's Colleges and Domesticity, 1875–1918," *History of Education Quarterly* 14 (Spring 1974): 31–47. Other notable sources highlighting the ironies involved in using domestic ideology as a professional creed include Sklar, *Catharine Beecher;* Mary Kelley, "At War with Herself: Harriet Beecher Stowe as Woman in Conflict within the Home," in *Woman's Being, Woman's Place: Female Identity and Vocations in American History,* ed. Mary Kelley (Boston: G. K. Hall, 1979), 201–19. Special references to women in the sciences include Rosenberg, *Beyond Separate Spheres;* Margaret W. Rossiter, *Women Scientists in America: Struggles and Strategies to 1940* (Baltimore: Johns Hopkins University Press, 1982). Some social-psychological pieces that attribute professional women's ambivalence to some type of traditional ideology are Matina S. Horner, "Femininity and Successful Achievement: A Basic Inconsistency," in *Feminine Personality and Conflict,* ed. Judith M. Bardwick et al. (Belmont, Calif.: Brooks-Cole Publishing, 1970), 45–74; Judith M. Bardwick and Elizabeth Douvan, "Ambivalence: The Socialization of Women," in *Readings on the Psychology of Women,* ed. Judith M. Bardwick (New York: Harper and Row, 1972), 52–58; Cynthia Fuchs Epstein, *Woman's Place: Options and Limits in Professional Careers* (Berkeley: University of California Press, 1970), 23–24, 52–53, 134–42; K. Patricia Cross, "The Woman Student," in *Women in Higher Education,* ed. W. Todd Furniss and Patricia Albjerg Graham (Washington, D.C.: American Council on Education, 1974), 29–50.

66. For other sociological works that in some manner discuss the semiprofessional status of woman's career work, see Ritzer, *Man and His Work,* 205–20; T. Leggatt, "Teaching as a Profession," in *Professions and Professionalization,* ed. J. A. Jackson (New York: Cambridge University Press, 1970), 155–77; Richard L. Simpson and Ida Harper Simpson, "Women and Bureaucracy in the Semi-Professions," in *The Semi-Professions and their Organization, Teachers, Nurses, Social Workers,* ed. Amitai Etzioni (New York: Free Press, 1969), 196–265; Talcott Parsons, "Implications of the Study," in *The Climate of Book Selection: Social Influences on School and Public Libraries,* ed. J. Periam Danton (Berkeley: University of California

School of Librarianship, 1959), 94–95; Patricia Cayo Sexton, "Schools Are Emasculating Our Boys," in *And Jill Came Tumbling After: Sexism in American Education,* ed. Judith Stacey, Susan Béreaud, and Joan Daniels (New York: Dell Publishing, 1974), 138–41; Louis H. Orzack, "Work as a 'Central Life Interest' of Professionals," *Social Problems* 7 (Fall 1959): 125–32; George Rosen, "The Hospital: Historical Sociology of a Community Institution," in *The Hospital in Modern Society,* ed. Eliot Freidson (New York: Free Press, 1963) 1–36; Elliot Freidson, *Profession of Medicine: A Study of the Sociology of Applied Knowledge* (New York: Dodd, Mead, 1970), 58–60; Barbara Melosh, *"The Physician's Hand": Work Culture and Conflict in American Nursing* (Philadelphia: Temple University Press, 1982); Ronald G. Corwin, "The Professional Employee: A Study of Conflict in Nursing Roles," *The American Journal of Sociology* 66 (May 1961): 604–15. Patrick B. Forsyth, "The Professions and the Predominant Gender Hypothesis," presented at the American Educational Research Association meeting, Montreal, April 1983.

67. An address from this chapter was given at the American Educational Studies Association Conference, Pittsburgh, Oct. 29, 1986.

2. The Presentation Sisters in Historical Perspective

☐

Although the Presentation's woman-centered ideology has served as a professionalization catalyst, the apostolic sisters have not necessarily aspired to be triumphant feminists, achieving personhood through their professional accomplishments. During the nineteenth and throughout much of the twentieth centuries, the nuns have resolved any conflicts between their professional and religious goals through compromise, sometimes redirecting but seldom curtailing their careers. Although an ideal of selflessness has motivated the Presentations' professionalization drive, this does not mean that they were or are semiprofessional or unassertive; various sisters have proven to be competent and hard-driving. Moreover, in making some concessions to maintain their internal and external ideological support system, Presentations during the eighteenth and nineteenth centuries readied their community for professionalization victories during the modern age.

Ambitious to do good in the world, Presentation Sisters were not unlike the subjects of Mary Ryan's historical work on women in Oneida County, New York, from 1780–1865. Ryan concludes that to combat the evils of modernization, a traditional ideology of separate spheres motivated many women to leave the home and form family protection agencies, yet working in the outside world did not alter the women's ideals. In fact, after earlier generations had firmly established various family support centers, later generations of married women, with greater frequency than had the women who preceded them, chose not to involve themselves in volunteer agencies outside of the home, thereby reasserting the primacy of woman's familial domestic role.[1] Although Presentations and other apostolic nuns have also maintained a traditional commitment, they have had neither husbands nor children to beckon them home. Therefore, they

31

have never retreated completely into the convent. In fact, any alterations in ideology that have occurred over time have not marked a deterioration of Nano Nagle's philosophy of separate spheres; rather, these changes represent an evolution from the original unequal status of women and men to an eventual argument for separate but equally important life-styles.

In order to understand the Presentations' dialectic of determination, conflict, and adaptation, we must first look back to Nagle, her early followers, and the social climate that would lure her scions to South Dakota. Born in 1718 to Garret and Ann Nagle, Nano was to be the first of seven children in this wealthy Irish family. In 1728, her parents sent her to study in France. The Nagle family could afford such a luxury because it managed to retain most of its property during the early eighteenth-century enforcement of English penal laws, enacted at various times from 1697 to 1746. The first important law commanded that all ecclesiastical Catholics leave the country. A life of poverty and obscurity became the lot of the many churchmen who defied the order and stayed. Further proclamations forbade Catholic acquisition of property and precipitated the breakup of holdings after a Catholic landlord's death. The result was that at mid-eighteenth century less than 10 percent of the country's profitable land belonged to Catholics. Other laws closed the professions to Catholics, and admittance to civil and military offices was possible only when an applicant took an oath denying the faith. Education, therefore, became the government's province, and parochial schools existed only outside the law. Dedicated but impoverished parishioners endured the greatest hardship because, unlike the Nagles, they could not afford to have their children privately tutored or sent to another country for an education. Thus discrimination finally wore many down, as large numbers of Catholics eventually sent their progeny to the state's charter schools or those run by Anglican charitable institutions.[2]

In France, on the other hand, Nano Nagle experienced the refinements of Louis XV's court, but eventually she was to grieve over the destitution of less fortunate Catholics, a concern that soon would redirect her life. Legend has it that the future educator's awakening came as she was returning from a ball during the wee hours. Passing a church, Nagle noticed a crowd of French laborers waiting to attend Mass before beginning their day's work. It was said that the commoners' dedication, contrasted with her own indolent life, lingered in Nagle's mind until she returned to Ireland during the early 1740s, destined to face sorrow and self-analysis. A few years after her return, Nano's father, mother, and her younger sister, Ann, all died. Ann and Nano had been close because they had spent some years together in France. Although Ann was four years younger than Nano, she had been the first sister to develop a social conscience. As a youngster, Ann had been concerned, especially in view of her family's wealth, by the poverty of a multitude of Catholics; consequently, she had helped those in need whenever possible. Devastated by society's loss and by personal bereavement when Ann died, Nano decided to return to the Continent and probably entered a Benedictine abbey. She hoped that through a monastic life of prayer and abstention she could make reparation for her own shortsightedness and for the sins of the world. After having spent only a few months in seclusion Nagle grew restless and returned to Ireland in 1748, moved in with her brother, Joseph, and opened her first school for Catholic poor. From this point on, she would be driven to seek monastic spirituality and to do apostolic deeds at the same time.[3]

Nano lived the next thirty-six years of her life obsessed with these passions for spirituality and good works. Heedless of the danger she incurred by defying the law, the teacher would devote her life and fortune to parochial education, establishing several small schools during the next two decades. In addition, the samaritan endured much public scorn because, unlike officially recognized orders of nuns, Nano walked the streets of Cork, visiting the sick, teaching pupils, and overseeing her schools. Subjecting herself to further ridicule from some quarters, Nagle took not only girls, but also boys, some of them delinquents, as students. That a lady of means would don plain, and in time worn-out, garb, would live alone for at least ten years after her brother left the country in 1761, and would work with commoners was a violation of eighteenth-century social standards. Nagle persevered, however, and continued to provide the needy with succor, religious instruction, moral training, and the opportunity to learn basic reading and writing skills. Moreover, she also insisted that pupils engage in manual labor. The educator's intent was to instill a sense of duty within "all my children . . . to be fond of instructing, as I think it lies in the power of the poor to be of [more] service that way than the rich."[4]

Although Nagle instructed both boys and girls, her contributions to girls and young women were particularly significant. While a student in France she had been exposed to the ideas of Cardinal Francois Fenelon who, by emphasizing women's potential as nurturers and ethical models for children, had prepared them through education to be practical, hard-working home managers. In so doing, he hoped to counteract the effete, lazy French aristocracy of Louis XIV's court.[5] Putting this ideal into practice in Ireland, Nagle helped to establish what one historian terms "a standard of domestic virtue . . . [and] a delicacy of female honor . . . among the Irish poor. . . ."[6] Thus, she did not defy gender roles; rather, she provided girls and boys with different occupational choices. In 1749, she even reported that reading was not being taught in two out of five of her schools for girls, but it was taught in all of those for boys.[7]

Nagle desperately needed help with her schools. In 1771, she enticed some French Ursulines to settle in Cork, but their observance of enclosure meant that students would have to come to the teachers, a practice that only select families could afford. Consequently, Nagle herself never entered the Ursuline order, but lived a short distance away, preferring instead to fulfill her personal promise to God. Nagle once explained that to do anything else meant running "a great risk of salvation. . . ."[8] Thus despite grave physical handicaps—her ulcerated limbs, respiratory problems, and numerous other ailments— she went to the poor day after day.[9]

Nagle fought other battles as well. In 1776, Father Francis Moylan, one of Nagle's ardent admirers, objected to Nagle chartering her own religious community that would operate before official papal recognition and call itself the Society of the Charitable Instruction of the Sacred Heart of Jesus. A Presentation annalist recorded that the tension was so great between Father Moylan and Nagle that the cleric threatened to have Nagle's new convent destroyed. Nagle was said to have countered, "'if he was pleased to drive her thence, she would never pursue her intended object in Cork. . . .' Not willing to lose the exertions of one, whom he saw was conducted by the spirit of God. . . . [Father Moylan] remained ever after silent on the subject."[10] Thus, Nagle's faith inspired her to defy all sorts of obstacles in order to perform her duty; yet unlike the assessments of other historians who have viewed similar behavior in other religious women as ultimately liberating them from a domestic ideology, Nagle remained true to her original ideals. Although her behavior pushed contemporary propriety to the limit, she ultimately performed her "world mother" obligation to impart domestic ideals and skills to young girls and to boys a sense of the responsibility born by heads of households.[11]

Nagle's followers continued her work after she died in 1784, but a year later they numbered only four. In Klegon's sociological frame of reference, the small community was in desperate need of the internal solidarity and external support crucial to their future as a group. For them, the absence of an inspirational leader, the lack of comfort and respect gained from papal recognition, and the existence of an oppressive routine were problems that needed to be solved. Therefore, soon after Nagle's death the sisters resolved to move toward full status within the Church hierarchy. This meant that they must accept the enclosure rule.[12]

Although they continued to teach within cloister walls, by accepting confinement the Presentations unavoidably limited the extent to which they could serve clients, especially the ill, thus they also perpetuated a long-accepted sexist bias toward women and revealed that their ideology of separate spheres was as yet separate and unequal to the analytical, intellectual, hard-working ideals of the male world. Directions for novice training in the nuns' constitution of 1793 reflected commonly held gender stereotypes of both Eve and Mary, each of whom resided within the historic woman's sphere—one the portent of woman's evil nature, the other a harbinger of woman's potential for good. Consequently, the Presentation documents explained that each new sister should learn modesty, meekness, and humility (characteristics of Mary), and that the novice mistress should teach her "to root out, as much as possible, those pettish and childish humours (inherited from Eve), which especially in persons of the female sex, weaken the spirit, and render it vapid and languid. . . ."[13]

Regardless of these depictions of womankind, like Nagle, the fledgling group strove to recognize the rejuvenating spiritual and occupational benefits that solitude and prayer could provide. Having once contemplated a purely monastic life, Nagle had eventually understood the importance of remaining in constant contact with the values that gave her work purpose. Although she had opposed the necessity of enclosure to insure that such regeneration could take place, she had acknowledged the benefits of some form of se-clusion, once instructing her followers to "never dine abroad or visit or go abroad only to the chapel, the schools or business. . . . I hope we will show the world that nothing makes us go out only where charity obliges us."[14]

Yet because Nagle's followers labored constantly within an in-hospitable environment in Ireland, they longed for the complete acceptance of some outside agent—the Catholic Church. Although penal law repeals gradually came in Ireland, beginning in 1778 and extending through 1793, and although de facto toleration of Catholic education had existed before that time, Catholics did not receive the franchise until 1793. Moreover, the impending Act of Union with England in 1800 threatened only to bolster Anglican hegemony in the troubled little country. Although it gave the country thirty-two members in the British House of Lords and one hundred mem-bers in the House of Commons, the law ended the Irish Parliament's independence and approved the continuation of the Church of Ire-land, an Anglican body.[15]

Fighting this Protestant hegemony, the Presentation Sisters, pre-pared for full papal approval, were also able to restructure the com-munity's rule, the edicts by which any religious order lives and works. The new constitution helped create a better working envi-ronment, which the sisters hoped would attract more candidates for membership. For a year after Nagle's death in 1784, Margaret Tobin, one of Nano's early followers, watched as three sisters returned to their homes to die, and one left the tiny band of teachers to become a recluse. Dedicated as she was to the founder's ideals, Tobin believed that Nagle's intense drive to work and suffer for God had become a physically destructive force, leading to some sisters' early deaths. Following a longstanding Irish monastic practice, Nagle had iden-tified with Christ's physical and psychological suffering, believing that if she too endured hardships and pain, she would help atone for her own sins and those of the world. Thus, not only did Nagle push herself and her charges to work despite inclement weather and her own health problems, but four times a week she also took what is referred to as "the discipline." This latter form of extreme bodily penance involved enduring pain, either self-inflicted or administered by a spiritual director.[16] T. J. Walsh, one of Nagle's biographers, records that even on her death bed the martyr received "an ordeal of blistering. . . [and] submitted without complaint. . . ."[17]

In the light of past travails, the 1793 constitution of the Society of Charitable Instruction eliminated "the discipline," even though as a whole the document resembled the Ursuline Rule that allowed for the ritual. The newer instructions reasoned that "The Sisters of this Congregation being by their Institute employed in the arduous and laborious functions of Instructing poor [*sic*] Children, they shall be obliged to fast and abstain only on the days Commanded by the Church, and on the eve of the Conception, Nativity, Presentation, and Purification of our Blessed Lady."[18]

Prayers also were shortened to accommodate the nuns' teaching schedule, but they still recited the Little Office (in Latin) and followed a daily schedule of prayer, meditation, work, and silence. Moreover, the routine and training of the postulant (an aspirant to religious life) and the novice (a sister who is not yet professed but has received the habit) was prescribed. Although a bishop could make exceptions, the postulant was to be nineteen years of age, and the noviceship was to extend for two years. Again, a bishop could approve early profession. Essential to protect the purity of the nuns' intentions, routine helped occupy the material mind in constant activity while the actual words of prayers, psalms, and hymns focused on spiritual matters. Thus, theoretically, a sister's heart was open to receive communication from God. Hence, historian M. Raphael Consedine appropriately entitles her history of the international Presentation Order *Listening Journey*. With this essential act of religious life preserved but rescheduled, and with the official Church recognition, the community increased in popularity. Although in 1793 it had only eight members, the newly named Sisters of the Presentation of the Blessed Virgin Mary numbered approximately fifty by 1805, due largely to the order's reorganization. That year Pope Pius VII gave official approval to their new rules and constitution.[19]

At this time other nuns were attempting to savor but reconcile their spiritual and apostolic lives. As a pupil of her brother, Frenchwoman Madeline Sophie Barat adroitly mastered a rigorous liberal arts curriculum, but Louis Barat rewarded her by meeting "her simple demonstrations of affection . . . with chilling discouragement while corporal mortifications were authorized with an unwise rigor. . . ."

Thus when in 1800 Madeline Barat founded the Society of the Sacred Heart, she made it a point to de-emphasize the corporal and stress positive reinforcement for students. "Never treat them with severity," she instructed.[20]

With similar sympathies the Presentation teaching philosophy continued to model Nagle's educational aims. Throughout most of the nineteenth century, the nuns specialized in primary education, offering a basic curriculum of religion, reading, writing, and arithmetic. Being middle-class in origin, they stressed values of cleanliness, responsibility, order, industry, and the belief that women and men had separate social responsibilities—the former to nurture God's children, the latter to manage. Once the Presentations founded a new school and motherhouse, they augmented the basic course of study. For example, the nuns' industrial schools enabled girls who had first obtained an elementary education to learn needlework, embroidery, crochet, and lace-making.[21] Although these were special domestic skills, the teachers helped move their pupils beyond using their new-found abilities only in the home, obtaining "regular buyers both in Ireland and overseas, for [the girls'] work. . . ." Like that of the Ursulines and Jesuits, the Presentations' methodology consisted of the monitorial system, in which the brighter, older students instructed the younger ones. Thus the sisters adopted an educational technique several years before it became popular in non-Catholic educational circles.[22]

In 1789, recognizing the need for Presentation expertise in Dublin, Teresa Mulally founded the motherhouse from which the South Dakota Presentations would hail. She sent two novices to receive teacher training at the South Cork convent, and in 1794 instruction in the Dublin schools began; but Mulally, who never took the veil herself, became very disappointed with the young nuns' lack of freedom. Having been acquainted with Nagle, Mulally knew that the matriarch would have worked whenever and wherever necessary, but the new Rule prevented the sisters from teaching uninterrupted day-long sessions, during the evening, and throughout the summer. Moreover, to engage in spiritual renewal the regulations included a mandatory eight-day retreat each year.[23] Mulally attempted to convince Archbishop John Troy of Dublin to change the edicts. In return, Mulally received the following letter from Margaret Tobin, by then Sister Francis Tobin:

You could never have proposed to yourself to get Religious who would be content to devote themselves entirely to the instruction of others and neglect their own perfection which should be the case were they deprived of their regular times of prayer and Retreat. . . . It is from the exact observance of the Rule that all Religious must expect that God will prosper their establishment. . . . The number of school hours observed in your house together with the other duties of the rules are in my opinion impossible to persevere in and at the same time maintain their health. . . . If every Bishop or person had to do with our Institute looked on themselves as authorized to change our Constitutions. . . I would look on our state not as that of Religious but a slavery.[24]

It seems that this letter ended the conflict, but, as in Nagle's case, Mulally's emphasis on the apostolate as the manifestation of one's dedication to God marked the Dublin and other Presentation foundations throughout the world. In the 1830s, the order established a convent at St. John's, Newfoundland, and one in Manchester, England, because each area contained a large settlement of Irish immigrants. The house at St. John's resulted from the vision of Newfoundland's Bishop Michael Anthony Fleming, who visited the women's headquarters at Galway and found four sisters willing to staff a school in far-away North America. The new motherhouse at Manchester resulted from a 2,000 pound gift from a wealthy Irish man, Patrick Lavery, who had immigrated to England. Made possible through charity, the Presentations' expanding professional activities generated a reputation that by 1854 would make places for them in the United States.[25]

Even before the Presentations were forming and expanding their order, other European predecessors were reaching out to the New World. In 1727, the New Orleans Ursuline educators became the first cadre of elementary schoolteachers in what later became the United States. A special outpost of religious culture, this school and then the other convent schools that followed stressed spiritual training along with a liberal arts course of study.[26] The ideal Ursuline educator possessed an "uprightness of conscience, strength of will, [and] kindness of heart and demeanor. . . ." that produced a compassionate but disciplined teacher. The educators' professional ethos manifested itself in a curriculum that encouraged girls to understand

and accept their future roles as children's moral guides. Similarly, the Society of the Sacred Heart, which in 1818 rooted itself in Louisiana, aptly explained that its pedagogical purpose was to form "complete women . . . [through] the full and harmonious development of the faculties [and] to train Christian women who shall be well informed and influential for good. . . ."[27]

To spread this idea, Bishop Carroll made a special effort to recruit more nuns as part of his drive to shape the nascent American Catholic family. From 1790 to 1870, fifty-six newly formed congregations answered the call. Because of immigration, but also because of conversion of American citizens, during the nineteenth century the total number of women religious increased from less than forty to forty thousand. Providing the ever-growing need for these women's services between 1851 and the turn of the century, 4,805,497 future parishioners poured into the country, hoping to obtain factory work in the cities or to cultivate land in the West. Immigrants, converts, and newborns together raised the total number of Catholics from approximately 24,500 in 1860 to 16,363,000 in 1910. Although eastern and northern cities were the first strongholds of these parishioners, the frontier's promise of equality lured many to settle on the Great Plains as well. Taking the guidance of the Holy See, which condemned United States public schools as irreligious, bishops all over the country undertook the overwhelming task of establishing Church schools in their dioceses.[28] In the words of Archbishop John Ireland, the clergy's grievances against secular education centered around the complaint that these establishments ignored religion, thereby eliminating it "from the minds and hearts of the youth of the country."[29]

The push for Catholic tutelage led to programs and legislation enacted at a number of the seven provincial Church councils beginning in 1829, and three plenary councils beginning in 1852. Delegates at many of the Baltimore meetings urged the multiplication of religious teaching communities to instruct in the new schools.[30] At the Second Plenary Council, convened in 1866, it was resolved, "that in every diocese schools—each close to the church—should be erected, in which the Catholic youth may be instructed in letters and the noble arts as well as religion and sound morals."[31] The Third Plenary Council published its directives in 1884, a year that also witnessed the publication of the Congregational Reverend Josiah Strong's book

Our Country: Its Possible Future and Present Crisis, which called on Americans to counteract "the perils which threaten our Christian and American civilization."[32] Thus, despite Protestant and Catholic differences over religious doctrine, they seemed to share common values of familial loyalty, honesty, industry, and respect for the genders' separate spheres. Catholic schools even used many of the same textbooks that appeared in public school classrooms. Apparently with a Catholic teacher present to add official Church interpretations to religious-related academic material, these texts were acceptable to Catholics throughout much of the nineteenth century. Even so, American Catholic officials did encourage Church educators to write school books. In addition, the plenary council directive instructed each parish church to support a parochial system, to be erected within two years of the church's founding. All Catholic parents were bound to send their children to the church-affiliated schools unless, at home or elsewhere, they could provide for their progeny's religious instruction. Armed with such a plan, bishops pressed priests in their dioceses to insist on parochial education for the Catholic youth, raise funds for building construction, and search for nuns to breathe life into the experiments.[33]

Although challenging to the point of driving many European and even American sisters back to their motherhouses or even to their own families, the expansion of opportunities for religious teachers and nurses, particularly in the American West, revitalized those who remained. Mother Teresa of Jesus, a member of the School Sisters, taught in "the backwoods of Pennsylvania"[34] and was to have exclaimed, "America has brought me nearer to God."[35] Historian Sister Julia Gilmore concludes that "The West . . . [was] a condition of development, a frame of mind," that molded the Leavenworth, Kansas, Sisters of Charity and their "psychological outlook. . . [into] one of vigor, of youth, and of progress in spite of temporary setbacks."[36]

In selecting the religious life, nuns also chose an alternative to motherhood or spinsterhood, adding a personal motivation to the strong altruism that already existed.[37] In their minds, however, this vocational choice always involved a type of mothering. Even so, a Sister of Charity, Catherine Mallon, wrote confidentially that she pitied "the poor women we met in our [begging] travels, with five or six children, and they [the mothers] trying to cook for twenty, thirty, and forty men. Oh! How often I thanked good God for saving me from such a fate."[38] Esther Pariseau, who joined Canada's Sisters of Providence in 1843, provided another example of individualism. Thirteen years later she immigrated to the United States, and as Mother Joseph of the Sacred Heart established a convent, school, and orphanage in the state of Washington. Although the leader had exhibited the reverence appropriate for a woman of her station, she displayed the courage necessary to survive and teach on the uncivilized frontier. The intrepid mother superior once scolded a robber who had snatched from her a bag full of money, shaming him into returning the stolen goods.[39] The diaries of Sisters of Charity Catherine Mallon in New Mexico and Blandina Segale in Colorado recorded a similar fortitude. Enduring an extended begging trip that lasted several months, Sister Mallon boldly confronted crass miners' rebuffs and continued to solicit money from everyone whom she encountered.[40] Neither did the world intimidate Sister Segale, who, like Mother Joseph, rebuked an outlaw, Billy the Kid, thereby gaining his undying respect. While in Trinidad, New Mexico, Sister Segale exhibited an act of bravery when she personally accompanied a prisoner to jail to prevent a lynch mob from murdering him. On yet another occasion, she took the bold stand that white settlers had committed crimes of thievery against Native Americans throughout the westward expansion period. "Poor Indians!" she lamented in 1873. "Will they ever understand that the conquerors claim the land?"[41] Thus, although Sister Segale's and other nuns' efforts to construct Christian settlements may have been ethnocentric, the efforts revived their mission as educators, nurses, and social workers. Moreover, although nuns intended to acculturate the Native Americans rather than perpetuate their ethnic heritage, they certainly did not support extermination.

The Presentations who migrated to San Francisco in 1854 could have fit a similar description beause they too answered a call to help cultivate a new society. The mid-century flood of migrants to the state and the unruly communities that had developed encouraged the Bishop of San Francisco, Joseph Sadoc Alemany, to seek the sisters' help. He instructed an associate, Father Hugh Gallagher, then in Rome, to visit Ireland on his return journey and enlist religious teachers for the diocese. Father Gallagher contacted the Presentations at Middleton, Ireland, who agreed to send five of their members on the long journey to western North America. In 1854, they reached San Francisco and soon began an educational system that attempted to mold young women into paragons of domestic purity.[42] Years later two Presentations, Sisters Mary Annetta McFeely and Patricia Marie Mulpeters, summarized their own order's mission and in so doing restated the now historic philosophical base for their colleagues' work commitment, explaining,

> [We have made girls aware of] . . . the exalted supernatural dignity of their rôle, [for] it is necessary that the education of girls be geared to a practical fulfillment of the ideal of womanhood. [We] . . . make the girl aware of all that she is supernaturally and of all that she owes in loving allegiance and dependence to Mary her Mother. [We] . . . emphasize the fact that woman is essentially mother, that biologically and physiologically she is fitted for motherhood, and in motherhood she will normally find the fulfillment of her being. Her natural tendency is to give herself in love and service. Thus, whether she marries and bears and rears children, or whether in virginity she serves others through works of mercy or of education, she can best fulfill herself through the expression of her maternal instinct. Only an educational program which imbues pupils with such concepts as these is worthy of woman.[43]

Knowledge of the Presentations' work in San Francisco spread to other regions. Bishops notified various motherhouses in Ireland, and before the close of the century eight congregations had arrived in the United States to staff educational facilities. Twenty-one years after the California founding, another western community developed in Dubuque, Iowa. In 1880, other Presentations immigrated to Dakota Territory, and by statehood in 1889, two houses existed—one in Fargo, and the other in Aberdeen.[44]

Throughout the nineteenth century, the Irish order formed other congregations in the American Northeast, each of which eventually developed into an autonomous body but affiliated historically and ideologically with the Irish foundations that originated them. Thus a tradition of independence and personalized commitment to fulfilling Nagle's intentions marked each new Presentation community in the United States. The sisters established one for teaching at Newburgh, New York, in 1874. Watervliet and Staten Island, New

York, witnessed additional Presentation immigrations in 1881 and 1884, respectively. Finally, Fitchburg, Massachusetts, became the last nineteenth-century site in 1886, although the spread of Presentation influence continued within the trans-Mississippi West and elsewhere during the twentieth century.[45]

Ironically, the Protestant and Catholic teachers, whose common goal was to save society through education and domestic socialization, often were at odds. Although prominent Protestant churchmen in South Dakota accepted that a few female parishioners would remain single and dedicated to a religious life, for the most part they maintained that women had a duty to marry. Presbyterians, for example, accepted the position of minister William Cox who stated that, "society would . . . commit suicide, [if it] tempt[ed] woman to a life of celibacy."[46] New England educator Catharine Beecher (who, like nuns, also never married) couched part of her argument for sending Protestant proselytizers west within the need to counteract the nuns' early influence.[47] Reflecting the Beecher family attitude, Catharine's father, Reverend Lyman Beecher, had warned, "The Catholic Church holds now in darkness and bondage nearly half the civilized world. It is the most skillful, powerful, dreadful system of corruption to those who wield it, and of slavery and debasement to those who live under it."[48] Women religious stationed in western America privately responded to such persistent rebukes, as Sister Seagle's diary reveals. In 1873, she wrote rhetorically, "Will the [Catholic] frontier missionaries in the South and West . . . fare any better in public records than did the first [Catholic] missionaries who staked all to bring the knowledge of God to those who inhabited the newly discovered land?"[49]

With other North American religious already in place, the last factor to lure more Irish Presentation sisters to the United States was the presence of pupils who were similar to Nagle's Irish poor. Initially the Dakota Sioux Indians were prime candidates because they had been the object of much abuse. Hailing from the eastern part of the Northern Great Plains during the mid-eighteenth century, their Native American ancestors had fled from Minnesota when their enemies, the gun-toting Chippewa, drove them from the woodlands. The Yanktonia and Yankton Sioux were members of a larger Dakota federation, composed of fifty thousand members who had roamed the grasslands while following the buffalo herds. By the 1850s, they began to feel pressure from advancing whites and soon agreed to relinquish part of their holdings and confine themselves on a reservation. In 1858, a United States treaty with the Yankton opened a vast area to settlers in what is now eastern South Dakota, while limiting the tribe to a small section east of the Missouri River and north of the Nebraska border. Officially, then, the Yankton did not participate in the uprisings of the 1860s and 1870s. In fact, the leaders proudly claimed that they never warred with whites. Other Indians and foreign invaders eventually changed the Yanktons' lives, however, when the federal government placed hostile Sioux on reservations along the Missouri after the Minnesota Sioux war of 1862. As a result, young warriors from the relatively docile tribes east of the Missouri River rode west to join the Teton Sioux in their 1876 battle against Custer at Little Bighorn.[50]

A harbinger of this inevitable clash between cultures was the organization of the Dakota Territory in 1861. From the beginning, white officials made it clear that they intended to educate only their own children, even though the first governor, Republican William Jane, gave a flowery speech about the social importance of education. Reflecting the perception of education as a panacea, he pontificated that "in communities where truth, virtue, intelligence and knowledge prevail, there crime is rare, and poverty almost unknown." In reality, however, even an all-white public school system was slow to develop because of a lack of funds.[51]

The dearth of public schools for both minorities and whites invited Protestant and Catholic teaching and missionary activities. Early greats in South Dakota history are Episcopalians Reverend Melanethon Hoyt and Bishop William Hobart Hare. Hoyt began work in 1862, and three years later he founded a college preparatory school for whites even before he built a church in 1868. Bishop Hare was very influential in regional politics as during the late nineteenth century Episcopalians received the lion's share of federal government-assigned Indian missions in Dakota Territory. Along with educator William Henry Harrison Beadle, the churchman was a key figure in gaining separate statehood for the southern half of Dakota Territory in 1889. Another religious educator was Reverend E. W. Cook, a Congregationalist. Particularly dedicated to Indian conversion and education were Presbyterian John P. Williamson and his close associate, Congregationalist Alfred Riggs. Bishop Martin Marty, a Catholic, was also a well-known cleric dedicated to educational and mission work. Although these men were not multiculturalists in the modern sense, they did realize the necessity of learning Indian languages and customs and of speaking different dialects in the schools. Thus, in 1888 they successfully resisted a Bureau of Indian Affairs' ruling requiring that all classes be taught in English, but when the federal government cut funds to church education in 1900, all of their efforts were severely restricted.[52]

Until that time President Ulysses S. Grant's "peace policy" of 1870 encouraged missionary designs as the federal government assigned to the Catholic Church the administration of Standing Rock and Fort Totten in Dakota Territory. These were two of the eight Indian agencies throughout the country that Catholics received, while various Protestant denominations were awarded another thirty from 1870 to 1880. To carry out its responsibility, the Bureau of Catholic Indian Missions sent an appeal in 1876 to the Benedictine Abbey at St. Meinrad's, Indiana, requesting two missionaries for the Standing Rock Agency. Marty, who was a Swiss immigrant and the first abbot of St. Meinrad's, and Father Chrysostom Foffe answered this call. Preceding the Presentations, then, the two men first began converting the Sioux of Dakota Territory.[53]

Despite initial government aid, Catholic and Protestant clerics experienced, from their point of view, both negative and positive encounters as they sought to be both missionaries to the Indians and shepherds to their imported Catholic flocks. Paucity of population and the shortage of financial resources plagued the bishop. Catholic organizations attempted to follow the frontier as diocesan divisions appeared according to the size of a given citizenry. Even though priests and bishops had been instructed to insist on parochial education, it was difficult to establish institutions where numbers were small and wealth was nonexistent. The wide distances between farms and towns further hampered ecclesiastical efforts, and anti-Catholic bigotry flared on occasion to remind the clerics that although they might, for Indians, be agents of white culture, Protestants also regarded them as second-class citizens.[54]

Undaunted, Marty began traveling throughout the southern part of Dakota Territory soon after his Standing Rock appointment, meeting with both potential and confirmed converts and making plans to establish churches, convents, and schools. In order to build a church and school, he negotiated in 1877 with a group at Wheeler, the seat of Charles Mix County near the Missouri River, one hundred miles above the territorial capital of Yankton. After receiving a ten-acre donation of land, Marty chose Father Jean Malo, a French veteran of mission activity among the Indians of Oregon, to direct the project and supervise the new parish.[55]

The two clergymen made plans to erect facilities and locate teachers. Father Malo relied heavily upon his parishioners to provide materials, asking Bruno Cournoyer, a Sioux-French trader who had donated the land for the mission site, to help collect funds from other families in the area and to supervise construction of a chapel, attached kitchen, and fence. Although Marty had tried with no success to obtain a community of nuns to run the school, the priest decided to continue construction with the hope that some women religious would eventually accept the assignment.[56]

Malo did not have long to wait. While visiting his brother, Monsignor John Baptist Marty, a chaplain of the Swiss guards at the Vatican, Martin Marty learned of his own appointment as Bishop of Dakota Territory. The assignment would begin on September 22, 1879, so before the new bishop's return trip to the United States he pondered the need for religious communities to educate the Dakota Indians. Stopping in Dublin, he talked with Mother John Hughes and the Presentations at George's Hill about teaching at Wheeler. Amenable to the plan, Mother Hughes then convinced her biological sister, Mother Agnes Hughes of the Presentation Convent at Doneraile, County Cork, and Sister Teresa Challoner of Manchester, England, to join her on the journey to Dakota Territory. Mother Agnes Hughes also recruited two young novices and, along with a servant who aspired to be a lay sister, planned to leave Ireland in the spring of 1880.[57]

The Presentations would soon realize that in the Dakotas, ironically, the Catholic and Protestant Churches were acting as both saviors and saboteurs as they encouraged the migration of white parishioners into what ethically was Indian land. Moreover, other settlers' and itinerants' lust for gold lured outsiders into the sacred Black Hills, which had been designated part of the Sioux reservation by a treaty between the tribes and the United States government in 1868. With the new encroachment came railroad company officials, who in turn recruited more homesteaders from Europe and eastern portions of the United States by advertising the territory as a potential garden spot and by reducing passage rates for newcomers. These businesses cooperated with the territorial government and the Catholic Church to lure Catholic emigrants as well—each of the three viewing the others as beneficial to its particular goal of making money, spreading religious influence, or organizing the polity.[58]

Catholic bishops had often encouraged the formation of religious colonies, sometimes founded on tracts furnished by a company's land grants. Bishop John Ireland successfully established ten villages in southwestern Minnesota with Catholics from Ireland, England, Germany, and Canada. In addition, Marty, who became Vicar Apostolic of Dakota Territory in 1879, negotiated with officials of the Northern Pacific Railroad for fifty thousand acres of land in his jurisdiction to form a Catholic settlement. The churchman abandoned his plans, however, when the Irish-American group he had obtained to underwrite the scheme failed to provide the necessary funds. One of the first successful Catholic commonwealths was in eastern Dakota Territory's Brown County. The settlers came from Flint, Michigan, and their pastor, Father Robert Haire, offered the first Mass in a sod shanty near the town of Columbia. The group had planned to reside in Texas, but in 1880 the news of the "Dakota Wonderland" advertised by various railroad firms persuaded them to set out for the northern prairies.[59]

Thus the inevitability of white domination in Dakota Territory beckoned to more and more of their own kind, and despite financial setbacks in the 1870s the ten-year period beginning in 1878 marked what is called the Great Dakota Boom. The earth that lay between the Minnesota border and the Missouri River was rich, and once the heavy layer of sod was broken and the prairie grass that covered it was removed, the fertile soil yielded abundant harvests. Because the rains had been steady and plentiful during the decade, water supplies did not appear to be a problem when outsiders' homesteading began in earnest. The prairies were treeless except along the banks of streams, and the wind was a constant companion, yet optimistic homesteaders accustomed themselves to the open sky and the incessant howl of the wind as they discovered that crops would grow. When winter did come, however, temperatures dropped below zero, and blizzards occurred frequently; but the arrival of spring was glorious as the prairie grew lush with grass and flowers, and meadowlark songs invited farmers to the fields. Consequently, during the ten years before statehood came in 1889, the population reached one hundred thousand as farms improved and harvests remained profitable.[59]

By 1890, the Catholic Church could count 25,720 of these 100,000 people as members of the flock, and that figure was the highest percentage in the state when compared individually to Lutherans (23,314), Methodists (12,116), Congregationalists (5,164), Presbyterians (4,778), Baptists (4,052), or Episcopalians (2,649).[60]

Although the Catholic Church would flourish in South Dakota, in 1880 the six Presentation pioneers faced a very tenuous future, for the sisters would endure more than two years of uncertainty as they sojourned from place to place. In addition, the nuns' original intention of working with the Sioux, who were their nineteenth-century version of Nano Nagle's eighteenth-century Irish poor, would be diverted in another direction before the women finally established a permanent motherhouse in South Dakota. Yet the sisters possessed a singular adherence to their order's ideals, and they could take comfort in the forbearance of other nuns who had made a place for themselves in the United States.

NOTES

1. Mary P. Ryan, *Cradle of the Middle Class: The Family in Oneida County, New York, 1790–1865* (New York: Cambridge University Press, 1981) and "A Women's Awakening: Evanglical Religion and the Families of Utica, New York, 1800–1840," in *Women in American Religion,* ed. Janet Wilson James (Philadelphia: University of Pennsylvania Press, 1976), 89–110.

2. T. J. Walsh, *Nano Nagle and the Presentation Sisters* (Dublin: M. H. Hill and Son, 1959), 25–26, 38–41; Sister Rosaria O'Callaghan, *Flame of Love* (Milwaukee: Bruce Press, 1960), 30; Mary Hayden and George A. Moonan, *A Short History of the Irish People: From the Earliest Times to 1920* (New York: Longmans, Green, 1922), 363–67.

3. M. Raphael Consedine, P.B.V.M., *Listening Journey: A Study of the Spirit and Ideals of Nano Nagle and the Presentation Sisters* (Victoria, Australia: Congregation of the Presentation of the Blessed Virgin Mary, 1983), xi, 20–27, 36, 45, 52. Records are unclear as to the exact founding date of Nagle's first school.

4. Consedine, *Listening Journey,* 42, 46, 48, 52.

5. Ibid., 14–15; Carolyn C. Lougee, " 'Noblesse', Domesticity, and So-

cial Reform: The Education of Girls by Fénelon and Saint-Cyr," *History of Education Quarterly* 14 (Spring 1974): 87–113.

6. M. Lechy, quoted in Consedine, *Listening Journey*, 42.

7. Ibid., 45.

8. Nano Nagle, quoted in Ibid., 28.

9. Walsh, *Nano Nagle*, xiii–xiv.

10. South Presentation annalist, quoted in Consedine, *Listening Journey*, 67.

11. Nancy F. Cott, "Young Women in the Second Great Awakening," *Feminist Studies* 3 (Fall 1975): 15–29.

12. Consedine, *Listening Journey*, 98, 100–1, 111, 188.

13. "The Rules and Constitutions of the Sisters of the Congregation of the Charitable Instruction," 1793, quoted in Ibid., 422.

14. Nagle, quoted in Ibid., 195.

15. Ibid., 95–98; Hayden and Moonan, *A Short History of the Irish People*, 418–22, 448; Harold J. Schultz, *History of England* (New York: Barnes and Noble, 1968), 187.

16. Consedine, *Listening Journey*, 100–1, 109, 116–17; Walsh, *Nano Nagle*, 124–25.

17. Walsh, *Nano Nagle*, 116.

18. "The Rules and Constitutions of the Sisters of the Congregation of the Charitable Instruction," 1793, quoted in Consedine, *Listening Journey*, 413.

19. Ibid., 116, 186, 205, 410–12; The Poor Clares of Reparation and Adoration, *Religious Communities in the American Episcopal Church and in the Anglican Church of Canada* (West Park, N.Y.: Holy Cross Press, 1956), 143, 144; Sister Alicia Dunphy to Courtney Ann Vaughn-Roberson, July 28, 1986.

20. Louise Callan, *The Society of the Sacred Heart in North America*, vol. 1 (New York: Longmans, Green, 1937), 12–13; vol. 2, 743. Also see page 16.

21. Consedine, *Listening Journey*, 146, 211, 224–25, 230, 298–99.

22. Ibid., 296, 220–1.

23. Sister Pauline Quinn, "Biographies of Major Superiors, Section II: Prologue, Teresa Mulally," Presentation Archives, Presentation Heights, Aberdeen, S.D.

24. Sister Francis Tobin, quoted in Sister Quinn, "Teresa Mulally."

25. Walsh, *Nano Nagle*, 253–65.

26. Mary Ewens, O.P., *The Role of the Nun in Nineteenth-Century America: Variations on the International Theme* (New York: Arno Press, 1976, repr., Salem, N.H.: Ayer Publishers, 1984), 22. For an account of early New England women professed as nuns in Canada, see Sister Mary Leo Clement Fallon, "Early New England Nuns" (Ph.D. diss., Boston College, 1936).

27. Sister Catharine Frances, S. S. J., "The Convent School of French

Origin in the United States, 1727 to 1843" (Ph.D. diss., University of Pennsylvania, 1936), 139, 69. Also see page 138.

28. James Hennesey, S. J., *American Catholics: A History of the Roman Catholic Community in the United States* (New York: Oxford University Press, 1981), 73, 86–87, 173; Ewens, *The Role of the Nun in Nineteenth-Century America,* 35–61, 86, 201 and "The Leadership of Nuns in Immigrant Catholicism," in *Women and Religion in America,* vol. 1: *The Nineteenth Century: A Documentary History,* ed. Rosemary Radford Ruether and Rosemary Skinner Keller (New York: Harper and Row Publishers, 1981), 101; Sara Maitland, *A Map of the New Country: Women and Christianity* (London: Routledge and Kegan Paul, 1983), 54; Gerald Shaughnessy, *Has the Immigrant Kept the Faith? A Study of Immigration and Catholic Growth in the United States, 1790–1922* (New York: Macmillan, 1925) 140, 159, 165, 169.

29. Thomas T. McAvoy, *A History of the Catholic Church in the United States* (Notre Dame, Ind.: University of Notre Dame Press, 1970), 294.

30. Harold A. Buetow, *Of Singular Benefit: The Story of Catholic Education in the United States* (London: Macmillan, 1970), 146–54.

31. Second Plenary Council, quoted in Buetow, *Of Singular Benefit,* 146.

32. Josiah Strong, quoted in Robert H. Wiebe, *The Search for Order, 1877–1920* (New York: Hill and Wang, 1967), 44.

33. Buetow, *Of Singular Benefit,* 148–54; Ruth Miller Elson, *Guardians of Tradition: American Schoolbooks of the Nineteenth Century* (Lincoln: University of Nebraska Press, 1964).

34. A School Sister of Notre Dame, *Mother Caroline and the School Sisters of Notre Dame in North America,* vol. 1 (St. Louis: Woodward and Tiernan, 1928), 30.

35. Covelle Newcomb, *Running Waters* (New York: Dodd, Mead, 1947), 125.

36. Sister Julia Gilmore S.C.L., *We Came North: Centennial Story of the Sisters of Charity of Leavenworth* (St. Meinrad, Ind.: Abbey Press, 1961), 475.

37. Marta Helen Danylewycz, "Taking the Veil in Montreal, 1840–1920: An Alternative to Motherhood and Spinsterhood" (Ph.D. diss., The University of Toronto, 1982).

38. Sister Catherine Mallon, quoted in "Sister Catherine Mallon's Journal: Part 2," ed. Thomas Richter, *New Mexico Historical Review* 52 (Summer 1977): 239.

39. Lucile McDonald, "Mother Joseph," in *The Women Who Made the West,* ed. The Western Writers of America (Garden City, N.Y.: Doubleday, 1980), 120–29.

40. Thomas Richter, ed., "Sister Catherine Mallon's Journal: Part 1," *New Mexico Historical Review* 52 (Spring 1977): 135–55 and "Sister Catherine Mallon's Journal: Part 2," 237–50.

41. Sister Blandina Segale, *At the End of the Santa Fe Trail* (Milwaukee: Bruce Publishing, 1948), 11–12, 43, 62, 78, 81, 99.

42. Walsh, *Nano Nagle*, 265–66.

43. Sisters Mary Annetta McFeely and Patricia Marie Mulpeters, quoted in Walsh, *Nano Nagle*, 270.

44. Consedine, *Listening Journey*, 405; see chapter 3 of this volume.

45. Consedine, *Listening Journey*, 405; Walsh, *Nano Nagle*, 265, 279–80.

46. William Cox, quoted in Dennis A. Norlin, "The Suffrage Movement and South Dakota Churches: Radicals and the Status Quo, 1890," *South Dakota History* 14 (Winter 1984): 323.

47. Polly Welts Kaufman, *Women Teachers on the Frontier* (New Haven: Yale University Press, 1984), xix, 8.

48. Lyman Beecher, quoted in Hennessey, *American Catholics*, 119.

49. Segale, *At the End of the Santa Fe Trail*, 54.

50. Herbert Schell, *History of South Dakota* (Lincoln: University of Nebraska Press, 1961), 20, 68–72, 85–86, 130–39; Sister M. Cabrini Di Donato, P.B.V.M., "A History of the Educational Work of the Presentation Sisters of Aberdeen, South Dakota" (master's thesis, Northern State College, 1966), 6–8.

51. William Jane, quoted in Cleata B. Thorpe, "Education in South Dakota 1861–1961," in *South Dakota Historical Collections* 36 (1972): 213. Also see pages 212, 247–49.

52. Ibid., 221–25, 393–403; Schell, *History of South Dakota*, 198–99, 211–12.

53. Sister Di Donato, "A History of the Educational Work of the Presentation Sisters," 2; *Diamond Jubilee Book* (Aberdeen, S.D.: Sisters of the Presentation of the Blessed Virgin Mary, 1961), 21–22; Buetow, *Of Singular Benefit*, 156.

54. McAvoy, *The Great Crisis in American Catholic History* (Chicago: Henry Regnery, 1957), 70; John Tracy Ellis, *American Catholicism* (Chicago: University of Chicago Press, 1955), 120.

55. *Diamond Jubilee Book*, 21–23; Sister Di Donato, "A History of the Educational Work of the Presentation Sisters," 2.

56. Sister Di Donato, "A History of the Educational Work of the Presentation Sisters," 2.

57. Ibid., 5; Sister Pauline Quinn, "Biographies of Major Superiors, Section III: Mother John Hughes, 1886–1892," Presentation Archives.

58. Schell, *History of South Dakota*, 88–89, 159.

59. James P. Shannon, *Catholic Colonization on the Western Frontier* (New Haven: Yale University Press, 1957), ix, 190–91, 248; Sister Di Donato, "A History of the Educational Work of the Presentation Sisters," 5; "Presentation Annals," Presentation Archives, Aberdeen, S.D.

60. Schell, *History of South Dakota*, 158–74.

67. Norlin, "The Suffrage Movement and South Dakota Churches," 310–11.

3. Sojourning and Settling
in South Dakota,
1880–96

□

For early South Dakota Presentation Sisters, a "continuous touch with the simplicity of primitive society" helped produce the resilience that became one of their community's major traits.[1] Nineteenth-century Presentations (especially Australians) stationed at mission sites all over the world experienced a similar regeneration. Historian M. Raphael Consedine described these Presentations as "generous-hearted women who had come to religious life with high ideals [and who] might well have felt cramped within a well-established enclosed community. [They] welcomed the opportunity of venturing along untried roads."[2] Truly this was the case for the Dakota Presentations, as their pioneer existence set in a sometimes desolate environment led the nuns to abandon their enclosure rule. This decision catalyzed the rekindling of Nano Nagle's ideological spirit, which heightened colleagueship and enabled the group to better serve the students, their families, and the secular settlement of which the nuns were a part. Moreover, a growing number of Catholics in South Dakota, and a compatibility of the Irish women's ideology with that of other western women, provided helpful external reinforcement for the nuns' special teaching mission. Looking back in 1980 on those frontier days, a group of South Dakota Presentations wrote, "the spirit of our early Sisters [is] . . . a prairie spirituality, . . . characterized by a grateful dependence on God, a hope for the future, a simplicity and hiddenness, [yet] a boldness and love for open space and for the people whose lives are rooted in the soil and the prairie environment."[3]

In March of 1880, exactly one hundred years earlier, three Irish Presentations and three Irish postulants left Ireland for the United

53

States, intending to become missionaries and teachers to the Sioux and their children. Led by Presentation superior Mother John Hughes, the small group had a strong-willed, stern, heavyset woman capable of steering the fledgling community through its infant days. "The sisters found in her leadership, a tower of strength and [an example] of a true apostolic woman."[4] Born in 1831, the trailblazer was the daughter of a lawyer. Educated in Belfast, she entered the Dublin convent in 1856 at the age of twenty-five. Before she left Ireland for the United States, Mother Hughes successfully ran and taught in an orphanage and founded another Presentation settlement in Granard. Harsh by modern standards, as was forebear Nano Nagle, Mother Hughes must have viewed suffering as a virtue.[5] As one biographer records, she "seemed to thrive on challenges and obstacles, and she inspired her companions (especially her own sister Mother Agnes and Sister Teresa Challoner of England) to unbelievable sacrifices due to privations, piercing cold and unstable conditions."[6]

Thus Mother Hughes was one of many strong-minded Irish women who immigrated to the United States during the nineteenth century. Due largely to depressed socioeconomic conditions in Ireland, particularly the Great Potato Famine that took its greatest toll from 1845 to 1848, Irish Catholic families began passing holdings only to their eldest sons. Moreover, because of the socially frustrated position of men in Ireland, it seems that women were held in lower esteem there than in the United States. This left a number of young single men and consequently unmarried women with specific motivations for entering a convent and/or seeking a new life in the United States. Even before the Potato Famine, one million Irish traveled to America between 1815 and 1845, and by mid-century, one-half of those immigrants to the United States were women.[7]

Although some of these Irishwomen, like Mother Hughes, were quite independent, most retained a commitment to some form of domestic ideology. Threats to Catholicism in Ireland and the prejudice of nativism in the United States encouraged them to focus on holding their families together. As late as 1975, studies of Irish Americans indicate that although they had lost much of their original commitment to the importance of grown children keeping in contact with parents or in-laws, Irish American women had retained a belief in the primacy of their roles as wives and mothers.[8]

At least throughout the nineteenth century and on into the

modern era, however, Irish immigrants still retained a dedication to the extended family. In 1850, only 5 percent of single Irish men and women lived in boarding houses rather than with family members. Moreover, the new Americans kept strong ties with kinfolk living in Ireland. Ironically, the success of the Irish National School system (established in 1831) facilitated this bond. By 1875, it had made the Irish people literate in English and therefore able to write letters to their Americanized relatives. These North American kinfolk did more than just answer the correspondence. Between 1848 and 1900, they mailed 260 million hard-earned dollars overseas to their struggling families.[9]

Because Presentation superiors in South Dakota continued to recruit Irish novices well into the twentieth century, traditional Irish attitudes were alive and well within the Aberdeen order; however, for the Presentations, life on the American frontier helped them expand, if not escape, domesticity's limitations. Social conditions in South Dakota fostered an ideological merger of religious and lay Irish women into what became the state's melting pot. Dakota Bishop Martin Marty was an advocate of Americanization. Irish immigrants had only a small identity group in South Dakota because the primary groups were Norwegians, Swedes, Germans, Dutch, and Bohemians or Czechs. The territorial government created an immigrant bureau in 1875 to help all newcomers adapt to the new milieu. Attempting to force the unwilling to assimilate, four years later the territorial legislature banned the instructional use of any language other than English in the public schools.[10] Whether or not immigrants initially aspired to the notion, most South Dakota women came to believe that the preservation of American culture was their domestic duty. Assessing the general impact of frontier life on all Dakota women, historian Glenda Riley notes that although they "represented a variety of heritages that occasionally manifested themselves through special foods, items of clothing, crafts or value systems in their new homes in the West, they were unified by their participation in what might be called the female frontier."[11]

Even Western American women who rejected a capitalist economic system still seemed to envision a world of separate spheres: the strong male providers in one and the good moral mothers in the other. Although the famous turn-of-the-century socialist Kate Richards O'Hare favored woman suffrage she, too, held that the male and female roles should be separate, reasoning that "our prehistoric ancestors settled the question of man's and woman's place in life ... when instinctively the men went out to hunt the game and left the women and children to tend the fires, prepare the food and dress the skins."[12] A depiction of socialist miners' wives from Colorado also portrays these women's desire to be contented, well-fixed housewives.[13]

Although as an institution the Catholic Church in the Dakotas and throughout the United States feared the threat of socialism to the centrality of religion in daily life, there were exceptions. One was Father Robert Haire, a convert to Catholicism and an intimate associate of Mother Hughes and the Presentations at Aberdeen. He migrated from Michigan to the Dakotas in 1880, and after having worked with struggling farmers for years became an avid supporter of the Populist cause, a rural collectivist political movement that was born in 1890 at Huron, South Dakota. After the demise of populism, Father Haire turned to socialism as a cure for the poverty that he witnessed every day. He accepted a leadership role in the state's Knights of Labor organization,[14] and although Catholics throughout the nation "were popularly identified as opponents of woman suffrage,"[15] he supported the cause. It is not known if Mother Hughes concurred. In 1891, Bishop Marty forced Father Haire to choose between his position within the Church and his political work. Although the priest selected the latter, he was reinstated in 1902 and retained close ties with the South Dakota Presentation nuns until he died in 1916.[16]

Regardless of the affiliation with Father Haire, if the early Presentations had supported suffrage their reason for doing so would never have contradicted their ideology. Probably their sentiments were echoed in the words of a Kansas Sister of Charity, Mother Mary Berchman. After national suffrage was granted in 1920, she encouraged nuns to vote and thus "restore spiritual values to a country rapidly becoming obsessed with a desire for tangible and material accomplishments and governed by an administration stigmatized as the most corrupt in history up to that time."[17] Reiterating this same argument, Bishop John Lancaster Spalding eventually favored the vote for women, maintaining that "woman was closer to the supreme reality, because she was guided by a 'divine instinct to understand that the infinite need is the need of love.'"[18]

Reflecting a more restrictive mood, the major religious denominations in South Dakota, including the Catholic Church, did not support suffrage, and the issue was defeated six times between 1890 and 1918. Yet religious women such as Methodist minister Anna H. Shaw spoke in the state for the cause, and a well-organized South Dakota Women's Christian Temperance Union included many suffragists. Even Territorial Superintendent of Schools General William Henry Harrison Beadle, who served from 1878 to 1885, favored the cause.[19]

If not through the voting franchise, then at least through education South Dakotans seemed to agree that moral women teaching in the public schools should mold the state's youth into God-fearing, responsible adults. Resembling teaching forces throughout the country, the South Dakota educators were predominantly female, numbering 1,056 women and 461 men in 1893. Although all teachers were expected to obey school board mandates such as "go[ing] to church regularly. . . ," one local edict posted in 1872 was for women only. It read, "women teachers who marry or engage in other unseemly conduct will be dismissed."[20] Of course it was assumed that most female public school teachers would marry eventually; then, according to tradition, their appropriate place would not be in the classroom but in the home.[21]

Because of these conservative attitudes, a shortage of funds, a sparse population, and an inadequate rural school system, nineteenth-century training of public school teachers was poor in South Dakota; however, this trend was reflected in many parts of the country, particularly the rural West. By 1860, the United States could boast of only twelve normal schools, and although there were 345 by the turn of the century, only about one-fourth of the national teacher work force had received any postsecondary preparation because most of them were trained through apprenticeship.[22]

The Catholic Church in the United States was aware of similar inconsistencies within its own teaching ranks. Some nuns were trained in programs within the motherhouse, priests taught others, and a few sisters studied at secular and/or Catholic postsecondary schools. In particular, the Plenary Council of 1884 sought to remedy the problem. It decreed that bishops were to appoint a diocesan board of examiners that would test all prospective teachers, religious and secular. The certification of each person would be good for five years and would be recognized in every diocese. At the end of the first five years, teachers were to take a second and final examination. The council also insisted that bishops in each diocese name school committees that once or twice a year would review every school in a given district, examining pupils and making other observations. The committee was then to report directly to the chairman of the diocesan board. Having set up a system all its own, the plenary council encouraged the writing of Catholic texts and forbade co-operative efforts with public schools such as those that had operated in Poughkeepsie, New York and Faribault, Minnesota.[23]

South Dakota public school certification was handled initially through examination and left solely to the county superintendents who were to "examine all teachers. . . in moral character, learning and ability to teach."[24] By 1883, the territorial superintendent wrote the test questions which, if passed with varying degrees of competency, resulted in the awarding of one of three types of licenses. To assist preparation of student teachers or to augment the skills of those already employed, the first one-week teacher institute was held at Elk Point in 1867. By the end of the century, county summer sessions were common, and the state provided additional teacher instruction at what became South Dakota State College at Brookings (founded in 1881) and at the University of South Dakota (established in 1862 but not opened until 1882). In the 1880s, the legislature created five state normal schools but provided them with no appropriations; three survived: Black Hills State College at Spearfish, Dakota State College at Madison, and the University of South Dakota at Springfield. Another would be established in Aberdeen after statehood. Further bolstering the professionalization of teaching, Superintendent Beadle encouraged the formation of the South Dakota Teachers Association in 1884.[25]

Denominational colleges speckled the state, and some of their students also became teachers. Speaking positively about this development, Superintendent Beadle stated in 1884 that "these Christian colleges and schools are all needed to help the State Schools. There is room for all and each is better for the others."[26] Reverend Joseph Ward, a Congregationalist, founded Yankton College in 1881. Two years later the Presbyterians erected what would become Huron College, and the Baptists opened what became Sioux Falls College. In 1883, Methodists opened Dakota Wesleyan University at Mitchell, and a year later Wessington Springs Junior College at Wessington Springs joined the others. Permanent facilities for Catholic higher education in South Dakota would not begin until the twentieth century.[27] Even so, the plenary council had spearheaded the development of Catholic high schools, academies, and colleges, particularly promoting Catholic University of America. The institution was initially closed to women; apparently, the churchmen at Baltimore seemed not to recognize women as an oppressed majority when it stressed the Christian duty of Catholics to address the educational needs of American blacks and Indians, the "forgotten people."[28]

It was with these children of God in mind that Mother Hughes and her five companions made their way to the United States in 1880. After a twelve-day sea voyage that brought the women to New York, they met Bishop Marty's envoys, Fathers Jean Malo and Arthur Donnelly. After receiving advice on teaching in American schools from a group of Presentations at St. Michael's Convent in Newburgh, New York (a congregation Donnelly had helped establish six years earlier), the missionaries traveled by train to Chicago, then to Omaha, to Sioux City, and finally to Yankton in the Dakotas. There they boarded the *Josephine* and began passage up the Missouri River to Wheeler, a town in the same vast territory. The steamboat encountered shifting sandbars and a spring storm that made the journey hazardous, yet even as the tumult subsided the women noticed the flat, treeless wilderness beyond the high banks of the river, which could only have offered desolation in place of the blinding rain.[29]

When the sisters finally arrived in Wheeler, they could not help comparing their new home to the one they had recently left. The primitive two-story, stone-and-sod structure was located between Fort Randall and the Yankton Indian Reservation, more than ninety miles northwest of the nearest railroad station, at Yankton on the Missouri River. Although the reservoir provided the prospective schoolkeepers with water, they had to haul it themselves and still pay 25 cents a barrel. There were a few pieces of furniture in the building. On the first floor, the room in which they were to conduct classes contained some log benches, a small table, and a students' desk that consisted of one long board lodged perpendicularly into the wall and kept stable by sticks that served as table legs. The sisters' living quarters on the second floor consisted of five small sleeping and meditation cubicles and three larger meeting rooms, all devoid of furnishings. The windows were poorly fitted, and the heat for the entire building radiated from an old woodburning stove in a corridor of the sisters' residence. The new setting was vastly different from their former home, a sturdy stone Irish convent cradled in gardens of blooming shrubbery. The old motherhouse must have seemed like a castle when compared to the rugged edifice silhouetted against the limitless sky of the northern prairie.[30]

Aside from any lamentations, there was work to do, so after making the living quarters as comfortable as possible, the women regrouped and soon opened St. Ann's Mission School. The Presentations' major contributions were teaching such rudimentary subjects as reading, writing, and arithmetic, and instilling basic Christian values to children ranging in age from seven to seventeen. An added social emphasis was present in home management course offerings taught to Indian female boarders, who earned their keep by helping with cooking, laundry, and cleaning. Especially for girls, the school's plan of study was designed to sustain the household while it prepared American Indian women to lift their values to what the Presentations felt were greater cultural heights.[31]

Much to the sisters' disappointment, fewer than twenty children enrolled, most of them from nearby mixed-blood French-and-Indian families. In fact, the large enrollment of two hundred pupils that Bishop Marty envisioned never materialized because many people had either moved farther west or had fled to Canada with Sitting Bull after the Sioux War of 1876–77. At one point there were only five students for the nuns to instruct. The classroom, which was forty feet by thirty-two feet, doubled as the chapel and was never crowded. Essentially, the teachers had major communication problems with the many pupils and parishioners who spoke no English. Because territorial school officials frowned on teaching pupils in various native languages, the nuns enlisted Emily Cournoyer, the daughter of Bruno Cournoyer, a French-Indian trader and farmer. Emily, who had studied at a Catholic school in Kansas, was hired to provide some help as an interpreter for the Indian children. To communicate with the mixed-bloods, the sisters used the French that they had learned in Ireland; but even when the instructors could explain a particular lesson effectively, the pupils often lacked the supplies necessary to carry it out. Paper was scarce, so slates often sufficed. The few available textbooks were ones the nuns brought from Ireland.[32] As to the curriculum, one of the nuns recounted that "education was restricted to the fundamentals . . . reading, writing, and arithmetic," which were memorized and recited. "Discipline," she continued, "was strict and demanded!"[33]

The Presentations' determination helped them and their school to survive during the first year, but the disastrous blizzard that raged during the winter of 1880–81, filling the sky and blanketing the prairies, made teaching harder than ever. From mid-October until the next April, storm followed storm, and temperatures fell below zero degrees Fahrenheit. The sisters lacked sufficient clothing to protect them from such brutal weather, and they suffered additionally because of the school's faulty heating system. Never easy even in the best of weather, travel was impossible, and often supply wagons did not reach them. Neighbors sustained the Presentations, occasionally sharing newly butchered meat. The only advantage of all the snow was that water no longer had to be purchased by the barrel, for the women could manufacture it by merely melting snow. When spring arrived, however, problems did not abate entirely because thaws caused the Missouri River to flood the surrounding area. Gradually the moisture crumbled the walls of the Presentations' home, and in June it finally collapsed, forcing them to seek refuge in huts abandoned by earlier settlers.[34] Mary Lynch, a boarder who had remained with the nuns through the Easter vacation, remembered the tragedy: "I was awakened in the middle of the night by a heavy crash. Everyone else was awakened too and there was a great excitement among the children, mostly Indian girls. Mother Agnes quieted us and told us to dress and go to another part of the building. There she explained that the outside wall of the dormitory had caved in. I have never forgotten that Good Friday because we ate our supper standing in honor of Christ's death. I don't remember the kind of food we ate except that we had dried apple sauce at each meal."[35]

After Bishop Marty learned of conditions at Wheeler he decided to give up the effort, for he had no funds for rebuilding and the small enrollment hardly justified construction even if he could find the money. Feeling badly defeated, three Presentations left their comrades. Sister Teresa Challoner went back to Manchester, and two postulants also returned to their families. This left the nuns with only four members besides Mother Hughes—Sisters Agnes Hughes, Alacoque Scallard, Magdalen Menahan, and M. Martin O'Toole. Not wanting to lose those women's influence, Marty suggested that they establish an academy at Deadwood in the Black Hills. This mining center was still booming as a result of the 1870s' gold rush, and the Catholic priest there, Father Peter Rosen, had requested the bishop's permission and assistance to erect an educational facility and to locate sisters to operate it. Marty explained to the Presentations that they could be of immediate help to Deadwood's largely non-Indian population and that in due time their school could receive Native American matriculants from the reservation south of the Black Hills.[36]

Mother John Hughes responded affirmatively to Father Rosen's request, but her flock apprehensively awaited the journey to this bawdy mining town in which the women were to begin teaching in September of 1881. They prepared to leave on the first boat up the Missouri River but were delayed three weeks until a steamboat finally appeared. At last the sisters gathered blankets and food, said goodbye to their Indian neighbors, who wished them a safe journey, and then embarked. The three-day trip upriver to Fort Pierre proved to be slower than expected, and from the fort they traveled miles by stagecoach across the plains. Sister Frances Menahan, one of the few Presentations whose recorded reminiscences survive, wrote of her relief at finally leaving the coach after being jolted from side to side for such a long distance.[37]

Upon arriving in Deadwood, the sisters were anything but favorably impressed. Built on the side of a hill, the town was scattered with brick and wooden buildings, and heavy rains had washed a large amount of hillside soil into the streets. Amid such disarray, Father Rosen must have been a welcome sight as he greeted his new associates and took them to rest in a private home. The next day the priest led the Presentations to a three-story brick building, which he said would be their home and school. The sisters, he explained, would have to attend Mass at the parish church located one mile away. Although the nuns would not stay in Deadwood, this event was the first of several that eventually forced the Presentations to realize that they must abandon enclosure. Initially, however, the thought of leaving the convent was disturbing because the Presentations had practiced enclosure for almost a century. Aggravating the nuns' anxiety were the rough-hewn Deadwood citizens, making the town "a seething cauldron of restless humanity" where "lawlessness and the usual pandering to man's frailties" abounded.[38] After only two days Mother Hughes and her small group resolved not to live without enclosure and began a return trip to St. Ann's by the next available stage.[39]

En route they took shelter in a hotel in Pierre, in which they slept on mattresses thrown into a room. A rough town, Pierre was located across the river from Fort Pierre. The nuns' hotel was apparently a brothel, and the sisters were so terrified that they took turns holding watch throughout the night. The next day they boarded a steamboat for a trip downriver and eventually arrived at Wheeler. They slept in their old ruined convent for one night then moved into a hut offered by an Indian neighbor. Eventually Marty found for the sisters an abandoned three-room log cabin that they inhabited for two months. During that time, despite the scarcity of food, the Presentations once again set up a school. Their facility was even more primitive than before, and they matriculated only a handful of youngsters.[40]

Bedraggled and almost defeated, the sisters wrote to Marty that it might be best if they returned to Ireland. Sympathetic toward their plight, he agreed to send them the necessary passages and money for incidental travel expenses. While they waited to return home, the Presentations' sense of commitment triumphed over their frustration and fear, and the nuns' change of heart brought about the decision to remain in Dakota.[41] Experiencing what one pioneer of the School Sister order would later write as purification "in the crucible of suffering,"[42] the Presentations persevered and endured hardships unusual for even the American West. For example, later in Fargo, a lay Catholic teacher, Minnie Farlin Stock, remarked that the Hughes sisters were even "reluctant to have heat in their cells in the severe winter until they received approval from their mother houses in Ireland."[43] Nano Nagle would have been proud.

While awaiting their next journey, the Presentations moved in with the Sisters of Mercy, who conducted a boarding school in Yankton. In June of 1882, they left for Fargo, in northern Dakota Territory, to teach in the parish of Father James Stephan. The priest had asked Marty to locate an order of educators, and the bishop in turn asked Mother Hughes to accept the responsibility. Eager to find a permanent location, she and her charges took the assignment. After reaching Fargo, the sisters stayed in the parish rectory until Father Stephan could have their living quarters completed, but on July 26,

1882, the women began to instruct and shape the region's children, holding catechism lessons in the church for several hours a day. That fall the Presentations started regular academic instruction in the first school for non-Indian children in North Dakota.[44]

Despite the sisters' changing clientele, the Irish order was becoming an agent for civilization in the West, as the Presentations' educational efforts gave students the knowledge and values to bridge into the inevitably more complex world of the next century. Moreover, the nuns' activities became so diverse that for all practical purposes the enclosure rule was becoming a thing of the past. Demands for a larger classroom and rectory building resulted in fundraising drives in which the sisters participated. A fair was held to raise money, and the nuns sold tickets at $1.00 each, traveling as far west as Mandan to peddle them, although, as one member put it, they met with "indifferent" success. The promotional event was the first of many to come, and even though it taxed the women, it also strengthened the group by weeding out the less determined. Two novices left. Sister Menahan transferred to a Rhode Island Presentation convent because, in her words, "I could not bring myself to go on a begging tour."[45] Sister Joseph Butler and Sister Martin O'Toole, two of the three nuns who remained, accomplished the job, and construction on the new edifice did begin. In fact, rather than teach, these two were to be chief mendicants of the Presentations during these early days. In this role, as one nun later wrote, "they approached railroad men, merchants and farmers," asking for any donation that the fellow Dakotans could spare.[46]

By the summer of 1883, the small Presentation community in Fargo needed more members to carry out its ever-expanding responsibilities. Mother Hughes requested temporary help from the Presentations in San Francisco until she could obtain more educators from Ireland. Four sisters from California served at the Fargo academy until 1885, when Irish Sisters Mary Clare Brown, Mary Aloysius Chriswell, Nora Tanner, and Mary Ellen Butler arrived. With the mission firmly established, Father Stephan transferred the property deed to Mother Hughes.[47]

At last it seemed that after five years of strife the Dakota Presentations had made for themselves a home, but because the women had proved to be so useful in the initial drive to civilize a frontier community the Church would call them away again. Four years earlier, in 1880, the same year that the Presentations had arrived at Wheeler, engineers had surveyed the town of Aberdeen as a stop on the Milwaukee railroad line through central Dakota Territory. A small band of German-Russian Catholics, which Father Robert Haire had led from Michigan, already had settled in the area. Under Bishop Marty's direction, Father Haire subsequently had received a large parish that encompassed territory between the Minnesota line and the Missouri River and from Huron in southern Dakota to Jamestown in the northern portion of the Territory. The railroad's completion brought a flood of pioneers, many of whom were European Catholics.[48] They created a settlement "in which necessity and expediency taught various nationalities to cooperate in the establishment of Catholic parishes," writes one South Dakota historian.[49] Together with Father Haire, the settlers established the Sacred Heart Church at Aberdeen. The first donor to the cause was Frank Hagerty, a non-Catholic who contributed the land for the site. After the church was built, the priest turned his attention to parochial education. A plea to Bishop Marty for teachers spurred the patriarch to elicit the skillful Presentations, whom Marty believed could perpetuate Christian ideals within the new region of his jurisdiction.[50]

In October of 1886, Mother Hughes and Sisters Chriswell and Mary Ellen Butler established a convent in Aberdeen, and they rang the first school bell that month. Fifty pupils, both Catholic and Protestant, first entered the classroom doors of a temporary facility. The shortage of equipment, facilities, and classroom space again was a handicap, but in addition to religious principles, the sisters, later in a new building, taught English, history, reading, spelling, arithmetic, geography, pedagogy, business courses, voice, piano, organ, and art. Sister Chriswell in particular was responsible for the fine arts curriculum.[51] An unnamed observer recorded that "she had a beautiful singing voice. Teaching piano, voice and organ lessons, . . . she was of sympathetic disposition and gentle demeanor which commanded the love and respect of all who knew her. . . ."[52] Aldea Cloutier, a student and boarder at the Academy from 1890 to 1893, added that Sister Chriswell "was a great favorite of the girls, remarkably attractive, very small and aristocratic in appearance, dark eyes and beautiful complexion, always smiling. Students found her extremely holy with a very distinctive and contagious laugh. . . ."[53]

Of a more serious sort, Mother Hughes was kind but a disciplinarian and probably ruled as the authority figure in the school.[54] Although the Presentations relied on instructional techniques such as recitation and memorization, the sisters' school exceeded territorial standards for curriculum, which in 1861 had stipulated that "spelling, reading, writing, English grammar, and arithmetic were to be taught in every school district."[55] The state of South Dakota later would offer them some formidable competition, especially in teacher training, when in 1901 it opened the chartered Northern Normal and Industrial School in Aberdeen. Nevertheless, Father Haire helped found this secular institution and served on its board of regents for a number of years.[56]

Also during their frontier period the Presentation educators at Aberdeen were competing with and supported by a growing territorial and soon state system of Catholic education. By 1890, five orders of nuns staffed thirteen parochial schools. Congregations included the following: the Sisters of Mercy at Yankton; the Sisters of St. Agnes at Mitchell and Yankton; the Sisters of the Holy Cross at Deadwood and Lead; the Benedictine Sisters at Maria Zell, Jefferson, Milbank, Sturgis, and White Lake; and the Ursuline Order at Sioux Falls. Each of these communities had its own story of strife and accomplishment. Benedictines teaching at Zell during the 1880s scarcely obtained "food sufficient to keep them from starving and fuel enough to keep them from freezing. . . ."[57] Yet sharing a commitment similar to that of the Presentations, only the Benedictines persevered.

The Presentations' competition with secular and religious institutions and the lack of satisfactory materials resembled Nano Nagle's plight a century earlier. Thus the Dakota sisters' situation seemed to feed their determination and cooperation. Like Nagle in Ireland and the Presentations in Fargo, the Aberdeen nuns soon accepted that they could not continue as an enclosed order. In some respects they had already violated the rule by joining Father Haire, the students, and their parents to raise money for a permanent school building. After receiving the first official dispensation from Bishop Marty to leave their cloister, the sisters traveled widely to ask for money. Parish fairs, private donations, and tuition ($3.50 a week per pupil for board and fees) also brought in revenue, but loans and the sale of bonds provided most of the balance. Published in the *Aberdeen American News* after the school's completion, Father Haire's statement of income and expenditures listed $8,609.14 as the total cost of the building, furniture, supplies, and operating expenses, and itemized donations and other sources of income, including a generous sum he himself provided (Table 1). Volunteers completed most of the construction work, and by November of 1887 Presentation Academy of the Sacred Heart of Jesus was ready for ninety young students. In a letter to the local newspaper, Father Haire thanked the people of Aberdeen for their support, including that from the substantial non-Catholic citizenry whose children attended the school.[58]

In encouraging interdenominational cooperation and acculturation, Father Haire and the Presentations sided with late-nineteenth-century liberals within the American Catholic Church. Unlike Father Haire, Bishops Spalding and John Ireland disapproved of socialism, but they did favor a denominational public school system in which the state fostered education through private institutions. In 1890, Archbishop Ireland addressed the National Education Association meeting to support this proposition and in so doing ignited a war of words with conservatives such as Bishops Bernard J. McQuaid of Rochester and Michael A. Corrigan of New York.[59] Describing the progressive proposition in action at Presentation Academy, Father Haire wrote in 1890, "Difference of religious belief is no bar to the attendance [at Presentation Academy] of non-Catholic pupils inasmuch as such pupils are protected in their civil rights and their religion is not interfered with. Among our most diligent and successful pupils are found the non-Catholics. . . ."[60] Even so, the Presentation Sisters and Father Haire had expanded the academy curriculum to include teachers' training courses for the young nuns and the female students, whom they hoped one day might join their now historic effort. Moreover, in offering education to settlers' children they had helped attract many parishioners, who by then numbered six hundred in a town of six thousand inhabitants.[61]

The Presentations at Fargo were also doing well. In 1890, they accepted Phoebe Selover from St. Paul, Minnesota, their first American candidate. That year four more members came from George's Hill Convent in Dublin. To benefit from a more spacious community facility, the Fargo novitiate was then transferred to Aberdeen and the academy.[62]

Although Father Haire soon left Aberdeen, he kept up with the

TABLE 1. ACADEMY ACCOUNTS: STATEMENT OF INCOME AND EXPENDITURE,
MAY 1, 1888–DECEMBER 31, 1889

General statement of the accounts of the Presentation
Academy from May 1, 1888 to December 31, 1889:

Total cost of academy building including land, lumber, hardware, paint, and work thus far paid including furnace, boiler, and steam heating apparatus, cistern, sidewalks, fences and other appurtenances	$ 7,546.60	
House furniture including piano, organ, and dormitory for boarders	1,062.54	
		$ 8,609.14

Operative expenses from October 1, 1888 to December 31, 1889:

Insurance on academy	150.00	
Making papers and recording	9.00	
Interest on mortgage loan	250.00	
Interest at bank on note	9.00	
Fuel for academy	197.00	
	$ 615.00	
Household expenses for academy and sisters for fifteen months from October 1888 to December 1889	944.55	
		1,559.55
	$10,168.69	

Sources of income for the aforesaid outlay:

Dec. 1886 fair given for the sisters	1,277.14
Nov. 1888 fair given for the sisters	945.00
Nov. 1889 fair given for the sisters	402.00
Sept. 1889 dinner at state fair	109.00
106 shares at $10 each	1,060.00
Private donations	45.00
Rebates of workmen	24.00
October 1888 amount of mortgage loan	3,500.00
Presentation Sisters	1,714.74
Rev. Robert Haire	1,091.61
	$10,168.69

Amount of unpaid debt per book	85.65
Amount of unpaid expenses	150.00
	$235.65

Source: Sister Di Donato, "A History of the Educational Work of the Presentation Sisters," 171.

Presentations and their dedication to education in the Dakotas, writing to Mother Hughes in 1891, "I received your last kind letter when you have not evidently received mine. . . . I will see you once more when you return. . . . I shall remember you and the community's great kindness and courtesy to me, and in case of need will do all in my power to prove myself not an ingrate."[63]

Thus by 1889, the year the Dakota Territory entered the Union as the separate states of North and South Dakota, the Presentations already had befriended local Church officials and established themselves as the agents of assimilation into Western Christian traditions for a handful of Indians and for many more Catholic and Protestant whites. Perhaps the fact that the Presentations' initial trials seemed to be waning gave them time to engage in some intracongregational strife. In any case, soon after statehood a conflict within the Dakota foundation led to a split between the North and South Dakota congregations. According to the Presentations' constitution, elections for mother superior took place every six years. When Mother Hughes's term expired in 1892, an election was held in December of that year. Mother Aloysius Chriswell was elected, and Mother Hughes so took the action as a personal insult that she promptly returned to Fargo and weakened connections with Aberdeen. One can only speculate on why the Presentations favored a change in leadership, but it seems likely that with the homeless pioneer days behind them, they needed a different kind of superior.[64] Although Mother Hughes had ably held the community together through her "faithful observance of the rule,"[65] and even faced the need for some change such as relinquishing the enclosure stipulation, still she was a taskmistress. Mother Chriswell was more flexible; students and Catholic clerics characterized her as "a warm, talented, dedicated person, freely sharing her musical and singing talents with the early settlers."[66]

In addition to these personality differences, a political reason arose for dividing the Fargo and Aberdeen establishments. After statehood, the vicarate was divided into two distinct dioceses, and the Fargo and Aberdeen convents fell into different arenas of episcopal jurisdiction. Therefore, the sisters resolved that the two communities should sever their six-year relationship. Archbishop John Ireland arbitrated the dispute and decided that the group at Aberdeen would receive clear title to its real estate and other property upon payment of $2,600 to the Fargo membership. While in Fargo, Mother

Hughes again worked especially hard to locate financial support for orphan children until her death in 1897. Left to their own resources, the South Dakota community would never again solve its internal problems through separation rather than resolve them within the order.[67]

Economic and environmental forces made it extremely difficult for Mother Chriswell and the South Dakota Presentations to solve their problems through any means. The nation suffered a financial depression in 1893, and throughout the 1890s a drought and the financial depression plagued much of the South Dakota countryside, homes, and other establishments nestled in the northern plains. Abruptly Mother Chriswell experienced a true test of her leadership ability. She had been born in Dublin in 1853, and there she had received her basic education in music and pedagogy before immigrating to the United States. As a student, she had specialized in teacher training and music, and at the age of eighteen she had entered the Granard Presentation convent that Mother Hughes had founded. When in 1885 the older woman left Fargo and returned to Ireland on a recruiting mission, Sister Chriswell gladly volunteered to follow Mother Hughes, first back to Fargo and then on to Aberdeen. Consequently, the property dispute with the Fargo motherhouse after the split in 1892 must have caused the younger nun much personal distress. Added to that, in the middle of a depression Mother Chriswell was forced to borrow from a bank the settlement money to pay the Fargo sisters. To repay the loan, the South Dakota sisters had only their income from her music lessons, begging, and boarder fees; moreover, enrollment at the academy declined in hard times, and the teachers discovered that their neighbors viewed education as a luxury to be dispensed with when money became scarce.[68]

The diminishing numbers of students meant that the Presentations might never hope to entice American women into the order, which then counted five members in South Dakota. Mother Chriswell, therefore, asked Irish Presentation convents for suitable novices. Although five postulants came in 1894, two left because they could not meet the challenge of frontier life. The three who stayed were Sisters M. Teresa Murphy, M. Benedict Murphy, and M. Veronica Houlihan. Also that year the Aberdeen women made a breakthrough by receiving the first American candidate, Annie McBride of Iowa. Soon renamed Sister Gertrude McBride, she proved a great help to the order by aiding their own assimilation into the South Dakota social clime. Moreover, Sister McBride had been an excellent teacher in the state's public school system, and she continued her career in the Presentation schools. Mother Chriswell lived long enough to see her group double in size, but she died of pneumonia in 1894.[69] Similar tragedies were repeated in other American western Presentation convents. Twelve young San Francisco Presentations died from 1867 to 1880, while "other communities knew similar griefs."[70] Yet there usually were others left to carry on. Mother Chriswell's successor, Mother Joseph Butler (previously Mary Ellen Butler), assumed office after her friend's death and held it for more than twenty years. Bishop Thomas O'Gorman, who was a good friend of Bishop Ireland and a professor of history at Catholic University, replaced Bishop Marty in 1896; at the sisters' request the new patriarch permanently dispensed them from their rule of enclosure so they could reach out even farther to the scattered South Dakota population.[71]

With the succession of Mother Butler, the uncertain years of the Presentations' history in Dakota Territory came to an end. They had arrived in 1880 with the hope of ministering to the Indians, but because environmental demands and pressures altered their original intention, they soon began teaching the children of European and American settlers in the farming country of northeastern South Dakota. Nevertheless, their dedication to building moral settlements of Dakota residents persisted, particularly by empowering women to be their families' ethical guides. With independence from the Fargo foundation and with the strong guidance of Mothers Chriswell and Butler, the South Dakota Presentations had built an occupational community, bound not by enclosure but by their Marian ideology and supported by many people whom they served. They stood ready to strive for professional goals in education and health care, as they participated in the twentieth-century modernization of the American West.[72]

NOTES

1. Frederick Jackson Turner, "Statement of the Frontier Thesis: Later Explanations and Developments," in *The Frontier Thesis: Valid Interpretation of American History?* ed. Ray Allen Billington (New York: Holt,

Rinehart and Winston, 1966), 10. According to some neo-Turnerians, the frontier environment alone was not enough to ensure emigrants' survival and self-reliance on the Northern Great Plains. American cultural similarities with Old World values were crucial elements, and as we discussed in chapter 1, the Presentations did share a similar ideological base with most of the Protestant educators in the United States. For works concerning similar emigrants' coping with their new home in the West, see Frederick C. Luebke, "Ethnic Group Settlement on the Great Plains," *The Western Historical Quarterly* 8 (Oct. 1977): 405–30. For further discussion of immigrant adapation to the frontier, see Brian W. Blouet and Frederick C. Luebke, eds., *The Great Plains: Environment and Culture* (Lincoln: University of Nebraska Press, 1979).

2. M. Raphael Consedine, P.B.V.M., *Listening Journey: A Study of the Spirit and Ideals of Nano Nagle and the Presentation Sisters* (Victoria, Australia: Congregation of the Presentation of the Blessed Virgin Mary, 1983), 272, 298.

3. "Draft of the Constitution of the Presentation Sisters, Passed by the 1980 Chapter," Presentation Archives, Presentation Heights, Aberdeen, S.D.

4. Sister Pauline Quinn, "Biographies of Major Superiors, Section III: Mother John Hughes, 1886–1892," Presentation Archives.

5. Sister M. Cabrini Di Donato, P.B.V.M., "A History of the Educational Work of the Presentation Sisters of Aberdeen, South Dakota" (master's thesis, Northern State College, 1966), 5,8.

6. Sister Quinn, "Mother John Hughes."

7. Marjorie R. Fallows, *Irish Americans: Identity and Assimilation* (Englewood Cliffs, N.J.: Prentice-Hall, 1979), 14–18, 98–102, 108; Carol Groneman, "Working-Class Immigrant Women in Mid-Nineteenth-Century New York: The Irish Woman's Experience," *Journal of Urban History* 4 (May 1978): 257.

8. Fallows, *Irish Americans*, 98–102, 108.

9. Ibid., 98–99; Carole Turbin, "And We Are Nothing but Women: Irish Working Women in Troy," in *Women of America: A History*, ed. Carol Ruth Berkin and Mary Beth Norton (Boston: Houghton Mifflin, 1979), 200–22; Groneman, "Working-Class Immigrant Women," 268.

10. Herbert Schell, *History of South Dakota* (Lincoln: University of Nebraska Press, 1961), 118–21; Cleata B. Thorpe, "Education in South Dakota, 1861–1961," *South Dakota Historical Collections* 36 (1972): 223–24; Sister M. Claudia Duratschek, O.S.B., *The Beginnings of Catholicism in South Dakota* (Washington, D.C.: Catholic University of America Press, 1943), 244.

11. Glenda Riley, "Farm Women's Roles in the Agricultural Development of South Dakota," *South Dakota History* 13 (Spring-Summer 1983): 92. Further evidencing the domination of a monolithic American female culture in other parts of the West, a study of Scandinavian immigrant women who settled in Seattle from 1888 to 1900 concludes that after a few years

the subjects had abandoned the custom of married women working outside to fulfill the American middle-class housewife ideal. For details, see Janice Reiff Webster, "Domestication and Americanization, Scandinavian Women in Seattle, 1888 to 1900," *Journal of Urban History* 4 (May 1978): 275–89.

12. Kate Richards O'Hare, quoted in *Kate Richards O'Hare: Selected Writings and Speeches*, ed. Philip S. Foner and Sally M. Miller (Baton Rouge: Louisiana State University Press, 1982), 98.

13. Elizabeth Jameson, "Imperfect Unions: Class and Gender in Cripple Creek, 1894–1904," in *Class, Sex, and the Woman Worker*, ed. Milton Cantor and Bruce Laurie (Westport, Conn.: Greenwood Press, 1977), 166–202.

14. Duratschek, *The Beginnings of Catholicism in South Dakota*, 150–51, 176–78, 236–40.

15. James Hennesey, S.J., *American Catholics: A History of the Roman Catholic Community in the United States* (New York: Oxford University Press, 1981), 232.

16. Schnell, *History of South Dakota*, 241; Dennis A. Norlin, "The Suffrage Movement and South Dakota Churches: Radicals and the Status Quo, 1890," *South Dakota History* 14 (Winter 1984): 312; interview with Sister M. Lelia Beresford, Aug. 11, 1976, South Dakota Oral History Center, The University of South Dakota, Vermillion; interview with Sister Alicia Dunphy, Aug. 6, 1976, South Dakota Oral History Center; Duratschek, *The Beginnings of Catholicism in South Dakota*, 240.

17. Mother Mary Berchmans, quoted in Sister Julia Gilmore, S.C.L., *We Came North: Centennial Story of the Sisters of Charity of Leavenworth* (St. Meinrad, Ind.: Abbey Press, 1961), 274.

18. Bishop John Lancaster Spalding, quoted in Merle Curti, *The Social Ideas of American Educators* (Totowa, N.J.: Littlefield, Adams, 1978), 371. Also see 372.

19. Mary Kay Jennings, "Lake County Woman Suffrage Campaign in 1890," *South Dakota History* 5 (Fall 1975): 390–409.

20. Thorpe, "Education in South Dakota," 216.

21. Courtney Ann Vaughn-Roberson, "Having a Purpose in Life: Western Women Teachers in the Twentieth Century," *Great Plains Quarterly* 5 (Spring 1985): 107–24.

22. Harold A. Buetow, *Of Singular Benefit: The Story of Catholic Education in the United States* (London: Macmillan, 1970), 151–54; John D. Pulliam, *History of Education in America* (Columbus, Ohio: Charles E. Merrill Publishing, 1982), 86; David B. Tyack, ed., *Turning Points in American Educational History* (New York: John Wiley and Sons, 1967), 415.

23. Buetow, *Of Singular Benefit*, 153; Curti, *The Social Ideas of American Educators*, 350.

24. Curti, *The Social Ideas of American Educators*, 217.

25. Ibid., 234–36; Schnell, *History of South Dakota*, 383.

26. William Henry Harrison Beadle, quoted in Duratschek, *The Beginnings of Catholicism in South Dakota*, 231.

27. Thorpe, "Education in South Dakota," 237–39, Schnell, *History of South Dakota,* 382. Both Wessington Springs and Freeman closed during the twentieth century.

28. Buetow, *Of Singular Benefit,* 151.

29. *Diamond Jubilee Book* (Aberdeen, S.D.: Sisters of the Presentation of the Blessed Virgin Mary, 1961), 23.

30. Sister Frances Menahan to Mother Joseph Butler (n. d.), Presentation Archives; T. J. Walsh, *Nano Nagle and the Presentation Sisters* (Dublin: M. H. Hill and Son, 1959), 280; Sister Di Donato, "A History of the Educational Work of the Presentation Sisters," 9.

31. Sister Frances Menahan to Mother Joseph Butler.

32. Ibid.; *Diamond Jubilee Book,* 23; Sister Di Donato, "A History of the Educational Work of the Presentation Sisters," 10.

33. Sister Di Donato, "A History of the Educational Work of the Presentation Sisters," 11.

34. Ibid., 10, 13.

35. Mary Lynch, quoted in Ibid., 15.

36. *Diamond Jubilee Book,* 22; Schell, *History of South Dakota,* 180–81; Sister Frances Menahan to Mother Joseph Butler; Sister Di Donato, "A History of the Educational Work of the Presentation Sisters," 16.

37. Sister Frances Menahan to Mother Joseph Butler.

38. Schell, *History of South Dakota,* 150–52.

39. Sister Frances Menahan to Mother Joseph Butler.

40. Sister Di Donato, "A History of the Educational Work of the Presentation Sisters," 16–18.

41. Sister Frances Menahan to Mother Joseph Butler.

42. A School Sister of Notre Dame, *Mother Caroline and the School Sisters of Notre Dame in North America,* vol. 1 (St. Louis: Woodward and Tiernan, 1928), 24.

43. Minnie Larkin Stack quoted in Sister Quinn, "Mother John Hughes."

44. Ibid.; Walsh, *Nano Nagle,* 280; Sister Di Donato, "A History of the Educational Work of the Presentation Sisters," 18; Sister Frances Menahan to Mother Joseph Butler; "Summary Data for Encyclopedia Dictionary of Canonical States of Perfection, 1968," compiled by Sister Alicia Dunphy, Presentation Archives. Sources disagree as to the spelling of Stephan's name.

45. Sister Frances Menahan to Mother Joseph Butler.

46. Sister Pauline Quinn, "Biographies of Major Superiors, Section V: Mother Joseph Butler, 1894–1915," Presentation Archives.

47. Sister Quinn, "Mother Joseph Butler"; Sister Di Donato, "A History of the Educational Work of the Presentation Sisters," 18–19; *Diamond Jubilee Book,* 24.

48. *Diamond Jubilee Book,* 27; Schell, *History of South Dakota,* 164; Duratschek, *The Beginnings of Catholicism in South Dakota,* 172.

49. Duratschek, *The Beginnings of Catholicism in South Dakota,* 176.

50. Ibid., 172–178. Sister Di Donato, "A History of the Educational Work of the Presentation Sisters," 22.

51. Sister Di Donato, "A History of the Educational Work of the Presentation Sisters," 20–21, 23; Walsh, *Nano Nagle*, 280.

52. Sister Pauline Quinn, "Biographies of Major Superiors, Section IV: Mother Aloysius Chriswell, 1892–1894," Presentation Archives.

53. Aldea Cloutier, quoted in Sister Quinn, "Mother Aloysius Chriswell."

54. Sister Di Donato, "A History of the Educational Work of the Presentation Sisters," 26–27; Sister Quinn, "Mother John Hughes."

55. Thorpe, "Education in South Dakota," 217.

56. Duratschek, *The Beginnings of Catholicism in South Dakota,* 229–30; Sister Di Donato, "A History of the Educational Work of the Presentation Sisters," 20.

57. Duratschek, *The Beginnings of Catholicism in South Dakota,* 162, 230.

58. Sister Di Donato, "A History of the Educational Work of the Presentation Sisters," 26; Walsh, *Nano Nagle,* 280; interview with Mrs. Aldea Cloutier by Sister DeSales, Nov. 18, 1957, Presentation Archives.

59. Curti, *The Social Ideas of American Educators,* 358; Buetow, *Of Singular Benefit,* 170–71; Sister Helen Angela Hurley, *On Good Ground: The Story of the Sisters of St. Joseph in St. Paul* (Minneapolis: University of Minnesota Press, 1951), 197–202, 204–7.

60. *Aberdeen American News,* Jan. 2, 1890.

61. Walsh, *Nano Nagle,* 25; *Official Yearbook of Sacred Heart Catholic Church* (Aberdeen, S.D.: Sacred Heart Catholic Church, 1901–02), 18; Sister Di Donato, "A History of the Educational Work of the Presentation Sisters," 25.

62. Sister Di Donato, "A History of the Educational Work of the Presentation Sisters," 27.

63. Father Robert Haire, quoted in Sister Quinn, "Mother John Hughes."

64. Sister Di Donato, "A History of the Educational Work of the Presentation Sisters," 27–28.

65. Sister Quinn, "Mother John Hughes."

66. Sister Quinn, "Mother Aloysius Chriswell."

67. Schell, *History of South Dakota,* 223; *Diamond Jubilee Book,* 28; Sister Di Donato, "A History of the Educational Work of the Presentation Sisters," 28.

68. Schell, *History of South Dakota,* 233; Sister Quinn, "Mother Aloysius Chriswell."

69. Sister Quinn, "Mother Aloysius Chriswell"; *Diamond Jubilee Book,* 29; Sister Di Donato, "A History of the Educational Work of the Presentation Sisters," 30.

70. Consedine, *Listening Journey,* 285.

71. Sister Quinn, "Mother Aloysius Chriswell"; *Diamond Jubilee Book,* 29; Walsh, *Nano Nagle,* 279; Hurley, *On Good Ground,* 132. "Summary Data," Presentation Archives. Pope Pius XII gave final approval of Bishop O'Gorman's dispensation in September 1946, when he accepted the revised

constitution of the Aberdeen Congregation of the Sisters of the Presentation of the Blessed Virgin Mary; Bishop William O. Brady, D. D. to Presentation Sisters, Dec. 13, 1947, Archives of the Sioux Falls Diocese, Sioux Falls, S.D.

72. Portions of this chapter were first published in Susan Peterson, "Religious Communities of Women in the West: The Presentation Sisters' Adaptation of the Northern Plains Frontier," *Journal of the West* 21 (April 1982): 65–70.

4. The Challenge of Professionalization: The Education Apostolate, 1898–1961

☐

By 1898, the Presentation teaching community was permanently settled in Aberdeen. At least during the first two decades of the twentieth century, the women were either trained in Ireland, at the Aberdeen motherhouse, or at Northern Normal School. During this period they also acquired much of their expertise through apprenticeship; however, both internal and external factors were pushing them into a new phase of occupational growth because the Presentation educators displayed a growing eagerness to be more highly educated themselves and to remain competitive with other nuneducators and public school teachers. Consequently, early in the century the Presentation educators adopted what were becoming nationally recognized goals for the members of any given occupational group. The nuns elected superiors who insisted that the career-bound sisters in all fields be prepared academically despite South Dakota's comparatively poor record in the area of teacher certification and despite comparatively low national standards for educators, especially when compared to professionals in other fields such as medicine and law. Always, however, superiors insisted that a nun's occupational improvements and her school lessons manifest the order's spiritual objectives. Thus each leader recognized the importance of keeping not only Presentation ideals, but also the concept of sisterhood alive, for, as already noted, such precepts comprised the essence and mechanics of the community's internal strength. Maintaining both internal consistency and external support proved to be a challenge, even in the face of success. Throughout the century, environmental circumstances and the nuns' individual dedication modified their traditional teaching techniques and opened up new career opportunities in administration, curriculum supervision, policymaking, and higher education. Yet each one of these innovations brought the nuns more and more into the secular world, forcing many of them to reassess the separate and unequal religious philosophy of Nano Nagle's day.

Attempting to maintain ideological consistency and to modernize, the Presentations and other religious educators blended their old axiology with progressivism, the new science of education popularized early in the twentieth century. This proved to be difficult because even the progressives sometimes contradicted each other. Nevertheless, the new educational movement grew in popularity during the nation's Progressive Era extending from 1900 to 1920. With it came a pressure on private and public educators to endorse efficient, centralized administration, school consolidation, pragmatic curricula, inductive teaching methodology, an enthusiasm for the reliability and validity of quantitative tests and measurements, and the advancement of teacher preparation.[1]

Established to further the relationship between higher education and educator training institutions, schools such as New York's Columbia Teachers College had been established as early as 1889. Other colleges and universities had created, or soon would form, departments of education, and by 1930 most states had phased out the nineteenth-century normal school concept. Within the private sector, Bishop John Lancaster Spalding pushed for the training of sisters outside their motherhouses. In 1908, Catholic University opened a department of education, and three years later it accepted female students. Hundreds of teaching sisters began attending summer classes, but even those nuns who still were schooled within their compounds were often exposed to modern methodological concepts. *The School Manual for the Use of the Sisters of St. Joseph of Carondelet* had been published in 1884 and was used widely in many religious teacher-education programs. The text stressed the importance of individualized instruction that led to internalization of curricular material in subjects such as history.[2] "Teaching chronological tables is not teaching history . . . ," the *Manual* read. In reference to language arts, it further instructed, "to awaken interest and develop the idea . . . begin each new lesson with conversation on objects or pictures illustrative of the reading lesson . . . . The mastery of our language should be the end aimed at in this study. Teaching mere rules and constructions will not accomplish this." Moreover the treatise recommended that a sister-directress supervise teaching sisters, encouraging a collegial exchange of information for teachers' self-improvement.[3]

Despite the *Manual's* popularity, traditional methods of rote memorization and repetition persisted within some teaching orders' preparatory programs. Attempting to arrest the timeworn techniques, in 1929 St. Paul, Minnesota, Reverend Rudolph G. Bandas, professor of dogmatic theology at St. Paul Seminary and of catechetics at Diocesen Normal School, criticized this methodology, pointing out that a progressive teaching style need not challenge the permanency of absolute truth.[4]

Regardless of what educational theories dominated religious teacher-training curricula, the idea of the necessity of receiving a higher education in order to acquire professional skills was becoming widely accepted within Catholic circles. In 1927, Sylvester Schmitz of Catholic University conducted a study to investigate nuns' comparative progress in this area. Using two years of advanced training beyond secondary school as the standard for adequate preparation, he found that slightly more than 57 percent of the nation's teaching sisters measured up, compared to a bit over 50 percent of the public school teachers. Assessing reasons for his finding, Schmitz wrote that for the nun "teaching is not a stepping stone to a life career. . . . [It] . . . is her life work. Not financial remuneration, but the most noble, . . . sublime . . . ideals and spiritual values are the dynamic, motivating principle underlying her professional work."[5] Serious about building on the early success, by 1930 many sisters were attending secular colleges in order to improve their education credentials. Other nuns pursued degrees from Catholic colleges and lived with other nun students. In so doing, these women were, as one historian observes, "well on their way from evangelism to professionalism."[6] In 1950, Pope Pius XII called an international congress of religious men and women to discuss future improvements in teacher training for religious. Answering the call, nationally known sister-scholars and several other nun-educators held a Sister Formation Conference in Everett, Washington, in 1956. The delegates drew up a document and sent it to motherhouses all over the country. The proposal recommended a teacher-training course of study thoroughly grounded in pedagogy and the liberal arts, including philosophy and religion. Notable international male clerics supported the nuns' suggestions. One was Leon Joseph Cardinal Suenens, who eventually became a Belgian archbishop and a moderator at the Second Vatican Council. Not all churchmen, however, supported formation because increased years of academic preparation for sister-educators meant that more of them would be taken out of the classroom to pursue advanced degrees. For example, John Cardinal O'Hara of Philadelphia promoted a short preparatory program that emphasized quantity over quality and thereby provided him with enough teachers so that every Catholic child in his diocese could be placed in a Catholic school.[7]

A disappointment to men such as Cardinal O'Hara, the number of teaching sisters decreased during the last half of the century as nuns began selecting professional fields other than teaching. Before World War II, lay teachers in the Catholic schools were rare substitutes for religious, whereas by 1950, they were 20,075 of a total 116,043 faculty members in religious schools. By the end of the decade, there were 49,648 lay teachers out of a total 171,181 educators. Although the lay work force was dedicated and underpaid, compensating its members was more costly than remuneration for the nuns had been.[8]

Earlier in the century the national Catholic Education Association had sensed this potential for conflict between the secular and religious educational worlds and feared the consequences of progressive education's epistemology, which held that through a scientific system of inquiry individuals defined their own values. Some Catholic educators attacked other progressive products such as standardized testing, which often challenged one of progressivism's own tenets, the primacy of individualism in the classroom.[9] Particularly protesting the measurement craze, in a Catholic education book Joseph Husslein announced in 1934 that the "robot theory of education . . . makes of a man a mere mechanism without a soul; [and] the materialistic philosophy . . . sees in his every action the inevitable resultant of [a] purely chemical and physical reaction; consequent rejection of all true freedom of the will, and so of the very possibility of morality itself."[10]

Despite such opposition and probably because the average parent and student remained relatively unaware of progressive philosophic positions, Presentations and other Catholic educators constantly compromised their essentially liberal arts curriculum. They employed progressive methodology and offered more courses associated with the new pragmatic era. These classes, families believed, would help their children compete for jobs and high salaries in the secular world. Although in 1925 the United States Supreme Court insured the continued existence of private education as an alternative to public schools by ruling that no state had a right to force students into a public school, in many respects Catholic education evolved into a mirror image of the public school system. In an effort during the first half of the twentieth century to meet national accreditation standards, the college division of the Catholic Education Association brought about a change in the six-year Catholic college curriculum, creating separate four-year college preparatory and four-year higher educational programs.[11] Sounding like progressive John Dewey himself, leading Catholic scholar Thomas Edward Shields declared as early as 1921 that "more and more educators are coming to realize that real education must be interpreted in terms of experience. The business of the curriculum, therefore, is chiefly to supply to the children the right kind of experience. . . . Education is not mere knowing or remembering; it is preeminently a matter of doing."[12] Echoing this same sentiment during the 1940s and 1950s, Sister M. Marguerite wrote the *Faith and Freedom Series* readers. Sister Marguerite stated that the books were designed "to bridge the gap which has existed for so long . . . between the teaching of religious truths and their translation into life situations."[13]

Throughout the second half of the twentieth century numerous other instances of Catholic and secular school intersection have existed. In 1956, a Kentucky Supreme court case sanctioned what was common practice in many quarters, that of employing traditionally dressed nuns to teach in public schools. In a series of United States Supreme Court cases, justices approved the granting of released time to Catholic students in public schools who wished to attend religion classes; the Court also sanctioned state support of transportation and nonsectarian books for students in religious schools. Other evidences of cooperation between private and public schools were the cross-listing of classes and combining other resources.[14]

The growing similarities between public and private schools was so extensive that by mid-century scholars criticized Catholic education for sacrificing its liberal arts tradition and suggested that the Church-sponsored schools reestablish themselves as a "bulwark against the erosion of the values derived from the Judeo-Christian tradition . . . ."[15] Many schools heeded such admonitions, for later investigations found that Catholic schools, more than public schools, gave copious amounts of homework and prescribed a rigorous curriculum.[16]

South Dakota public education flirted with progressivism and other aspects of modernization but held to the past in some respects. For years the state seemed unable to support any curriculum well. South Dakota poverty, the archaic school funding systems based largely on property taxes, and an anti-intellectualism pervasive in parts of the American West were all contributing factors. Between 1900 and 1960, South Dakota's entire population increased only from 401,570 to 680,514. Rural schools were especially unsophisticated, as they were in many sparsely populated areas across the Great Plains. Salaries were comparatively low for both public school and Catholic school teachers, but always lower for the nuns. Janitorial assistance and the necessary equipment to conduct classroom assignments were both in short supply. As late as 1961, South Dakota rated forty-eighth in a national ranking of teachers' salaries; Arkansas and Mississippi were the only states with poorer records. At this time in South Dakota, an average Presentation nun teaching in higher education earned only around $1,500, whereas public school teachers earned an average of $3,725 compared to the national figure of $5,174. The lower figure in South Dakota was generally representative of the West.[17]

As salaries suggest, South Dakotans devoted scant attention to the importance of teacher training. In 1901, a normal school graduate still had to pass certification exams to receive a license to teach, but a degree holder from any of the state's denominational colleges, not necessarily skilled as a teacher, could obtain a five-year teaching certificate. In 1920, however, the legislature did insist that all first grade certificate holders must have attended an approved normal school for twelve weeks, and those applying for a second or third grade certificate must have attended six weeks. The body upgraded the state's normal schools to teachers colleges in 1923, but eight years later the institutions at Springfield, Spearfish, and Madison were cut back to two-year programs that prepared elementary teachers only. In 1946, Springfield and Madison were reinstated as four-year colleges, and in 1931 the legislature had made some college credit essential before one could instruct in a high school; however not until 1953 did South Dakota establish a state board of education to plan and oversee its educational development. Four years later the new agency did decree that a college degree was required to teach high school and stipulated that particular amounts of college credits were necessary in order to qualify a future educator for different types of elementary certificates.[18]

South Dakota public educators were slow also to update their school curricula. From statehood until 1903, no prescriptions for appropriate courses of study existed; however, extending from 1903 to 1906, during Superintendent George W. Nash's administration the state established a uniform guide for high school students, which included basic college preparatory subjects and electives in Latin and German. M. M. Ramer, the next superintendent, designated three types of high schools, those of two, three, and four years. Each was to implement its own standard curricula, so by 1912, South Dakota was one of a handful of states in the Northwest that conducted no supervision of its high schools. Nevertheless, some of the state's high schools had applied for and received accreditation from the North Central Association of Colleges and Secondary Schools. Yankton High School, for example, was approved in 1905.[19]

The state public school curriculum evolved slowly throughout the following decades. Hazel Ott, who was the state superintendent of elementary education, and E. C. Griffin, who was the state superintendent of schools, worked with Columbia Teachers College officials to revise the accepted course of study and published the new version in 1936. The course included an array of subjects for students of all grades from the fields of fine arts, English, history, science, and foreign language. Unfortunately for individualists, however, the course represented the rigidity and routinization that were sometimes a product of progressive educational thought. An outline was provided for each subject, including what was to be taught every six weeks and how instructors were to break down a unit into daily teaching lessons. Objective testing also became quite popular in South Dakota, although some educators criticized it for encouraging students' mechanical rather than conceptualization skills. Pragmatic courses such as homemaking and industrial arts became part of the schools' curricula, while moral education, life adjustment programs, and special accelerated courses grew in popularity during the 1950s.[20]

Funding for all of the programs remained tight, partially because of the recalcitrance of many citizens to give up rural schools, which were not cost effective because of their small numbers of students. Thus, at various times throughout the century South Dakota ranked quite high in per-pupil costs when compared to all other states in the union. By 1960, state income tax receipts were $65.58 per $1,000 as compared to the national average of $43.50, and yet the state still could not muster sufficient funds to thrust its educational system out of the ranks of the nation's poorest funded schools.[21]

Because of a lack of money and the traditional attitudes of many South Dakotans, public education continued to reflect a conservative educational philosophy. The states' Catholic educators concurred with their counterparts in the public sector. One such educator was Father Sylvester Eisenman, who throughout much of the twentieth century until he died in 1948 ran Marty Mission, one of several state Catholic mission schools for Indian children. Including kindergarten through the twelfth grade, the school was founded in 1918 at St. Paul, South Dakota, and was run by Father Eisenman, the Sisters of the Blessed Sacrament, and Catholic lay instructors. A Benedictine priest, Father Eisenman disapproved of the progressives at Columbia Teachers College. Guided by his religious beliefs, Father Eisenman claimed that these professors used agencies like the Bureau of Indian Affairs to obtain subjects for their experiments, for example, to determine the value of an elective curriculum. He also rejected ideas made popular in the 1930s by government officials like John Collier, whom President Franklin Roosevelt appointed in 1933 to head the Bureau of Indian Affairs. Collier promoted a multicultural approach to teaching Indians, but Father Eisenman thought this would forever perpetuate their separate and unequal social status and hinder their Christian development. Marty was traditional, and reportedly the students had a reverential respect for the churchman, who believed in the benefits of a basic academic curriculum, hard work, and self-sufficiency. Consequently, the school produced many graduates who acculturated successfully into the white Anglo-Saxon world. They became business people, professionals, and successful homemakers. On the other hand, the school perpetuated the Indian separatism that Father Eisenman purportedly disdained: The Oblate Sisters of the Blessed Sacrament, an order of Indian women, originated at Marty.[22]

Residing at their own mission sites, Presentation educators attempted to replicate their motherhouse community structure. Together they kept a community schedule of prayers and silence periods, although each of these mission groups usually were and still are less structured than the one living in the motherhouse. Many of the Presentation teachers worked twelve- to eighteen-hour days. In the early days and throughout the 1930s and 40s, usually the Presentations comprised 95 percent of the personnel employed anywhere they were stationed. The sisters rarely owned the institutions that they conducted, but they often supplied domestic help from their own ranks and paid to keep a school's physical plant clean. Early in the century it was customary to send only one person to town for supplies because the sisters tried to concentrate solely on their spiritual and professional lives. A sister-principal usually supervised the nuns' educational and community activities. The sisters' salary checks went into one fund for the entire Presentation order, and the motherhouse bursar paid for the expenses at each mission.[23]

Until mid-century, the Presentations maintained the basic educational tenets held by Father Eisenman and many other Catholic pedagogues throughout the country. For years the Presentations remained skeptical toward progressive education, although eventually they were to make methodological adaptations, and always they strived to equal or better the qualifications of South Dakota public school educators. Foreshadowing this sentiment, a nineteenth-century Presentation Sister from San Francisco wrote, "as the attraction of science seems to be a principal weapon in the hands of the enemies of the faith here, we endeavor to have our schools progress so as not to be behind them, but rather in advance; and thus we have . . . [kept] our schools in good repute and gain[ed] youth for God."[24] Moreover, in 1907, Australian Presentations were quick to meet the Victorian government's national standards for registration of the country's educators.[25] Similarly, South Dakota Presentations often adopted the same textbooks as those used in the South Dakota or Minnesota public schools.[26] These adaptations had an impact on many of the students who graduated from Presentation schools all over the world. Due to the modernization of Catholic curricula, their roles after graduation gradually shifted from homemaker to professional or incorporated both. One Presentation nun explained that well into the twentieth century, "girls who came under the Sisters' guidance left them to fill the traditional influential roles of wives and mothers. As new fields of activity opened to women, they found places, often high places, in the arts, the professions, [and] the world of business."[27]

Always with the basic philosophical mission in mind, however, early in the century the Presentations relied heavily on their own discipline and solidarity not only to remind them of their apostolic purpose, but also to combat anti-Catholic prejudice. Cooperation between Protestants and Catholics in South Dakota towns such as Aberdeen apparently had given way to hostility in many quarters. Taking a cue from national sentiments during the early twentieth century, South Dakota became an area of rebirth for the Ku Klux Klan (originated during the 1860s in Tennessee). Catholics' numerical strength in South Dakota probably helped provoke the phenomenon, and yet it provided strength necessary to fight prejudice. By 1960, only the Lutherans counted more members, numbering 96,604, while Catholics recorded 89,001. Other groups ranked far below. For example, Methodists, who were in third place, listed only 23,928; Congregationalists, Presbyterians, Episcopalians, Baptists, and a few others had even smaller state memberships.[28]

In response to anti-Catholic prejudice and by virtue of large numbers of members, a collective sense of Catholicity eventually superseded any separate, immigrant identity because churchgoers tended to bond together to combat a common foe. Although the South Dakota Poles originally insisted on having Polish priests, and while Irish and Germans sometimes quarrelled over leadership roles in local Catholic Church affairs, by the early twentieth century it seems that South Dakota Catholics identified more with their religion than with their nationalities. Presentation Sister Martha Raleigh provides in her life story an example of this evolutionary process of Americanization. An Irish immigrant, she recalled that the first moment she saw the frame building that was the Aberdeen convent in 1923, "I was terribly disappointed, . . . the convents in Ireland [were] . . . really quite beautiful."[29] Soon, however, teaching in a country where Catholics were an unaccepted minority strengthened her resolve and made her concentrate on molding new kinds of Americans: assimilated to some degree but respectful of their Catholic heritage, nevertheless. Consequently, through her teaching, Sister Raleigh tried to give students "a sense of hope and . . . of . . . [being] accepted."[30]

Thus, discrimination by others had mobilized and strengthened many of the Irish Presentations. Sister Mary Stephen Davis (born in 1914) remembered growing up in Sioux Falls where the Klan exerted a strong social influence, where living "was a . . . challenge for the average Catholic." Yet, she claimed, through Catholic solidarity parishioners were empowered to fight back.[31] Catholic determination also won converts to its ranks. Sister Bonaventure Hoffman's story provides a good example. The child of a strong Lutheran clan, she was admonished by a family member, "don't let the Catholics get you" while attending nursing school at the Presentation's St. Luke's Hospital in Aberdeen.[32] The warning became a prophecy because Sister Hoffman became a nun, although it would take some of her family members twenty years to forgive her. Mother Viator Burns, who was the superior at the time of Sister Hoffman's profession of vows, knew the value of good community relations and encouraged the young novice to reconcile with her parents.[33]

Unlike Sister Hoffman's experience, urban-environmental pressure to conform to Protestantism often drove the immigrant Catholic, particularly the Irish, into public schools and away from their faith. As one historian writes, the ostracized minority member viewed "the public school as his passport . . . out of the ghetto," and as a result "many upwardly-mobile Catholic immigrants became public-school teachers." Some big-city priests like Edward McGlynn of New York City "believed that the problems of social welfare were so overwhelming that neither priest nor people had time or money to spare" on education.[34] Ironically, however, in rural South Dakota where Catholics had made a strong stand, the Catholic Church exerted the same acculturative effect that Protestant hegemony had catalyzed in the Northeast. South Dakota conservatism mirrored the national fear of communism. Thus faced with South Dakota laws passed in 1918 and 1921, banning school instruction in foreign language and requiring teachers to sign loyalty oaths, Catholics faced legal mandates to assimilate.[35]

Because many South Dakota Presentations became a part of the dominant American Western culture, the order did not attract racial minorities such as Indian women. Only a few ever joined the Presentation community, and they did not remain. Native American women were more attracted to separatist communities like the Oblate Sisters. In line with an emergent American Catholic vision of a homogenous Catholic Church, however, the Oblate order eventually integrated. By and large, however, in South Dakota most Indians remained an isolated subculture as were the state's German Mennonites and Hutterites.[36]

Despite the Presentations' eventual amalgamation into the Great Plains social milieu, for at least one-half of the twentieth century the predominantly Irish-born South Dakota Presentation order elected Irish women to lead them. Irish immigration to the United States had dwindled from a high of 914,119 during the 1850s to 339,065 during the first ten years of the twentieth century, but Mother Joseph Butler was a part of that continuous flow of seekers. Born in February of 1859 in County Cork, Mary Ellen Butler was from an affluent family. An intellectual of sorts, she received her basic education in Ireland and higher education in Belgium. Purportedly, she entered a Sisters of Mercy order for a short while, but perhaps the need to serve the poor rather than those of her own socioeconomic class directed her toward the Presentation convent in Bandon, County Cork, where she had become a postulant by 1885. That same year she immigrated to the Dakotas with Mother Hughes, who was returning home from a recruiting trip to Ireland. A frail girl, Sister Butler risked her life to join her pioneer sisters in the United States, and after settling in the Dakotas, overcame her health problems for a time. A few years later in Fargo, a lay teacher described her as blonde, stately woman eager to accomplish much. That she did, raising money on begging tours and enduring rugged pioneer conditions that led to the death of her dear friend Mother Chriswell. Even after Sister Butler became the superior in 1894, she sent other nuns in search of contributions when starvation seemed imminent. In fact, the tradition probably extended on through Mother Butler's tenure, although she invented other ways of obtaining food such as flying a flag out a convent window or ringing the cloister bell to alert the charitable that the sisters were hungry. Because during these days each Presentation had to be from durable stock, soon after becoming superior Mother Butler ceased recruiting young women from wealthy homes.[37] Although "the order she started . . . was [created by] taking in rich girls," one sister explained, soon "she had nothing to do with them; she wanted poor ones."[38]

Despite its hardships, the little community of nuns grew. While superior, Mother Butler retained the role of novice mistress, and by 1911 the order increased from four to sixty-one members, many of whom staffed the eight parochial schools that the sisters helped found in eastern South Dakota during the superior's tenure. Mother Butler recruited postulants and teachers for these institutions, as would her successors until the 1940s, by acquiring young women from Newfoundland and by making numerous journeys back to Ireland. There she met with likely candidates and persuaded them to accompany her to the northern Great Plains. One such young woman, Sister Eucharia Kelly, remembered Mother Butler as patient, capable, and strong. Even though the convent head "came from a . . . [wealthy Irish] family," Sister Kelly reminisced, she managed in South Dakota with "nothing really."[39] "All the money she could get," another nun recalled, "she used it on the poor."[40]

Other sisters assessed that because Mother Butler was an educated woman from a family of means, she had a good head for business and administration. Moreover the superior appreciated the need to augment Presentation teachers' academic expertise. To this end she located priests and laypersons able to instruct the nuns whose mission was to be professional. In addition, Presentation educators were to observe classes and give written reports to an experienced adviser before assuming responsibilities. Then the neophytes submitted formal lesson plans to a supervisor, attended weekly meetings with advisers, and had daily conferences with methods instructors. To make sure her schools ran smoothly, Mother Butler journeyed by train from one location to the next, engaging a horse and buggy to transport her from the station to each town or country school. Because she was worn to the point of exhaustion, in 1903 Bishop O'Gorman and Mother Butler's physicians advised her to go to California for a rest. Accompanied by a Presentation nurse, Sister Margaret Mary Grainger, Mother Butler made the trek in January of 1904 and returned in late spring of 1905. Apparently reinvigorated, she then served as superior another eleven years. Although Mother Butler had affection and dedication for the poor, even after her term was over in 1915 she continued to rely on her upper-class upbringing and familiarity with the ways of the wealthy to raise money, negotiate business deals, and supervise Presentation-run schools until she died in 1935.[41]

In 1898, Mother Butler had received the first request to staff a school outside Aberdeen when Father John Hogan of Holy Family Parish in Mitchell, South Dakota, asked for teachers to instruct in Holy Family School. The Sisters of Saint Agnes, from Fond du Lac, Wisconsin, had operated the institution from 1886 to 1895, and the Benedictine Sisters from Yankton from 1895 to 1898. Mother Butler sent four women—Sisters M. Agatha Hartnett, M. Paula Roche, M. Martin O'Toole, and M. Teresa Murphy —to begin the fall term, and the pattern that emerged in the following story of Holy Family history would be repeated many times as parochial schools opened throughout eastern South Dakota communities.[42]

Holy Family School had been built in the 1880s at a cost of $5,000, and parishioners hoped that it would induce the bishop to make his residence in Mitchell. The wooden building housed eight grades until high school courses were added to the curriculum in 1912. Father Dean Shea, who replaced Father Hogan, worked with Bishop O'Gorman to establish the school's philosophy and rules (Table 2). Father Coleman O'Flaherty became pastor in 1912. Confronted with the school's overcrowding and crumbling walls, he decided to remodel and enlarge the campus facilities. Presentation teachers conducted classes in the church basement during construction, while Notre Dame (Academy) High School was started in 1912 and continued until 1970. The first faculty consisted of twelve people, seven of whom were Presentations. The curriculum and instructors (Table 3) reflected the standard liberal arts program infused with a traditional emphasis on separate gender roles.[43]

Parishioners were conscious of maintaining a curriculum competitive with that in the public schools, and the Presentations were proud to advertise that Sister Holland, the principal, had earned a college degree.[44] A 1914 contract with her, her staff, and the Presentation Order required that each nun-educator be certified by the state and that "at least one or more teachers ... be qualified to [instruct] ... chorus and the theory of music as prescribed in the State Course of Study. ... One Sister shall also be competent to drill or train pupils in the general principles of expression and elocution [and] ... be able to conduct ... school plays and entertainments."[45] Meeting these and other needs, the nuns taught for a low salary of $180 for the school year, compared to an average of $468 for South Dakota rural public educators and of $525 for the nation. Sacrifices

TABLE 2. PHILOSOPHY AND RULES OF HOLY FAMILY SCHOOL

General Rules of the School

I. The pastor of the parish is superintendent of the school.
II. The teacher of the highest grade is principal of the school.
III. No agent or other person shall be allowed to exhibit in the school any books, articles or apparatus unless specifically authorized by the superintendent.
IV. There shall be no session of the school on Saturdays and legal holidays: Labor Day, National Thanksgiving Day and Friday following, Christmas, New Year's, Washington's Birthday, (February 22nd), Decoration Day, or any holiday appointed by the state or general government.

Pupils

1. No person affected with any contagious disease or directly exposed to the same shall be allowed to attend the parochial schools.
2. Pupils coming to school without proper cleanliness of person or dress shall be sent home to be properly prepared for the school room.
3. Each pupil shall be assigned by the teacher to a particular seat and be required to keep the same, with the desk and floor beneath in a neat and orderly condition. The eating of food or fruit or nuts during school hours and the use of tobacco or gum are strictly prohibited.
4. Pupils shall not at any time play, run, jump, scuffle, or make any boisterous noises within the school building.
5. Any pupil who shall in any way cut or mark or otherwise injure any part of the school building, furniture, trees, outbuilding, or other property; use or write any profane or obscene language; or make any obscene pictures or characters on the premises or other school property shall be liable to payment of damages, expulsion, or other punishment, according to the offense.
6. Any pupil absent or tardy for whatever cause shall on his return to school bring to the teacher a written excuse from his parents or guardian for such absence or tardiness, unless a parent or guardian shall make an excuse in person. Any pupil who shall be absent without an excuse from parent or guardian (given in person or writing, and satisfactory to the principal) may be suspended, and the principal shall immediately notify the parents or guardian of such suspension.

(continued)

such as this allowed schools to buy supplies and keep physical plants standing. In return for the Presentations' charity, the parish did provide a shelter for the nuns because the women's community life gave them mental and emotional strength to do their work.[46]

After Father O'Flaherty left Mitchell to serve as a chaplain in

TABLE 2. PHILOSOPHY AND RULES OF HOLY FAMILY SCHOOL *(continued)*

7. No pupil shall leave school or be withdrawn therefrom for a grievance of any kind without consulting the Reverend Superintendent.
8. The promotion of pupils from one grade or class to another shall be made at such times as the interest of the school may require. No pupil shall be promoted from one class or grade to another until he is able to pass an examination (judged by the principal to be satisfactory) in all the studies of the grade or class from which the student is to be transferred.
9. Pupils shall not be permitted to leave the school before the close of the session for other reasons except sickness or some pressing emergency or for the purpose of attending any other lessons, when absence would interfere with the studies pursued in the schools or with any class with which the pupils are connected. Students shall not leave the school room during school hours or leave the yard at recess without permission from their teacher.
10. The teacher of any room shall report to the Reverend Superintendent the name of any pupil guilty of truancy and the name of any pupil whose conduct in school or out is such that the teacher considers him an unfit member of the school.
11. Any pupil suspended by the teacher may be restored to school by the principal at her discretion. No pupil shall be finally expelled from the school without the approval of the Reverend Superintendent.
12. Pupils shall strictly adhere to the course of study prescribed for the grade to which they belong; but pupils whose health or circumstances at home will not permit them to take the full work may select their studies under the direction of the principal, provided such selection be from not more than one grade.
13. Any pupil who shall absent himself from any regular examination or special exercise of the school, without valid excuse, shall not be permitted to advance with the class until the neglected duty is performed in a satisfactory manner. Any pupil suspended from school by virtue of any of the foregoing rules can be restored only on such conditions as the reverend Superintendent shall determine.
14. Persons aggrieved by the application or administration of any of the foregoing rules and regulations may seek redress by application to the Reverend Superintendent of the school.

Source: Sister Di Donato, "A History of the Educational Work of the Presentation Sisters," 35–37.

France during World War I, Father John M. Brady became the new pastor, holding the position for forty years until he died in 1959. Father Brady and the sisters worked together to enlarge the academy, improve the curriculum, and insure that each student take the work

TABLE 3. FACULTY AND CURRICULUM AT NOTRE DAME HIGH SCHOOL, 1912

Principal, English, Latin, Mathematics	Sister Francis Holland
Voice, Elocution, Calisthenics	Miss Ethel Dowdell
Didactics, History	Sister Agnes Gilmore
Christian Doctrine	Father O'Flaherty
Catechism and Bible History	Father M. J. Harte
Domestic Science	Sister M. Bernadine Baldwin
Piano	Miss Edith Smith
Violin	Mrs. Genevieve McLean
Grades seven and eight	Sister M. Attracta Deecy
Grades five and six	Sister M. Loretta Houlihan
Grades three and four	Sister M. Conception Hamilton
Grades one and two	Sister M. Winifred Daly

Source: Sister Di Donato, "A History of the Educational Work of the Presentation Sisters" 38–39.

seriously. Sister M. Alexius Steinman, who taught in the school, recalled that the number of students in a class varied from ten to sixty.[47] Not all of them were ideal pupils, however. One year two boys in a class of forty-eight ninth graders decided to drive Sister Steinman away by misbehaving continually. She countered by making them write compositions explaining why they were in school. When one boy wrote that he was there to have a good time, the sister showed his paper to Father Brady. Offended at such flippant behavior, the priest confronted the two youngsters, grabbing one "by the neck until his eyes bulged" and expelling the other. That was the end of Sister Steinman's trouble.[48] Due partially to the nuns' efforts, most of their students displayed a belief in the traditional American values that were common to both Catholic and Protestant faiths, despite their differences. Sister Grace Farrell, who taught at Notre Dame for twenty-three years, reminisced that at a reunion of students who had attended the school during the 1930s, many former pupils proudly boasted to her that they were upholding high moral standards in their personal lives and were still married to the same spouses after many years.[49]

Founded before the junior college, Notre Dame's coeducational elementary school and its secondary school were later housed under the same roof as the junior college that Father Brady and the nuns established in 1921. Admission to grades one through twelve was free to day scholars whose parents contributed money to the parish church, as well as to those who were too poor to give; the church charged a $50 a month fee to outsiders. Other financial support came from an offering of $1 per family, collected at Mass on the first Sunday of every month. As years passed, the high school curriculum met the state-accepted South Dakota course of study requirements, emphasizing a combination of liberal arts and individualized student self-selection—four years each of English, history, and science, two years of Latin, and two years of electives.[50]

Because the program that Notre Dame came to offer modernized over the years and responded to its clients' requests, enrollment continued to grow. In particular, the 1950s was a period of expansion and change. The parish added a new gymnasium, an auditorium, and more classrooms to accommodate the multiplying student population. By the time of the Presentations' seventy-fifth jubilee in 1961, Notre Dame High School had an enrollment of 194, with forty-two in the graduating class; the elementary school contained 623 pupils. The staff consisted of twenty-three nuns but included five lay teachers, indicating that the school had grown beyond the Presentations' ability to run it independently. In so evolving, the institution joined the national trend of the use of lay teachers in Catholic education. Nevertheless, the sisters' ranks had also grown as their influence had drawn into their community more than sixty-five young women whom the nuns had contacted through the high school and the junior college at Mitchell.[51] Despite the recruiting success, older Presentations such as Martha Raleigh later lamented that they had compromised their predominantly liberal arts and religious course of study. "But there were pressures put upon us by . . . parents . . . and students," and to remain in business, we could not ignore them, Sister Martha Raleigh explained.[52]

This constant demand dispersed Presentations to many more schools in the Sioux Falls Diocese. By 1900, the jurisdiction contained more than 35,000 Indian and non-Indian Catholics. For them, the sisters helped open twelve parochial schools and four academies, enrolling a total of 1,803 persons. Even though thirteen other religious orders had convents in the state, Bishop O'Gorman relied heavily upon the Presentations to staff schools in the eastern part of South Dakota. Between 1900 and 1910 the Presentations worked in Milbank, Jefferson, Bridgewater, Woonsocket, and Dell Rapids. They also opened short-lived schools at Marion, Bristol, and Elkton.[53]

As a girl, Sister Sylvester Auth lived with the nuns at Elkton. Her remembrances suggest the great impact that Presentations had on many of their pupils. Sister Auth's father was a farmer who sent his daughter to live with the Presentations at Elkton while she attended the town's only high school, a public facility. Sister Auth remembered how Mother Butler coaxed her into the congregation during one of the superior's inspection tours: "The morning she [Mother Butler] left, she went on the five o'clock train. . . . [The nuns] let me walk to the depot with her, and her train was . . . three hours late. . . . We sat in the depot and visited. . . . It was the anniversary of my mother's death, and she said . . . , 'God had taken your mother . . . now you can join the Presentation Sisters and take blessed Mother for your mother,' . . . . She went on her train, and three months later I was in the convent."[54]

Also exerting an influence over students, in 1885 Benedictine sisters from Yankton first opened St. Lawrence School in Milbank. Six years later they were forced to abandon the effort, but Father John Wulf and three Presentations—Sisters M. Benedict Murphy, M. Thaddeus Holmes, and M. Benignus Saunders—reopened it in 1901. Until a new brick structure stood completed in 1910, the pupils studied in a frame building that had formerly been the pastor's home. The second story served as a church for several years until a new one was built. From an original membership of twelve families, the parish experienced slow but steady growth, and by 1961, a faculty of eight taught 214 pupils in grades one through nine.[55]

Father Charles Robinson of St. Peter's parish in Jefferson followed Father Wulf in asking Mother Butler for teachers. The priest had worked formerly with the Yankton Benedictines, but they had withdrawn when the parish could no longer support them during the depression years of the early 1890s. In 1902, four Presentations— Sisters M. Benedict Murphy, M. Cecelia Sullivan, M. Bernard McWalters, and M. Paul Connery—went to St. Peter's to teach grades one through six, where they were so successful that a few years later town officials asked several more of the nuns to work in the public school. This arrangement continued successfully more than twenty years because Jefferson was an overwhelmingly Catholic community. The lower grades remained in the nuns' hands, while lay persons taught the older children. Over the years, parishioners paid to remodel and enlarge the original structure. In 1952, they built a new school to accommodate the increasing enrollment, which by 1960 had reached 165 students in the first eight grades.[56]

Continuing to follow in fellow church members' footsteps, in 1901 the Catholics of St. Stephen in Bridgewater started their first school—this time, in an old Protestant church. Three years later Father Bunning acquired five Presentation educators, Sisters Holmes, M. Teresa Murphy, Crowley, M. Clare Wallace and M. Gabriel Barron. Sister Murphy was the mission superior, and Sister Wallace shared her music-teaching talents with pupils at Bridgewater and Mitchell and had forty students. A new building erected in 1922 housed the school, a convent, and pupil dormitories. Up to seventy-five scholars, as they sometimes were called, boarded each year until the rural bus system was introduced in the late 1930s. By 1961, enrollment had stabilized at one hundred day pupils, with a faculty of three teachers for grades one through six.[57]

Another parish, St. Wilfred's in Woonsocket, under the leadership of French Eudist Father Haquin, became the site for a Presentation-run school. With four nuns—Sisters Murphy, Holmes, Hickey, and M. Agnes Gilmore—it began classes in 1908. Two years later, St. Joseph School was completed there, and in 1911 a secondary program, enrolling seventeen students, was added to the curriculum. Regardless of the ancient portrayal of the corruptible woman (a picture that had discouraged nuns from teaching boys) these Presentation Sisters instructed both genders. Unfortunately, a drought and economic hardship forced the parish to close the high school during the mid-1920s.[58]

Up to that time the institute had served more than two hundred pupils, of whom seventy-five had been boarders. In August of 1932, the Catholic orphanage at Turton moved into the abandoned high school dormitories, where the nuns would take care of the homeless children until the Bishop of Sioux Falls moved the orphans to a Sioux Falls residence in 1934. Dwindling under the weight of a harsh climate and sparse population, by 1961 the enrollment at St. Joseph had declined to 116.[59]

Evincing interethnic cooperation, the Irish and German Catholic families of St. Mary's parish in Dell Rapids requested in 1910 that the Presentations staff their new academy. Seven women—Sisters Holmes, Murphy, M. Regis McCarthy, M. Hyacinth Brummel, Hickey, M. Josephine Mitchell and Gilmore—began teaching 125 youngsters in grades one through eight and, one year at a time, added levels of a high school curriculum. The first class of seniors, seven in number, graduated in 1915. Illustrating the rural atmosphere of many Presentation schools, each day one of the nuns had barn duty. She supervised the hitching of horses to buggies and the safe passage of children to and from the teams. The nuns' quarters were located within the school building, which also housed a dormitory on the second floor and a kitchen and dining room in the basement. Before World War II, Father Walter Roche organized a transportation system for St. Mary's, and students no longer lived at school.[60]

Just after World War I, an influenza epidemic ravaged the area around Dell Rapids, forcing schools to close for several months. St. Mary's Presentation teachers became volunteer nurses in the homes of the parishioners. Some sister-teachers became ill also. Years after this ordeal, Sister Sylvester Auth never forgot one particular girl's suffering: "I don't remember that she ate anything that morning . . . [before she died], but I washed her up anyhow and got her settled. . . . I said, 'Now you turn over and we'll say some prayers together.' . . . She went to sleep and pretty soon she woke up and . . . was struggling. . . . I called her [mother] and said, 'You'd better come in. I'm afraid she's dying.' I got things ready for a dying person, and she [the mother] went out to call one of the men in the barn, and by the time she got back the girl was dead. She died right in my arms."[61]

The epidemic passed after placing many people in their graves. Subsequent years saw St. Mary's grow in academic stature, receiving state accreditation in 1924 and boasting a curriculum that included four years of religion, English, science, and Latin, and one year of speech. Yet even as the school persisted, the small agrarian community that sustained it continued to suffer the neverending whims of nature and economics. Dry weather and subsequent fiscal depressions periodically plagued the Great Plains, and after 1930 the entire nation joined countless farmers who feared the permanent end of prosperity. One Presentation teacher remembered that the nuns, like many public school teachers, received no salary during much of the Great Depression, although people furnished facilities and utilities and often gave them food in exchange for their expertise. St. Mary's transportation system did provide some revenue because the parish had purchased the buses and routinely charged families whose children used the service.[62]

By 1951, a new church and rectory stood as proof that more affluent times had returned to St. Mary's. Presentation educators moved into the priest's vacated rectory and converted their former living quarters into classrooms, while Monsignor Peter Meyer supervised the construction of a new $300,000 high school in 1958 and made plans to erect another convent. Encouraged by growing rural clientele, St. Mary's remained viable through an arrangement with Dell Rapids Public High School. That institution agreed to offer agricultural courses to the Catholic students, who would then use these credits toward graduation from St. Mary's. Because of the nuns' insistence, however, St. Mary's did retain a reputation for its classical offerings, of which some public school students took advantage. This proved an excellent strategy for growth, so by 1961, the high school faculty consisted of twelve sisters, two lay teachers, and the assistant pastor; the same year, twenty-eight students attended commencement and claimed their diplomas. The sisters' influence on many of these graduates' lives was evident because by 1961, more than thirty-five of St. Mary's female graduates had entered the Presentation order.[63]

Located in Aberdeen, Sacred Heart was the last school that Mother Butler staffed. It came into existence inadvertently, beginning with the sisters' need for expanded classroom facilities at Presentation Academy, which had been operated by the nuns since 1888 and had, by 1900, become crowded. Fourteen years later, the sisters ceased teaching at Presentation Academy because Mother Butler decided to shift needed personnel into running the nuns' first hospital, St. Luke's. She did conclude that her order could spare sisters to instruct the less extensive curriculum of Sacred Heart parochial school, which opened in September of 1914. Four Presentations —Sisters M. Saunders, M. Regis McCarthy, M. Columba Daly, and M. Perpetua McCullen —composed the faculty that educated the first year's 158 pupils. Three others—Sister Crowley (an art teacher from Presentation academy), Sister M. Cecelia Sullivan (a choir leader), and Sister M. Borgia Fitzgerald (a secretarial instructor)—offered part-time assistance. During the 1920s, one nun reported that she was responsible for forty-five students in the third grade and part of the fourth.[64]

In the 1940s, the educators added a ninth grade to the Sacred Heart curriculum so that graduates could transfer directly to Aberdeen's Central High School. During the next decade the laity also built a youth center that provided a meeting place for the community's young people. By 1961, enrollment had reached almost six hundred pupils, several of whom would later dedicate themselves to a spiritual life. The faculty consisted of twenty-two lay instructors, eight priests, and twelve nuns.[65]

Also a significant figure in the growth of these schools, Mother Aloysius Forrest served the Presentation community from 1915 to 1921 and from 1927 to 1932. A Cork native, Hanna Forrest was born in 1872. Because she entered the Irish convent when she was a bit older than most, she was still a postulant when Mother Butler recruited her and seven other women in 1899. A well-educated teacher, Sister Forrest assumed several leadership positions within the Presentation community before her election to the chief executive's job in 1915. In 1906 she became novice mistress, resuming the office once again during the period between her two terms as superior. She pushed her novices to receive state certification. Sister-teachers usually attended Northern in Aberdeen, but nuns such as Sister Grace Farrell were educated at other institutions. Sister Farrell earned her bachelor's degree from Columbia College in Dubuque, Iowa, in 1920, and received a master's in 1926 from Notre Dame in Indiana. When any nun left to pursue her studies outside Aberdeen, superiors made every effort to find for her a community of nuns with whom she might live and share a common bond.[66]

Tending to the sisters' other needs, Mother Forrest recognized that all work and no relaxation could be oppressive. At the motherhouse she encouraged the sisters to relax and enjoy themselves during evening recreation periods. She promoted the playing of card games such as pinochle.[67] Bishop Lambert Hoch recalled celebrating the Feast of Saint Aloysius with Mother Aloysius and the Presentations shortly after he had become a priest. Some of the women were "just young sisters, and they were very much Irish," he recounted.[68] At the festival they did the Highland fling and other dances. Despite Mother Forrest's efforts to ease the burden of work, however, during her two terms thirteen sisters died prematurely, harbingers of her own death from cancer in 1932.[69]

Serving as superior six years between Mother Forrest's two stints in office, Mother Agatha Collins was another advocate of educational professionalization. Also born in Cork, she came to Aberdeen in 1904 at the age of thirty-two and enjoyed a long life in South Dakota, living until 1954. Yet a postulant upon arrival, she did not receive the habit until a year later and finally pronounced her vows in 1907. One nun, Sister M. Martha Raleigh, remembered Mother Collins as a kind, friendly, and generous spirit who loved all people. A nurse by training, she nevertheless kept a vigilant eye over the educators and their schools.[70] Sister M. Alexius Steinman remembers Mother Collins holding up a stack of teaching sisters' first-grade certificates (a highly ranked state license to teach school) and declaring "educated by gosh!"[71] She also persuaded pastors to increase the teacher's earnings, which during her term probably hovered around $200 for nine months' work. This compared to a national public school teachers' average annual salary of $871 in 1920 and $1,420 in 1930.[72]

Finding an ally for many of their professionalization causes, Mothers Collins and Forrest established a working relationship with Bishop Bernard J. Mahoney, who was appointed in 1922 soon after Bishop O'Gorman died. Attesting to this support, Sister Bonaventure Hoffman remarked that South Dakota churchmen had joined the Presentation superiors in encouraging the career-minded sisters to join their fields' state and national professional associations and to remain competitively prepared for their work. Although many of the nuns made these connections eagerly, a few clung to the past, fearing the vitiating effects of the order's growing secular affiliations. Their sentiments, however, would become more and more a vestige of days gone by as the nuns became part of the modern age.[73]

Mothers Forrest and Collins were able to provide increasingly well-trained teachers to establish another three institutions—St. Ann at Humboldt, St. Teresa at Huron, and St. Thomas at Madison. The first of these schools began in 1921. St. Ann included boarding facilities until 1950, and by 1961 the school's faculty of five women— Sister M. Clare Wallace (the superior and music teacher), and Sisters Saunders, Gilmore, M. Viator Burns, and Sister Aurelia Cronin—was teaching 144 students in grades one through eight. Despite setbacks, especially during the days of financial depression during the 1930s, the Presentations worked doggedly to keep schools going.[74] Although begging tours had ended, Sister Sylvester Auth remembers that during the depression the nuns at St. Ann found many homeless children on the streets. "I'd take one of the little girls from our school," she reminisced. "We'd ... stand at the church door with a little plate or a box or something, and Father would announce [to parishioners] that when you leave today there will be a sister at the door . . . [taking] . . . offering[s] for the orphans."[75]

Construction on St. Teresa began in 1921, but because of difficulty in obtaining building materials the workers did not finish it until 1929. The first year's enrollment of 175 pupils in eight grades had increased to 405 by 1961. Difficulties in erecting the St. Thomas school, however, were no barrier to seven Presentations—Sisters M. Benedict Murphy, M. Clare Wallace, M. Regis McCarthy, M. Loyola Mullally, M. Hyacinth Brummel, Sister Teresa Murphy, and M. Clotilda Gully—who in 1929 began holding sessions for sixty children in the church basement. Finally, the structure was completed, and from 1933 to 1944 the women continued to teach elementary and secondary classes. The new facilities were then deemed inadequate, leading to a loss of state accreditation. Eventually, the upper grades were phased out. Elementary enrollment, on the other hand, had stabilized at approximatley 100 students; then it increased to more than 170 in the early 1960s. Plans were then made to build new quarters for the nuns and to convert their old rooms into much needed classrooms.[76] St. Thomas School, which included grades one through twelve, was opened in 1928 by Father Eugene Eagen. Sisters Thaddeus Holmes, M. Carmel Harney, and M. Eunice Staudenraus taught there. The first graduating class of eleven members produced one diocesan priest—Father Joseph Deragisch—and two Presentations: Sisters M. Mildred Sullivan and M. Carmelita McCullough, (the latter becoming a Presentation superior). In 1944, the high school closed its doors, funneling all of its resources to the lower grades. Because the earlier years in a child's life mark a time of crucial values formation, Catholic officials faced with limited resources judged the elementary school to be more important than the high school.[77]

Mother Raphael McCarthy was another notable catalyst for the growth of Presentation-staffed schools. Born in 1888 in Bandon, County Cork, Margaret McCarthy was fortunate to have a father who was a teacher. In 1907, Mother Butler met her in Ireland and convinced the nineteen-year-old woman to return with her to South Dakota. Although eager to be part of the pioneer teaching community, in a few years Sister McCarthy had completed nurses' training at St. Luke's; however, she never lost interest in education, even though her major responsibilities before becoming superior were as superintendent of St. Joseph's and McKennan hospitals and as assistant to Mother Forrest until the older woman died in 1932.[78]

Facing a multitude of challenges, in 1932 Sister McCarthy was elected superior. She worked closely with Bishop Mahoney until he died in 1939. Bishop William Brady took his place, and together he and Mother McCarthy managed to promote professionalization despite the financially troubled and war-torn decades of her term, which extended until 1946. Mother McCarthy's energy, practicality, and perseverance were sources of her successes: she opened a home and school for orphans, began a kindergarten in Aberdeen, and extended the order's influence into Minnesota. Mother McCarthy's decision to set up a uniform bookkeeping system for the motherhouse and hospitals brought about further improvement in the Presentations' financial situation, although the schools and hospitals that the sisters operated brought in little income.[79]

A shortcoming within the education apostolate that Mother McCarthy attempted to solve was the intermittent higher education of nuns in summer sessions. Moreover, Sister M. Cabrini Di Donato observed, "schools were getting old. . . ; . . . visual aid equipment was rare; libraries were neglected or did not exist; physical education was considered a luxury . . . ; art and music were often taught as a reward . . . ; [and] methods had not progressed with the times. . . ."[80] Thus Mother McCarthy requested that Sister M. Winifred Daly obtain a master's degree in educational supervision and administration in preparation for a new role in the education apostolate—community school supervisor. In this capacity Sister Daly guided and standardized the schools' curricula, correcting some of the problems that Sister Di Donato had noted. According to Sister Di Donato, Sister Daly accomplished this through a quietly assertive "ladylike" leadership style. From 1951 to 1959, when Sister Rose Anne took the post, the Presentations did without a supervisor because Sister Daly joined the Presentation Junior College faculty.[81]

Continuing her professionalization efforts, Mother McCarthy campaigned actively for a new campus facility at Aberdeen that would include a motherhouse, a girls' high school, and especially a junior college so that more and more Presentations would have easy access to at least two years of higher education.[82] The superior's skill in promoting such projects was evidenced in the 1946 letter to South Dakota Senator Karl Mundt, whom she contacted for help in obtaining a building permit: "We are really very handicapped in our work, and if we could build this new Motherhouse and School on the piece of property we have secured, it would give us the facilities we need and the opportunity to develop our teaching. There is no Girls' Catholic High School in Aberdeen, and one is really needed. I am sure a word from you to Mr. Caulk or 'the powers that be' would insure us this permission. . . . We always follow with interest the splendid work you are doing in Washington. God bless you for it. . . ."[83]

Mother McCarthy further documented her resolve in letters to Reverend J. J. O'Neil of the St. Theresa's School in Huron, S.D. and Reverend T. J. Manning at St. Ann's in Humbolt. In both, she explained that a contract she was sending each priest requested a special payment for Presentation music teachers to staff his school. She wrote: "The terms stated in this contract, Father, are the same as have been in force in your parish for several years. We have . . . added the clause regarding the choir, because I feel that where so much choir work is done by the Sisters, some compensation should be made, as education of music Sisters is most expensive."[84]

Reflecting again her sense of professionalism, during the mid-1930s, Mother McCarthy conducted a study on the activities and qualifications of religious elementary school teachers. The report she submitted to the community recorded that in the twelve parochial schools in which South Dakota Presentations worked, fifty-seven of the sister-teachers received, in addition to facilities and utilities, an average salary of $270 for the nine-month school year, a figure that was overshadowed by approximately $807 for the state and $1,283 for the national averages.[85]

Ever mindful of the Presentations' ideological linchpin, Mother McCarthy generated administrative policies that flowed from her belief that the Presentations' "first . . . purpose . . . was to manifest God's glory and honor [by being] . . . faithful religious" and top educators as well. To this end, Mother McCarthy required "spiritual retreats, summer school courses, canon law institutes, congresses for religious, workshops and pilgrimages. . . ."[86]

Using their skills to provide quality services, the Presentations began running a children's home under Mother McCarthy's direction. In 1932, a fire destroyed an orphanage at Turton, and Bishop Mahoney put the home's thirty-five children under Presentation care because the childrens' previous caretakers, the Sisters of St. Louis of Montreal, Canada, intended to return home. Once again the Presentations' unenclosed community structure made them open to accept the new responsibility. Mother McCarthy made temporary arrangements for the children to stay in Graham Hall, a dormitory on the Northern State Teachers College campus. After a four-week stay, Mother McCarthy saw to it that the orphans journeyed safely by train to Woonsocket, where they occupied the old dormitories of St. Joseph's School. After two years in Woonsocket, the children moved on to Sioux Falls and into a building of what had been Columbus College until it had closed in 1935. That year, however, the Marianhill Fathers, intending to open a seminary, asked to take over the facility. Thus the boys were placed in Bishop Mahoney's residence, and the girls were sent to the parochial school at Bridgewater. By the late 1930s, the total number of children had reached sixty, so Mother McCarthy received permission from the city of Sioux Falls and requested federal Works Progress Administration funds to construct a new home for the children. Government workers under President Franklin Roosevelt's administration completed a new building in September of 1940. Other funding came from private donations and the diocesan aid program. Presentation Children's Home, as it was called, initially accommodated fifty-four children, but during its existence the dwelling sheltered anywhere from sixty to ninety boys and girls between the ages of three and fifteen, several of whom were non-Catholic. Bishop Brady instructed the resident chaplain that the nuns were to have complete authority over running the facility and caring for the children. While with the nuns, the children studied grades one through eight. Then, following tradition, the males went to Boys' Town school in Nebraska, and the girls attended either Notre Dame in Mitchell or Mount Marty, a girls' school and Catholic college in Yankton. Girls also could go to St. Mary's in Dell Rapids.[87]

As always, the sisters relied on donations to run the children's home and school. Parishes throughout the diocese donated food, clothing, toys, and school supplies. Several charitable organizations in Sioux Falls held bi-weekly sewing circles, a yearly Christmas party, and special lawn socials to raise money. One group, called the Presentation Club, contained eight couples who provided transportation when the sisters or children needed to run errands or visit a physician. The participants also took young people on picnics or to movies, for which several Sioux Falls theater operators provided free admission. Church and civic organizations provided significant help.[88] Bishop Lambert Hoch, who had attended the Presentation-run school at Elkton and who became their bishop beginning in 1958, said that administering Presentation Children's Home proved to be the sisters' "finest hour."[89]

Despite the Presentations' dedication to the orphan children, during the 1960s federal and state authorities laid down a number of new regulations that the nuns were to follow. These reflected the increasingly popular contention among psychologists and sociologists that parentless children needed guidance from trained social workers holding master's degrees.[90] Bishop Hoch countered that "no state mandate is going to supply any institution . . . with the love, devotion, care, and concern that the sisters gave those children."[91] Even so, by 1965 the Presentations decided that they had ventured out of their area of professional specialty, closed Children's Home, and placed the children with families. The sisters, some of whom had labored as professionals, teachers, cooks, and laundresses, departed with warm memories of their past work; regardless of the level of their expertise, satisfaction had filled those days devoted to running Children's Home. Feeling the same way, five girls and one boy had bonded with various nuns and decided to join religious communities.[92]

More in line with the work for which the Presentations were trained, Mother McCarthy established a kindergarten on the convent grounds in Butler Hall. In 1934, she had returned from a visit with the Presentation Sisters of Dubuque, enthusiastic about their work with preschool children. The matriarch then asked Sister Holmes to attend Pestalozzi-Froebel College in Chicago and prepare to open a kindergarten inspired by the two great educators for whom the college was named.[93] Employing Montessori principles as well, during the mid 1930s Sister Holmes designed a curriculum intended to create "well-adjusted," "independent" children who could also "play well with others."[94] To do so she used the gift method that she described as " 'Gift' because advancement from one stage of learning to another is introduced by a gift. For example . . . the first gift is a wooden ball and a crocheted ball to teach hard and soft. This learning experience is accompanied by a song. The second gift is blocks from which the child learns manipulation . . . and number readiness, [and] to follow directions, listen . . ., [and] concentrate. . . . The third is a tin box with a hinge-on-cover in which are colored beads. These are used to teach numbers, colors, materials, direction, comparison, and safety. Each gift advances the student to the next stage of learning until he has completed eight stages."[95]

Presentation sisters accepted other teaching responsibilities during Mother McCarthy's term. In the fall of 1939, she responded to a request from the Archbishop of St. Paul for catechism teachers at Mound, Minnesota; four nuns—Sister M. Gerard Hilliard, the superior, and Sisters M. Consolata Grace and M. Ambrose Muldoon—left Aberdeen and moved to the old Mound rectory at Our Lady of the Lake Parish. There they lived upstairs, and on the first floor held classes for 145 youngsters. An arrangement with the city superintendent of schools enabled other Catholic children to attend public schools in response to a Minnesota state law but to have released time each week to receive religious instruction; children from rural areas attended such religion classes on Saturdays. Eventually the institution became a full-fledged school, with a new convent purchased in 1941, and with another classroom building for grades one through eight constructed ten years later. Located in suburban Minneapolis, the parochial school grew rapidly, from an attendance of 280 in 1951 to nearly 450 students and a faculty of ten by 1961. As part of the expansion program that began in 1960, the parish eventually added eight classrooms and a library.[96]

In 1939, Presentation teachers had also begun teaching catechism at Willmar, Minnesota, but there the educational developments had been slower than in Mound. In fact, the sisters remained for fifteen years before an elementary school opened, traveling throughout the Willmar area to teach religion to nearly seven hundred students each week. The school, named for St. Mary, finally opened in 1954. During the first year, Sister Brendan Fitzgerald served as principal. Other educators included Sisters M. Imelda Kelly, M. Virginia Hallauer, M. Ancilla Russell, M. Lucia Schulte, and a laywoman, Helen McGowan. They taught 219 students in grades one through six. Seventh and eighth grades soon augmented the curriculum, and in 1960 the faculty consisted of five sisters and four lay persons, who watched with pride as ninety-nine students graduated from the middle school that year. Although the Presentation teachers had waited many years to be a part of this formalized school, during the mid-1960s the nuns spent most of their time journeying to Willmar and Mound, teaching religion classes to children whose parents could not afford to send them to a parochial school.[97]

Mother McCarthy extended the Presentation's professional teaching services further into Minnesota, eventually accepting an offer in 1943 from Father E. S. de Courcy to replace the Sisters of St. Joseph at St. Ann's school in Anoka.[98] At first Mother McCarthy hesitated to accept the job because she believed that Mother Agnes Gonzaga, the St. Joseph Sisters' superior, would be offended. Mother McCarthy explained to Father de Courcy, "Our communities have always been good friends, and . . . I hesitate to do any thing that would disturb that friendship."[99] Yet Father de Courcy was determined to replace the seven St. Joseph Sisters—six teachers, and a cook. Although they owned and ran the school, instructing approximately 250 students in grades one through eight, the St. Joseph Sisters' rule prevented them from tending the altar and sanctuary, conducting the choir, and training the altar boys. Moreover, Father de Courcy may have been concerned over the friction between the St. Joseph's Sisters and leading women within the Anoka Catholic community.[100] Expecting to be replaced, Mother M. Gonzaga wrote to Father de Courcy: "I hope the Mother you will assign in charge of our school will be a woman of tact and experience because we have some would-be socialites who are more critical of the Catholic school than the ordinary ignorant non-Catholic. It is just another example of what Christ said: 'one's worst enemies are those of . . . [one's] own household.' They will play the part of the Pharisee and will be delighted to point out our faults and weaknesses. I have ignored them since I came here and that is the unforgiveable sin in their eyes. Hence because this change is being made in my administration both you and I will be legitimate targets for their malicious shafts."[101]

Mother McCarthy wrote to Mother Gonzaga asking if the St. Joseph Sisters resented the Presentations working at St. Ann's. Mother Gonzaga assured her friend that the two congregations would remain close, even if Mother McCarthy accepted the assignment. Thus the St. Joseph Sisters transferred ownership of the school to the Anoka parish in 1943 but continued to run the institution until Presentation sisters—M. Brendan Fitzgerald, Consolata Grace, Jeanne Marie Farrell, M. Lucia Schulte, M. George Jurgens, M. Fabian Martin, M. Raymond Aherne, and M. Myron Martin —could take charge in 1945. The South Dakota nuns never did assume ownership of what became St. Stephen's school. Presentation elementary teachers agreed to a contract that entitled them to $40 per month, while any high school teachers were to hold at least a bachelor's degree and earn a $45 monthly salary. These sums were about $5 more per month than Presentation educators were making at the same time in South Dakota towns such as Humbolt, but they compared disfavorably to the 1949 state ($230) and national ($335) public school teacher salaries. Initially the Presentations in Anoka were responsible for 350 students, and by the 1960s, sixteen faculty members taught 660 pupils.[102]

Ever ready to prove the nuns' usefulness, Mother McCarthy sent various Presentations to instruct hundreds of children not only in Catholic schools, but also in more than thirty religious vacation summer schools in Minnesota and other northwestern states. The superior continued to assign sisters to nonprofessional duties, providing all of the professional Presentations and Bishop Brady with domestic services. Like other superiors before her, she saw that within the convent and the Church the housewife role could free the other professional nuns to perform their duties. We can only speculate about any conflict resulting from the various domestic and semiprofessional tasks that different Presentations assumed. Probably some strife did occur just as it has erupted in other hierarchical structures—between the housewives and breadwinners of the traditional American family and between teachers and administrators within the nations' schools. Existing evidence does document strife within the health care field, between Presentation administrators and nurses and within the Presentation nursing ranks as well; but the nuns at least tolerably resolved their differences for the sake of meeting commonly inspired goals.[103]

Largely the result of these efforts, in 1946 the congregation numbered 221 and owned $2,370,579.54 worth of property with an indebtedness of $123,000: a motherhouse, four hospitals, and one children's home. Moreover, the nuns helped operate eleven parochial schools, two high schools, one normal school and junior college, and two catechetical schools. After her tenure in office, Mother Mc-Carthy continued to pursue her administrative objectives to keep these Presentation-run or -owned institutions operating. In 1952, she was elected bursar-general and continued to serve the community, particularly as a financial expert, until her death in 1966.[104]

Twenty years before, Mother Viator Burns had succeeded Mother McCarthy, becoming the first Presentation superior who was a native of the United States. In other countries that hosted Presentation motherhouses the same acculturation trend was being repeated. (For example, at mid-century, East-Indian women became predominant within Presentation mission sites in India.) A native of South Dakota, Honoria Burns was born in 1892 in Rowena. After a year of teaching in a rural school, at the age of twenty-two she applied to enter the convent at Aberdeen. By the time she became superior, the South Dakota sisters had evolved from an original, homogeneous Irish unit into a mixture of various Caucasian nationalities. By mid-century, a majority of the nuns was no longer Irish, and this trend was reflected in the national decline of Irish immigrants, which had fallen to a comparative trickle of 25,377 between 1941 and 1950. Moreover, national sociological studies done on Irish women during the second half of the twentieth century showed that although they retained traditional values such as the notion that a mother's place is at home with young children, they had lost much of their ethnic identity. Presentation Sister Colman Coakley, who arrived from Ireland in 1948, was one of the last immigrant candidates.[105]

Hailing from this rugged part of the United States, Mother Burns inherited from her parents the grit she needed to lead the order that comprised 238 sisters and twenty novices, soon after she took office in 1946. Emphasizing the empowering effect of internal camaraderie, in 1947 she wrote: "Almighty God has given all of us certain talents which He wishes us to share with the others and it is this sharing of ideas which often tends to make a school function successfully. No sister should feel that she stands alone. She has the responsibility to further the interests of the school and should have the humility to be able to seek and to accept help from others in her group."[106]

Inspired by a belief in God, Mother Burns continued professionalization during her years at the helm, and she "disappointed pastors" to whom she refused to send unprepared teachers. As a result of her urging, many Presentations earned academic degrees and won honors. As a result greater numbers of lay persons replaced the nuns in many jobs, thereby enabling them to attend colleges and

universities on a full-time basis.[107] Sometimes Church officials outside of the state had to be convinced just how important these
achievements were. One such churchman was Bishop William J.
Condon, of Great Falls, Montana, who wrote to Mother Burns ex-
pressing vaguely masked impatience at her refusal to send ill-trained
women into the classroom. "It would be for the good of the Church
and religion as well as a more natural and desirable arrangement if
the Presentation Sisters could take over the assignment [of teaching
in Miles City]. Heretofore, you have not been able to see your way
clear to send a minimum number of Sisters to staff the school. . . ."[108]

Mother Burns held her ground. In 1950, assessing her order's
hard-fought victories for professionalization, she once again took
inventory and issued another progress report similar to Mother
McCarthy's document issued in the 1930s. Within the organization,
it stated, almost all of the nuns' educational institutions resembled
typical public schools. In those small schools with fewer than one
hundred pupils in grades one through eight, faculties consisted of
only four or five sisters and a pastor. All the sisters held state certificates, and most principals had bachelor's degrees. At mid-century,
none of the schools maintained boarding facilities because most
students arrived daily by bus, the parishes either owning vehicles
or sharing them with the public schools. No hot-lunch programs
were yet in effect. The teachers administered IQ and state achievement tests for those students transferring from nonaccredited schools
in order to determine their pupils' abilities and levels of performance.
Reflecting national Catholic policy, textbooks came from the
Church's suggested list for courses in history, language, reading, and
literature, but there was no uniform adoption of books. Such decisions rested with the faculty in each school, which typically gave
preference to Catholic authors, although public and private schools
used many of the same books. Libraries usually were limited in size
but did contain Church-sponsored newspapers and magazines. Ex-
tracurricular activities included drama, music, and in a few cases
basketball. Such evidence of acculturation into the secular world
was apparent, especially in the larger, more heterogeneous, Presentation-staffed schools. They typically had more money to offer a
wider variety of athletic programs and clubs and subscribed to a
larger number of non-Catholic newspapers and magazines than did
the smaller institutions. The bigger schools also employed lay in-

structors, and a greater percentage of their teaching sisters held bachelor's degrees even though South Dakota was relatively slow to enforce the undergraduate degree requirement for all of its licensed teachers. It seems the minimal state standards did not discourage many Presentations from pursuing advanced degrees, because they continued to attend schools such as Northern State Teachers College in Aberdeen, Marquette University in Milwaukee, and Catholic University.[109]

Under Mother Burns, qualified Presentation educators Sisters M. Rose Anne Melmer and Marie Patrice Moriarty began teaching sixty-nine children in St. Mary's parish in Sioux Falls. Initially, they held classes in the church. The school was not built until 1950, just a short time before Catholics at Willmar had built theirs. Thus the Presentation teachers lived at and commuted across town from McKennan Hospital. In 1952, a convent was built for the women on the St. Mary's campus. The nuns offered instruction to 140 students in grades one through eight, and by 1961, the Sioux Falls school boasted 500 pupils. That year, 150 South Dakota Presentation nuns were working statewide with 5,339 elementary and secondary school students, saving South Dakota taxpayers $1.8 million in 1961 alone.[110]

During these years after her term in office, Mother Burns continued to serve the Presentation professional movement as chief administrator of McKennan Hospital and, beginning in 1964, as first councillor or assistant to the superior. During her last years, she suffered severe back pain, and she died in 1966. As if this nun had reincarnated the trials of Nano Nagle, one Presentation historian wrote of Mother Burns, "Her burning desire to serve God was alive to the end, as on her deathbed she continued to offer her pain for the Community and those who needed her prayers."[111] Such records indicate the nuns' persistence in seeing suffering as a virtue.

By 1960, the Presentations had seen their area of educational influence grow. The nuns had constantly revised their curricula to meet client-defined needs. They also had professionalized their own teaching skills and assumed stereotypically male occupational roles in administration and policymaking. Thus, some of the sisters had demonstrated an increasing sense of authority and autonomy, continually advocating higher standards for themselves and their schools and supporting organizational efforts to standardize the South Dakota Catholic school system. As one nun pointed out, it had been years since "the priest was boss."[112] For at least some Presentation educators then, although the separate-but-unequal professional philosophy remained separate *from*, it was coming to be viewed as equal *to* that of the male world. Female ideals such as the concept sisterhood had rationalized all of the nuns' professional career goals within and without women's traditional sphere.

NOTES

1. T. M. Stinnett, "Teacher Education, Certification, and Accreditation," in Jim B. Pearson and Edgar Fuller, eds., *Education in the States: Nationwide Development Since 1900* (Washington, D. C.: National Education Association of the United States, 1969), 391–94; David Tyack and Elisabeth Hansot, *Managers of Virtue: Public School Leadership in America, 1820–1980* (New York: Basic Books, 1982), 105–201.

2. Harold A. Buetow, *Of Singular Benefit: The Story of Catholic Education in the United States* (London: Macmillan, 1970), 187–93, 215. David B. Tyack, ed., *Turning Points in American Educational History* (New York: John Wiley and Sons, 1967), 417–19.

3. *The School Manual for the Use of the Sisters of St. Joseph of Carondelet*, quoted in Buetow, *Of Singular Benefit*, 192.

4. Ibid., 242.

5. Sylvester Schmitz, quoted in Ibid., 248.

6. Ibid., 249.

7. B. Meyer, "Sister Formation Movement," *New Catholic Encyclopedia*, vol. 13 (New York: McGraw-Hill, 1967), 261–62; Buetow, *Of Singular Benefit*, 251–53; Leon Joseph Cardinal Suenens, *The Nun in the World: Religious and the Apostolate* (London: Burns and Oates, 1963), 148–50; Karl Fleckenstein and Leon Heinz, *Joseph Cardinal Suenens: Open the Frontiers: Conversations with Cardinal Suenens* (New York: Seabury Press, 1981). For more information, see Sister Maria Concepta, C.S.C., *The Making of a Sister-Teacher* (Notre Dame, Ind.: University of Notre Dame Press, 1965).

8. Buetow, *Of Singular Benefit*, 249–50.

9. H. Warren Button and Eugene F. Provenzo, Jr., *History of Education and Culture in America* (Englewood Cliffs, N. J.: Prentice-Hall, 1983), 179–262; Tyack, *Turning Points in American Educational History*, 412–76. For an interesting essay on the ironies of the progressive movement, see Peter G. Filene, "An Obituary for the Progressive Movement," *American Quarterly* 22 (Spring 1970): 20–34. For a good revisionist work on ideology and education, see Henry A. Giroux, *Ideology, Culture, and the Process of Schooling* (Philadelphia: Temple University Press, 1981). On the necessity for an ideological underpinning for American education, see Richard Pratte, *Ideology and Education* (New York: David McKay, 1977); Paul Julian Schu-

ler, "The Relation of American Catholics to the Foundations and Early Practices of Progressive Education in the United States, 1892–1917" (Ph.D. diss., Notre Dame University, 1970), 129–32, 250–333; William H. Howick, *Philosophies of Education* (Danville, Ill.: Interstate Printers and Publishers, 1980), 29–46, 61–74.

10. Joseph Husslein quoted in Buetow, *Of Singular Benefit*, 235.

11. Ibid., 280; Andrew M. Greeley, *From Backwater to Mainstream: A Profile of Catholic Higher Education* (New York: McGraw-Hill, 1969), 13, John D. Pulliam, *History of Education in America* (Columbus, Ohio: Charles E. Merrill Publishing, 1976), 187.

12. Thomas Edward Shields, quoted in Buetow, *Of Singular Benefit*, 237.

13. Sister M. Marguerite, quoted in Ibid., 239.

14. Ibid., 267–77, 280.

15. Rev. Neil G. McCluskey, S. J., "Catholic Schools after Vatican II," in *Trends and Issues in Catholic Education*, ed. Russell Shaw and Richard J. Hurley (New York: Citation Press, 1969), 335–47. Also see Greeley, *From Backwater to Mainstream*, 15; John Tracy Ellis, "American Catholics and the Intellectual Life," *Thought: Fordham University Quarterly* 30 (Autumn 1955): 351–88.

16. James Coleman, "Public Schools, Private Schools, and the Public Interest," *The Public Interest* 64 (Summer 1981): 19–30.

17. *Census of the Population, Characteristics of the Population, South Dakota*, vol. I, pt. 43 (Washington, D. C.: U.S. Government Printing Office, 1961), 43–11; Cleata B. Thorpe, "Education in South Dakota, 1861–1961," *South Dakota Historical Collections* 36 (1972): 386; *Digest of Education Statistics, 1983–1984* (Washington, D. C.: U.S. Dept. of Education, 1984), 56; interview with Albert Harrington, June 14, 1978, South Dakota Oral History Center, Vermillion; David B. Tyack, *The One Best System: A History of American Urban Education* (Cambridge, Mass.: Harvard University Press, 1974), 13–39; Andrew Guillford and Randall Teeunen, "Country School Legacy: Humanities on the Frontier" (Colorado Springs: Mountain Plains Library Association and the National Endowment for the Humanities, 1981).

18. Thorpe, "Education in South Dakota," 258–62, 283, 290, 323, 346, 367.

19. Ibid., 261–62.

20. Ibid., 319–23, 362–63.

21. Ibid., 280, 388.

22. Interview with Monsignor Louis Delahoyde, July 19, 1978, South Dakota Oral History Center; Sister M. Claudia Duratschek, O.S.B., *The Beginnings of Catholicism in South Dakota* (Washington, D. C.: Catholic University of America, 1943), 106; Buetow, *Of Singular Benefit*, 361; Margaret Connell Syasz, *Education and the American Indian: The Road to Self-Determination Since 1928* (Albuquerque: University of New Mexico Press, 1974), xix, 76. In 1986, three religious Indian schools remained in South

Dakota. Two of them, St. Francis at Rosebud and Holy Rosary at Pine Ridge, were Catholic-run, while St. Mary's at Springfield was in Episcopalian hands.

23. Interview with Deanna Butler, June 20, 1978, South Dakota Oral History Center; interview with Sister Lynn Marie Welbig, Aug. 10, 1976, South Dakota Oral History Center; interview with Sister Helen Freimuth, Aug. 5, 1976, South Dakota Oral History Center; interview with Sister Judith O'Brien, June 19 and 21, 1978, South Dakota Oral History Center; interview with Sister M. Eucharia Kelly, Aug. 12, 1976, South Dakota Oral History Center; Sister Alicia Dunphy to authors, Feb. 14, 1986.

24. Sister M. Teresa Comerford, quoted in M. Raphael Consedine, P.B.V.M., *Listening Journey: A Study of the Spirit and Ideals of Nano Nagle and the Presentation Sisters* (Victoria, Australia: Congregation of the Presentation of The Blessed Virgin Mary, 1983), 295.

25. Consedine, *Listening Journey*, 306.

26. Interview with Sister M. Alexius Steinman, June 21, 1978, South Dakota Oral History Center.

27. Consedine, *Listening Journey*, 318–19.

28. Thomas A. Bailey and David M. Kennedy, eds., *The American Spirit: United States History as Seen by Contemporaries*, vol. 2 (Lexington, Mass.: D.C. Heath, 1984), 704–7; Herbert Schell, *History of South Dakota* (Lincoln: University of Nebraska Press, 1961), 382.

29. Interview with Sister Martha Raleigh, Aug. 10, 1976, South Dakota Oral History Center.

30. Ibid.

31. Interview with Sister Mary Stephen Davis, Aug. 7, 1976, South Dakota Oral History Center.

32. Family member, quoted in interview with Sister Bonaventure Hoffman, June 26, 1978, South Dakota Oral History Center.

33. Ibid.

34. Buetow, *Of Singular Benefit*, 213, 217.

35. Thorpe, "Education in South Dakota," 272, 284.

36. Buetow, *Of Singular Benefit*, 361–66; interview with Monsignor Louis Delahoyde; interview with Sister JoAnn Sturzl, Aug. 5, 1976, South Dakota Oral History Center; interview with Sister Judith O'Brien; Schell, *History of South Dakota*, 380.

37. Martin W. Sandler, Edwin C. Rozwenc, and Edward C. Martin, *The People Make A Nation*, vol. 1 (Boston: Allyn and Bacon, 1971), 63; Sister Pauline Quinn, "Biographies of Mother Superiors, Section V: Mother Joseph Butler, 1894–1915," Presentation Archives, Presentation Heights, Aberdeen, S. D.; interview with Sister Eucharia Kelly; Sister M. Martha, "Brief History of the Presentation Community in Aberdeen 1886–1976," Presentation Archives.

38. Ibid.; interview with Sister M. Sylvester Auth, Aug. 9, 1976, South Dakota Oral History Center; Sister Quinn, "Mother Joseph Butler."

39. Interview with Sister Eucharia Kelly.

40. Interview with Sister M. Sylvester Auth.

41. "Report of Activity of Religious Communities of Women in the Preparation of Religious Elementary Teachers," Presentation Archives; interview with Sister M. Sylvester Auth; Sister Quinn, "Mother Joseph Butler"; Sister M. Cabrini Di Donato, "A History of the Educational Work of the Presentation Sisters of Aberdeen, South Dakota" (master's thesis, Northern State College, 1966), 38.

42. Sister Di Donato, "A History of the Educational Work of the Presentation Sisters," 34; *Diamond Jubilee Book: 1886–1961* (Aberdeen, S. D.: Sisters of the Presentation of the Blessed Virgin Mary, 1961), 29–30.

43. Sister Di Donato, "A History of the Educational Work of the Presentation Sisters," 35–39.

44. Ibid., 41.

45. "Teaching Contract, State of South Dakota, County of Brown," 1914, Presentation Archives.

46. Ibid.; *Bicentennial Edition,* 375; Thorpe, "Education in South Dakota," 265.

47. *Diamond Jubilee Book,* 31; interview with Sister M. Alexius Steinman.

48. Interview with Sister M. Alexius Steinman.

49. Interview with Sister Grace Farrell, June 19, 1978, South Dakota Oral History Center.

50. *Diamond Jubilee Book,* 31; "Notre Dame Academy Historical Data," Presentation Archives; Greeley, *From Backwater to Mainstream,* 17.

51. Sister Martha, "Brief History."

52. Interview with Sister Martha Raleigh.

53. *Diamond Jubilee Book,* 42; "Jubilee Data," Presentation Archives; Sister Di Donato, "A History of the Educational Work of the Presentation Sisters," 47.

54. Interview with Sister M. Sylvester Auth.

55. "Jubilee Data"; *Diamond Jubilee Book,* 43; Sister Di Donato, "A History of the Educational Work of the Presentation Sisters," 46. For a source on the Presentations' early practice of teaching only younger boys, see "Teaching Contract, State of South Dakota, County of Brown, 1914."

56. Sister Di Donato, "A History of the Educational Work of the Presentation Sisters," 48; "Jubilee Data." Sources disagree on the denomination of the Protestant church—Baptist or Methodist.

57. "Jubilee Data"; *Diamond Jubilee Book,* 47; *The Dakota Catholic,* Oct. 1922; Sister Di Donato, "A History of the Educational Work of the Presentation Sisters," 49.

58. Ibid., 50; "Jubilee Data"; *Diamond Jubilee Book,* 46.

59. Ibid.; "Jubilee Data."

60. *Diamond Jubilee Book,* 46; Sister Di Donato, "A History of the Educational Work of the Presentation Sisters," 51–52; Sister Martha, "Brief History."

61. Interview with Sister M. Sylvester Auth.

62. Interview with Sister Helen Freimuth; "Jubilee Data"; *Diamond Jubilee Book*, 44; Sister Martha, "Brief History."

63. "Jubilee Data"; interview with Dan Heinemann, July 16, 1978, South Dakota Oral History Center; *Diamond Jubilee Book*, 44–45; Sister Di Donato, "A History of the Educational Work of the Presentation Sisters," 52–53.

64. Sister Di Donato, "A History of the Educational Work of the Presentation Sisters," 53–54; *Diamond Jubilee Book*, 48; interview with Sister M. Alexius Steinman; *Official Yearbook of Sacred Heart Catholic Church* (Aberdeen, S. D.: Sacred Heart Catholic Church, 1901–2), 9.

65. *Diamond Jubilee Book*, 48.

66. Sister Pauline Quinn, "Biographies of Major Superiors, Section VI: Mother Aloysius Forrest, 1915–1921, 1927–1932," Presentation Archives; Sister Martha, "Brief History"; interview with Sister Grace Farrell.

67. Interview with Sister M. Alexius Steinman.

68. Interview with Bishop Lambert Hoch, June 28, 1978, South Dakota Oral History Center.

69. Sister Quinn, "Mother Aloysius Forrest"

70. Sister Pauline Quinn, "Biographies of Major Superiors, Section VII: Mother Agatha Collins, 1921–1927," Presentation Archives.

71. Interview with Sister M. Alexius Steinman.

72. *Bicentennial Edition: Historical Statistics of the United States Colonial Times to 1970* (Washington, D. C.: U.S. Dept. of Commerce, Bureau of Census, 1975), 375; Sister Di Donato, "A History of the Educational Work of the Presentation Sisters," 100; "Teaching Contract, State of South Dakota, County of Brown," 1914; "Teaching Contract between Mother M. Raphael and Msgr. J. M. Brady," 1943, Presentation Archives.

73. Sister Quinn, "Mother Agatha Collins"; Sister Martha, "Brief History"; interview with Sister Bonaventure Hoffman; interview with Sister Martha Raleigh.

74. *Aberdeen American News*, March 30, 1932; Sister Martha, "Brief History"; Sister Di Donato, "A History of the Educational Work of the Presentation Sisters," 98–99; *Diamond Jubilee Book*, 51.

75. Interview with Sister M. Sylvester Auth.

76. *Diamond Jubilee Book*, 52; "Jubilee Data"; Sister Di Donato, "A History of the Educational Work of the Presentation Sisters," 99–100.

77. Sister Di Donato, "A History of the Educational Work of the Presentation Sisters, 98–99.

78. Sister Pauline Quinn, "Biographies of Major Superiors, Section VIII: Mother Raphael McCarthy, 1932–1946," Presentation Archives.

79. Sister Quinn, "Mother Raphael McCarthy"; Sister Martha, "Brief History"; *Diamond Jubilee Book*, 58.

80. Sister Di Donato, "A History of the Educational Work of the Presentation Sisters," 123–24.

81. Ibid., 124–25.

82. Sister Quinn, "Mother Raphael McCarthy."

83. Mother M. Raphael McCarthy to Senator Karl Mundt, Dec. 3, 1951, Presentation Archives.

84. Mother M. Raphael McCarthy to Rev. J. J. O'Neil, July 19, 1943, Presentation Archives; Mother M. Raphael McCarthy to Rev. T. J. Manning, July 19, 1943, Presentation Archives.

85. "Report of Activity of Religious Communities of Women in the Preparation of Religious Elementary Teachers," Presentation Archives; *Digest of Education Statistics*, 56; *Bicentennial Edition*, 375..

86. *Diamond Jubilee Book*, 58.

87. "Jubilee Data"; Sister Martha, "Brief History"; interview with Sister Edward Lucas, Aug. 6, 1976, South Dakota Oral History Center; interview with Sister Mary Stephen Davis; *Diamond Jubilee Book*, 55–56; "News Release on Mother Joseph Manor," Presentation Archives; Mother Raphael McCarthy, "History of the Orphanage," Presentation Archives.

88. Interview with Sister Mary Stephen Davis; interview with Sister Edward Lucas.

89. Interview with Bishop Lambert Hoch.

90. Ibid.; "Jubilee Data."

91. Interview with Bishop Lambert Hoch.

92. "Jubilee Data."

93. Sister Di Donato, "A History of the Educational Work of the Presentation Sisters," 103.

94. Sister Thaddeus Homes, paraphrased in Ibid., 104.

95. Ibid.

96. Ibid.; Sister Martha, "Brief History"; *Diamond Jubilee Book*, 57; "Jubilee Data"; Sister Di Donato, "A History of the Educational Work of the Presentation Sisters," 106–7.

97. Ibid., 107; Sister Martha, "Brief History"; "Jubilee Data"; *Diamond Jubilee Book*, 56.

98. E. S. de Courcy to Mother Raphael McCarthy, Oct. 2, 1943, Presentation Archives.

99. Mother Raphael McCarthy to Rev. E. S. de Courcy, Oct. 5, 1943, Presentation Archives.

100. E. S. de Courcy to Mother Raphael McCarthy, Oct. 2, 1943 and Feb. 9, 1945, Presentation Archives.

101. Mother M. Gonzaga, quoted in E. S. de Courcy to Mother Raphael McCarthy, March 12, 1945, Presentation Archives.

102. Sister Di Donato, "A History of the Educational Work of the Presentation Sisters," 107–8; E. S. de Courcy to Mother Raphael McCarthy, Feb. 9, 1945; "Anoka Contract Agreement," March 1945, Presentation Archives; *Digest of Education Statistics, 1983–1984*, p. 56.

103. Sister Quinn, "Mother Raphael McCarthy." In 1933, Catholic church officials launched a full-scale effort to open CCD schools. The Most Reverend Edwin V. O'Hara, Bishop of Great Falls, Montana, and from Kansas City, Kansas after 1939 was a central figure in this movement. For a source,

see Buetow, *Of Singular Benefit*, 266. Sources for conflict in the workplace and at home include Wayne K. Hoy and Cecil G. Miskel, *Educational Administration: Theory, Research, and Practice* (New York: Random House, 1982), 110–35 and Carl N. Degler, *At Odds: Women and the Family in America from the Revolution to the Present* (New York: Oxford University Press, 1980), 55, respectively.

104. Mother Raphael McCarthy to Most Reverend William J. Condon, D.D., Jan. 15, 1946 Presentation Archives; Sister Quinn, "Mother Raphael McCarthy."

105. Sister Pauline Quinn, "Biographies of Major Superiors, Section IX: Mother Viator Burns, 1946–1958," Presentation Archives; interview with Sister Colman Coakley, Aug. 7, 1976, South Dakota Oral History Center; interview with Sister Martha Raleigh; Consedine, *Listening Journey*, 324; Marjorie R. Fallows, *Irish Americans: Identity and Assimilation* (Englewood Cliffs, N.J.: Prentice-Hall, 1979), 106–9. Sandler, Rozwenc, and Martin, *The People Make a Nation*, 63.

106. Sister Quinn, "Mother Viator Burns."

107. *Diamond Jubilee Book*, 60; Sister Di Donato, "A History of the Education Work of the Presentation Sisters," 109.

108. Bishop William J. Condon to Mother M. Viator Burns, July 25, 1950, Presentation Archives.

109. "Report of Parochial Schools Taught by the Presentation Sisters of the Blessed Virgin Mary, 1949–50," Presentation Archives; Stinnett, "Teacher Education," *Education in the States*, 394.

110. Sister Di Donato, "A History of the Educational Work of the Presentation Sisters," 110; *Sioux Falls Argus Leader*, Jan. 8, 1961.

111. Sister Quinn, "Mother Viator Burns."

112. Interview with Sister Lynn Marie Welbig.

5. Anticipating the Diamond Jubilee and After: The Twilight of the Education Apostolate, 1960–85

☐

For the South Dakota Presentations, the 1960s and 1970s proved to be a time of rejoicing and yet fear because the numbers of nuns available to operate schools increased and then fell dramatically. This attrition threatened to detract from the community spirit generated within the groups of teaching sisters at any given mission. By 1985, Presentations made up only about 5 percent of the staff at most of the schools that they administered or in which they still taught. Dedicated to their purposes despite diminishing numbers of fellow sisters, the Presentation nuns continued to professionalize. They cooperated with lay educators and adopted what could be seen as renovated progressive educational methods, but their goals remained exemplified in the following statement:

> . . . we—the School Community
> admit our need for conversion
> develop a sense of self-worth and respect for life
> foster relationships based on love, truth and freedom
> train students in leadership and give them a real say in school life
> create an environment where discipline aims at responsible freedom
> educate to be reflective
> develop programmes which train students to be constructively critical
> show concern about justice in the home and school
> provide opportunities for social work in school and parish
> . . . .[1]

The saga of the South Dakota Presentation's recent educational history reflected national occurrences in Catholic education. Fewer nuns entered convents during the 1960s, and many of those postulants who were interested in religious life did not select education as their career. Those nuns who were in the field remained dedicated, however. For example, the Sisters of St. Joseph of Carondelet in St. Louis worked summer jobs so that they could donate their salaries to keep Catholic schools open. Ever interested in professionalization, these and other nun-educators continued to improve their credentials. A study conducted in 1966 showed that although just over 7 percent held bachelor's degrees in 1952, the figure had climbed to almost 42 percent in 1964. Some nuns whose home states maintained relatively low requirements for certification, or whose members feared the ideological deterioration brought on when nuns attended secular colleges and universities, kept this average figure lower than it might have been. Religious actively participated in joint professionalization ventures with public and lay-Catholic teachers, for example, during the 1960s, Rhode Island provided inservice training for all of the state's educators.[2]

As nuns continued to pursue secularly accepted professionalization goals, Catholic educators in South Dakota and throughout the country evidenced modernization trends in their classrooms. By the 1960s, a "learning-by-doing" approach had replaced the strict regurgitation of facts in many Catholic elementary and secondary schools, particularly in religion classes.[3] Sister JoAnn Sturzl remarked in 1976 that even the texts and curriculum for South Dakota's Presentation-run catechetical classes evolved throughout the century from the rote memorization and recitation of the Baltimore Catechism to a course involving problem-solving lessons that did, nevertheless, lead the student to discover a set of absolute truths.[4]

Similarly, South Dakota education officials moved teacher preparation and curricular norms toward nationally popular expectations. The state's course of study was updated in 1960, 1970, and 1973, moves that brought more practical offerings into the program. Moreover, the baccalaureate degree finally became a requirement for teacher certification in 1968.[5]

Just as South Dakota's educational system came to resemble those in other states, South Dakota Catholics joined fellow Catholics throughout the country and assimilated into American culture.

Loosing much of its ethnic identity, in 1976 less than 15 percent of the South Dakota Presentation Order was Irish. Thus, although by 1980 the 138,387 Catholic parishioners in the state were still comparatively numerous (outnumbered only by 151,797 Lutherans), their ethnic character had greatly diminished. The Presentation Order had still managed to grow under Mother Burns and her successors by attracting postulants from the student bodies of Presentation schools and hospitals that they had established in the American Northwest. Encouraging acculturationist trends, by 1970 the Catholic Church had come out against the establishment of parishes based on nationality and for intermarriage as a means to combat racism.[6]

Marking the onset of the crucial transition into the new era of Vatican II and the turbulent decade that spawned it, Sister Carmelita McCullough held office as The South Dakota Presentation's superior in 1958. Sister McCullough was a quiet, self-confident woman who had been born Loretta McCullough in 1915. A native of Madison, South Dakota, McCullough had attended St. Thomas School (which opened in 1928). She entered the convent while only fifteen years old, quite younger than the average age of approximately twenty. After completing high school at Notre Dame Academy in Mitchell, she prepared for and taught in the elementary grades, the high schools, and in college. Eventually Sister McCullough earned a bachelor's degree in business education at Aberdeen's Northern State Teachers College. She became the first elected secretary-general of the community, a job that introduced her to the inner workings of the order. She was in the last phase of studies for a master's degree in business administration at Notre Dame when she was elected to serve what then was a congregation of 360 women.[7]

Although another school, Butler Hall Music Department, was founded at Aberdeen in 1958, and Presentation membership peaked in the early 1960s, some sisters rightly observed that health care, higher education, and other Presentation ministries had drawn sisters into careers other than teaching in the grade and high schools. This trend among Presentation professionals reflected the national tendencies for career-bound women. In 1900, many bright young females made teaching their occupational choice, but by the 1960s, this group was just as likely to attend law or medical school or to select a career from any number of other fields. To help attract enough postulants so that the Presentations could fill any and all of the order's professional posts, Mother McCullough engaged a Kansas production company to make a recruiting film that described all phases of the novitiate and professional preparation for ministries.[8]

Significantly, Mother McCullough's term in office parallelled the overwhelming popularity of the national Sister Formation Movement (discussed in chapters 1 and 4), and the superior nurtured the ideological fervor of those career-oriented women who continued to work toward advanced degrees. She also encouraged those Presentations to keep community with other nuns wherever they attended college. One such sister was Sister Anthony Dempsey, who received a scholarship to study at Loretto Heights College (founded in 1891) in Denver. While a student there from 1959 to 1961, Sister Dempsey lived with nuns from other orders and became very good friends with a Sister of St. Joseph. By 1966, some 152 of Sister Dempsey's South Dakota Presentation sisters held baccalaureate degrees. Fifty-three had obtained master's degrees, and three held doctorates. Even those sisters who were to perform the community's domestic work were then encouraged to attend at least three years of college. Before the new decade of Vatican II they had not been allowed to obtain more than two years of college work.[9] (A list of institutions that Presentations attended appears in Table 4.)

In 1960, Mother McCullough established a dormitory near Marquette University in Milwaukee, calling it Presentation Hall. Initially it housed five sisters. Sister Carmel Harney was the superior and Sister Adrienne Dorn was the housekeeper, indicating that regardless of their augmented education, the domestic services of some Presentations continued to enable others to professionalize. Because it was the first dormitory for religious in Milwaukee, the Jesuits who ran the college praised the Presentations for their groundbreaking efforts. The first year the shelter opened, it welcomed six sisters from other orders, and over the next few years it remained intercommunal until it closed in 1968. Sisters of Mercy and Sisters of the Holy Name were two such orders represented at Presentation Hall. Because of variations in the rule of each community of nuns, the guest sisters did not always share the Presentations' schedule or community routine. Living solely with nuns who respected silence periods and other restrictions, however, afforded each sister the opportunity to nurture her spiritual life. Thus, despite slight variations in ideology, the mechanism of sisterhood helped perpet-

TABLE 4. HIGHER EDUCATIONAL INSTITUTIONS ATTENDED
BY SOUTH DAKOTA PRESENTATIONS, 1966

Aberdeen, S. D.: Northern State College; Presentation College	Missoula: Montana State
Austin: University of Texas	Mitchell, S. D.: Notre Dame Junior College
Boston: Boston University	New York: New York University
Champaign-Urbana: University of Illinois	Notre Dame, Ind.: University of Notre Dame
Chicago: Cardinal Stritch College; Holy Rosary College; Loyola University	Omaha: Creighton University
Davenport: St. Ambrose College	Orono: University of Maine
Denver: Loretto Heights	San Francisco: University of San Francisco
Detroit: Mary Grove College	Seattle: Seattle Business College
Dublin, Ireland: University of Dublin	Sioux Falls, S. D.: Augustana College; Columbus Normal School; Nettleton Commercial School; Sioux Falls College
Dubuque: Loras College	St. Joseph, Minn.: St. Benedict College
Huron, S. D.: Huron College	
Lincoln: University of Nebraska	St. Louis: Fontbonne College; St. Louis University
Madison, S. D.: General Beadle College; Madison Normal	St. Paul: St. Catherine College
Manhattan: Kansas Agricultural School	Vermillion: South Dakota State University
Miles City, Mont.: Custer Junior College	Washington, D.C.: Catholic University
Milwaukee: Alverno College; Marquette University	Xavier, Kan.: St. Mary College
Minneapolis: University of Minnesota; McPhail School of Music	Yankton, S. D.: Mount Marty

Source: Sister Di Donato, "A History of the Educational Work of the Presentation Sisters," 138, 140.

uate each order's commitment to some form of a Marian professional goal. Moreover, young Presentation novices who attended Marquette also received guidance from a juniorate directress who assisted and encouraged them to study diligently but also to remember the purpose for it all.[10]

Mother McCullough experienced a spiritual lesson of her own when during the early 1960s she became exhausted and ill. After hospitalization at St. Luke's and at the Mayo Clinic, she took a rest with relatives who lived near Seattle. Emerging from this period with an ever-keener awareness of the importance of her community's historical philosophy and of the value of contemplation to realize it, she reminded the sisters in 1961 that "the virtue of silence can be practiced in thought and deed as well as in word . . . . Silence is a challenge to a courageous and mortified religious . . . . It is only the strong religious who will . . . remain silent in the midst of those who will not." Instructing her flock further, the leader cautioned that "in the early days of our Community, our sisters were deprived of many of the necessities of life . . . . Now we should be careful not to demand the latest or best of everything or all the recreation afforded lay people." Determined that each nun remain dedicated to the order's original intent, Mother McCullough cautiously lead the group through a decision to alter habits, giving the nuns more freedom of movement. She and her sisters reasoned that these modernization and professionalization trends were justified because they met the community's traditional objective, to serve people in the names of Mary and Christ.[11]

In 1961, the Presentations celebrated their Diamond Jubilee, which catalyzed a renewal of this ideal. Church and state civic leaders attended a banquet and pageant in Aberdeen commemorating seventy-five years of hard work and rewards for the Presentations in South Dakota. As part of the spirit of that year, Sister Rosaria O'Callaghan, a native of County Cork, wrote *Flame of Love*, a biography of Nano Nagle, whose example Sister O'Callaghan had sought to emulate since childhood.[12]

Also following Nagle's example, the Presentations reached out to even more schools during Mother McCullough's term. One was St. Pius X Parochial School in Bowie, Maryland, near Washington, D.C. Mother McCullough accepted the assignment so that sisters attending Catholic University could live with other Presentations. Sister M. Loretta Stoltz was principal; Sisters Jeanne Marie Farrell and M. Maurice Crowley were teachers. Proving to be a short-lived experiment, the Presentation teachers began working in 1962 with 180 children in five grades, but withdrew three years later when the school had reached an enrollment of 430 students. Accustomed to wide open spaces, at least these Presentations had found it difficult to commute in heavy traffic and fog. Moreover, sources suggest that the nuns discovered that their basic frontier conservatism conflicted with the far from reverential attitude of their students. Unwilling to alter their basic notions about students' respect for authority, the

Presentations returned to the familiar rural areas and small towns of the Great Plains. Truly, these spiritual daughters of Irish immigrants had made their home the American West.[13]

Continuing to educate students within the Presentations' familiar culture, in 1963, several of them traveled to Miles City, Montana, to replace Dominican nuns who had taught in the town's Sacred Heart High School (founded in 1935). It was affiliated with a grade school established in 1884. The first principal had been an Ursuline nun named Mother Genevieve, who with her fellow sisters initially had opened the school for fourteen students. In 1954, the Ursulines withdrew, and the Dominican Sisters of Everett, Washington, took their place. When almost a decade later they too decided to withdraw, four Presentations arrived to begin taking their places. They were Sisters M. Louise Erne (principal), M. Helen Freimuth, M. Ruth Ann Evans, and M. Isabel Schneider.[14]

Although the Presentations worked with the Dominicans who stayed in Miles City for a time, friction existed between the two orders of sisters. Apparently the Dominicans, whose motherhouse was in Seattle, viewed themselves as overqualified to teach in a backwoods state like Montana. According to a lay teacher at the school, after the Dominicans left the Presentations behaved a bit defensively, giving the impression that "Aberdeen was the hub of the universe."[15] Yet, paradoxically, the quality of the Presentations' work soon restored their humility by bolstering their professional self-esteem. By 1966, the high school was housed in a new building accommodating 156 students. Moreover, Sister M. Edmund Walsh (a principal) and Sister M. Robert Even were then assigned to the grade school. Laymen with whom they worked were proud of the school. Although salaries were well below the 1979 national ($8,840) and state ($3,725) averages, Joe Cadlo, a social studies and religion teacher, maintained that he was attracted to Sacred Heart because of the enthusiastic involvement of parents with the school and what he called the "academic freedom" to address more than just the intellectual aspects of learning.[16]

Sacred Heart did, however, share some things in common with the public schools. Although Catholic American history books did highlight Catholic Church activities, the Catholics used many of the texts employed in the public sector. Secularization occurred during the 1970s to compensate for the lack of nonessential courses and activities at Sacred Heart. Presentation administrators arranged for Sacred Heart students to take shop and mechanics classes in a public school and to share athletic tickets with other institutions. Moreover, public bus service was provided to Sacred Heart. The school also enjoyed some indirect federal support without inviting much government interference because some students received publicly funded remedial instruction and supplies through Title I and III of the 1965 Elementary and Secondary Education Acts.[17]

After the Diamond Jubilee, the Presentations witnessed other adaptations to help fund the schools in which they taught. Parishes in South Dakota cities with populations large enough to support Catholic education had begun to combine their resources for the joint funding of secondary education. O'Gorman High School in Sioux Falls and Roncalli High School in Aberdeen, both coeducational and founded early in the 1960s, had strong enough financial bases to allow construction of modern, well-equipped buildings. Faculties of well-trained religious and lay teachers offered curricula that rivaled those of other cities' public schools. Sisters M. Aloysius Clarke, M. Helen Freimuth, M. Phyllis Marie Calmus, and M. Annette Stumpff were the first four Presentations located at O'Gorman. Presentation nuns headed the mathematics and home economics departments and served as the dean of women. In so doing, they worked side by side with ten Dominican Sisters, nine priests, ten laymen, and two laywomen. In the fall of 1964, Mother Myron Martin assigned Sisters M. Loyola Mullally, A. Anne Hamm, and Sister M. Julia Behselich to Roncalli. Five years later Roncalli had an enrollment of more than 430 students taught by fourteen priests and nuns and thirteen secular teachers, all of whom had earned bachelor's degrees. Between eight and nine hundred students attended O'Gorman, receiving instruction from twenty-six religious and twenty other faculty members, nine of whom had master's degrees. Annual tuition ranged from $120 plus fees at Roncalli to $190 at O'Gorman. Reflecting the centralization efforts in South Dakota public schools, interparish school boards coordinated operations and received support from the Diocesan Office of Education. In turn, the parish councils financed the sisters' living arrangements and paid their salaries, which at the time were several thousand dollars a year lower than the average South Dakota teaching wage. Nevertheless, Presentation Sisters instructed at both schools and provided leadership in the drive for quality education in them and also at Holy Spirit School in Mitchell.[18]

Ever a part of new responses to educational challenges, Mother McCullough became personally involved in education and renewal after stepping down as superior in 1964. She spent a short time at Presentation Hall, and in 1965 became superior-principal of St. Mary's High School at Dell Rapids. Two years later she was transferred to Notre Dame High School, where she served on the faculty until the school closed in 1970. Then Mother McCullough started an eleven-year-long assignment at Holy Trinity School in Winsted, Minnesota, living and teaching in an intercommunity arrangement with the School Sisters of St. Francis of Omaha. She thus continued the tradition of shared sisterhood with other nuns. Besides her Winsted teaching duties, she donated her bookkeeping skills to the school and rectory and gave invaluable tips to Winsted businesses on how to better manage financially. In July of 1981, before her death later that year, Mother McCullough spent several weeks at Mound, Minnesota, renewing her faith with profession classmates as they prepared for their Golden Jubilee observance.[19]

Seventeen years earlier, Sister Myron Martin had been elected to assume leadership of the Presentation community. Born Eva Martin in 1922 at Cavour, South Dakota, she had received her elementary and secondary education there. She then attended Notre Dame Junior College before entering the convent in 1940. Sister Martin taught in South Dakota and Minnesota Catholic schools, also serving as a local superior and principal. When she was elected, Sister Martin was the juniorate directress to the yet unprofessed sisters and had just completed her bachelor's degree at Marquette.[20]

Although Mother Martin was described as a quiet and patient listener, she asserted herself when necessary in order to remind the sisters of their ideological roots. Although she supervised changes in the liturgy, prayers, life-style, and habit, according to one nun Mother Martin was "dissatisfied with post-Vatican adaptations."[21] Consequently, she strove to reinforce the community's internal solidarity of purpose by stressing "*authentic*" renewal, checking rampant individualism, and fostering the notion that "what benefits one, benefits the whole." Always reminding the nuns of the appropriate direction for their apostolic work, she continued, "since we are not poor materially let us be generous in other ways."[22]

Another of Mother Martin's worries was the attrition in numbers of sisters during her tenure. During the 1964–65 school year, the nuns faced the responsibility of staffing twenty-three schools plus the children's home (Table 5). Since the South Dakota foundation began, during each decade a few members left the fold for health or other personal reasons. Beginning late in the 1960s, the number of professions decreased dramatically, reflecting a national trend. Mother Martin witnessed a shrinking of membership unprecedented in the community's history. Dissatisfied with the changes in the church, apparently both prospective and professed Presentations felt it was no longer a mark of distinction to be a sister. Illustrating the seriousness of this situation throughout the country, the South Dakota congregation remained the largest of all the other autonomous Presentation houses in the United States: Fitchburg, Massachusetts; Staton Island, Newburgh, and Watervliet, New York; and San Antonio, Dubuque, San Francisco, and Fargo.[23]

For the South Dakota nuns the decline in membership reflected internal problems within the education apostolate. Early-twentieth-century trailblazers had become old, and many of their ideas were outmoded. Because they were not forced to retire, by the mid-1960s many of them held important administrative roles, although some had become ineffective. Consequently, younger nuns were frustrated because they were placed into subordinate professional roles. As one Presentation nun observed, under such circumstances the younger women's "decision-making talents atrophy, and when at last they succeed to power and responsibility, they, in turn, feel threatened and insecure, and are quite frequently incompetent [themselves]."[24]

Counteracting such trends, the South Dakota Presentations increased professional contacts with colleagues in the secular world and with other Catholic orders of religious women (Table 6). They began attending the Minnesota Catholic Education Association meetings, and although South Dakota had no comparable affiliate, all of the state's teaching sisters met occasionally with members of the then twelve other South Dakota orders of religious women, such as the Dominicans and Benedictines, to discuss new developments in education. These South Dakota educators' goals were more association- than union-oriented, but this was not the case for other nuns living in cities like Philadelphia, Newark, and Chicago.[25] There, during the 1960s, religious joined the 1916-founded American Fed-

TABLE 5. SCHOOLS STAFFED BY THE PRESENTATION SISTERS OF
ABERDEEN, S. D., FOR THE 1964–65 SCHOOL YEAR

School	Year Founded	Location	No. of Sisters	No. of Pupils
Notre Dame High School	1898	Mitchell, S. D.	7	271
St. Lawrence School	1900	Milbank, S. D.	7	210
St. Peter's School	1902	Jefferson, S. D.	5	133
St. Stephen School	1904	Bridgewater, S. D.	3	75
St. Joseph School	1908	Woonsocket, S. D.	4	114
St. Mary High School	1910	Dell Rapids, S. D.	6	134
St. Mary Grade School	1910	Dell Rapids, S. D.	7	321
Sacred Heart School	1914	Aberdeen S. D.	14	720
St. Ann School	1921	Humboldt, S. D.	6	130
St. Thomas School	1928	Madison, S. D.	6	218
St. Teresa School	1929	Huron, S. D.	9	279
Presentation Kindergarten	1936	Aberdeen, S. D.	1	40
Our Lady of the Lake School	1939	Mound, Minn.	11	460
St. Mary's School	1940	Willmar, Minn.	8	450
Presentation Children's Home	1945	Sioux Falls, S. D.	10	39 orphans
St. Stephen's School	1945	Anoka, Minn.	15	800
St. Mary's School	1949	Sioux Falls, S. D.	12	605
Butler Hall Music Department	1958	Aberdeen, S. D.	2	30
O'Gorman High School	1961	Sioux Falls, S. D.	4	900
St. Pius School	1962	Bowie, Md.	6	450
Sacred Heart School	1963	Miles City, Mont.	8	156
Roncalli High School	1964	Aberdeen, S. D.	3	190
Holy Family School	1964	Mitchell, S. D.	13	453
Holy Spirit School	1964	Mitchell, S. D.	4	245

Source: Sister Di Donato, "A History of the Educational Work of the Presentation Sisters," 206–7.

TABLE 6. PRESENTATION EDUCATORS' PROFESSIONAL AFFILIATIONS, 1966

American Library Association	National Catholic Music
Archdiocesan Teachers'	Association
Association	National Catholic Theater
Association for Student Teachers	Conference
Association of Sacred Doctrine and	National Education Association
Theology	National English Council
Biology Teachers' Association	National Guild of Piano Teachers
Catholic Library Association	National Home Economics
Catholic National Sociological	Association
Association	National Science Teacher's
Catholic Renaissance Society	Association
Catholic School Press Association	North Central Association of
College Teachers of Sacred	Junior Colleges
Doctrine	Notre Dame Alumni
English Teacher Association	Notre Dame English Association
Guidance Association	Parent-Teachers' Association
Kappa Delta Pi	Psi Chi
Latin Teachers South Dakota	Social Science Association
Classical Association	South Dakota Association of
Medical Technicians' Association	Women Deans and Counselors
Minnesota Catholic Education	South Dakota Guidance
Society	Association
National Association of Social	South Dakota Music Teachers'
Workers	Association
National Business Education	South Dakota Speech Association
Association	South Dakota Teachers of English
National Catholic Education	St. Ambrose College Alumni
Society	St. Louis University Alumni
National Catholic Kindergarten	University of Minnesota Alumni
Association	

Source: Sister Di Donato, "A History of the Educational Work of the Presentation Sisters," 141–42.

eration of Teachers. Attempting to explain why South Dakota religious may have seemed slow to form professional attachments of any kind, Sister Helen Freimuth reasoned, "We are so isolated and our schools are all so far apart that . . . we never ever really united like Minnesota [nuns] did."[26]

This situation was changing, however, as a specific opportunity to promote educational centralization had come early in Mother Martin's administration. In 1964, the bishop created the Diocesan Office of Education, which included fifteen members: five priests, five sisters, and five lay people, all of whom various parish councils or school boards elected. The participants served as advisers to the bishop and set policies in his name for the diocese. In its attempt to provide more uniformity of education throughout the region, the new executive arm offered training workshops for educators, installed a central bookkeeping system, and coordinated preschool education and catechetical classes. Members established salary guidelines and studied parish schools that were threatened with closure, but the council did not interfere with internal academic operations.[27]

Five years after its founding, the Office of Education administered a survey to determine the status of Catholic education—its faculties, finances, and curricula. The assessment revealed that the diocese contained thirty-three elementary and nine secondary schools with total enrollments of 7,871 and 2,346, respectively; faculties consisted of thirty-three priests, 313 nuns (including more than ninety Presentations), and 228 lay people. Despite these impressive numbers, the report indicated that many Catholic parents sent their children to public schools. In an effort to revive the Church school's unique role in students' educational experience and thereby to attract more families' attention, the document urged South Dakota's Catholic schools to be genuine centers of religious formation and dedicated academically to serving all people. To effect this end, it proposed area centers to deal with the academic education and religious formation of all children, with the most efficient use of available personnel and materials in areas where schools were no longer feasible or were already closed. The diocese would thus support twenty-one programs, seventeen in cooperation with academic and four with only the catechetical curricula.[28]

Further indicating that Catholic ideological fervor had become subdued in an increasingly secular age, investigations exposed the fact that many South Dakota sisters had gradually lost interest in teaching. It became apparent that Catholic schools must expand nuns' freedom to experiment, and that sisters must rekindle the apostolic spirit of days gone by. Perhaps to assist communities in this process, the Office of Education began appointing certain numbers of sisters each year to the diocese rather than to individual parishes. The Presentations generally viewed such innovations in a positive light. As an order they embraced the concept of group planning, the monitoring and directing of their own progress through periodic self-studies and reports. Presentation Sister Lynn Marie Welbig, who served on the diocesan council for six years, regretted the recalcitrance of rural schools' leaders who fought centralization and who refused to use their sisters' full professional capacities.[29]

Nevertheless, the new planning efforts did lead to several changes in the Presentation-staffed institutions. During the late 1960s, the schools in Bridgewater, Woonsocket, and Humboldt, South Dakota and Willmar, Minnesota had to close because of various factors such as finances and enrollment. Eventually, Presentation Kindergarten and Butler Hall Music Department were closed, too. Many parishioners sadly accepted these occurrences, and a few mistakenly blamed the sisters for closing schools that financially or legally never belonged to them. In fact, it was because of the sisters' inexpensive salaries that many institutions were able to stay open as long as they did. A council memorandum encouraged pastors to upgrade their faculties and to allow parish boards of education to take greater responsibility in directing the educational activities that remained. The evaluators suggested that St. Mary's elementary school at Dell Rapids needed more enrichment courses in music and modern languages, and that the economic feasibility of keeping the secondary school open was questionable. In Mitchell, the two parish grade schools appeared secure, but the coeducational Notre Dame High School was earmarked for extinction.[30]

Even so, as late as 1966 Notre Dame had produced an impressive institution. The seventeen faculty members held bachelor's degrees, and six of those instructors held master's. Course offerings comprised a blend of religious, practical, and liberal arts offerings (Table 7). In 1969, Notre Dame claimed a student body numbering 283 young people from two different parishes—Holy Spirit (created in 1961) and Holy Family. Those from the former paid no tuition because the school received its financial support from collections, chiefly from an annual $50 assessment from Holy Spirit Parish members. The Office of Education recommended that both areas support the facility equally and that administration should be under a joint board of education rather than under only Holy Family Parish. The central agency further directed the diocese to provide a subsidy to help the school through financial difficulties incurred during the early sixties when Mitchell Junior High School—fully equipped with language

TABLE 7. NOTRE DAME HIGH SCHOOL CURRICULUM, 1964–65

Freshmen	Sophomores	Juniors	Seniors
Religion	Religion	Religion	Religion
English	English	English	English
Modern	Biology	American	American
geography	*Geometry	history	government
Algebra	*Bookkeeping	*Typing I	*Typing II
*Latin	World History	*Mechanical	*Shorthand
*General	*Home	drawing	*Mechanical
business	economics	*Home	drawing
Physical	Physical	economics	*Home
education	education	*Spanish II	economics
*Chorus	*Chorus	*German II	*Trigonometry
*Band	*Band	*Advanced	*Solid geometry
*Athletics	*Athletics	algebra	*Physics
	*Latin II	*Chemistry	*Electronics
	*Spanish I	*Chorus	*Spanish III
	*German I	*Business law	*German III
		and	*Business law
		arithmetic	and
			arithmetic

Source: Sister Di Donato, "A History of the Educational Work of the Presentation Sisters," 45.

* indicates elective courses.

laboratories, an auditorium, and even a swimming pool—lured many Catholic students into the secular school system. After completing the eighth grade in public school, these Catholic students were likely to go on to Mitchell's high school, thus undermining the enrollment at Notre Dame.[31]

Despite the rivalry, relations between Mitchell's high school and Notre Dame had always been cordial. The city had sold the vacated public school building to Holy Family Parish, and the Church remodeled it to accommodate Notre Dame. The two systems also cross-listed courses, offering a mixture of the traditional course of study and the more modern, progressive curriculum that included economics and physical education courses. Because a public school's average daily attendance provided the basis for state funding, South Dakota officials still allowed Robert McCardle, the city school superintendent, to add the part-time Notre Dame students to the rolls.

The public high school obtained several thousand dollars each year for doing nothing but cooperating with Notre Dame.[32]

Even with coordination, however, advocates of Catholic education feared that because of financial problems, their high school would cease to exist. During the 1969–70 school year, Holy Family spokespersons asked members of both parishes for donations and tried to organize a committee to run the eduational program, but Holy Family parishioners claimed that Holy Spirit members were not willing to share fairly the burden of supporting Notre Dame. Holy Spirit representatives fired back that they were heavily in debt because of an ambitious building program for their own elementary school and a new church, and that they resented the implication that they were not prepared to make sacrifices for Catholic education.[33]

The misunderstanding between parishes, combined with parents' and students' demands on Notre Dame for an even more up-to-date course of study than it was offering, eventually closed the school's doors. Once the decision was made, on the surface the procedure was carried out smoothly, although there still existed an underlying sadness if not a tension within the communty. McCardle, himself a member of the Holy Family parish, recalled being personally moved when he saw Sister Helen Freimuth, a long-time Notre Dame educator, quietly packing up books in an unnaturally quiet hallway.[34] Sister Grace Farrell confessed that after twenty-three years at the school she, too, "felt terrible" when it closed.[35] Within the Catholic community, Keith Fitzpatrick, a physical therapist at St. Joseph Hospital who had helped raise $100,000 to keep the school open, blamed the failure on the loss of a strong Catholic identity within parishioners. He believed that his fellow Catholics could have continued to support the school had they only had the dedication to do so. Like the Irish, however, the Catholic descendants of the various nationalities who had settled Mitchell had successfully fought nativism by merging their religious and social ideologies with those of white Anglo-Saxon Protestant Americans. In so doing, they had ceased in some respects to be a distinctive group. Symbolizing the merger, the school boards met together and worked closely with McCardle and both principals to set policies. The public school administrators provided whatever help they could during the transfer. By the time public school classes began in the fall of 1970, the process was over, and some people in the community had forgotten the controversy.[36]

Thus, by 1974 Mother Martin completed a term that had been filled with educational problems. Handing them to Sister JoAnn Sturzl, Mother Martin took Sister Sturzl's job as the order's personnel director. Sister Sturzl's experience in this role had kept her in touch with not only the nun-educators, but also with other Presentations. As a delegate to the Special General Chapter of 1968 and as chairperson of the Religious Life Commission following the meeting, she was well attuned to movements and needs of the historical times and the Great Plains region. A native of Pipestone, Minnesota, she had been born Josephine Sturzl in 1933, and attended local elementary and secondary schools with her twin sister, Mary. She graduated from the Presentation School of Nursing at McKennan Hospital in Sioux Falls in 1954. Entering the convent that same year, she received the religious habit and the name Sister Joseph Ann in 1955. After her basic religious training, she pronounced her temporary vows in 1957 and was made head nurse at McKennan Hospital. She completed the requirements for the bachelor of science in nursing at Marquette and continued her studies at Boston College, receiving a master's degree in nursing in 1969.[37]

Sister Sturzl was keenly aware of the need to promote the orders' apostolic purpose amid a turbulent changing social climate. Soon after becoming superior, she staged a special ceremony before sending each sister to her ministry. About the occasion she wrote, "I pray that our coming together will be a visible sign of our unity, strengthening us to go forth to minister to the needs of God's people." Consequently, like her predecessors, Sister Sturzl perceived a danger in adaptation without renewal of commitment, a phenomenon that had led to an "emptiness and darkness" within the American Catholic Church. Thus, she wrote, "Reflecting on God's faithfulness to us, as [a] Presentation Community is a source of great strength and joy for us . . . [we must] continue to enflesh Nano's charism of love and service."[38]

Consequently, Sister Sturzl displayed a determination and assertiveness not unlike the international Presentation's Irish founder. These qualities surfaced as a result of Sister Sturzl's educational policymaking role. In 1975, she wrote to Paul V. Dudley, the new bishop of Sioux Falls: "We realize [that the decrease in numbers of

135

Presentations] creates intense difficulties for Catholic schools. We encourage you to approach this situation with realism and planning. While Presentation Sisters will surely continue to assist with Catholic schools, the continuation of the schools cannot and should not depend on our numbers."[39]

Sister Sturzl did attempt to keep as many Presentation educators as possible in the Catholic schools. By 1976, Sacred Heart elementary and junior high schools were still open in Aberdeen. The enrollments of Roncalli and O'Gorman combined totalled approximately one thousand students in two parishes. Dell Rapids, South Dakota, and Miles City, Montana, had grade and high schools that enrolled a total of about 450 students in each city's school. Also in South Dakota, Madison (with at least 150), Millbank (with 280 students), Huron (with 220), Sioux Falls (with 600), and Jefferson (with 100) had grade schools, instructing the first through the eighth grade. Anoka, Minnesota, had a similar institution that housed 600 pupils. In Mitchell, South Dakota, two schools with a kindergarten through sixth grade were in operation for 200 students; and in Mound, Minnesota, approximately 220 were instructed in the first through sixth grade elementary school.[40]

After retiring from office in 1982, Sister Sturzl continued her own professional work outside the education apostolate. She enrolled at the Jesuit College in Toronto, Canada where she spent the school year of 1982 and 1983 studying theology so she could become a parish minister in Montebell, California, differing only from a priest in that she could not hear confessions. In this role she showed a special care and concern for the poor and the elderly, organizing lay groups to assist those in greatest financial and spiritual need.[41]

Sister Sturzl's successor, Sister Mary Denis Collins, was born in Wibaux, Montana, in 1934. She entered the Presentation Congregation in 1952 and then attended Presentation College, Northern State College, and Colorado State University—taking majors in business and sociology and a minor in counseling. Sister Collins's first assignment was at St. Joseph Hospital in Mitchell, where she was the business manager for one year. From 1958 to 1968, she performed the same function at St. Luke's Hospital, followed by five years at Holy Rosary Hospital in Miles City, Montana, as assistant administrator. Before her four-year appointment as secretary general of the Presentation Sisters beginning in 1974, she served as personnel director at Presentation College. In 1978, she was elected to the General Council, a job that she held until becoming president in 1982.[42]

Sister Collins watched the Presentations adapt and change over the years, in many respects leaving the school-teacher image behind. The Roncalli Catholic schools—the junior high with 130 students and eight lay faculty, and the elementary with 208 students and eight lay teachers, employed no Presentations. The Sacred Heart schools in Aberdeen and St. Stephen's at Anoka had been phased out, but Presentation educators were associated with schools at Hoven and Watertown, South Dakota and Maplewood, Minnesota. Because of shrinking numbers of those nuns willing and able to educate, however, Sister Collins feared for the Presentations' ability to fulfill their existing commitments.[43] The leader reflected in 1984, "We are being challenged at this point in history, [we are] faced with many questions about our future and the choices that we need to make as Presentation Sisters." She continued that the nuns had survived thus far through "teamwork" and the sense of "spiritual purpose," apparent in the "Gospel vision . . . of . . . foundress, Nano Nagle."[44]

Thus, although Presentation educators diminished numerically, particularly from the late 1960s to the present, they and their other sisters continued to give their students elements of a timeless morality, the chance for employment, and (when they could) an appreciation for classic academic subjects. Moreover, many of the nuns believed that due to their impact on children their profession provided the order with its most powerful social change agent and our democratic society with an alternative to public education. Recent years may indicate that Presentation perseverence has been rewarded, because a renewed interest in traditional family values during the late 1970s and early 1980s coupled with public cries for a more basic academic curriculum have led many Catholic and non-Catholic clients to rediscover the Catholic school.[45]

In addition, the younger women's quest for greater responsibility and flexibility within the education apostolate seems to have been realized. This adaptation documents the flexibility of the nuns' Marian ideology, which seemed continually to rationalize ever-innovative career opportunities for Presentation educators to organize and deliver their talents and services. Some Presentations, however, continue to question the propriety of too much intersection between the two genders' spheres and the value of comparing the relative

137

importance of each, as later discussions of renewal and its aftermath will reveal.

NOTES

1. Sisters of the Union, quoted in M. Raphael Consedine, P.B.V.M., *Listening Journey: A Study of the Spirit and Ideals of Nano Nagle and the Presentation Sisters* (Victoria, Australia: Congregation of the Presentation of the Blessed Virgin Mary, 1983), 370–71.

2. Harold A. Buetow, *Of Singular Benefit: The Story of Catholic Education in the United States* (London: Macmillan, 1970), 309, 347–48, 363–64.

3. Buetow, *Of Singular Benefit*, 241–42.

4. Interview with Sister JoAnn Sturzl, Aug. 5, 1976, South Dakota Oral History Center, Vermillion.

5. Cleata B. Thorpe, "Education in South Dakota, 1861–1961," *South Dakota Historical Collections* 36 (1972), 319–23; *Secondary School Standards: Policies, Minimum Standards, Regulations for Accreditation of Secondary Schools*, Bulletin No. 21-C (Pierre: State of South Dakota Department of Public Instruction, 1960); *Minimum Standards for Accreditation of K–12 School Systems for the State of South Dakota*, Bulletin 99 (Pierre: State of South Dakota Department of Public Instruction, 1970); *Minimum Standards for Accreditation of K–12 School Systems in the State of South Dakota*, Bulletin 99-A (Pierre: State of South Dakota Department of Public Instruction, 1973); communication between Sylvia Starr and Wyland J. Borth, Aug. 25, 1986.

6. Bernard Quinn et al., eds., *Churches and Church Membership in the United States, 1980: An Enumeration by Region, State and Country Based on Data Reported by 111 Church Bodies* (Atlanta: Glenmary Research Center, 1982), 249–54; interview with Sister Colman Coakley, Aug. 7, 1976, South Dakota Oral History Center; Buetow, *Of Singular Benefit*, 366; interview with Sister Judith O'Brien, June 19, 1978, South Dakota Oral History Center. Also see chapter 4 of this volume.

7. Sister Pauline Quinn, "Biographies of Major Superiors, Section X: Mother Carmelita McCullough, 1958–1964," Presentation Archives, Aberdeen, S. D.

8. Sister Quinn, "Mother Carmelita McCullough"; J. Myron Atkin, "Who Will Teach in High School," *Daedalus: Journal of the American Academy of Arts and Sciences* 110 (Summer 1981): 91–104; interview with Sister Kay O'Neil, Aug. 9, 1976, South Dakota Oral History Center; Sister M. Cabrini Di Donato, "A History of the Educational Work of the Presentation Sisters of Aberdeen, South Dakota" (master's thesis, Northern State College, 1966), 207.

9. Sister Di Donato, "A History of the Educational Work of the Pres-

entation Sisters," 138–40; interview with Sister Anthony Dempsey, June 27, 1978, South Dakota Oral History Center.

10. Sister Quinn, "Mother Carmelita McCullough"; communication from Sister Myron Martin, in Sister Alicia Dunphy to the authors, Feb. 14, 1986; *Diamond Jubilee Book*, 71; interview with Sister Rita Coss, Aug. 13, 1976, South Dakota Oral History Center.

11. Sister Quinn, "Mother Carmelita McCullough," also see chapter 9 of this volume.

12. Sister Quinn, "Mother Carmelita McCullough."

13. Ibid.; Sister Di Donato, "A History of the Educational Work of the Presentation Sisters," 128.

14. Ibid., 128–30.

15. Interview with Joe Cadlo, July 13, 1978, South Dakota Oral History Center.

16. Interview with Joe Cadlo; *Digest of Education Statistics, 1983–1984* (Washington D.C.: U.S. Department of Education, 1984), 56; Sister Di Donato, "A History of the Educational Work of the Presentation Sisters," 130.

17. Interview with Joe Cadlo.

18. "Statistics: Total Education Program," Presentation Archives; "Summary of Criteria," Presentation Archives; interview with Sister Helen Freimuth, Aug. 5, 1976, South Dakota Oral History Center; Sister Di Donato, "A History of the Educational Work of the Presentation Sisters," 127, 135.

19. Sister Quinn, "Mother Carmelita McCullough."

20. Sister Pauline Quinn, "Biographies of Major Superiors, Section XI: Mother Myron Martin, 1964–1974," Presentation Archives.

21. Sister Quinn, "Mother Myron Martin."

22. Mother Myron Martin, quoted in Ibid.

23. Sister Quinn, "Mother Myron Martin"; interview with Sister JoAnn Sturzl; Consedine, *Listening Journey*, 405.

24. Sister Di Donato, "A History of the Educational Work of the Presentation Sisters," 144.

25. Interview with Sister Helen Freimuth; Buetow, *Of Singular Benefit*, 347.

26. Interview with Sister Helen Freimuth.

27. Interview with Sister Lynn Marie Welbig, Aug. 10, 1976.

28. "Final Report of Executive Committee," Presentation Archives; "Statistics."

29. "Statistics"; "Summary of Criteria"; interview with Sister Helen Freimuth; "Missions," Presentation Archives.

30. Interview with Sister Lynn Marie Welbig; "Missions"; "Summary of Criteria"; Sister Quinn, "Mother Myron Martin."

31. "Summary of Criteria"; "Statistics"; interview with Robert McCardle, July 29, 1978, South Dakota Oral History Center.

32. Interview with Robert McCardle; interview with Keith Fitzpatrick,

June 5, 1978, South Dakota Oral History Center; Sister Di Donato, "A History of the Educational Work of the Presentation Sisters," 46.

33. Interview with Keith Fitzpatrick.

34. Ibid.; interview with Robert McCardle.

35. Interview with Sister Grace Farrell, June 19, 1978, South Dakota Oral History Center.

36. Interview with Keith Fitzpatrick; interview with Robert McCardle.

37. Sister Quinn, "Mother Myron Martin"; Ibid., "Biographies of Major Superiors: Section XII: Sister JoAnn Sturzl, 1974–1982," Presentation Archives.

38. Sister JoAnn Sturzl, quoted in Ibid.

39. Sister JoAnn Sturzl to the Most Reverend Paul V. Dudley, D.D., Feb. 21, 1979, Presentation Archives.

40. Sister Quinn, "Mother Myron Martin"; "Sister JoAnn Sturzl"; interview with Sister Lynn Marie Welbig.

41. Sister Quinn, "Sister JoAnn Sturzl."

42. Sister Pauline Quinn, "Biographies of Major Superiors, Section XIII: Sister Mary Denis Collins, 1982-," Presentation Archives.

43. *The Official Catholic Directory, 1986* (New York: P.J. Kenedy and Sons, 1986), 348–51, 731–33, 797–806, 887–91. Also see chapter 10 of this volume for a discussion of the extended education apostolate.

44. Sister Quinn, "Sister Mary Denis Collins."

45. Interview with Bishop Lambert Hoch, June 28, 1978, South Dakota Oral History Center; James Coleman, "Public Schools, Private Schools, and the Public Interest," *The Public Interest* 64 (Summer 1981): 19–30.

6. *Ventures in Higher Education: Notre Dame Junior College and Presentation College, 1922–85*

☐

The Presentations' desire to improve their educational credentials first prompted them to become involved with Notre Dame Junior College in Mitchell, which opened in 1922. When Notre Dame closed in 1951, members of the order who were students there continued their schooling at the motherhouse, and in the fall of that year the nuns opened Presentation Junior College, which they would rename Presentation College in 1965. Many nuns hoped that the institution would teach timeless truths through instruction in religion and liberal arts, but from its early years it also offered teacher training and secretarial courses. In the 1960s, medical technician courses became important, and the first class of associate degree nursing students graduated from Presentation College in 1968. By the early 1970s, with Presentation College's economic standing fairly stable, the Presentations rejuvenated their original interest in liberal arts by chartering a curriculum in general education. A revised form of classical study, and a direct product of their own holistic professional ideology, it was designed to counteract the "fragmentation" of students' lives and intellect by providing them with a " 'common learning' . . . [and] a comprehensive understanding of the Western tradition. . . ."[1]

Given the history of higher education in America, it was inevitable that from its inception the Presentation College would have to struggle in order to maintain its ideological source. Reflecting the Presentations' belief in absolutes, during the twentieth century a perennialistic philosophy advocating the existence of timeless, abstract truths had inspired a Great Books course of study at Catholic private colleges such as St. John's located at Annapolis, Maryland,

and St. John's at Santa Fe, New Mexico. Inasmuch as the program was thought to be unpractical and elitist, similar ones have existed only in abbreviated form at other Catholic and non-Catholic colleges and universities. For the most part, a smattering of courses from a variety of disciplines has been considered adequate to provide college students with the knowledge and depth to become broadly educated, for pragmatism dictates that the more important courses are those that prepare one for work. This attitude generally has pervaded the two-year college curriculum, but in 1900, all of the country's eight junior colleges were private, and most of them emphasized a course of study that prepared students for upper-division college work. Some 137 of the 207 junior colleges that existed by 1922 were private, but by 1961, only 273 of the 678 total were. This proliferation of public junior colleges continued into the 1980s. Vocationalism, which the federal government has promoted since the World War I era, has dominated a good portion of the degree certification and diploma programs in both the public and the private community and junior colleges.[2] In so doing, the two-year college often has become an institution that has perpetuated the social order by what Burton R. Clark has termed the "cooling out" of the lower socioeconomic class: its members are trained for a job but dissuaded from seeking high-status professional careers in fields already overcrowded by the more well-to-do.[3]

Job training has also made up a significant part of independent higher education in South Dakota. Rivaling Presentation College's specialty in medical training, in the early 1970s, Dakota Wesleyan University began offering an associate degree in registered nursing; by 1985, it provided training in a number of other health care fields such as medical laboratory technology and x-ray technology. The twentieth century brought other religious-oriented institutions that developed technical programs in South Dakota. The Mennonites founded Freeman Junior College at Freeman in 1903; the Lutherans moved Augustana College from Chicago to Sioux Falls in 1918; and Mount Marty College (conducted by the Benedictine Sisters) was established at Yankton in 1936. By 1985, a few of the certificates awarded at each institution included those in farm and ranch management and in television electronics. An associate degree in licensed practical nursing operated at Freeman until the school closed in 1986. A bachelor of arts in aviation, hospital administration, and nursing were offered at Augustana by 1985, and certificates in criminal justice and secretarial science existed at Huron College. Although Mount Marty's original expertise was liberal arts, by 1985 it offered a bachelor's degree in nursing, an associate degree in recreational leadership, and certificates in early childhood education and in secretarial science. Blending practical and classical studies, Mount Marty also listed courses of study in American historical awareness and in religious education. In 1941, the independent National College of Business was founded in Rapid City, and by 1985 it granted both two- and four-year degrees. During the 1960s, Wessington Springs College closed, but in 1977, another private institution, Kilian Community College, was built at Sioux Falls. It, too, prepared students specifically for employment.[4]

By the mid 1980s, public colleges and universities in South Dakota also included an associate degree and other one- and two-year certificate programs. The South Dakota School of Mines and Technology (founded in 1885) had always offered a pragmatic scientific curriculum. Black Hills State College, Dakota State College, South Dakota State University, and the University of South Dakota (located at Vermillion and Springfield) listed numerous job-training classes such as air-conditioning and refrigeration at the University campus in Springfield. The University at Vermillion offered an associate degree in registered nursing. Northern State College at Aberdeen, which has trained many Presentation educators, also listed two-year technical programs such as electronic data processing, and it granted certificates in subjects as diverse as wood technology, secretarial science, and being a teacher's aide. Oglala Lakota College at Kyle and Sinte Gleska College at Rosebud were erected in 1970 and 1971, respectively. The Oglala Sioux tribe ran the former, while the Rosebud Sioux Tribal Council operated the latter. Each school primarily served Native Americans, and, like Presentation College, Oglala Lakota provided two-year preparation for prospective registered nurses. Criminal justice and other such programs have been available at Sinte Gleska.[5]

As racially imbalanced as Oglala and Sinte Gleska, Notre Dame and Presentation Colleges attract white students, often the offspring of struggling farmers. Through the Presentations' desire to provide these youths with the means to make a living, the sisters may also have restricted their clients' professional vision, concentrating on limited, readily obtainable goals rather than the more grandiose dreams of lucrative careers. Yet empowering graduates to earn large sums of money has never suited any aspect of the nuns' professional mission. Rather, they have considered it much more important to give job training in modestly paid fields and instruction in ethics and morality.

With ethics and some degree of practicality in mind, the sisters and Father Brady developed a one-year teacher-training course at Notre Dame High School in 1921. Sister M. Francis Holland, principal of Notre Dame Academy, and Sisters M. Bernard McWalters, M. Clement Fitzgerald, and M. Perpetua McCullen were a few of the Presentations with whom the priest worked closely. The school offered a one-year normal training course that lead to a South Dakota first-grade certificate valid only in the state's rural schools. A teacher could earn full certification by attending summer courses that amounted to ninety quarter hours. With Notre Dame's addition of a new wing in 1921, a second year of teacher training was approved by the South Dakota Department of Public Instruction, and a two-year arts and sciences preparatory program became part of the curriculum. By the 1930s, Dean W. W. Ludeman of Southern State Teachers College, one of the school's accrediting officials, stated that Notre Dame Academy ranked first among private teacher-training schools in South Dakota. Although then officially accepted as part of the South Dakota higher education establishment, it retained an Old World Presentation charm, as students often enjoyed Father Brady's Irish brogue or were entertained by Sister Margaret Mary Grainger, who was said to have imparted as much Irish history to her students as she did Latin. Sister Cabrini Di Donato wrote of the Notre Dame schools that "nowhere else in the United States was there a parochial school where Catholic parishioners could send their children to receive fourteen years of Catholic education—all under one roof."[6]

The junior college continued to grow. By 1939, a total of 117 men and women were enrolled in a teacher-preparatory course of study. In 1941, the State Director of Nursing Education approved a one-year nursing preparatory curriculum. Moreover, Sister M. Rosaria O'Callaghan instituted a two-year secretarial science program which, together with the nursing classes, represented the college's move toward vocational offerings rather than liberal arts.[7] Apparently some of the Presentations had a hard time accepting that fact. Sister Marie Patrice Moriarty, a one-time Notre Dame student, confided that "Sister Anna Marie [Weinreis] and Sister [M.] Martha won't like me for saying [this] . . . but [when] I went to Notre Dame . . . it was career oriented . . . [toward] . . . teacher education."[8] Nevertheless, the adaptation helped promote the college. Because Notre Dame was accredited, graduates could transfer their credits to four-year colleges and universities without taking an examination or losing units of instruction. After taking a general course of arts and sciences leading to the associate degree, many of these graduates chose to matriculate at the University of South Dakota at Vermillion.[9]

With its broad curriculum, Notre Dame truly became a community college, serving the eastern portion of South Dakota for twenty-nine years and graduating approximately 1,300 students before it closed in 1951. The Presentation educators had made every effort to keep the institution open by taking only a small salary, arranging for their own janitorial service, and supervising the care of any boarding students. In 1943, for example, they each earned only $350 per year. It compared miserably with averages in 1940 of approximately $540 per nine months for the state's Catholic lay teachers, $807 for South Dakota public school teachers, and $1,441 for public educators nationally.[10]

Notre Dame helped eliminate teacher shortages during World War II. Whereas in 1940 there had been 1,394 fully trained teachers in South Dakota, four years later the number had fallen to 397. Some teachers went off to fight, and others took jobs in munitions factories. Consequently, the state lowered its requirements for teacher certification, and Notre Dame opened its doors to high school graduates who took ten weeks of summer classes and were then licensed to teach in the South Dakota rural schools. Ninety to 145 students went through this program each summer.[11]

Throughout the college's history it not only educated those secular and nonsecular school teachers, but it also provided a means by which the Presentations could improve their own level of education without losing contact with their religious community. As a result, most of the group's teachers could easily enroll in the education courses, thereby upgrading their own skills and the standard of instruction in Catholic elementary and secondary schools.[12]

For many Presentations, the higher educational process proved to be a catalyst for career expansion that would continue long after Notre Dame closed and Presentation College opened in 1956. The nuns developed pride and self-reliance because of their educational achievements. These inner changes supported the sisters' choices to enter such professions as nursing, hospital administration, or the higher education professorate. To prepare for these fields, Presentation administrators and high school teachers and post-secondary educators worked toward and received master's and doctoral degrees at institutions such as Catholic University, the University of Texas, Marquette University, and De Paul University. Although the University of South Dakota and South Dakota State College began offering the doctorate in the 1950s, the Presentations gravitated toward Catholic institutions where they could continue to live with their own sisters or with those from other orders. For example, while pursuing a master's degree during the 1960s, Sister Anthony Dempsey lived with other religious at Catholic University. Thus the Presentations' progress toward professionalization remained inspired but also bound by their ideological commitment.[13]

Not only the Presentations, but also other South Dakota nuns throughout the century have endorsed the professionalization of the higher education apostolate. In 1943, Sister M. Claudia Duratschek, a Benedictine nun from Yankton, took a Ph.D. in history from Catholic University, later publishing her dissertation on Catholicism in South Dakota. Thus emboldened by their charge to educate, Presentation educators and their South Dakota religious colleagues carefully entered what was once considered a male professional sphere, working for and receiving doctoral degrees.[14]

At Notre Dame the Presentations stimulated less dramatic yet significant changes within their students. Students usually came from the small towns and farms around Mitchell, and regardless of any or no religious affiliation they could board on campus or with families nearby. Winnifred Peterson commented that during the early 1940s she paid $100 tuition for a one-year teacher-training course and worked for her room and board in the mayor's home. Peterson was able to acquire the beginnings of a bachelor's degree even though she started school just after the end of the Great Depression, an economic ordeal that residents of South Dakota were still suffering because of persistent drought. As the daughter of a farmer, she was thankful that Father Brady and the Presentation staff provided her and other rural people a chance to obtain a college education and to reach for greater personal and economic heights.[15] Despite both the success and the promise of professionalization, during the late 1940s the future of Notre Dame Junior College became questionable, ironically because the area's population was beginning to recoup losses from the Great Depression and the war years, providing incentive to young couples who had postponed having children to start their families. Consequently, Notre Dame's elementary and secondary divisions became crowded with students, and the two-year college became less important. It so dwindled in size that it was relegated to only the building's top floor. Most parishioners favored the move, believing that the Presentations should reserve any available classrooms for the elementary grades and high school so that a maximum number of young people would benefit. For a time Monsignor Brady considered expansion of the entire educational institute, but in the final analysis he determined that such a project would overextend the parish resources.[16]

Another problem for the college division of Notre Dame was the loss of accreditation. Higher-education institutions of South Dakota that the North Central Association had not evaluated came under the jurisdiction of the University of South Dakota, which conducted periodic reviews. At Notre Dame during the late 1940s, University representatives assessed facilities, budgets, the faculty, and the library. Spokespersons then decreed that because the physical plant was overcrowded and because not enough faculty members were available, Notre Dame Junior College should be terminated. Without state accreditation the institution was doomed. Accepting the criticism, Brady reluctantly planned to close the school.[17]

Brady and the Presentations, however, did not retreat from higher education. As Sister Alicia Dunphy put it, Monsignor Brady "didn't want to die," and he believed if the nuns would continue to run the college he would, in a sense, live on. Thus, Mother Viator Burns and her council agreed to move the facility from Mitchell to Aberdeen. Presentation educators continued for a while to operate Notre Dame in the motherhouse near St. Luke's Hospital, but in May of 1951 the parish closed the college, ending the institution's twenty-nine-year history. Then, with land purchased north of Aberdeen, the nuns planned to build a new convent and additional facilities for an all new Presentation Junior College for women.[18]

Three months after Notre Dame's demise, the Presentation Junior College opened its doors but, although it eventually developed into a solid institution, the beginnings were uncertain. Capable but overburdened, Presentation superior Mother Burns became president of the college, as would Mother Carmelita McCullough after her. Moreover, Sister Anna Marie Weinreis recalled, "Sister Augustine [Phelan] was the first academic dean ... [but] she didn't seem to have any idea of what it meant to run a college." The initial enrollment exceeded 150 students, 127 of whom were part-time. Although sisters composed a majority of students in the early years, by 1964 they were only 6 percent of the total. The nuns' residence, the hospital, and the parochial school on the east side of the city were all part of the higher-education project. Those students who were not sisters were boarded at private homes or in the dormitory. The curriculum included three academic programs: a junior-college degree, the South Dakota general certificate, and the state's first-grade certificate. Many of the part-time students also were enrolled in nurses' training at the four Presentation hospitals in South Dakota and Montana because the Presentations insisted that all vocational preparation must include some type of general education sequence. Thus, apprentice nurses schooled largely in hospital training programs attended Presentation Junior College for courses in sociology, psychology, and religion, which were all components of what would later become a two-year associate degree.[19]

Curriculum development and accreditation decisions filled the school's early years. Although the sisters had hoped initially to re-dedicate their own college to the liberal arts, they soon resigned themselves to emphasizing teacher training and commercial courses as directors of Notre Dame had done. Sister Marie Patrice Moriarty lamented, "We'd like ... more liberal arts because we believe it's important for students to become someone and then do something for humanity."[20] Yet the power of client demands, which had forced the secularization of many Catholic institutions with much older histories than that of Presentation Junior College, proved insurmountable for a time. Thus the Presentations relented, concentrating on health care programs that combined internships in their hospitals with a general education sequence at the junior college and with a few courses at Northern in Aberdeen.

In 1953, after the first Presentation Junior College class completed its sophomore year, the college applied for and received approval from the university accrediting committee to grant degrees, although selected university personnel continued to tour the college every two years to ensure that the institution maintained standards and followed university recommendations. The sisters hoped that because the requirements were similar to those of the North Central Association, compliance with the state guidelines eventually would lead to North Central accreditation.[21]

Despite the sisters' willingness to professionalize and work, Presentation Junior College's early years were marked with difficulties because of space shortages and because of the effort involved in transferring records from Mitchell to Aberdeen. Sister Anna Marie Weinreis, who became a dean at the college in 1953, remembered that an old wing of the convent in Aberdeen housed most of the school, including the first student dormitory facilities. She recalled that there was very little office space, and few supplies were available. In the interest of sustaining continuity between the old and the new colleges it was necessary to transfer copies of all student records. In the manner of medieval scribes, several Presentations had to hand copy grades from nearly 1,400 transcripts so that the new facility would have complete files and the alumnae from Notre Dame could consider Presentation Junior College their alma mater. In spite of the early procedural problems, during Sister Weinreis's seventeen years as a college administrator the institution became a landmark on the northern Great Plains.[22]

The college's future was further secured when the order moved into a new building on the north side of Aberdeen, where the sisters had purchased one hundred acres of land in 1944. Mothers Raphael McCarthy and Burns took great care in planning construction of the new motherhouse and college, and they spent more than $2,000,000 before the three-winged structure stood completed. Besides classrooms it housed a convent for 364 nuns, a cafeteria, a recreation room, a bookstore, an auditorium, a chapel, a library, a student lounge, and a dormitory. Designed for future expansion, the excellent laboratory facilities allowed for curriculum growth. Now students from the Presentation nursing schools could complete all pre-clinical classes at the college instead of taking science courses at Northern as they had done in the past.[23]

Eager to become part of this nationally recognized system of higher education, Mother Burns and her colleagues were polite and diplomatic when dealing with secular authority figures. A University of South Dakota representative who supervised both the closing of Notre Dame and the opening of its successor commented that the Presentations in Mitchell had been most cooperative. The sisters willingly accepted those proposed recommendations which, they believed, would improve the quality of their institution if implemented.[24]

In turn, the fledgling college received important cooperation from outside evaluators. Although the evaluators strived to enforce nationally accepted standards, Albert W. Harrington, dean of the College of Arts and Sciences and head of the University of South Dakota accrediting team, noted that he and his colleagues respected the philosophical differences between Catholic and public colleges. For example, Harrington interpreted a low salary schedule as an early warning signal that a college's future was in jeopardy predicting that the institution was in serious financial trouble. "I never did that [with] . . . Mount Marty or Presentation College," he recalled, "because . . . that would have been intruding [on the prerogatives of religious] whose dedication went beyond money." Typically during the 1950s, he noted, private school educators made an average of $1,500 per year, while other college professors and instructors commanded as much as $4,000 to $5,000 per year; however, rather than discouraging Presentation Junior College or Mount Marty, Harrington praised them both, even encouraging Mount Marty to become a four-year school.[25]

Buttressed by both internal and external forces, therefore, Presentation Junior College grew steadily as its relevance to South Dakotans and especially to Aberdeen residents flourished. Reviving the nineteenth-century collaboration of homemaker-volunteers with professionals such as teachers (both of whom together civilized the West), a group of local Catholic and Protestant women organized the Presentation Auxiliary. They held fund drives and conducted publicity campaigns to finance a school newspaper and to inform local people about Presentation Junior College activities. To raise additional money, they held bridge luncheons, sponsored movies, and presented a fall arts festival. Other promotional events came from the students themselves. In 1958 they organized a homecoming celebration that commemorated the Presentations' Irish origins, declaring green and gold to be the school's colors and selecting a leprechaun as their mascot.[26]

In the same year the administration expanded the curriculum to include medical technology, utilizing many of the nursing students' pre-clinical courses in conjunction with intern experience at St. Luke's Hospital. By September 1960, when Presentation Junior College's calendar switched from three quarters to two semesters, enrollment had reached 212. Included were forty-seven women in teacher training, twenty-nine in general education, twenty-one in secretarial courses, six in medical technology, and seventy-two in the preclinical nursing program.[27]

From 1960 to 1965, many curricular changes occurred at Presentation Junior College, some not without conflict between traditional and progressive protagonists. Pragmatic Presentation educators successfully implemented a medical secretary course. Moreover, although some of the nuns feared that a greater and greater commitment to nurses' training could further blur the college's focus on liberal arts, college administrators executed a plan to reorganize the nursing program toward an associate degree.[28]

The success of these innovations promoted the addition of courses and the expansion of the physical plant, both of which enhanced an already positive rapport with the community outside the order. In 1963 they contracted for the construction of a northeast wing of the college's main building. This addition enabled the sisters to triple the size of the library, enlarge the cafeteria, and increase dormitory space. A health center and several recreation areas were included, as well as a remodeled laboratory for the study of foreign languages. The more spacious accommodations also made way for new coeducational offerings for adults. Often taught in the evening, these classes made the townspeople appreciate the college.[29]

During the 1960s, Presentation Junior College administration and faculty worked toward North Central approval. Following the University of South Dakota accrediting team's suggestions, Presentation educators began conducting a self-study in 1962. Two years later, they submitted their report, but the authorities turned the college down for immediate approval. North Central suggested that the sisters obtain a consultant to help them identify the institution's weaknesses and assist them in planning for the future. Undaunted but compliant, in 1964 Mother Myron Martin and her general council (the college's corporate board) incorporated the school separately from the motherhouse and changed the institution's name from Presentation Junior College to Presentation College—a symbol of the educators' quest for an improved image. The board hired Donald B. King, the consultant who advised the college administrators to apply for candidacy in the North Central district as a preliminary step to full membership. Also in 1964, Sister Alicia Dunphy became the college's first full-time president.[30]

The new president's three-year term was trying because of turbulent changes in students' social and political demeanor that were occurring in Aberdeen as on college campuses all over the country. An anti-establishment attitude prevailed, manifesting itself in social movements such as the civil rights and New Left movements. Sister Dunphy often felt as if she were "starting from scratch."[31] Sister Rita Coss, instructor of theology, commented that the turbulence of the times surfaced in her classes as students seemed embarrassed to admit their religious feelings. Many other students demonstrated their lack of interest by not even attending class, while others protested and succeeded in eliminating the school dress code. Attempting to alter but not sacrifice an authoritarian administrative style, Sister Dunphy tried to maintain control over the students but at the same time allowed the students' government association a voice in running the college.[32]

Besides incorporating student attitudes into the college bureaucratic machinery, throughout the late 1960s and early '70s, Presentation College continued to create a variety of vocational offerings, primarily in the allied health fields. Various associate degree and certificate programs in the dietetic, radiologic, and laboratory technician fields, as well as classes on the administration of health care facilities, swelled the curriculum. Along with the national push for increased academic training for future teachers, the sisters phased out the inadequate one- and two-year teacher certification programs. By 1969, associate of arts and associate of science courses prepared a person to continue baccalaureate work at colleges and universities in fields such as elementary or secondary education. The school also initiated associate degrees in child development and instructional aid, while the business schedule expanded to offer one- and two-year secretarial diplomas.[33]

Exemplifying the ever-increasing professional attitude at Presentation College, the institution's leaders strove to make connections with other state colleges and with national professional organizations. When Sister Frances Mary Dunn became president in 1967, the school was an active member of the South Dakota Association of Private Colleges (founded in 1950) and gained full North Central recognition in 1971. The organization was dedicated to establishing good public relations and to working for federal tuition grants and a scholarship program for students of private schools. The South Dakota Foundation of Private Colleges, also established early in the 1950s, at first excluded two-year colleges, displaying what one Presentation nun thought was a typical bias among South Dakota higher educators. However, Presentation College officials badgered the organization's leaders, the rule was changed, and Presentation College was finally admitted in 1975. The foundation typically conducts fund-raising drives for the state's private colleges, sending representatives to cities such as Minneapolis to collect contributions from corporations with business interests in South Dakota. Making contacts in a more personal fashion during the 1970s, Presentation Sister Francene Evans taught classes at Sioux Falls College. On a national level and in addition to the North Central affiliation, Presentation College joined forces with the National Catholic Education Association, the American Association of Community and Junior Colleges, the National Association of Independent Colleges and Universities, and the American Association of Collegiate Registrars and Admissions Officers.[34]

Individual nuns also involved themselves in professional outreach activities. In 1966, Sister Di Donato enumerated a few of the accomplishments achieved during that decade: "Sister M. Sheila Crampton received an appointment to the Commission of American Citizenship. As a member of this group, she writes for the *Faith and Freedom* readers being published by Ginn and Company. . . . Sister M. Richard Caron was selected to serve the Surgeon General on a committee appointed to evaluate the effectiveness of Federal grants for nursing education. . . . Sister M. Judith O'Brien participated in a major research project in social service with the Metropolitan Youth Commission of Saint Louis while studying at Saint Louis University."[35]

Presentation higher educators have always been aware of the importance of maintaining good relations with officials at Northern.

As noted earlier, Father Robert Haire had served on the college's board of regents. Some of the nuns did not have such positive experiences with Northern faculty members. For example, Sister Martha Raleigh, who eventually received a master's degree elsewhere, attended the college for one year during the 1930s. As part of her experience she remembered sparring with an economics teacher who was opposed to private education. Conversely, Sister Jane Francis, who held a master's in microbiology from Catholic University, taught chemistry at Northern during the early 1950s. Although she wore her habit to class, she recalled no prejudice because people were accustomed to the nun students being on the campus. Moreover, Sister Anna Marie Weinreis, an early physics teacher and dean at Presentation College, relied heavily on professors at Northern and at Dakota State College in Madison for advice and council regarding preparation for accreditation. Late in the 1960s new fears arose, however, when South Dakota officials began requiring the bachelor's degree for elementary certification. Presentation College lost students who, rather than transferring to Northern after two years' work at the Catholic school, began the freshman year at the state institution. Speculating that a similar phenomenon would occur if Northern administrators ever decided to go into the health care training fields, Sister Dunn stated flatly that Presentation College might be forced to close. Presentations have therefore been quite interested in cooperating with Northern in any new curricular areas. Under the guidelines of Title III of the 1965 Higher Education Act, during the 1970s Presentation College cooperated with Northern's adult education department. Together the two schools staffed a higher education center at Eagle Butte on the Cheyenne River Reservation in western South Dakota. There the sisters' major role was offering a nursing course, a satellite of their college's own curriculum.[36]

Another major component of Presentation College's higher education agenda was constructing a specially equipped edifice funded in part by the federal Department of Health, Education, and Welfare, which oversaw implementation of the Nurse Training Act of 1964. Connected to the main building by a tunnel, the structure contained classrooms and seminar areas, offices, a lecture hall, and an audio-tutorial laboratory. It provided individual study carrels equipped with tape recorders, additional rooms for simulated hospital and nursing-home settings, and a cache of audio-visual equipment. Renovations to the main college structure included additional seminar rooms and a new residence for fifty female students. When Presentation College became coeducational in 1968, new male students had to acquire off-campus residences. That year male students were a rare sight, but the ratio of men to women soon leveled off at approximately one to twenty. With an expanded physical plant, the college was able to accept one hundred male and female nursing students a year. Sister Mary Eleanor Joyce, the college registrar (beginning in 1973) commented that if space permitted, the school could enroll as many as 150 students because the demand for nurses in northern South Dakota far exceeded the supply.[37]

Thus during the 1970s Presentation College established an even more intimate relationship with South Dakota citizens, which was due in part to additional curricular developments. Founded in 1966, a Presentation College advisory board, including lay members from the Aberdeen area such as state senator Margaret Lamont and Northern administrator Wendell Jahnke,[38] served as a liaison between the school and the townspeople, advising the administration in public relations and assisting in recruitment of students. Consequently, the college began to offer many more adult and continuing education courses, refresher classes in the fields of nursing, home health care and laboratory technology, and a prenatal and postnatal care series. The sisters made areas of the college available to local groups needing facilities for workshops. The Presentations also showed an interest in working with members of other religious denominations. For example, the college's curriculum has included courses and special programs spotlighting Aberdeen community church leaders. A local Methodist minister has offered a course in social problems, and from time to time various speakers from other denominations, such as a Mormon elder, have addressed religion classes.[39]

The drive to extend the college's horizons paved the way for the Office of Community Services, which opened in 1972. As officially stated, this department supervised community projects in Aberdeen and elsewhere in order to fulfill local educational needs. It also provided solutions for economic, cultural, and civic problems not met by formal collegiate training. The office developed four basic kinds of services: special college-coordinated programs, contractual training agreements with other agencies, retraining or refresher courses, and facilities for workshops and meetings. During its first year of operation, the new agency involved more than 3,000 local people in programs it sponsored or directed. In 1975, approximately 3,500 persons were involved in seventy-eight different workshops, training series, and conferences. The sisters charged the lowest possible fee and even ran some of the sessions free of charge. Much of their time went to seeking sources of funds to continue the expansion of offerings. The results were positive, with projections indicating growth for the new office.[40]

The success at Presentation College was accomplished originally by preparing women and a few men for the female's traditional role as a community-builder, teacher, or nurse. Despite such success, which seemed to reside within the nuns' accepted ideological framework, some Presentation educators believed that the college was not fulfilling Nano Nagle's intentions. Sister Francelle Clarke, who served as a counselor in a 1957-founded guidance program, maintained also that by the 1970s the college's middle-class white students were inappropriate Presentation clients. A "number of them throw money around like they've got a lot of it," she remarked. She did, however, approve of the counseling policy that, during the mid-1970s, assisted nontraditional, impoverished students such as twenty Indians and approximately twelve welfare-supported divorced women who, after graduating, became gainfully employed. Sister Clarke maintained that in accordance with the order's mission it was her job to give these people a feeling of self-confidence, which she did.[41] Regarding a ballet course originated in the 1970s, Sister Weinreis expressed sentiments similar to those of Sister Clarke: "I'm really against this dance program that they're starting. . . . I think it would be all right to have ballet as an elective but . . . it's [not] our type of work. It's the wealthy people that take ballet. . . . It is really more Mount Marty's role, than it is ours [that of Presentation College] to provide cultural programs such as this," Sister Weinreis concluded.[42] Sister Joyce disagreed, claiming that the typical Presentation College student had always been one worthy of Presentation services. "I really think that we have a majority of the lesser middle class [students] . . . going to school here, and most of them . . . come from farming areas and big families. They all need [financial] help. . . ." Even so, a majority of the student body in the mid-eighties was neither Irish, nor Catholic, nor poor, those to whom Nagle had devoted her life.[43]

Other controversies have stirred between the Presentation College educators—some favoring a philosophically based curriculum, and others maintaining that technical-training courses have been the economic lifeblood of their college. Like most colleges and universities throughout the country, what the institution called the liberal arts course of study during the late 1960s consisted of a number of credit hours representative of the freshman and sophomore levels of a baccalaureate degree: English grammar and composition, history, language, science, mathematics, physical education, philosophy, literature, sociology, speech, psychology, social science, and a few electives. Even though Presentation College students in this program took classes in religion as part of a general education requirement for the associate degree, some sisters were concerned that an emphasis on ethics was not central to all or even any of the college programs. In an attempt to resolve the problem, Sister Moriarty researched and in 1973 completed her doctoral dissertation for the purpose of formulating an interdisciplinary course of study in general education, largely for those students preparing for upper-division college work. The notion was not new. In fact, as early as 1919, Columbia University had created an Introduction to Contemporary Civilization Program. By the early 1930s, the American Association of Junior Colleges had proposed that two-year college curricula infuse continuity into what had become the typically disjointed liberal arts offerings, thereby providing students with the personal and philosophical unity needed to cope with a rapidly changing modern age.[44]

As part of her research, Sister Moriarty worked with a team of Presentation College representatives to conduct a feasibility study and to establish a rationale for implementing a program that in her words was "value-centered and aimed toward an intellectual and emotional development of the person. It is not so much content-oriented as process-oriented, aiming to develop skills for [an individual's continuous] . . . education." Working from this basic concept the college faculty articulated several specific goals: "to develop a deeper realization of . . . [the student's] potentialities in relationship to God, self and others; . . . to develop and live Christian values realistically within and outside the college setting; . . . to prepare for job opportunities and/or upper division courses; . . . to develop a desire and facility to continue to educate himself in a *dynamic* society."[45]

TABLE 8. PROPOSED GENERAL EDUCATION COURSE OF STUDY,
PRESENTATION COLLEGE, 1973

First Semester	Second Semester
Theology	Theology
Literature	Literature
Communications	Communications
Enrichment	*Enrichment*
Science	History
Fine arts	Fine arts
Third Semester	**Fourth Semester**
Sociology	Ethics
History	Communications
Communications	
Enrichment	*Enrichment*
Science	Related readings
Literature	Seminar

Source: Sister Marie Moriarty, "A Feasibility Study of Adopting a Program of Interdisciplinary General Education for a Two-year Curriculum at Presentation College, Aberdeen, South Dakota," unpub. Ed.D. diss., Lawrence University, 1973, 93.

The implementation of these intentions evolved into the two-year course of study outlined in Table 8. As these listings suggest, the new program was primarily a perpetuation of what perennialist or essentialist educators have earmarked as classic, foundational educational material; and like their national counterparts, Sister Moriarty and the Presentation College faculty believed that only with an emphasis on the values and ideas that contain timeless truth can an individual work out her or his own relationship to an often-mercurial, material world. Remaining traditional in substance but borrowing contemporary rhetoric, Sister Moriarty's argument was that this program assisted "students in the process of synthesizing information and applying it to their existential situation." Explaining how one might accomplish this, she nevertheless recommended modern methodology, stating that an instructor should "work out thematically a *progressive* [emphasis added] program which would present a total concept of man's development, his experiences and communication with other men, his development with regard to his environment, and his relationship to God."[46]

Although contested by some nuns, other Presentations claimed that the initiation of an associate degree in dance and ballet was one manifestation of the revived interest in tradition and the arts. The nuns hired a lay person to instruct classes, and they also provided a well-equipped practice room. Women such as Sister Weinreis objected, evidencing differing positions within what could be considered the traditional camp. Yet Aberdeen citizens' initial responses were enthusiastic, as twenty-four students committed themselves to this program in 1976.[47]

Leaving a record of conflict and consensus, by the 1980s Presentation College seemed to have survived its philosophical crisis and remained a viable institution of service at the same time. In 1985, students could choose from four parallel associate of arts degrees in liberal arts, classical ballet, general education, and teacher education. They also had a choice of seven areas leading to the associate of science degree: business, child development technology, instructional aide, medical laboratory technology, nursing, radiologic technology, and social service technology. Moreover, five certificate programs—in surgical technology, religious education, secretarial skills, business/accounting, and computer science—augmented the list of offerings. From the beginning, directors of these programs had reached for state and nationally recognized professional distinction. For example, in 1948, Sister Veronica Ogden had been the first president of the South Dakota Society of Medical Technologists and later served in various offices of the national organization. Professional involvements such as these attracted students who augmented matriculation in all of the new areas because it climbed steadily from 150 students in 1951 to an annual enrollment of 312 students thirty-two years later. In 1951, tuition for full-time students had been $100 a semester but had increased to $1,710 by 1985, while part-timers paid $35 to $95 a credit hour. The full-time administrative and faculty ranks at Presentation College had grown to thirty members, and, although fourteen of them were still Presentations, salary costs had increased as the percentage of sisters on the staff gradually declined over the years to slightly less than 50 percent in 1985.[48]

After more than five decades, Notre Dame and Presentation College were monuments to the sisters' interest in higher education, their adaptability to external demands, and yet their internal commitment to age-old philosophical principles. Although their comparative numerical domination of the faculty and administration had dwindled, they maintained ideological control of Presentation College. For instance, a college official wrote in 1985 that the college "received its tradition of concern for human persons from the Sisters of the Presentation of the Blessed Virgin Mary. This community of Catholic women religious had been committed to serving human and spiritual needs through education and health care for more than two hundred years.... In this tradition the Presentation College community addresses life-long learning needs which are intellectual, spiritual, cultural and social. Presentation College has the capability to humanize learning ... [which] flows from the Christian community experience [and] ... supports the students['] ... total growth."[49] Motivating themselves in this fashion, the nuns provided through the college the first steps in their own professional preparation as teachers, nurses, and hospital administrators. Yet professional developments in the health care fields merit the telling of their own stories, as they too involved internal and external polemics also resolved within the Presentations' contextual ideological base.

NOTES

1. Daniel Bell, *The Reforming of General Education* (New York: Columbia University Press, 1966), 282. For a nineteenth-century source on the classic liberal arts tradition, see Cardinal John Henry Newman, *On the Scope and Nature of University Education* (London: J. M. Dent and Sons, 1915).

2. William H. Howick, *Philosophies of Education* (Danville, Ill.: Interstate Printers and Publishers, 1980), 61–74; Gregory L. Goodwin, "The Nature and the Nurture of the Community College Movement," *Community College Frontiers* 4 (Spring 1976): 5–13; Charles R. Monroe, *Profile of the Community College* (San Francisco: Jossey-Bass, 1972), 1–21; John S. Brubacher and Willis Rudy, *Higher Education in Transition: A History of American Colleges and Universities, 1636–1976* (New York: Harper and Row, 1958), 18, 274–78, 298.

3. Burton R. Clark, "The 'Cooling-Out' Function in Higher Education," *American Journal of Sociology* 65 (May 1960): 569–76.

4. James Cass and Max Birnbaum, eds., *Comparative Guide to Two-Year Colleges and Career Programs,* "South Dakota," (New York: Harper and Row, 1976), 300–2; Andrea E. Lehman, ed., *Peterson's Guide to Two-*

Year Colleges (Princeton: Peterson's Guides, 1985), 223; D. Parnell and J. W. Peltason, eds., *American Community, Technical and Junior Colleges* (New York: Macmillan Publishing, 1984), 647; Andrea E. Lehman, ed., *Peterson's Guide to Four-Year Colleges* (Princeton: Peterson's Guides, 1985), 859–60.

5. Cass and Birnbaum, eds., *Comparative Guide to Two-Year Colleges*, p. 299–302; Lehman, ed., *Peterson's Guide to Four-Year Colleges*, 40, 273–74, 348–49, 623–24, 625–26, 731.

6. "Notre Dame Academy Historical Data," Presentation Archives, Aberdeen, S. D.; *Diamond Jubilee Book* (Aberdeen, S.D.: Sisters of the Presentation of the Blessed Virgin Mary, 1961), 31; interview with Sister Grace Farrell, June 19, 1978, South Dakota Oral History Center, Vermillion; Sister M. Cabrini Di Donato, "A History of the Educational Work of the Presentation Sisters of Aberdeen, South Dakota" (master's thesis, Northern State Collge, 1966), 41–42.

7. Sister Di Donato, "A History of the Educational Work of the Presentation Sisters," 42–43.

8. Interview with Sister Marie Patrice Moriarty, Aug. 12, 1976, South Dakota Oral History Center.

9. Sister Di Donato, "A History of the Educational Work of the Presentation Sisters," 41.

10. Ibid., 42; "Teaching Contract between Mother M. Raphael and Msgr. J. M. Brady," 1943, Presentation Archives; *Digest of Education Statistics, 1983–84* (Washington, D.C.: U.S. Department of Education, 1984), 56; interview with Sister Eucharia Kelly, Aug. 12, 1976, South Dakota Oral History Center; interview with Sister Mary Eleanor Joyce, Aug. 12, 1976, South Dakota Oral History Center.

11. Cleata B. Thorpe, "Education in South Dakota, 1861–1961," *South Dakota Historical Collections* 36 (1972): 339; interview with Sister Eleanor McCall, June 22, 1978, South Dakota Oral History Center.

12. "Notre Dame Acadamy Historical Data"; interview with Sister Eucharia Kelly.

13. Interview with Sister Anna Marie Weinreis, Aug. 10, 1976, South Dakota Oral History Center; interview with Sister Marie Patrice Moriarty; interview with Sister Helen Freimuth, Aug. 5, 1976, South Dakota Oral History Center; interview with Sister Anthony Dempsey, June 27, 1978, South Dakota Oral History Center; interview with Sister Mary Eleanor Joyce; Thorpe, "Education in South Dakota," 378.

14. Sister M. Claudia Duratschek, *The Beginnings of Catholicism in South Dakota* (Washington, D.C.: Catholic University of America Press, 1943); also see chapter 1 of this volume.

15. Interview with Winnifred Peterson, July 29, 1978, South Dakota Oral History Center; interview with Sister Helen Freimuth.

16. "Jubilee Data"; "Notre Dame Academy Historical Data"; interview with Sister Alicia Dunphy, Aug. 6, 1976; interview with Sister Eleanor McCall, June 22, 1978, South Dakota Oral History Center.

17. Interview with Albert Harrington, June 14, 1978, South Dakota Oral History Center; interview with Sister Anna Marie Weinreis.

18. *Diamond Jubilee Book*, 58–59; (Mitchell) *Daily Republic*, April 28, 1958; Sister Pauline Quinn, "Biography of Major Superiors, Section IX: Mother Viator Burns, 1946–1958," Presentation Archives.

19. *Outline*, Winter 1975; Sister Di Donato, "A History of the Educational Work of the Presentation Sisters," 112. The Presentations attended Northern State Teachers College in Aberdeen for science courses.

20. Interview with Sister Marie Patrice Moriarty; also see James Michael Galvin, "Secularizing Trends in Roman Catholic Colleges and Universities, 1960–1970" (Ed.D. diss., Indiana University, 1971), 86; Andrew M. Greeley, *From Backwater to Mainstream, A Profile of Catholic Higher Education* (New York: McGraw-Hill, 1969), 1–19; John Tracy Ellis, "American Catholics and the Intellectual Life," *Thought: Fordham University Quarterly* 30 (Autumn 1955): 351–88.

21. *Aberdeen American News*, May 2, 1976; interview with Albert Harrington.

22. Interview with Sister Anna Marie Weinreis; interview with Sister Eleanor McCall.

23. Sister Quinn, "Mother Viator Burns"; *Aberdeen American News*, May 2, 1976; *Diamond Jubilee Book*, 58–59; *Bishop's Bulletin*, Dec. 1966, Aug. 1960; Sister Di Donato, "The History of the Educational Work of the Presentation Sisters," 111. From 1954–56, the sisters operated a high school for girls, which shared facilities with the college.

24. Interview with Albert Harrington.

25. Ibid.

26. *Outline*, Winter 1976.

27. *Aberdeen American News*, May 2, 1976; *Outline*, Winter 1975.

28. Interview with Sister Alicia Dunphy; interview with Sister Marie Patrice Moriarty; *Aberdeen American News*, May 2, 1976.

29. Interview with Sister Frances Mary Dunn, Aug. 5, 1976; *Outline*, Winter 1975. A board of directors was created in 1964.

30. Sister Pauline Quinn, "Biographies of Major Superiors, Section XI: Mother Myron Martin, 1964–1974," Presentation Archives; Sister Di Donato, "A History of the Educational Work of the Presentation Sisters," 119–22; *Outline*, Winter 1975, Winter 1976; interview with Sister Frances Mary Dunn; *Aberdeen American News*, May 2, 1976.

31. Interview with Sister Alicia Dunphy. For one source on student rebellions during the 1960s, see William L. O'Neill, *Coming Apart: An Informal History of America in the 1960's* (New York: Quadrangle, 1971), 275–305.

32. Interview with Sister Alicia Dunphy; interview with Sister Rita Coss, Aug. 13, 1976, South Dakota Oral History Center; interview with Sister Anthony Dempsey.

33. Interview with Sister Alicia Dunphy; interview with Sister Frances Mary Dunn; interview with Sister JoAnn Sturzl, Aug. 5, 1976, South Dakota Oral History Center; *Aberdeen American News*, May 2, 1976.

34. Interview with Sister Frances Mary Dunn; *Presentation College Catalog*, vol. 21 (Aberdeen, S.D.: Presentation College, 1984), n.p.; "Presentation College Catalog Supplement," in Ibid., n.p.; communication between Sylvia Starr and Rex Swanson, Oct. 20, 1986; interview with Mother Myron Martin, August 12, 1976, South Dakota Oral History Center. Also see note 30.

35. Sister Di Donato, "A History of the Educational Work of the Presentation Sisters," 120.

36. Ibid.; Interview with Sister Martha Raleigh, Aug. 10, 1976; interview with Sister Jane Francis, June 20, 1978, South Dakota Oral History Center; interview with Sister Anna Marie Weinreis.

37. Elizabeth M. Jamieson, Mary F. Sewall, and Eleanor B. Suhrie, *Trends in Nursing History: Their Social, International, and Ethical Relationships* (Philadelphia: W. B. Saunders, 1966), 311–12; interview with Sister Mary Eleanor Joyce, Aug. 12, 1976, South Dakota Oral History Center; *Aberdeen American News*, May 2, 1976; *Outline*, Winter 1975; interview with Sister JoAnn Sturzl.

38. Interview with Sister Frances Mary Dunn.

39. Interview with Sister Frances Mary Dunn; interview with Sister Anthony Dempsey.

40. Interview with Sister Frances Mary Dunn; *Aberdeen American News*, May 2, 1976.

41. Sister Di Donato, "A History of the Educational Work of the Presentation Sisters," 116; interview with Sister Francelle Clarke, Aug. 13, 1976, South Dakota Oral History Center.

42. Interview with Sister Anna Marie Weinreis.

43. Interview with Sister Mary Eleanor Joyce; interview with Sister Anna Marie Weinreis; interview with Sister Francelle Clark.

44. *Presentation College Catalog*, 24–26. For a reference to trends in higher education, see Brubacher and Rudy, *Higher Education in Transition*, 272; Sister Marie Patrice Moriarty, P.B.V.M., "A Feasibility Study of Adopting a Program of Interdisciplinary General Education for a Two-Year College Curriculum at Presentation College, Aberdeen, South Dakota" (Ed.D. diss., Lawrence University, 1973), 13, 30-32.

45. Sister Moriarty, "A Feasibility Study," 90, 101.

46. Ibid., 93, 106.

47. Interview with Sister Alicia Dunphy; interview with Sister Anna Marie Weinreis.

48. Interview with Sister Alicia Dunphy; interview with Sister Marie Patrice Moriarty; interview with Sister Mary Eleanor Joyce; interview with Sister Frances Mary Dunn; interview with Sister Veronica Ogden, Aug. 13, 1976, South Dakota Oral History Center; *Presentation College Catalog*, 3–4; "Presentation College Catalog Supplement"; *Outline*, Winter 1975; Parnell and Peltason, eds., *American Community, Technical and Junior Colleges*, 647.

49. *Presentation College Catalog*, 2.

7. Another Arena for Professional Growth and Conflict: The Health Care Apostolate, 1901–85

□

When the tragedy of a diphtheria epidemic struck South Dakota in the early 1900s, the Presentations were literally and spiritually called to tend the afflicted. Consequently, the sisters became interested in establishing and staffing hospitals and so entered an administrative field already occupied by other nuns and some physicians since the nineteenth century. By 1925, most doctors had bequeathed hospital administration to an emergent cadre of health care managers, but women religious remained in charge of many Catholic hospitals, retaining what was to many a man's job.[1] Once again the Presentations and other apostolic nuns based their somewhat innovative behavior on traditional ideological tenets. "To do the best possible job, a hospital must meet constantly changing demands; equipment, medications, and methods must be revised frequently. In complying with these forces, the hospital staff [members] has a higher purpose to guide them; namely, service to man for the love of God."[2] Elaborating on this mission, Bishop William Brady wrote in 1948 that "Catholic hospitals are called charitable institutions . . . because the staff[s] . . . are pledged to serve every patient as if the patient were Christ Himself."[3] In pursuit of this goal, Presentation health care leaders made strong bonds with clients, state and federal government authorities, and the church whose interests the nuns served; however, by the 1960s, these managers, like their educator colleagues, found that the very process of professionalizing—constructing buildings, establishing programs, balancing budgets, raising money, striving to make autonomous decisions, and complying with a variety

164

of client and governmental expectations—had diverted their attention from the order's original focus. Eventually, they resolved their feelings of loss by hiring institutional managers. The nuns thus were freed to become hospital ministers and remained active policymakers, founding new health care programs and outreach agencies and maintaining professional contacts with colleagues throughout the state and nation.[4]

Aberdeen residents and settlers in surrounding areas were the first to receive Presentation health care. There had been a county hospital in the town in the 1880s, but because its financial status was not secure, it had operated only a few years before closing. Records show the existence of a small, short-lived Good Samaritan Hospital in operation during the early years of the twentieth century, but in general Aberdeen's growing population suffered from a shortage of medical services.[5]

It was fortunate coincidence that a new Presentation candidate arrived in South Dakota early in the century and introduced the sisters to nursing. She was Sister Dominic Boysen (Charlotte Boysen), a graduate nurse from Winona, Minnesota. In 1900, her training and ability proved invaluable to the order and to the Aberdeen citizens who were victims of a diphtheria epidemic that struck the Northern Great Plains only a few months after her arrival. The city was totally unprepared for such an emergency, so the Presentations offered part of their convent for use as a temporary hospital. Sister Boysen supervised the other nuns who took care of patients, and city leaders soon commended their efforts. Once the crisis had passed, Father Robert Haire (still pastor of Sacred Heart Parish), Mayor J. E. Adams, Dr. H. J. Rock, and the Presentation Sisters realized that a permanent hospital was essential. Recognizing the nuns' abilities and that Nano Nagle herself had visited the sick, Mother Joseph Butler and her council therefore resolved to establish a medical facility.[6]

Several obstacles were removed so that the women could commit themselves to the new venture. First, the Presentations sought Church approval for their decision to enter health care as an apostolate. Mother Butler worked with Bishop Thomas O'Gorman of the Sioux Falls Diocese to win the necessary sanctions from the Holy See for the change in the order's structure.[7] Then the order's revised constitution in 1946 officially sanctioned the development of nursing education as an agent of professionalization for the Presentations' new apostolate, stating that the "Sisters assigned to the care of the sick shall have special and careful preparation for their duties so that their labors may insure both the temporal and the spiritual welfare of their patients."[8]

Despite early groundwork and aspirations, initially the sisters did not possess sufficient funds to finance the construction of a hospital, and no aid was forthcoming from diocesan headquarters. Mother Butler obtained a loan from Isaac Lincoln, president of a local bank, to underwrite the building of a fifteen-bed facility to be called St. Luke's Hospital. She served as its first administrator when it opened to the public in 1901.[9] Steve Palank, a young Austria-Hungarian immigrant who worked at St. Luke's during the early days, remembered that "Mother Joseph was very kind . . . and fair . . . ." She was also "strict . . . and would not tolerate dishonesty."[10] Immediately the sisters began using the facility to provide training for future Presentation nurses, initiating a hospital-based program with Sister Boyson as supervisor. The first class enrolled three Presentations. When Father Robert Haire rededicated himself to religious rather than political life a year after St. Luke's opened, Bishop Thomas O'Gorman reinstated him and assigned the priest to the chaplaincy at St. Luke's. There he stayed, offering spiritual comfort and support to his old friends the Presentations until he died in 1916.[11]

Armed with an educational program, health care services, and religious reinforcement, the major thrust during St. Luke's first forty years concerned expansion of facilities and services. In 1902, Sacred Heart Church published an article for the parish's official yearbook describing the hospital's original physical plant and procedures for admittance. The attitudes expressed therein were quite progressive and ecumenical:

> It possesses all advantages of gas and city water. The Hospital is a three story building and basement, substantially built of brick and . . . Kesota stone. The floors . . . are doubled, with a layer of heavy felt to guard against transmission of noise. On the third floor are operating and sterilizing rooms, the boiler and ventilating systems are perfect. Everything pertaining to the comfort and convenience of the patient has been considered; bath and toilet rooms, electric call bells, telephone and elevator . . . . The Hospital has no medical or surgical staff, it is open to all reputable physi-

cians who may desire to have their patients treated in the hospital. Should patients come who are not recommended by any physician they must abide by the decision of the Board of Directors . . . . Patients are admitted irrespective of religious belief and all are assured the same treatment without regard to creed or color. All clergymen have free access at all times to patients of their denominations. . . . Accommodations in the Hospital to either medical or surgical patients range from $6.00 to $12.00 per week, according to location of the room.[12]

The hospital project proved such a success that in just a few years the original building became inadequate, requiring the nuns to build a new addition in 1908; however, the institution was still quite primitive by modern standards. There existed no electric lights (electricity was added in 1912), the elevator was operated by hand, and physicians traveled to and from work by horse and buggy. As St. Luke's grew, Aberdeen also grew in population and became a regional railroad center, with twenty-four passenger trains arriving daily. Disasters such as the flu epidemic of 1918 and 1919 and outbreaks of typhoid, smallpox, and other forms of influenza put the hospital additions to good use.[13]

St. Luke's was approved in 1919 by the American College of Surgeons, which had begun an accrediting service in 1913. The American Medical Association accredited the hospital in 1924. During Mother Agatha Collins's term as superior, the American College of Surgeons apparently reevaluated the institution and then concluded that the original structure had become obsolete. Disturbed by the monumental task of completely rebuilding the structure, Mother Collins and Sister M. Monica Parkinson (St. Luke's chief administrator) nevertheless complied with the accreditation agency's mandate. In 1926, the order razed the original hospital, made a nuns' residence out of the earlier additions, and built an all new hospital that was completed in 1928.[14] Sister Cabrini Di Donato praised the new facility: "The modern, fireproof, five-story, concrete, steel and brick structure was large enough to accommodate one hundred and twenty-five patients. Its medical surgical, obstetrical, pediatric, physiotherapy, and nutritional departments were fitted with the most modern equipment."[15]

As their hospital grew, so grew the Presentation's involvement in any number of health care fields, not only in numbers of nuns, but also in the extent of their professionalization. Because their responsibilities involved life-and-death matters, these Presentations necessarily became part of the scientific era of modernization and change, their nursing services and the medical staff's qualifications expanding to meet burgeoning patient needs. The community's involvement grew, also. Aberdeen needed the hospital, which in turn required the community's financial support. Aberdeen citizens formed an auxiliary association headed by physicians' spouses. The primary task of the organization was to raise money to pay for the care of financially indigent hospital patients.[16]

Because of what seemed to be an unending demand for quality health care, in 1940 the Presentations again needed more room at St. Luke's. Mother Raphael McCarthy, superior of the order since 1932, realized that new construction would severely weaken the community's pecuniary status, so she decided to purchase a suitable building instead. She and Sister M. Cornelia Swanton, St. Luke's administrator, selected one located ten blocks from St. Luke's, a four-and-one-half-story brick-and-concrete structure, formerly the short-lived Lincoln Hospital. In September of 1940, Mother McCarthy had it moved and placed adjacent to St. Luke's. Although many people believed that the five-thousand-ton edifice could not be relocated without crumbling, the structure incurred only limited damage when workers transferred it. When refurbished and refurnished, it became an eighty-bed medical annex located across the street and north of the main hospital building. The two were connected only by a tunnel until 1947, when a covered crosswalk was completed.[17]

Adding to the hospital proved to be an insightful move because during the 1940s and 1950s the Presentations were better able to meet the inordinate health care demands of a country coping with accelerating technological change. In 1948, Doctor Paul V. McCarthy, diplomate of the American Board of Radiology, and Sister Gertrude Nemers and Nelda Cronk, both registered technicians, opened the St. Luke's School of X-Ray Technology. The Council of Medical Education, a branch of the American Medical Association, approved the program in 1950 (Table 9). A year before, Doctor A. J. Miller and Sister M. Veronica Ogden opened the St. Luke's School of Medical Technology, and that year the American Medical Asso-

TABLE 9 ST. LUKE'S SCHOOL OF X-RAY TECHNOLOGY

Objectives

1. To develop in the student sound principles of Christian living
2. To inculcate ethical principles involved in X-ray technology
3. To teach the importance of the technician's relationship with other members of the medical team and with the patient as the primary focus
4. To assist the student in the acquisition of knowledge and technical skills necessary to the practice of their profession
5. To prepare the student to assume responsibility to function effectively as a graduate X-ray technician

Curriculum

Subject	Hours
Anatomy and physiology	100
History of the x-ray	5
Ethics	8
Darkroom chemistry	13
Elements of technique	20
X-ray therapy	9
Special procedure	14
Radiographic physics	25
Medical terminology	11
Radiation protection	6
Standard positioning	39
Office procedures	10
Nursing procedures in radiology	5
Department administration	5
Electrical physics	40
Isotopes	12
Radiologist instructions	15
Elective	72
Total	409 hours

Source: Sister Di Donato, "A History of the Educational Work of the Presentation Sisters," 72–73. Table edited slightly.

ciation for the training of laboratory technicians accredited the school. Its students could take affiliated classes at Northern State Teachers College and receive a bachelor of science degree in medical technology. During the 1950s, a new agency, the Joint Commission on Accreditation of Hospitals, began its work and, because of St. Luke's success, officially approved the entire hospital operation in 1956.[18]

In the wake of their initial success in establishing and administering St. Luke's, the Presentations had built, opened, and were running three more hospitals by 1911. The first of these was St. Joseph Hospital in Mitchell, South Dakota. Beginning in 1906, a group consisting of Dr. Byron A. Bobb and several of the city's inhabitants, impressed with the sisters' work at Notre Dame Academy and St. Luke's, appealed to Mother Butler for help in establishing an area hospital. Mitchell residents were in dire need of a health care facility because physicians and nurses had to travel long distances to practice medicine in rural areas and in the homes of small-town residents living within commuting distance of Mitchell. They performed surgery on kitchen tables and often received food as payment for their services.[19]

In response to the requests, Mother Butler and the Presentations decided to found and direct another hospital. The venture's first and almost perennial obstacle, the lack of money, was overcome by a skillfully orchestrated drive: a citizens' league sold bonds, the sisters borrowed an additional $20,000, and local business leaders donated several lots in the eastern part of Mitchell on which a four-story building would eventually stand. Sister M. Anthony Murphy, who became St. Joseph's first Presentation superintendent, remembered that while she and two other nuns—Sister Margaret Mary Grainger (a registered nurse) and Sister Paul Conroy—were making beds and organizing the rooms, a man offered to help them. The nuns later found out that their handyman was Dr. Bobb. His actions suggested that a holistic definition of professionalism existed for some early South Dakota physicians. Throughout the twentieth century, the Presentations have attempted to maintain this attitude within themselves and the other professionals with whom they have worked, although some scholars of medical history have pointed out that many contemporary American doctors have lost their caring skills. A labor of love and financial acumen, St. Joseph Hospital opened in November 1906, with a capacity of thirty beds. Local residents continued to assist the nuns by contributing linens, towels, and small amounts of money to be used to purchase furnishings. Five sisters comprised the original staff, and they opened a school of nursing during their first year.[20]

Problems did arise, but the years on the Great Plains frontier had taught the Presentations resourceful survival skills. When the first water supply proved unusable because of its high degree of rust, the women requested that the hospital custodian prepare a soft water system from steam in the boiler room. Presentation administrators also transported barrels of water from a farm well a short distance outside town. Moreover, most of the patients' food originated in a hospital greenhouse, chicken coop, and garden run by the younger sisters who tended the crops and gathered eggs as part of their daily routine.[21]

St. Joseph Hospital, like St. Luke's, experienced steady growth for many years, from one hundred persons admitted in 1907 to more than one thousand in 1921. Surprisingly, this occurred even though in the late 1910s some local promoters built a second facility, Methodist Hospital. A driving force behind St. Joseph was Dr. William A. Delaney, a Catholic physician whom the Presentations had recruited in 1910. Although according to one nun he and Mother McCarthy "could fight like the dickens" over day-to-day operational decisions, by and large Delaney received enthusiastic support from the nuns with whom he worked. The physician even helped plant trees and shrubbery on the hospital grounds. He and Father John Brady of Holy Family Parish also raised money so that the Presentations could pay off the old debt and expand the facility. To complete the funding, the Presentations then raised $225,000, and a Catholic women's group donated more than $4,000 to pay for new furnishings.[22]

The addition was dedicated in September of 1922. Creating a significant news story for Mitchell, the health care facility was described in detail in a *Mitchell Daily Republic* article: "The fireproof, soundproof structure contained four stories and a basement. The basement housed the kitchen, some classrooms, and two isolation areas. The first floor held offices, a lobby, several private enclosures, a diet kitchen, and sun parlors. The second floor had private and semi-private rooms, and the third level was devoted to nursery and obstetrics care. Operating and anesthetizing departments, as well as x-ray, bacteriology, and pathology laboratories, occupied the top story. Features included only in the most modern hospitals during the 1920s were a switchboard, telephones in private rooms, an electric elevator, and fireproof stairways."[23] So complete was the new facility that the sisters converted the old building into a nurses' residence. By 1921, the hospital, with eighty-five beds and eighteen bassinets, measured 5,500 square feet.[24]

Throughout the next two decades St. Joseph expanded and developed as a result of the fourteen- and sixteen-hour days that Presentation managers devoted to their jobs. Sister Monica Parkinson, one former administrator, remembered that she even visited the critically ill patients when she was not taking care of office emergencies. Such efforts reaped rewards when in 1932 the facility received approval from the American College of Surgeons, the American Medical Association, the Catholic Hospital Association, the South Dakota Hospital Association, and gained membership in the American Hospital Association. Five years later the nuns completed additions of a new chapel, classrooms, and an isolation unit. With Mother Raphael McCarthy as superior of St. Joseph for the second time, in 1946 the nuns added an east wing, which made the institution into a 145-bed facility. Nine years later, the hospital again received full accreditation from the Joint Commission of Hospital Accreditation.[25]

In 1910, the Presentation order assumed authority over another hospital in Miles City, Montana. A year earlier two missionary priests from eastern South Dakota, vacationing in Montana, had met Father John O'Carroll of Miles City. Father O'Carroll had been trying to find a congregation of women to deliver health care in Miles City as a supplement to the county hospital. The missionaries told him of the Presentations' success with St. Luke's and St. Joseph, so Father O'Carroll traveled to Aberdeen to speak with Mother Butler and ask her to manage a county hospital, later named Holy Rosary. At the same time, Milwaukee Railroad Company officials became concerned that the existing hospital in Miles City was insufficient for a town that was rapidly becoming a large railroad center. Dr. A. I. Bouffleur, a surgeon for the firm, also took his own delegation to Aberdeen to petition Mother Butler, who agreed to undertake the hospital venture. Bishop Mathias C. Lenihan of Great Falls welcomed the order's decision to begin working in the diocese because he, too, realized that the Miles City area was sorely in need of good health care. Thus, in August of 1910 the commissioners of Custer County, Montana, transferred management of the county hospital to the Presentation Sisters. Sister M. Anthony Murphy was the hospital's

first administrator, and Sisters M. Michael O'Brien, M. Ursula Con-
roy, and M. Monica Parkinson worked under her. The order wasted
no time purchasing Miles City land on which to augment the old
physical plant. They renamed the institution Holy Rosary.[26]

Although management of the county building was transferred
speedily, ownership was delayed. The women had to lease Holy
Rosary for several years because the county, not they, had sold bonds
to finance construction. Finally in 1919 the Presentations became
the official proprietors after purchasing the institution from the county
for $25,000. By then, generous patrons and cooperative physicians
had helped improve the hospital until many professionals rated it
as highly as hospitals in metropolitan areas. Indeed, in 1919, Holy
Rosary received recognition from the American College of Surgeons.
Three years later the nuns added on to the building, making it an
eighty-five-bed hospital with more modern medical and surgical
units.[27]

After a decade of expansion, the hospital entered several trying
years as the Great Depression devastated Montana. The state's fifteen Catholic hospitals attempted to give each other moral support,
forming in 1932 the Catholic Hospital Association, an affiliate of
the national organization of the same name. Drought and crop failure
ruined many ranchers, who were forced to ship their cattle and sheep
to other states to feed. Private donations fell off completely, and
Holy Rosary's deficit grew at an alarming rate. Consequently, the
nuns asked Bishop Edwin V. O'Hara, then bishop of the Great Falls
Diocese, for permission to liquidate their interest in Holy Rosary.
Although he could give the nuns no financial assistance, O'Hara
encouraged them to hold on just as their predecessors had persevered
earlier. Thus, the Presentations of Holy Rosary reached deeply within
their hearts and memories, unearthed that pioneer commitment to
survive, and convinced bankers not to foreclose. Finally, in 1939,
the Presentations were solvent enough again to meet their major
financial obligations, although problems with crowded conditions
and personnel shortages would plague hospital managers in the years
to come. Under Mother M. Viator Burns, Sister M. Fanahan Casey
and others began conceptualizing plans for an addition to and ren-
ovation of Holy Rosary. The improved structure was finished in
1950 at a cost of $1,500,000.[28]

In 1911, just one year after assuming control of Holy Rosary, the Presentations founded McKennan in Sioux Falls, their fourth and final hospital. That year Helen McKennan, a resident of Sioux Falls, died, bequeathing $25,000 in trust to the city for the founding of a hospital. McKennan had asked for the "construction and equipment of a public hospital within the city limits of . . . Sioux Falls . . . according to such plans as may be adopted by them [the trustees] and their successors."[29] The city commissioners and local doctors sought Bishop O'Gorman's assistance in securing an order to operate the hospital, and Bishop O'Gorman asked the Presentations to take on the task, which apparently was not easy because another hospital, Sioux Valley, had been located in Sioux Falls since 1896. The first Presentation health care team consisted of Sister M. Agatha Collins, superior and chief administrator, Sister M. Rose McCormick, an anesthetist, and Sister M. Magdalene Murphy, a dietician. Although details are not available, the competition emerging between the two institutions, one secular and the other religious, proved to be a source of tension within the local health care community. Yet another participant was added during the late 1930s, after the Marianhill Fathers abandoned their seminary (formerly Columbus College) to the federal government, which then converted it into a veterans' hospital.[30]

Truly from the first, McKennan Hospital had a distinct identity: in accord with the Presentations' mission, Helen McKennan's will further asserted that the hospital admit charity patients. Furthermore, although the institution could receive gifts of money and property, the operation would be strictly nonprofit. In assuming their new responsibility, the nuns borrowed more than $100,000 to complete the forty-five-bed building and opened in December 1911. Putting finishing touches on the project, Helen McKennan's attorneys vested controlling interest in the hospital with McKennan Hospital, Incorporated, an entity composed of Mother Butler, Dr. L. Edwin Perkins, and the will's trustees.[31]

Like the other three hospitals under Presentation auspices, McKennan experienced steady growth in its early years as it responded to both everyday and extraordinary public needs. According to one observer, Sister Collins's "kindly and friendly disposition and her keen business mind played an important part in . . . [McKennan's success] and [in] . . . endearing it to the people of Sioux Falls." Sister

Collins supervised the building of another section in 1919, bringing the hospital to 131 beds, double its original size.[32]

One of Sister Collins's major problems as chief administrator was the national influenza epidemic of 1918 and 1919. Sioux Falls was particularly hard hit because it was the largest city in South Dakota. Although the greatest number of afflicted people recovered at home, McKennan recorded 173 hospitalized cases. The illness attacked the patient's respiratory system, and sometimes caused death within three or four days. In the summer of 1918, rainy, cold weather only aggravated the outbreak, which lasted until March the following year. Further problems took place because many local doctors were still engaged in overseas military service connected with World War I. The existing staff was faced with a hospital so crowded that beds were set up in corridors and in all other areas where space was available, and the higher than usual death rate severely taxed the city's mortuary facilities.[33]

With the catastrophe's passing, several changes took place from 1919 to 1943 at McKennan. A reorganization of the hospital corporation made borrowing money possible; the Massachusetts Life Insurance Company agreed to underwrite the hospital (for $235,000) through the Presentation order. Because the women already owned several other hospitals, they were qualified financially to assume another large debt. As a result of the transaction, in 1925, hospital administrators established Presentation Sisters, Incorporated, a body that officially ran the hospital. Sister Raphael McCarthy, who ran the hospital from 1927 to 1932, oversaw two major additions and renovations that included a new chapel, chaplain's quarters, and more office space. However, during the depression it became almost impossible for the institution to make payments on the hospital's note, so the sisters asked for a reduction in interest rates, which their lending agency granted. By the early years of World War II, the hospital was fiscally stable and had reached a capacity of 185 beds.[34]

These and other efforts to economize made the hospital a success. According to Bishop Lambert Hoch, who was the McKennan chaplain during the 1930s and 40s before becoming Bishop of Sioux Falls, the nuns worked day and night for no remuneration to speak of: "They didn't know what a forty-hour week meant."[35] Mother McCarthy found other ways to save funds by asking Father Hoch to use his mechanical and technical expertise to find ways of cutting energy costs. As a result they brought the heating bill down one year from $12,000 to $4,000. The sisters' cash outlay had been minimal because of nonexistent sister salaries and no amortization of expenses (depreciation of the physical plant), so during the 1940s the nuns found that they had few recorded expenses that could be used as documentation for federal rebates on military families' maternity cases. Thus the nuns changed their bookkeeping methods, enabling them to receive federal money.[36]

Even with federal help, during World War II all four hospitals that the Presentation Sisters owned continued to experience monetary, space, and staffing problems. In an attempt to stay abreast of national colleagues' remedies to these dilemmas, convent superiors and other sisters involved in running the order's hospitals attended national professional meetings. For example, in 1941, Mother McCarthy and Sister Viator Burns attended the American Hospital Meeting in Atlantic City. Sister Burns was an official representative of the South Dakota Hospital Association, and, as noted earlier, after retiring as superior, Mother McCarthy took the job of chief administrator of St. Joseph from 1946 to 1952. Then, acting as the convent's chief executive, Mother Burns kept up with all the workings of state agencies that controlled federal health care allotments.[37] To further insure Presentation hospitals' economic future, she wrote Bishop Brady in 1947 to request "a Public Relations man, who would . . . represent us at civic meetings, clubs, and other public affairs."[38] Presentation managers also helped plan the South Dakota Catholic Hospital Association, a capstone of the nuns' effort to professionalize and make their health care centers fiscally sound. Essentially, the organization's purpose was "to exchange information that will be of common interest . . . [and] to form a group ready for united action, whenever united action may be of value for our hospitals, the church or our country."[39]

In the spirit of this organization the Presentations decided on two solutions to counteract the shortage of doctors and nurses during World War II—both plans relying on the secular world for support. First, to increase the supply of nurses, the nuns' hospitals participated in the United States Cadet Nurse Corps program. This plan awarded full scholarships to female nursing students, who in return would become available for military or other federal service for the

176

duration of the war. Second, attempting to solve further personnel problems, the Presentation managers also cooperated with organizations designed to assist nurses—such as the American Red Cross Gray Ladies and Nurses' Aides—and in so doing aided the professionalization of the hospitals' nursing staffs. Assistants who were provided under these programs were often former nurses themselves who would leave their duties as full-time homemakers to return to hospitals. They visited patients, sometimes writing letters for them and reading to those who were unable. By performing these duties and the housekeeping chores that student nurses had done previously, they helped center the latter's educational program around more academic concerns. The aides proved so valuable that once the war was over Presentation hospitals continued to train assistants, paying them regular salaries to do the routine work that Red Cross volunteers had done so well. To insure the utmost efficiency, the nursing schools of all four institutions were centralized into one operation.[40]

Dealing with and solving other novel problems, Holy Rosary at Miles City became involved in potentially controversial war-related activities. German soldiers who were captives in a nearby prisoner-of-war camp situated at the Custer County fairgrounds worked in the beet fields near the sisters' hospital. The nuns' professional dedication to healing encouraged them to provide the internment facility with medical care and supplies, a job that involved them in a dramatic incident. One morning as prisoners were transported to the fields by truck, the vehicle swerved off the road and overturned, injuring more than twenty men. Many of them fell down a forty-foot embankment and had to be rushed to the hospital for treatment. Attention to their wounds had been so professionally administered that after the war several of the Germans returned to the town to show their gratitude.[41]

Large-scale emergencies were not rare events for Holy Rosary. Because Miles City was a railroad center, catastrophes involving trains occasionally took place, requiring the Presentations' cool-headed skills. One disaster occurred in 1938 during a rainstorm that had washed away part of a track. Several victims died, and seventy-seven of the 132 survivors were hospitalized at Holy Rosary. Another train wreck occurred in 1943 and proved to be even more taxing than had the previous one, as more than nine hundred passengers had to be examined and treated, most on an outpatient basis. Even so, all available bed space in the hospital became occupied, so some victims had to be attended in chairs. Again relying on community solidarity, the nuns accepted help from volunteers to process these patients. As a result, the hospital cared for the more than seventy passengers who were seriously hurt and for the 150 who experienced minor injuries. In part because of their civil defense training, the Presentation hospital officials and staff proved equal to the emergency.[42]

Soon after the war ended, the nuns' hospitals responded once again to a health hazard of epidemic proportions: poliomyelitis. Fortunately, St. Luke's was one of the few hospitals on the northern Great Plains to be supplied with the latest equipment and to use the latest methods. As a member of the National Foundation for Infantile Paralysis, it possessed polio emergency quarters and was able to solicit aid from the Red Cross and other volunteer associations. In 1946, more than one hundred persons were treated for the disease. Most of them recovered completely, often with the help of an iron lung, hydromassage tanks, and pack heaters. Two years later the National Foundation for Infantile Paralysis selected St. Luke's as a site for a permanent polio clinic. Local doctors studied the crippling disease, and Mother McCarthy worked with nearby Northern State Teachers College to arrange a study schedule so that youthful patients could keep up with their school work. In addition, a specialist from Denver, Dr. I. E. Hendryson, organized a therapeutic clinic; visiting monthly, he worked with therapists who studied curative methods for the victims.[43]

Presentation hospital policymakers also took advantage of the Hill-Burton Amendment to the National Hospital Survey and Construction Act passed in 1945, as well as Public Law 380 passed in 1945 and 1949. The latter legislation released federal funds for the construction of hospitals through June 1955. The 1949 measure also increased the government's share of costs from approximately 30 percent to 50 percent of a given project.[44] Specifically, it allowed "grants-in-aid for construction of hospital[s], [and] help[ed] local communities . . . obtain facilities fundamental not only to the provision of necessary care but also to the development of local health programs generally." Legislators hoped also to encourage regional coordination of hospitals to provide smaller institutions with interns, radiology, consultation specialists, and administrative programs. Encouraging this, the legislation instructed the surgeon general to authorize research money for projects made in the interest of coordinating these regional hospital systems. The result was that many nonprofit and county hospitals that could not afford the earlier one-third federal subsidy now found the new level within their reach.[45]

During the mid-1950s, three of the Presentation facilities received additional financial assistance in the form of Ford Foundation gifts, which enabled the sisters to continue expansion. At St. Joseph, the sisters built a 2,600-square-foot addition in 1951, bringing the hospital's total to 81,000 square feet. St. Luke's, St. Joseph, and McKennan received grants from a $200,000,000 award given to 3,550 private hospitals. Such opportunities, extended several times in the 1950s and 1960s, made growth and recognition easier than ever before. McKennan received full recognition from the Joint Commission on Accreditation for hospitals in 1954.[46]

The recognition proved the beginning of a new era of building for McKennan. The fund-raising strategy that the sisters used there had become their standard procedure. With local business people and doctors, they raised $400,000, secured a mortgage loan that totaled $550,000, and received other pledges of $380,000 to fund the construction of a new hospital wing. The federal government awarded McKennan two Hill-Burton grants totaling $285,000, and, culminating the fund drive, the Ford Foundation donated approximately another $97,000. The addition was completed in 1957, a year before Mother Burns ended her term as superior of the order and became McKennan's chief executive. Included in the new facility under her direction was a psychiatric ward, which brought the hospital's total capacity to 264 beds and forty bassinets. An eleven-bed addition was added in 1960.[47]

The capacity and number of patients that each Presentation hospital treated in 1966 are listed in Table 10, and an example of the composition of staffs at each hospital lies in a sample from St. Luke's during the mid-1960s (Table 11). The fourteen nuns out of a total thirty-seven employees marked a larger number of religious at St. Luke's than at the other Presentation hospitals. St. Luke's was, however, the second largest Presentation hospital and, given the

179

TABLE 10. PRESENTATION HOSPITAL CAPACITIES, 1964–65

Hospital	Year Founded	Location	No. of Sisters	No. of Beds	Number of In-patients	Number of Out-patients
St. Luke's	1900	Aberdeen, S.D.	30	225	9,869	9,600
St. Joseph	1960	Mitchell, S.D.	15	140	3,847	4,510
Holy Rosary	1910	Miles City, Mont.	18	121	4,044	1,696
McKennan	1911	Sioux Falls, S.D.	22	280	12,110	14,763

Source: Sister Di Donato, "A History of the Educational Work of the Presentation Sisters," 206.

accelerating demands for educational and health care experts, it is remarkable that the nuns were able to extend themselves as far as they did.[48]

Thus, all four Presentation hospitals developed a variety of health care training programs in conjunction with the nursing schools, Presentation College, and other four-year higher educational institutions. Together they had real practical worth as well as altruistic value to the sisters, assuring them the availability of a labor supply for their facilities because many students were likely to settle in the region in which they received training. As early as 1947, the American Medical Association had approved McKennan to prepare interns for general practice. They studied surgery, orthopedics, obstetrics, gynecology, urology, pediatrics, radiology, and pathology, all on a rotating system. Other courses of study filled the list for x-ray technicians, medical technologists, laboratory technicians, and physical therapists. The McKennan School of Medical Technology was affiliated with the University of South Dakota and offered a twelve-month internship after one earned sixty semester hours of college credit.[49]

Despite the growth, during the 1950s some financial problems threatened to close Holy Rosary. In order to rescue the institution, Mother McCullough assigned the seasoned Mother McCarthy as the institution's chief administrator in 1958. Her job of keeping the facility open would be difficult because of a building debt that was incurred after World War II to offset construction costs and other expenses and that totaled $65,000 by 1958. Relying on her fund-raising skills, Mother McCarthy called on local friends of Holy Rosary, who then organized a fund drive through which they raised

TABLE 11. PERSONNEL OF ST. LUKE'S HOSPITAL, ABERDEEN, 1964–65

Marjorie Aadland, head nurse in surgery—R.N.
Lyle Anderson, pharmacist—B.S. in pharmacy
Jeanette Arlt, asst. director of nursing—R.N.
Neal Auble, director of anesthesia—C.R.N.A., B.S.
Sister M. Jeanne Bauhs, x-ray supervisor—R.T.
Harold E. Brady, administrator—M.S.W.
Barbara Busch, annex night supervisor—R.N.
Sister M. Aurelia Cronin, head nurse in central supply—R.N.
Cecilia Dahlmeier, psychiatric nursing—R.N., M.S.
Sister M. Denis Dauven, business manager
Sister M. Jude Deis, culinary department
Marguarite Dorman, head nurse—R.N.
Dean Driscoll, chief engineer—B.S. in Engineering
Sister M. Benita Engelhart, director of medical records—R.R.L., B.S.
Sister M. Evarista, supervisor in surgery—R.N.
Sister M. Fanahan, night house supervisor—R.N., C.R.N.A.
Helen Fleming, head nurse on surgical floor—R.N.
Sister M. Agnes Foley, head nurse on medical floor—R.N.
Sister M. Alacoque Geppert, director of physical therapy—B.S.
Phyllis Gloss, head nurse on medical floor—R.N.
Opal Hild, head nurse on urology floor—R.N.
Mary J. Hixson, director of nursing—R.N., B.S.
Daniel Kraft, special training in inhalation therapy, E.E.G. technician
Lavonne Maurseth, relief house supervisor—R.N.
Paul V. McCarthy, M.D.—Radiologist
Rosamond Perrizo, head nurse on E.E.N.T. unit—R.N.
Sister M. Declan Regan, laundry supervisor
Sister M. Richard, religious superior—R.N., M.S.N.
Sister M. Marcia Scheele, head nurse on orthopedic unit—R.N.
Ramona Schumaker, medical coordinator—R.N.
Judith Seyer, head nurse in pediatrics—R.N.
Marjorie Sheppard, head nurse on acute care unit—R.N.
Sister M. Alma Staudenraus, dietitian—B.S.
William T. Sweeny, M.D.—pathologist
Frances Walz, supervisor on O.B. unit—R.N.
Harold Walz, director of housekeeping and sanitation
Sister M. Joachim White, laboratory supervisor—R.T., A.S.C.P, B.A.

Sister Di Donato, "A History of the Educational Work of the Presentation Sisters," 174.

$70,000 to pay the bill and put the hospital on a more secure footing than it had been on since before the depression.[50]

Other more contemporary health care related projects included the development and operation of four facilities for the aged: two nursing homes, one hospital ward for the Presentations, and one retirement community for the diocese of Sioux Falls. Both completed in 1961 and open to Catholics and non-Catholics alike, Brady Memorial Home in Mitchell and Mother Joseph Manor in Aberdeen resulted as part of a drive throughout South Dakota to improve conditions for the aged. Each of the nursing homes contained dining, cleaning, and recreation facilities, as well as physical and occupational therapy departments. To make the new facilities operational, as managers of the homes the Presentation order hired qualified nuns and lay people to serve as nurses, aides, cooks, resident-services directors, and therapists. During the mid-1960s, eight Presentations served on the staff of Brady Memorial, which accommodated fifty-nine clients. Eight more of the nuns worked at Mother Joseph Manor, which housed and cared for fifty-seven persons. During Mother Myron Martin's term as superior from 1964 to 1974, the medical annex at St. Luke's was transferred to the Presentation Sisters and renamed Lourdes Hall, providing rooms for sisters under long-term medical care. By 1985, construction had begun on Prince of Peace Retirement Community in Sioux Falls.[51]

Assisting the first two centers for the elderly, some budget money came from patients' fees, by 1976 a little more than $20 per day from each patient, but the need for government subsidies led the Presentations to accept the government's supervisory role, an indication of secular society's ever-constant presence in the sisters' professional lives. Because federal grants through Hill-Burton legislation had built both centers, the women came under regulation from the Department of Health, Education, and Welfare. To better deal with the federal agency, the Presentations reorganized their corporate structure and made the nursing homes into top quality geriatric centers employing nurses around the clock. Consequently, Brady Memorial and Mother Joseph Manor received high federal government ratings, while the clients and their families also appreciated the clean, professional, and caring atmosphere that the sisters provided.[52]

Complying further with national government regulations, Presentation officials cooperated with the 1960s' Medicare and Medicaid legislation guidelines so that their patients could receive benefits. Before those procedures were established, federal reimbursement to Presentation hospitals had been confined chiefly to Hill-Burton funds; but by the 1970s that had changed. For example, nearly 50 percent of St. Luke's operating costs then came from government sources, and 52 percent of the patients received Medicare or Medicaid subsidies. The National Health Planning and Resources Development Act of 1974 established a board to survey professional standards, health needs, and cost-containment procedures, and during the 1980s each state was to develop a long-range scheme that the state health department was to supervise. To insure that health care operations actually met the needs of the population, a certificate of need was required before the nuns could undertake any hospital additions costing more than $150,000.[53]

It is ironic that the external support that had facilitated Presentation institution building eventually dampened and threatened to extinguish the administrators' ideological fervor, the same zeal that initially had motivated their professional ambitions. Although the order as a whole and certain individuals in particular continued to claim ultimate control over hospital policy, by 1970 each hospital had acquired a lay person to function as director. Many of the sisters were glad to relinquish that administrative position, which they claimed was routine and uninspiring.[54] Some of the older, more conservative sisters even reasoned that as long as the order remained ideologically in control, the world of finance and business really belonged within the male domain. One such woman, Sister Bonaventure Hoffman, explained that she always felt her job had been "a position for a man, because a man . . . is able to go out and make . . . contacts. . . . Many policies are formulated in hotel rooms with men . . . . Well, that was no place for a woman, let alone a sister."[55]

The case of Sister Mary Stephen Davis, chief administrator of St. Luke's from 1958 to 1964, illustrates the emotional drain on anyone, man or woman, whose central purpose was to maintain high policymaking ideals but who can become detrimentally encumbered with the bureaucratic squabbles of running a large institution. Her first major problem was with a group of local women whose motto, according to Sister Davis, was "Down with St. Luke's and the medical staff" because the hospital had recently increased its customary charges for services despite the fact that Aberdeen was a very low-wage city. Consequently, she set up an advisory board to harmonize public relations, an act that helped solve the problem. Another of Sister Davis's challenges involved her discordant relationship with a surgeon, Robert Bormes, who longed to create an open-heart surgery center at St. Luke's. Attempting to accommodate him, Sister Davis conducted a feasibility study that concluded that St. Luke's should refrain from building such a unit because federal funds for such a move had already gone to a hospital in Minot, North Dakota, and because such an operation was really more suited to a larger city such as Minneapolis. Unwilling to accept Sister Davis's response, Bormes reportedly convinced some members of St. Luke's advisory board to support his plans. Apparently he harrassed Sister Davis to such an extent that, she recalled, "When I left St. Luke's . . . I'd say that I was [headed toward a] . . . mental breakdown."[56]

The situation at St. Luke's also caused conflict within the Presentation community. Some of the nuns blamed Sister Davis when, during the 1960s in Aberdeen, Bormes promoted the establishment of Dakota Midland Hospital and its open-heart surgery center. Run by the Health Central Association of Minneapolis, the hospital became St. Luke's major competitor. Apparently the organization proposed a merger with St. Luke's, which caused subsequent administrators some agonizing decision making. One resentful Presentation administrator told Sister Davis, "Well, we'll undo everything you've done now."[57]

Despite any internal conflicts and despite who supervised the Presentation hospitals' day-to-day operations, the nuns corporately asserted themselves as the institutions' ultimate authority figures. As early as 1952, in a letter to Bishop William Brady of the Sioux Falls Diocese, Mother Viator Burns revealed her order's expectations when taking over any hospital, stating flatly, "I think I should mention to you, Bishop, that if in the future Sisters should be taking over this hospital [in Madison, South Dakota], there should be a very definite understanding that the [lay] Staff will relinquish . . . some of the [policymaking] rights they are now holding on to . . . ."[58]

In more recent years Presentations such as Sister Mary Denis Collins continued to serve in selected administrative roles, such as being associate to the director at Holy Rosary from 1968 to 1973. Yet because of the external and internal strife emanating from various Presentations' direct administrative functions, by the 1970s the

South Dakota Presentations decided that a new organizational structure was in order.[59] Presentations in other states were experiencing similar revelations. Sister Catherine Haertzen of the North Dakota congregation voiced her concerns: "certain tasks of Christian service should be performed by lay persons, thus freeing religious for forms of charity not so easily undertaken by [others]. . . ."[60] What resulted in South Dakota was a system that enabled those who were interested to participate in policymaking, not necessarily bureaucratic roles. The women elected a corporate board that oversaw a health care council comprised of Presentation Sisters and lay people appointed by the corporate board from the cities being served. Each hospital then selected its own board of trustees, which in turn supervised the activities of its executive director. The health care council assisted the corporate board in reviewing programs and providing consultative services. Each administrator coordinated the financial operation and, because the fiscal year began on the first day of October, prepared the budget each spring. The administrator met with department heads to make cost and revenue projections, next the board of trustees' finance committee reviewed the proposed plan, and finally it was presented it to the health care council for final approval.[61]

The Presentations' continued strong voice in the hospital governance was heard in one controversial incident. In 1974, Holy Rosary became involved in a lawsuit over the issue of sterilization and abortion, practices to which the sisters took moral exception. That year a physician on the hospital's staff, Dr. James Hamm, requested permission to perform tubal ligation, a request denied by the corporate board because the Catholic Church forbade such procedures. After trying to persuade the sisters to change their policy, he decided to force the issue by accepting a patient who was due for a Caesarean section and who also wanted the physician to sterilize her. Both patient and doctor filed suit against the institution for refusing to authorize the service—claiming that her civil rights were being denied and asserting that his alleged prerogative to practice was being obstructed. Because each plaintiff filed suit just a month before the woman was due to deliver, the court issued an injunction allowing Hamm to perform the surgery.[62]

David Patton, Holy Rosary's chief administrator, consulted with the Bishop of Great Falls, Most Reverend Eldon B. Shuster, D. D., and then authorized the controversial operation. Patton did, however, advise the staff that if any members had moral or ethical reservations they could refuse to participate. A few months later, the Montana Supreme Court handed down a summary judgment in favor of the Presentations' original stance. When Hamm appealed, the sisters won again. The court held that the tubal ligation was an elective procedure that any consenting clinic could have performed; in winning the case, the private hospital had regained the right to establish its own rules and regulations. Although many people in Miles City disagreed, the majority of citizens believed that political authorities should not force the nuns to go against their ethical standards. Even so, the turbulence in Miles City over the issue was part of a conflict brewing within the entire American Catholic Church. Despite the fact that many local Catholics publicly were willing to grant the Presentations the right to support Church values, they themselves harbored serious uncertainties about the ruling. For example, at informal gatherings, various Catholic women told Patton that they, too, had violated Vatican rulings by using birth control devices, some with their priests' tacit approval. Adding further to the confusion, by the late 1970s, St. Vincent's Hospital in Billings, Montana, owned by the Sisters of Charity of Leavenworth, Kansas, did perform some sterilization surgeries.[63]

During the 1980s, Holy Rosary has had to struggle to accommodate yet not be absorbed by the external forces that the Presentations needed. During the early 1960s, the revised Hill-Burton Amendment brought on many concerns. Despite the existence of a veterans' hospital in Miles City, Holy Rosary's 120-bed unit was the major medical center for eastern Montana. Yet the new legislation threatened to change all of this because it offered to fund the establishment of small town, ten-bed hospitals. Subsequently, by 1978 there existed an "overbeddedness" in Holy Rosary's service area. Further illustrating the two-edged scalpel of federal involvement in national health care developments, chief administrator Douglas Atkinson commented that the federal Medicare-Medicaid program increased Holy Rosary patients' purchasing power but brought the hospital many additional bookkeeping responsibilities. Nevertheless, growth and changes occurred. Michael R. Piper replaced Atkinson, and by September of 1985, the 115,506-square-foot structure totaled $6,297,636 in assets and had served 13,332 patients during that fiscal year.[64]

By 1970, McKennan Hospital also employed a lay administrator, Henry Morris. He was a Catholic and dedicated to the Presentations' ideals. In 1962, he was the first lay chief executive hired to run Mercy Hospital in Detroit. During his administration at McKennan (which he turned over to Roger C. Paavola in the 1980s), the facility moved from being a community hospital to a regional tertiary care medical center that served primarily clients who lived within a hundred-mile radius of Sioux Falls. By September 1985, McKennan consisted of 545,794 square feet, was valued at $89,339,710, and had treated 92,489 patients in that year. This happened primarily because McKennan became part of the University of South Dakota's four-year, degree-granting medical school in 1973 and so attracted more specialists. The nuns involved the community with hospital decision making by giving up seats on the governing board to local citizens; however, McKennan ideals remain the same, dedicated as much to the art as to the science of medicine.[65]

During the 1970s, St. Joseph Hospital's officials were also increasing their community involvement while maintaining their ideals when they served on a community-wide committee with Methodist Hospital representatives. Together they worked to bring in more physicians to both hospitals, thereby limiting competition and maximizing cooperation. David Rykus, St. Joseph's chief administrator, stated that having two hospitals in Mitchell also helped St. Joseph avoid the sterilization question because Methodist could perform the controversial operation.[66]

Free from conflict with other health care agencies, St. Joseph administrators concentrated on augmenting and improving the facility. A 5,400-square-foot building project completed in 1974 brought St. Joseph's total square footage to 147,250, while by 1985, under the guidance of a new lay administrator, Fred Slunecka, the hospital recorded $7,692,062 in assets, and in September of that fiscal year had treated 15,820 patients.[67]

Despite successes, from time to time all of the Presentation hospitals have been faced with physician shortages. The creation of a family practice residency at McKennan in conjunction with the state medical school at Vermillion eased the problem in the Sioux

Falls area. St. Luke's also had a medical intern program, but its administrators along with those at Holy Rosary and McKennan seemed always to be searching for doctors. Medical students were reluctant to settle in semi-rural areas, and even offers of guaranteed incomes did not attract large numbers of the much-needed doctors. Those who were in South Dakota during the 1960s and 70s, most of them near retirement, found themselves overworked, and patients complained about crowded clinics because they often had to wait three to four hours for an examination. To help alleviate the problem, in 1977, under Sister Sturzl, the Presentation health care specialists established the Presentation Health Services, Incorporated (Presentation Affiliated Cooperative Effort, known as PACE), an agency that coordinated the sharing of resources and personnel between five hundred hospitals, nursing homes, schools, and clinics of seven states within or contiguous to the northern Great Plains area. The plan had been originated in 1946 when all the Presentation hospitals made a group purchasing agreement. In 1982, PACE hired a marketing director, and the agency began leasing and purchasing contracts to assist small hospitals and clinics.[68]

Also augmenting the efficient administration of the Presentations' health care apostolate, in 1979 a revision of the corporate bylaws initiated the Presentation Health System, governed by a management council. Two years later, the agency hired a corporate health planner and incorporated the Presentation Health System Foundation, which was designed to promote monetary contributions to the Presentation health care projects. Using their new vehicle of centralization, the nuns continued to strengthen their relationship with colleagues outside their own institutions. In 1983, the Presentation Health System formed an alliance with the North Dakota Health Group headquartered in Valley City and overseen by the Presentation Sisters of Mary. A year later the South Dakota sisters held a leadership conference for the Presentation Health System trustees, administrators, and physicians and brought St. Joseph Hospital of Polson, Montana, into the network of agencies. The sisters further refined medical services by incorporating Presentation Health System, making the Health Care Council its board of directors. Other organizational incorporations that year created the Clinic Management Services and Accounts Management.

The bureaucratic innovations were guided by a mission coordinator, a position that the sisters first filled in 1980. A year later the nuns' Health Care Ministry Group was established to advise the Health Care Council and helped establish hospices in Aberdeen and Mitchell. By 1985, the Ethics Committee became an official advisory body for the Presentation Health System. Extending their philosophy beyond their own agencies, the nuns placed Presentation sisters at other health care agencies. Sister Theodora Paul, for example, became an activities director in a community hospital in Chamberlain, South Dakota.[69]

Under Mother Martin, one particular manifestation of the nuns' ideals was the initiation of pastoral care departments in all four of their communities' hospitals. McKennan was the first to organize the service formally, but all the hospitals eventually established a special team of nuns who served as ministers, making sure that the patients' spiritual and emotional needs were met. For sister-administrators, developing these programs was much more rewarding than the administrative jobs of the past. Sister Judith O'Brien explained that by working with the new and yet old health care concept she gained "a much greater understanding" of herself and a renewed sense of purpose.[70] There are numerous examples of Presentation assertiveness manifested through their new hospital role. In one anonymous hospital the nuns encouraged an "inactive chaplain" to leave and found another who was willing to give more of himself. Moreover, at all of the institutions Presentations were able to provide individual counseling for hospital personnel and medical staffs, while the nuns coordinated all other collective religious activities. They ran workshops to prepare local clergy for its role in the project and established public relations activities to inform people about their hospitals' renewed holistic approach. Some sisters coordinated activities, while others led families of patients through times of crisis, offered prayer on request, and provided follow-up visits after their clients left the hospital. These outlets provided a double benefit: order members saw them as a valuable adaptation to their traditional apostolate of ministering to God's people, while recipients commented that they were gratified to see numerous sisters working in the hospitals once again. Moreover, in many respects the job of minister evidenced another professional situation in which the sisters relied on traditional ideology to rationalize participation in another long-standing male field, the ministry.[71]

Despite all of these innovations, during the administrations of Mother Martin and Sister Sturzl the order still lost many sister hospital workers who apparently did not feel that their work was distinguishable enough from that of the lay health care specialists to require their living apart from the secular world. For those who remained, however, the challenge proved exhilarating. For example, in 1978, Patton, who had become St. Luke's new director, commented on the notable success of pastoral care at the hospital. By 1985, the nuns and their new administrator, Dale Stein, controlled a 247,616-square-foot structure that claimed $26,151,522 in assets and served 37,178 patients during that fiscal year.[72]

Because of Presentation administrators' expertise, the order's dedication to principle, and a significant amount of community, state, and national support, over the years all four institutions completed ambitious construction and modernization projects. In 1985, the corporate structure was sound financially, and the Presentations' hand-picked managers ran the organizations well. The pastoral care program maintained a religious atmosphere in all of the facilities, and the Presentation Health System represented an ever-greater extension of medical services on the northern Great Plains. The sisters had illustrated that the holistic dedication to healing and nurturing, originating from Nano Nagle herself, could be used to professionalize and to derive variations on the role of the health care manager and the services made available.

NOTES

1. Jo Ann Ashley, *Hospitals, Paternalism, and the Role of the Nurse* (New York: Teachers College Press, 1976), 12; interview with Sister JoAnn Sturzl, Aug. 5, 1976, South Dakota Oral History Center, Vermillion.
2. Sister M. Cabrini Di Donato, "A History of the Educational Work of the Presentation Sisters of Aberdeen, South Dakota" (master's thesis, Northern State College, 1966), 95.
3. Bishop William Brady, quoted in Sister Di Donato, "A History of the Educational Work of the Presentation Sisters."
4. For a classic reference to the deterioration of ideals in large organizations, see William Foote Whyte, Jr., *The Organization Man* (Garden City, N.Y.: Doubleday, 1957).
5. *Aberdeen American News*, June 17, 1956; *Diamond Jubilee Book* (Aberdeen, S.D.: Congregation of the Presentation of the Blessed Virgin

Mary, 1961), 46. The hospital, referred to as both Brown County Hospital and Good Samaritan Hospital, did reopen for a time in the early 1900s, but again failed to achieve permanence.

6. *Aberdeen American News*, Oct. 14, 1951, Nov. 12, 1939; J. T. Walsh, *Nano Nagle and the Presentation Sisters* (Dublin: M. H. Hill and Son, 1959), 281; *Diamond Jubilee Book*, 46; Sister Di Donato, "A History of the Educational Work of the Presentation Sisters," 57–59.

7. Walsh, *Nano Nagle*, 281; William O. Brady, D.D. to Venerable Sisters, Dec. 13, 1947, Office of the Chancery, Diocese of Sioux Falls, Sioux Falls, S.D.

8. *Constitutions of the Congregation of the Sisters of the Presentation of the Blessed Virgin Mary* (Aberdeen, S.D.: The Sisters of the Presentation of the Blessed Virgin Mary, 1946), 89.

9. Sister Pauline Quinn, "Biographies of Major Superiors, Section V: Mother Joseph Butler, 1894–1915," Presentation Archives, Presentation Heights, Aberdeen, S.D.; *Aberdeen American News*, June 17, 1956; "Jubilee Data," Presentation Archives, Presentation Heights, Aberdeen, S.D.

10. Steve Palank, quoted in "Jubilee Data."

11. *Presentation School of Nursing Bulletin, 1960–62*, (n.d.), 8; *Diamond Jubilee Book*, 27; Sister Alicia Dunphy to Courtney Ann Vaughn-Roberson, Aug. 11, 1986; Sister M. Claudia Duratschek, O.S.B., *The Beginnings of Catholicism in South Dakota* (Washington, D.C.: Catholic University of American Press, 1943), 237–40.

12. *Official Yearbook of Sacred Heart Catholic Church* (Aberdeen, S.D.: Sacred Heart Catholic Church, 1901–2), 2.

13. *Aberdeen American News*, Scrapbook, Presentation Archives; *Diamond Jubilee Book*, 32–33; Sister Di Donato, "A History of the Educational Work of the Presentation Sisters," 61.

14. Sister Di Donato, "A History of the Educational Work of the Presentation Sisters," 62; *Aberdeen American News*, Scrapbook; Sister Alicia Dunphy to the authors, Feb. 14, 1986; Sister Pauline Quinn, "Biographies of Major Superiors, Section VII: Mother Agatha Collins, 1921–1927," Presentation Archives. For a source on organizational foundings see Katherine Gruder, ed., *Encyclopedia of Associations* (Detroit: Gale Research, 1987).

15. Sister Di Donato, "A History of the Educational Work of the Presentation Sisters," 63.

16. "Jubilee Data."

17. Ibid.; Sister Di Donato, "A History of the Educational Work of the Presentation Sisters," 66; *Aberdeen American News*, June 17, 1956, Scrapbook; *Diamond Jubilee Book*, 33.

18. Sister Pauline Quinn, "Biographies of Major Superiors, Section VIII: Mother Raphael McCarthy, 1932–1946," Presentation Archives; Sister Di Donato, "A History of the Educational Work of the Presentation Sisters," 71–74; Sister Alicia Dunphy to the authors, Feb. 14, 1986.

19. "History of St. Joseph Hospital," Manuscript, Office, St. Joseph Hospital, Mitchell, S.D.

20. "History of St. Joseph Hospital"; interview with Sister Lelia M. Beresford, Aug. 11, 1976, South Dakota Oral History Center; Eliot Freidson, *Profession of Medicine: A Study of the Sociology of Applied Knowledge* (New York: Dodd, Mead, 1970), 62–63; *Diamond Jubilee Book*, 38; Sister M. Lelia Beresford, "Review of the History of St. Joseph Hospital," Office, St. Joseph Hospital.

21. Sister Beresford, "Review of the History."

22. Interview with Dr. W. A. Delaney, June 6, 1978, South Dakota Oral History Center; Sister Beresford, "Review of the History"; interview with Sister Judith O'Brien, June 19 and 21, 1978, South Dakota Oral History Center; Sister Alicia Dunphy to Courtney Ann Vaughn-Roberson, Aug. 11, 1986.

23. Mitchell *Daily Republic*, Sept. 23, 1922.

24. Communication between Sylvia Starr and Norbert Goergen, Oct. 1, 1986; Sister Di Donato, "A History of the Educational Work of the Presentation Sisters," 83.

25. Sister Di Donato, "A History of the Educational Work of the Presentation Sisters," 83; interview with Dr. W. A. Delaney; Sister Monica Parkinson to Mrs. Maxine Horman, Office, St. Joseph Hospital; "Jubilee Data"; Sister Beresford, "Review of the History."

26. "Holy Rosary manuscript," Jubilee Data; *Miles City Star*, Scrapbook; Sister Di Donato, "A History of the Educational Work of the Presentation Sisters," 85–86; Sister Alicia Dunphy to Courtney Ann Vaughn-Roberson, June 27, 1985.

27. "Holy Rosary manuscript," Jubilee Data; *Miles City Star*, Scrapbook; Sister Di Donato, "A History of the Educational Work of the Presentation Sisters," 86.

28. *Diamond Jubilee Book*, 39, 40; "Holy Rosary manuscript," Jubilee Data; Sister Di Donato, "A History of the Educational Work of the Presentation Sisters," 87, 110; Sister Alicia Dunphy to Courtney Ann Vaughn-Roberson, June 27, 1985; Sister Quinn, "Mother Viator Burns."

29. "The Will of Helen McKennan," Heritage Room, McKennan Hospital, Sioux Falls, S.D.

30. Interview with David Rykhus, June 2, 1978, South Dakota Oral History Center; Sister Alicia Dunphy to the authors, Aug. 11, 1986; Mother Raphael McCarthy, "History of the Orphanage," Presentation Archives; Sister Di Donato, "A History of the Educational Work of the Presentation Sisters," 88–89.

31. Dolores Harrington, *A Woman's Will ... A Sister's Way, the McKennan Hospital Story, 1911–1961* (Sioux Falls, S.D.: McKennan Hospital, 1961), 5–10; "McKennan manuscript," Jubilee Data.

32. Sister Quinn, "Mother Agatha Collins."

33. Harrington, *A Woman's Will*, 23–24.

34. "McKennan manuscript," Jubilee Data; Harrington, *A Woman's Will*, 30–31; Sister Quinn, "Mother Raphael McCarthy"; Sister Di Donato, "A History of the Educational Work of the Presentation Sisters," 90.

35. Interview with Bishop Lambert Hoch, June 28, 1978, South Dakota Oral History Center.

36. Interview with Bishop Lambert Hoch.

37. Mother Raphael McCarthy to the Sisters, Sept. 10, 1941, Presentation Archives; Sister Quinn, "Mother Raphael McCarthy."

38. Mother Viator Burns to Most Reverend William O. Brady, D.D., Oct. 23, 1947, Presentation Archives.

39. Bishop William O. Brady to Sister Superior, Feb. 2, 1948, Office of the Catholic Chancery Records, Diocese of Sioux Falls.

40. *Presentation Nurse*, Nov. 1942; "Holy Rosary manuscript," Jubilee Data; Harrington, *A Woman's Will*, 35–37, 60; *Aberdeen American News*, June 17, 1956; Elizabeth Jamieson, Mary F. Sewall, and Eleanor B. Suhrie, *Trends in Nursing History* (Philadelphia: W. B. Saunders, 1966), 293–95; *U. S. Statutes at Large*, 78th Cong., 1st sess., vol. 55, pt. 2 (Washington, D.C.: U.S. Government Printing Office, 1942), 484; Jubilee Data.

41. Interview with Sister Irene Talbot, June 7, 1978, South Dakota Oral History Center.

42. Interview with Sister Irene Talbot; "Holy Rosary manuscript," Jubilee Data; interview with Sister Fanahan Casey, June 20, 1978, South Dakota Oral History Center.

43. "St. Luke's manuscript," Jubilee Data; *Aberdeen American News*, June 17, 1956.

44. *United States Code, Congressional Service, 81st Congress, 1st Session* (Washington, D.C.: West Publishing and Edward Thompson, 1949), 2192, 2198; *U. S. Statutes at Large, 81st Congress, 1949*, vol. 63, pt. 1 (Washington, D.C.: U. S. Government Printing Office, 1950), 898.

45. *United States Code*, 2192, 2199, 2201.

46. *Sioux City* (Iowa) *Journal*, Dec. 13, 1955; "St. Joseph manuscript," Jubilee Data; *Aberdeen American News*, June 17, 1956; communication between Sylvia Starr and Norbert Goergen, Oct. 1, 1986; Sister Di Donato, "A History of the Educational Work of the Presentation Sisters," 91; interview with Douglas Atkinson, July 12, 1978, South Dakota Oral History Center.

47. Sister Di Donato, "A History of the Educational Work of the Presentation Sisters," 91; "Files of Newspaper Clippings," 1952–60, Heritage Room, McKennan Hospital; *Sioux Falls Argus-Leader*, Oct. 27, 1957; Sister Quinn, "Mother Viator Burns."

48. Sister Di Donato, "A History of the Educational Work of the Presentation Sisters," 174, 206.

49. "St. Luke's manuscript," Jubilee Data; *St. Joe Happenings*, Aug. 1976, 8; "Files of Newspaper Clippings," 1952–1960; Sister Quinn, "Mother Viator Burns"; *Sioux Falls Argus-Leader*, Oct. 12, 1948.

50. *Miles City Star*, Scrapbook; Sister Quinn, "Mother Raphael McCarthy."

51. Sister Alicia Dunphy to the authors, Fall 1985; Sister Pauline Quinn, "Biographies of Major Superiors, Section XI: Mother Myron Martin, 1964–

1974," Presentation Archives; interview with Sister Irene Talbot; Sister Di Donato, "A History of the Educational Work of the Presentation Sisters," 207; "Newspaper Scrapbook," Presentation Archives; *Diamond Jubilee Book,* 71.

52. Interview with Sister Irene Talbot; "Newspaper Scrapbook"; *Diamond Jubilee Book,* 71; interview with David Patton, June 26, 1978; interview with David Rykhus; interview with Mary Stephen Davis, Aug. 7, 1976; interview with Sister Colman Coakley, Aug. 7, 1978, South Dakota Oral History Center; "Long Range Plan," St. Luke's Hospital, Aberdeen, S.D.

53. Interview with David Rykhus; interview with David Patton; interview with Douglas Atkinson; "Long Range Plan."

54. Interview with David Rykhus; interview with Sister Bonaventure Hoffman, Aug. 6, 1976; interview with Sister Judith O'Brien.

55. Interview with Sister Bonaventure Hoffman.

56. Interview with Sister Mary Stephen Davis.

57. Anonymous Presentation nun, quoted in Ibid.

58. Mother Viator Burns to Most Reverend William O. Brady, D.D., April 26, 1952, Presentation Archives.

59. Sister Pauline Quinn, "Biographies of Major Superiors, Section XIII: Sister Mary Denis Collins, 1982–," Presentation Archives; interview with Sister Colman Coakley; "Long Range Plan"; interview with David Patton; interview with Sister Mary Stephen Davis; interview with David Rykhus.

60. M. Raphael Consedine, P.B.V.M., *Listening Journey: A Study of the Spirit and Ideals of Nano Nagle and the Presentation Sisters* (Victoria, Australia: Congregation of the Presentation of the Blessed Virgin Mary, 1983), 378.

61. Interview with David Rykhus.

62. Interview with David Patton; interview with Douglas Atkinson; interview with Sister Fanahan Casey.

63. Interview with Sister Fanahan Casey; interview with David Patton; interview with Douglas Atkinson; Sister Alicia Dunphy to Courtney Ann Vaughn-Roberson, June 27, 1985.

64. Interview with Douglas Atkinson; Sister Stephen Davis to Sister Alicia Dunphy, March 24, 1986, Presentation Archives; communication between Sylvia Starr and Sister Colman Coakley, Oct. 1, 1986.

65. Communication between Sylvia Starr and Sister Colman Coakley; interview with Henry Morris, June 30, 1978, South Dakota Oral History Center; Sister Stephen Davis to Sister Alicia Dunphy, March 24, 1986.

66. Interview with David Rykhus.

67. Sister Stephen Davis to Sister Alicia Dunphy, March 24, 1986; communication between Sylvia Starr and Norbert Goergen, Oct. 1, 1986.

68. Interview with Douglas Atkinson; interview with David Rykhus; interview with Sister Colman Coakley; "Long Range Plan"; Marshall Ause, "Shared Services, Trend for the Future," *All of Us* 9 (Sept. 1980): 2; Sister Alicia Dunphy to the authors, Fall 1985.

69. Sister Alicia Dunphy to the authors, Fall 1985; interview with Mother Myron Martin.

70. Interview with Sister Judith O'Brien.

71. "Long Range Plan"; "Department of Pastoral Care," Holy Rosary Hospital, Miles City, Mont.; Sister M. Gerald, "Areas of the Hospital Apostolate," Presentation Archives; "Draft for CPE Accreditation," Holy Rosary Hospital; interview with David Patton.

72. Sister Pauline Quinn, "Biographies of Major Superiors, Section XII: Sister Jo Ann Sturzl, 1974–1982," Presentation Archives; interview with David Patton; Sister Stephen Davis to Sister Alicia Dunphy, March 24, 1986; communication between Sylvia Starr and a St. Luke's representative, Oct. 1, 1986.

8. Using Head and Heart: Nurses' Training Throughout the Century

□

When the Presentation Sisters decided to extend their apostolate to include health care, they developed schools of nursing at the four hospitals that they operated. From 1901, when the first one opened at St. Luke's, until the 1980s, the nursing programs grew—but not without conflict within the order. To a degree, the Presentation nurses took part in a historic national struggle against hospital administrators and doctors to obtain professional autonomy and higher education for nurses, and they have at times argued among themselves over the appropriate amounts of academic course work and practical experience needed within the nuns' nurses' training programs.[1] By and large, the Presentation nurses have resolved these conflicts, maintained their order's unity, promoted the professionalization of numerous Presentation and lay nurses, and continued to attract clients by keeping in mind the order's holistic goal of preparing for "duties so that . . . [our] labors may insure both the temporal and spiritual welfare of [our] . . . patients."[2]

In so stating, the Presentations have identified themselves with countless other sisters who have cared for the sick. The French Ursuline nuns, who first established their New Orleans convent in 1727, had long been engaged in health care as well as education. Along with other women religious, the Ursulines constituted a substantial part of the total number of American nurses until the Civil War. Largely a product of apprentice training, these sisters learned most of their skills by taking care of victims of war and natural disasters. For example, Canadian Ursulines nursed both British and American soldiers during the American Revolution, and the New Orleans community did the same during the War of 1812. Another order, the Emmitsburg Sisters of Charity in Baltimore, became so well known that in 1823 the federal government requested their services in a local Marine Corps hospital. Similarly, the Sisters of Mercy proved invaluable during nationwide cholera epidemics during the 1830s, 40s, and 50s. In 1854, they were the only persons on the West Coast with any knowledge of how to treat the disease.[3]

The nineteenth-century Protestant woman's nursing role model, England's Florence Nightingale, believed that as a Christian woman she had a similar call to care for the sick. In the fall of 1854, Great Britian sent her to Scutari, Turkey, to nurse wounded soldiers who were fighting in the Crimean War against Russia. Nightingale's country called upon her primarily because the British press had popularized the deeds of Sisters of Charity who for months had been caring for wounded French allies. Nightingale took with her twenty-four nuns from various religious orders.[4] She forswore marriage, believing that because of the subordinate position of wife to husband, matrimony would have been to her a form of "suicide." Yet she had compassion for the idle, well-to-do homemaker and speculated that the lady of leisure "longs for a profession . . . [and] struggles to open to woman the paths of the school, the hospital, [and] the penitentiary. . . . Without the right cultivation and employment of all . . . the powers . . . there can be no repose, . . . [but] with it repose may be found in a hell, in a hospital of wounds and pain and operations and death and remorse and tears and despair."[5]

Like Nightingale and her Catholic sister compatriots, Americans Clara Barton and Dorothea Dix cared for injured soldiers during the bloody Civil War. Barton functioned apart from the Superintendent of Women Nurses, Dorothea Dix, who headed the federal government's corps, but almost six hundred sisters from more than twenty religious communities volunteered to work with Dix and other Protestant women who staffed the military hospitals. The Emmitsburg Daughters of Charity contributed 232 members to the cause, tolerating from Dix an antagonism that evidenced the persistence of age-old religious enmities between Protestants and Catholics.[6]

Although after the war many women religious retreated somewhat from the nursing professionalization movement, for some nuns the carnage had proven the need for medical sophistication that Nightingale had originally supported in tandem with her insistence on women's spiritual and personal dedication to care for each patient's moral and emotional needs. Nurses' training programs began to develop in the United States during the 1870s. Two of the more notable institutions were those begun at Bellevue Hospital in New York and at Johns Hopkins in Baltimore. In the eyes of some nuns and other Catholic Church members, these trainees and nurses, who now assisted in surgical procedures, were necessarily brought closer to the inner workings of a person's mortal body, a symbol of the original sin. These students were also challenged to reach new intellectual heights—another objectionable alteration of the status quo. These changes unearthed lingering medieval apprehension of women's corruptible nature and limited powers of reason, prompting Church officials to discourage sisters' involvement in such innovations.[7]

Quite the opposite were the views of late nineteenth- and early twentieth-century American nursing leaders such as Adelaide Nutting, who was the Johns Hopkins superintendent of nurses until 1907, when she became the first professor of the graduate nursing program at Columbia Teachers College, and Lavinia Lloyd Dock, who was a Columbia Teachers College faculty member and editor of the *American Journal of Nursing*. Following these early professionalization advocates, nursing leaders over the years attempted to ween their occupation from part of the Nightingale image (that of a pious, nurturing female) toward the stereotypically male-linked dedication to science. Yet, despite their efforts to the contrary, these leading American nurses tended to perpetuate rather than refute Nightingale's "secular nun" stereotype, choosing to remain single and almost exclusively dedicated to their work lest they appear too domestic. Thus, their programs and rhetoric increasingly emphasized the autonomy and the academic training long thought to be intrinsically male.[8]

Certainly, the defining of nursing's appropriate ideological base has been a major source of conflict within the secular nursing field throughout the century. A persistent division has existed between national leaders and grass-roots nurses working either in their communities or in hospital wards. Often substantiating hospital administrators' view of nurses and of women in general, practical nurses' entire reason for practicing has resembled the traditional rather than scientific orientation. Even though public health nurses have had some of the greatest autonomy from any hospital administrator's power to define their professional level, frequently they have chosen to embrace a craft-oriented rather than an academic perspective on their work.[9]

To augment members' professional status, nurses' associations also waged bloodless wars with foes outside their occupational community as more and more hospitals evolved away from charity and into money-making institutions. Competition promoted an exploitive mentality among hospital managers, who took advantage of the traditional, at best semiprofessional, nurses' emphasis on apprentice training to provide hospitals with cheap labor. From 1900 to 1910, an impressive 1,651 hospitals were built; and by 1930, 7,000 American health care facilities existed, with a capital investment of more than $3 billion. Resembling progressive managerial principles, new economical means to manage these institutions were continuously published by administration journals. One common practice developed was to incorporate schools of nursing into the hospital bureaucracy and to hire students who—at reduced salaries—could perform most of the nursing tasks. Illustrating the trend, fifteen schools of nursing functioned in 1880, but thirty years later, 1,129 existed. By 1910, one in four hospitals offered an apprentice-based nursing course of study leading to a diploma, even though the volume of knowledge was multiplying rapidly.[10]

Physicians' apprehension of nurses' potentially superior preparation posed a more subtle barrier against improving nurses' academic credentials. For example, although the Johns Hopkins University had established a school of nursing in 1873, it was not until twenty years later that its medical school was founded as a graduate institution, and by "1905 only five of the [country's] 160 medical schools required college work for admission."[11] In 1910, the Flexner Report exposed the poor state of medical education in America, and as a result many doctors who feared being upstaged by the highly skilled nurses with whom they worked made few attempts to advance national nursing leaders' professionalization designs.[12]

Throughout the century then, as the average nurse's workplace changed from settlement houses, community service agencies, or patients' homes to hospital settings, professionalization proponents combatted powerful authoritative and economic constraints. Undaunted, during the 1940s the National Nursing Council commissioned researcher Ester Lucile Brown to conduct a study on the vocation's status. The result was the 1948 Brown Report, which strongly advocated that the bachelor's degree be each nurse's goal. Fourteen years later, only 14 percent had attained it. In 1952, the first two-year associate-degree program was implemented as a compromise between hospital-diploma and college or university programs. In 1965, the American Nurses' Association issued a position paper declaring open support for the undergraduate degree as the ideal minimum qualification. Progress again was slow; nearly twenty years later, only 25 percent of the working nurses held baccalaureate degrees.[13]

In many respects the birth and growth of the South Dakota nurses' training program has reflected national historical trends. In 1927, Rapid City Regional Hospital began a three-year diploma program for registered nursing, a course that is still in operation even though similar preparatory programs are no longer common throughout the state. By the early 1980s, however, South Dakota still offered an array of programs that appeared to be guided by varying definitions of professionalism. Until it closed in June of 1986, Freeman Junior College was the only higher educational institution to offer training for the licensed practical nurse. Opening in 1971, Sinte Gleska awarded the associate degree in registered nursing until 1983. In 1962, the University of South Dakota chartered an associate degree in nursing, accredited four years later by the South Dakota Board of Nursing (as are all the existing state programs) and by the National League of Nursing in 1975. That year Dakota Wesleyan University graduated its first class of associate-degree registered nurses. Four years later the institution received accreditation through the National League of Nursing. The Dakota Wesleyan program accounted for one of the higher percentages of the school's total enrollment. It provided students with clinical experience in facilities such as the Presentations' St. Joseph Hospital and Brady Memorial Home. In 1972, the University began a satellite associate degree program in nursing at Oglala Lakota College. Twelve years later, Oglala Lakota took complete control of the course of study, becoming the only nursing program taught on an Indian reservation through an Indian college. The Oglala Lakota staff looked forward to National League of Nursing accreditation after two classes graduated.[14]

During the twentieth century, Mount Marty, Augustana, and

South Dakota State at Brookings all began offering bachelor's degrees in nursing, and South Dakota State originated a master's program in nursing. The South Dakota State program began in 1935 and was accredited by the National League of Nursing in 1960. Despite the development of graduate nurses' training, the directors claimed to promote a "holistic client-centered" philosophy, combining scientific and nurturing ideals into the nurse's professional training. In 1961, Mount Marty chartered its course of study, which was soon approved by the National League of Nursing. Augustana graduated its first class in 1968, advertising the curriculum as certified by the National League of Nursing in 1969 and leading to one of the few bachelor of arts nursing degrees in the United States.[15]

The four Presentation diploma schools of nursing—at St. Luke's, St. Joseph, Holy Rosary, and McKennan—opened in 1901, 1907, 1911, and 1912, respectively. These programs extended three years, with physicians teaching most of the academic classes, which included anatomy, physiology, bacteriology, and pathology. Nursing supervisors organized the curriculum and handled practical instruction, although they had no state guidelines to follow until 1917, when the South Dakota State legislature passed the first nursing-practice act. For two or three decades, nursing at the Presentation hospitals remained as it was throughout much of the country, more an art than a science. Therapy and medication were limited, and the practitioner had to rely on common sense, careful hands, strength, compassion, and prayer. Duties of students and nurses with hospital diplomas included reading temperatures, giving baths, making beds, administering medicines, and fulfilling physicians' instructions for patient care. Nurses spent many hours performing routine, unskilled chores. They poured drinking water, served meals, and changed dressings, while a senior student would sometimes give medications and prepare meals in her superior's absence. It was not uncommon for neophytes to work seven days a week, each day shift beginning at 7:00 a.m. and lasting until floor duty was over at 7:00 p.m. The nurses then wearily attended classes for three hours every evening, sharing the plight of colleagues elsewhere: little control over their professional training.[16]

Nursing educators and administrators gradually took over more actual instruction of classes, although from the beginning the Presentations' administered their programs. Sister Dominic Boysen organized the St. Luke's School of Nursing curriculum. Sisters Peter Buckley, Vincent Hennessey, and Margaret Mary Grainger were her first pupils. Sister Boysen taught techniques of nursing and assigned to doctors and other hospital personnel the instruction of "anatomy, physiology, bacteriology, *materia medica*, hygiene, medical and surgical diseases, chemistry, and obstetrics."[17] In 1919, a laywoman known in records only as Mrs. Earling took over Sister Boysen's role. She oversaw the building of a nurses' residence, an examination by the Board of Nurse Examiners, and the implementation of the state's nursing curriculum.[18]

Thus, nurses gradually replaced doctors as the nursing school's principal educators. During each hospital's first course of study, doctors' total lecture hours averaged 312, while those of nurse instructors and other hospital personnel equalled about 117. Throughout the remainder of the program, a student was supervised as she performed the various techniques she had learned. Through the efforts of national organizations like the American Nurses' Association, by 1920 nurses everywhere (except in Nevada) had to pass state boards and had to register. That year, the South Dakota State Board of Nursing Examiners granted accreditation to St. Luke's School of Nursing, and the Presentations' other institutions welcomed approval a few years later.[19]

A true test of skills had come a few years before when all four hospitals provided nurses who served valiantly during the trying months of the nationwide influenza epidemic of 1918 and 1919. Hospital patronage mushroomed after the epidemic, and the nursing schools increased their enrollments, accommodating between twenty and thirty in a class in order to meet the growing number of patients. An improved curriculum expanded to include new courses such as chemistry, pediatrics, ethics, and social problems. Physicians still taught most of these subjects, but as the Presentation Sisters earned college degrees, they became qualified to share lecturing chores with doctors, thereby becoming the doctors' academic peers. Despite the achievement, the holistic dedication to the order's ideals continued to imbue the nurses' training curriculum, as it did at several other of the state's training centers throughout much of the twentieth century. Of course, for the Presentations and other nuns such as those who came to study from Fargo, the commitment to religious principles had an added emphasis.[20] Veronica Goebel, a South Dakota nurse who trained under the Benedictine Sisters headquartered in Yankton, remarked that due to the nuns' sacrificial attitude, "we put them on a pedestal."[21] As the national attitude of nurses gradually changed throughout the century to embrace the more male-oriented emphasis of the scientific technique over nurturing qualities, then perhaps the laywomen's attitudes toward nun colleagues changed, but leading Presentation nurses would strive always to balance both in all of their training programs.

In the 1930s, the State Board of Nursing Examiners and the National Catholic Hospital Association conducted grading studies that included all four Presentation training programs. The agencies judged faculty, instruction, students, and residences. The most serious weakness that examiners discovered reflected the commonly debated issue over appropriate amounts of practicum and instruction. The reports attempted to encourage more instruction, criticizing the fact that after the first month the trainees spent five hours a day in the wards, and that this increased to eight hours by the fourth month—too much practicum. They did commend the Presentations' policy of granting free tuition and $6-$8 monthly stipends. Overall, the sisters' nursing programs received favorable assessments from both overseeing agencies, although each encouraged the school to strive for more theoretical instruction and to employ more full-time instructors.[22] An example is Mary Ayres Burgess's report for St. Luke's (Table 12).

In 1936 and 1941 representatives of the State Board of Nurse Examiners re-evaluated St. Luke's School of Nursing. The process once again aided the nun's professionalization efforts because the agency's recommendations pushed the nuns to strive for typical professional, progressive goals, for example, increased educational preparation, tighter organizational structure, and use of the laboratory method in teaching.[23] All of the board representatives' observations for each year are listed in Tables 13 and 14.

Agreeing with the assessment, Sister Bonaventure Hoffman became a champion for national standards. Armed with a holistic ideology and the intellectual tools to articulate it, Sister Hoffman became chief administrator of the McKennan School of Nursing in 1938, the year she received her baccalaureate from St. Louis University. At McKennan, she found that her goal to make the program more academic would be a challenge because she served simultaneously as

TABLE 12. GRADING SCHOOL COMMITTEE REPORT, 1932

Faculty and Instruction
(a) The director is the only faculty member with an office.
(b) Chemistry (80 hours) is being taught by Mr. Jensen, an instructor at Northern State Teacher's College.
(c) Teaching facilities are limited. There exists no film or slide projectors and no laboratories for bacteriology, anatomy, and physiology.
(d) The faculty makes an attempt to follow the National Curriculum for Schools of Nursing.
(e) The library consists of 150 reference books.

Students
(a) Students receive stipends of $6, $7, and $8 per month according to their classification. No tuition is charged, and the hospital supports the school.
(b) The preclinical period lasts four months. The first month students take a daily five hours ward practice, seven hours the second and third months, and eight hours the fourth month.
(c) There are forty-eight students enrolled in the school.
(d) All but one student has high school diplomas.
(e) Seniors have individual subscriptions to the *American Journal of Nursing*.

Students' Residence
There is only one housemother, and she is part-time.

Registered Nurses
There are only ten graduate nurses in the hospital and school of nursing. The most serious problem is that the nurses and supervisors have little time to teach the students.

Source: Sister Di Donato, "A History of the Educational Work of the Presentation Sisters," 63–64. Table edited slightly.

director of nursing services. This dual role required that she provide staff members for the hospital and concurrently educate them to be nurses. Reminiscing about the first faculty meeting in which she presented a class schedule that included more course work than had previously been required, Sister Hoffman remembered that fellow administrators, "would not approve it," claiming that "they needed the students for work on the floors. This surprised me and, to be truthful, I cried. After the meeting Mother Agatha consoled me and said, 'Sister, it will all work out in time.' " Crestfallen, Sister Hoffman recalled thinking, "Here I had been sent away to school to educate nurses and I can't get them off the floors for class." She discovered a solution, although it involved considerable self-sacrifice

TABLE 13. STATE BOARD OF NURSING EVALUATION, 1936

Faculty and Instruction
(a) The school does not appear to be organized on sound principles. Authority is divided.
(b) The chemistry laboratory and library are combined.
(c) Only one faculty member has a degree.
(d) Teaching on the ward is more or less casual.
(e) Three courses are taught by Miss Parden (Superintendent of Nurses), and eight by Sister Conception (Director of Nurses).

Students
(a) All forty-nine students are high school graduates.
(b) No allowances are given, and no tuition is required. The hospital supports the school.
(c) There exists ward practice for students: fifty-two hours per week exclusive of class hours. Night duty consists of four to six months during the three years.
(d) Classes are offered once or twice a year, depending upon hospital needs.
(e) There exists an attractive residence with maid service for general cleaning.

Recommendations
(a) A full-time housemother is needed. The director and educational director are overworked; therefore another instructor is needed to assist in teaching.
(b) Instead of two weeks, four weeks vacation should be given annually to students.
(c) Affiliations in pediatrics, psychiatry, and communicable diseases are indicated.
(d) The basic sciences should be taught with the proper proportion of laboratory.
(e) There should be regular meetings of the faculty.
(f) The required time on duty, including classes, is excessive. The maximum for both should be forty-eight hours.
(g) Bathing and toilet facilities are inadequate and require immediate attention.
(h) Faculty members should strive to become as well prepared for their work as members of other professions.
(i) A definite plan for rotating students through the clinical services should be arranged and adhered to.

Source: Sister Di Donato, "A History of the Educational Work of the Presentation Sisters," 64–65. Table edited slightly.

TABLE 14. STATE BOARD OF NURSING EVALUATION, 1941

Faculty and Educational Program

(a) The Catholic Hospital Association accredits the educational program of the school.

(b) An affiliation is arranged with the Children's Hospital in Milwaukee for pediatrics and communicable diseases.

(c) A library is set up in a large room on the first floor. A part-time librarian is employed, and books are being catalogued.

(d) Sister Conception's Procedure Manual is well done. The chemistry class of Sister Jane Frances is excellent.

Students

(a) More dormitory space is provided for nurses by connecting another building to the nurses residence.

(b) A student handbook is published.

Source: Sister Di Donato, "A History of the Educational Work of the Presentation Sisters," 66. Table edited slightly.

by instructors such as herself because the educator offered two identical blocks of course work, thereby freeing a continuous supply of some student personnel for the hospital while upgrading their education at the same time.[24]

Although Sister Hoffman juggled schedules to provide students with more classes, she also stressed experience and made practicums an integral part of the curriculum. For example, honor students participated in pediatric and medical nursing at the Minneapolis General Hospital. Sister Hoffman also encouraged students such as Marie McNamara to earn at least a bachelor's degree. McNamara took her mentor's advice and received a B.S. in nursing from Creighton and then a master's degree from Marquette University. Fueled by a strong sense of spiritual as well as professional dedication, she then joined the Presentation Order and became an instructor of anatomy and physiology at the McKennan School.[25]

Sister Hoffman cooperated well with the secular world to assist the nurses and trainees in performing their increasingly sophisticated responsibilities. She and the faculty whom she inspired soon eliminated the long-sleeved nursing uniforms and arranged for the trainees to have reinvigorating rest by allowing some time off from duty and studies. This reform was predictable; the first paper she had given after receiving her baccalaureate degree was an address to the South Dakota Nursing Association, "The Eight-Hour Day for

Nurses."[26] After administering the program for four years, she stepped down to enter full-time teaching. Concerning the classroom, Sister Hoffman wrote, "I had a lay instructor over me which was a good experience . . . because I respected her and we . . . complemented and supplemented each other."[27]

Other changes would involve Presentation nurses' right to make their own professional decisions. In the early days, the mother superior, often a hospital administrator, decided whether a sister should become a teacher or a nurse and where she would serve. Until the 1950s, most women unquestioningly went where they were told to go. Sister Lelia Beresford's experience was typical. Mother Butler assigned her to teach grade school, but during a summer vacation Sister Beresford assisted some nurses at St. Luke's Hospital. She did such a good job of taking care of an eye patient that Mother Butler transferred her to a nursing school. Although Sister Beresford exercised little choice of careers, she confessed later in her life, "I'm not sorry . . . because I . . . [gave] . . . help to others."[28]

The entry of the United States into World War II put added pressure on hospital administrators to impede the further professionalization of nurses who were more useful in practice than in study. Because trained health specialists were needed in military facilities, the local hospitals underwent losses of nurses and other health employees. To remedy the problem, in 1942, the federal government authorized the United States Public Health Service to solicit cooperation from hospitals all over the country to establish a Cadet Nurse Corps. Most students were young women who received financial aid, textbooks, uniforms, and monthly allowances. In return, the students promised to remain in some type of government service for the duration of the war. In order to be approved for conducting a cadet training program, nursing schools had to accelerate their curricula to provide the last six months of training for service in either a military or a civilian hospital, depending on which had the greater need at any given time. Often the American Red Cross would recruit graduates to work in hospitals or public health offices. Through this plan thousands of graduates—supposedly not lacking in adequate preparation—were then released for military service overseas.[29]

Despite the potential long-term ill effect on the professionalization of nursing, any hospital involved in the Nurse Cadet Corps had a good chance of attracting many students and improving its facilities; Mother Raphael McCarthy, who had completed the three-year nursing diploma program at St. Luke's, no doubt weighed the benefits against the handicaps that entering such a venture might have on Presentation nursing education. She decided that the first order of business was keeping the schools in operation and thus sent Sister Conception Doyle of St. Luke's Hospital and Sister Viator Burns (bursar of the order) to the nation's capital to inquire about St. Luke's Hospital's becoming involved in the Corps. While in Washington, the women discovered that only McKennan was large enough to meet the federal requirement that participating hospitals have a daily census of more than one hundred patients. United States Public Health Service officials therefore suggested that the sisters centralize the administration of their hospitals and of the four schools of nursing, thereby swelling the total patient count to well over the minimum.[30]

Sisters Doyle and Burns hurried home with their news because the application deadline was imminent. Mother McCarthy called the four schools' directors to Aberdeen, and they decided to follow the recommendation. Planners began reorganization of the nurses' training system to consolidate the courses into two-and-one-half instead of three years and to designate each school as a branch of what became the Presentation Central School of Nursing. Sister M. Conception Doyle became the director, assisted by Magdalene McArthur, the financial director. In April 1942, the operation was the fourth in the nation to receive the surgeon general's approval for participation in the Cadet Nurse Corps, and in June the first class of 103 students enrolled. St. Luke's functioned as the school's headquarters because college science courses and facilities were easily accessible at Northern State Teacher's College.[31]

The Corps brought the Presentations more than $30,000 in federal funds, operated from 1942 to 1946, and under federal provisions graduated four classes from the Presentation Central School of Nursing. Apprentices completed preclinical studies in Aberdeen and then went to one of the four units for the remainder of their education. In keeping with at least some of Sister Hoffman's goals, the candidates enjoyed an eight instead of a ten-hour day, and they also received more days off duty than earlier students had experienced. Some professional goals were sacrificed, however. Sister Richard

Caron, who had graduated from St. Louis University in 1939 with Sister Hoffman and soon became a nursing instructor, believed that although trainees were quite patriotic and proud of the cadet uniforms they wore, some of the graduates were less prepared than they should have been. Although the State Board of Nursing had approved the plan, the great need for nursing services, Sister Caron held, had caused the Corps to lower standards in order to meet the demand. Other sister-nurses, too, believed that shortening the program lowered its quality.[32]

In one respect the Cadet Nurse Corps positively transformed the Presentations' nursing schools because administrators and nursing supervisors afterward retained the centralized nursing program and continued to use pre-entrance tests and grade-point requirements in order to screen applicants. Controlled by a board of administrators comprised of each hospital's nursing superintendent and the school of nursing director, by the late 1940s the central school attained capacity for nearly six hundred enrollees, and the faculty had increased to nearly four times its previous size. Advantages of the four-branch consolidation of the nuns' growing educational effort included a sound financial system as well as improved budgeting practices that enabled the director to know in advance how much line-item money was available for daily institutional operation costs.[33]

The Cadet Nurse Corps adventitiously inspired a renewed sense of camaraderie within the hospitals and within the Presentation order. Some of the students eventually chose the religious life. Above all, the idea of serving one's country during a military emergency had given nursing a bolstered career status and greater prestige within the general population. School spirit, spurred on by patriotism, stimulated the order's desire for professional growth and for upgrading education techniques to achieve national accreditation. For example, in 1947, Sister Doyle represented the school on a panel at the National League of Nursing convention in Seattle, where she shared her order's progress and learned how it could be continued in the years to come.[34]

The nuns' traditional unity sustained them through yet other eras of changes in technology, science, and custom. Even the introduction in 1947 of men into nursing and other of the Presentations' allied health-training programs did not pose a threat to the traditional female values of a Marian ideal because the males accepted the nuns' professional philosophy to strive for intellectual, scientific, and nurturing ideals and therefore managed to adapt very well.[35]

Despite the development of the national polio center at St. Luke's in 1946 and other advances that offered nurses an ever more sophisticated training ground, throughout the 1950s the Central School's major concerns were finances and accreditation. Sister Hoffman received some reprieve when in 1950 Sister Vincent Fuller earned her master's from Catholic University and a year later became associate director of nursing at St. Luke's; however, the fact that Sister Fuller worked free of charge could not stem the tide. Increasing operational costs were because of medical advances that called for more modern classroom techniques and equipment, clinical work, and the employment of instructors with academic degrees. Continuing a trend, physicians were no longer responsible for directing as many formal courses as they had been in the past. Pharmacists, dieticians, physical therapists, and bacteriologists began to share their podium. Increasing medical costs and the discontinuance of federal funds forced the sisters to begin charging tuition. It was no longer possible for the Presentations to support nearly the entire cost of educating nurses as they had done in the past. By 1955, tuition had risen to $400 for the three-year course of study, not including the cost of books and uniforms. Pupils paid a low $25 a month for room and board during the first six months and an escalated fee after that time. The increased charges helped defray the expense of recruitment, supplies, library maintenance, and instructors' salaries. The hospitals still partially subsidized the educational institution: the total from St. Luke's was $4,300 each month.[36]

State accreditation meant working closely with the South Dakota League of Nursing, but this was no problem for the Presentations because they were already active in that organization. Founded in 1952, this affiliate of the National League of Nursing cooperated with the South Dakota Board of Nurse Examiners to encourage standard concepts of professionalization such as enhanced academic training. Sister Hoffman served on the league's board of directors for four years, during which time she and the other board members studied health-related problems and the status of nursing education in the state. The league included professionals and lay people and became the accrediting agency for nursing education, but its sanction was not a legal prerequisite for state approval. Nevertheless, a school that possessed the National League of Nursing seal did gain recognition as one with a superior program.[37]

Soon after the league established its rating procedure in 1952, the Presentations applied but failed in 1954. Examiners informed the sisters that the four units were too far apart geographically to provide adequate sharing of facilities and instructors, and thus the students received unstandardized learning experiences. Furthermore, not enough planning went into elective course choices, and no supplemental plan existed for evaluating the entire curriculum. The experts concluded that the sisters appeared to have, rather than one school, four separate institutions that shared the same program.[38]

This assessment led to further professionalization within the Presentations' Central School. Soon after being denied accreditation, the order cordially ended its diploma program affiliation with Northern State Teachers College and took complete control of the educational sequence.[39] In 1953, the American Association of Nurse Anesthetists approved the School of Anesthesia founded at St. Luke's in 1951. Initially headed by Sister M. DePazzi Zimprich and in 1953 by Sister Rene Regner, the program added alternative training to those seeking "scientific and professional knowledge and practical skill [in] . . . the field of anesthesia."[40] To benefit from other order's medical expertise, also during the mid-1950s, the Central School joined the Conference of Catholic Schools of Nursing.[41]

After much study and thought, administrators of the unified Presentation nursing program decided in 1957 to separate and stratify their nurses' training, thereby producing at least some registered nurses who, as products of a diploma program, then stood for state examinations. St. Luke's school, which together with Presentation College would eventually offer an associate degree program, remained part of the Presentation School of Nursing and achieved league recognition in December of 1957. Holy Rosary School of Nursing closed by August 1960, but during the mid-1970s, Holy Rosary Hospital still provided clinical training for the students of the associate degree nursing program under the administration of a community junior college located in Miles City. During the mid-1970s, the training centers at McKennan and St. Joseph hospitals became affiliated with the public school systems of Sioux Falls and Mitchell, where in each city the nuns utilized facilities of both hospital and school to prepare licensed practical nurses. The programs involved one year of study, after which the graduates took certification examinations. If they passed, the licensed practical nurses joined hospital staffs as medical personnel who basically worked under registered nurses, although they performed some of the same tasks. Today, St. Joseph Hospital offers intern experience to Dakota Wesleyan nursing students.[42]

Through stratification the Presentations bolstered the hierarchical satisfaction of nursing. By providing LPNs to perform the less technical of nursing's traditional duties, Presentation nursing-educators boosted the image of the registered nurses. The nuns also promoted the status of all nurses by continuing a program started by the wartime American Red Cross: a six-week training course that produced aides competent to handle the more menial tasks. The evolving structure of Presentation hospitals, state laws, and professional standards dictated that RNs administer medications and that they delegate personal patient care to LPNs, who in turn were assisted by aides and orderlies.[43]

Although these echelons of service enabled some nurses to reach for ever higher professional recognitions, all hospital nurses have occasionally tolerated arrogance and authoritarianism from a doctor, a potential infringement on nursing's professional autonomy. This infringement has been curtailed somewhat at Presentation and other parochial hospitals because the nuns, not doctors, have been administrators and policy-makers. Some of the Presentations' physician-employees have been reluctant to bow to the nuns' administrative authority, however. The nuns have attempted to keep these recalcitrant doctors (primarily men) in line, but it has been no small task. As Sister Richard Caron remarked, the nuns were not able to "retrain them overnight" because during the early twentieth century, doctors had been treated like "little tin gods." At one time nurses were even expected to rise to their feet when a doctor entered the room.[44] Reflecting on this conflict of autonomy between two professional groups, in 1954, Sister Hoffman advised Mother Burns that "the only one [who] . . . can handle those doctors . . . [at McKennan Hospital] . . . is Mother M. Cornelia Swanton," a fellow nun from another hospital.[45] Nevertheless, Mother Burns asked Sister Hoffman to become the chief administrator, a position she accepted and held until 1962. A nurse by training, Sister Hoffman secured greater autonomy for the nursing program and set an example for other Presentation hospitals by making the director of nursing responsible for only the education of students, no longer for the additional duty of staffing the hospital. With the struggle far from over, Sister Hoffman commented that in general the nurses still fight doctors' arrogance as they strive to be the physicians' professional peers.[46] Finding strength in numbers, Presentation nurses have sought higher degrees and made affiliations with state and national health care associations (Tables 15 and 16).

Right in line with state and national professionalization goals, in 1965, Presentation nurses and higher educators led by Sister Alicia Dunphy and Sister Hoffman took another step toward improving the nursing education program by beginning to conceptualize an associate degree of science.[47] Earlier, during the late 1950s, Sister Anna Marie Weinries, who had earned her Ph.D. in college administration from the University of Texas, had proposed the innovation at Presentation College. Mother Burns, who was the college president at the time, was ardently opposed to such a move and forbade her ever "to even bring this matter . . . up [in a] . . . faculty meeting."[48] Times changed, however, because the Presentations of 1965 eventually accepted many progressive goals. Moreover, Sister Hoffman, herself a nurse who had received her master's degree a year earlier at the University of Minnesota, supported the associate degree of science program and was well prepared to build one. To assist in the effort, in 1965 she and Sister Fuller attended a National League of Nursing Conference in San Francisco. That year the league approved the Presentations' associate degree plan, and the Presentations kept in close touch with the league, which approved of their actions from the outset.[49] A description of the diploma program, just before the transition was made, appears in Table 17.

Although Sister Hoffman and her cohorts were capable of designing the new curriculum, they knew that implementing it would be more difficult. "Even the mention of an Associate Degree Nursing Program [provoked] much controversy and defensiveness," she wrote.[50] Therefore, when possible she mollified the academic departments in which the most potential resistance existed by selecting various individuals from them to conduct feasibility studies and to analyze means of modifying the diploma program into a college degree sequence. The possibility of establishing an associate degree program at Presentation College was confirmed, and after its im-

TABLE 15. PROFESSIONAL AFFILIATIONS OF PRESENTATION
HEALTH CARE PERSONNEL, 1966

American Association of Hospital
Accountants
American Association of Medical
Record Librarians
American Association of Nurse
Anesthetists
American Association of
Registered Nurses
American College of Hospital
Administrators
American College of Nursing
Midwifery
American Nurses' Association
American Organization of
Registered Nurses
American Red Cross Nursing
Service
American Society of Radiographic
Technologists
American Society of X-ray
Technicians
Association of Catholic Schools of
Nursing
Catholic Conference of Schools of
Nursing in South Dakota
Catholic Hospital Association
Dietitians' Association
District Nurses Association
District Nursing Association
Alumni
Medical Technicians Association
Montana Association of Medical
Technologists

Montana Nurses' Association
Montana Society of Medical
Technologists
Montana State Association of
Teachers
National Association of Practical
Nurse Education and Service
National League of Nursing
Education
National Organization of Public
Health Nursing
National Student Nurses'
Association
Presentation School of Nursing
Alumni
Sigma Theta Tau—National Honor
Society of Nursing
Sodality of the Blessed Virgin Mary
South Dakota Association of
Homes for the Aged and Nursing
Homes
South Dakota Division of
American Cancer Society
South Dakota League of Nurses
South Dakota Nursing Association
South Dakota Society of Medical
Technologists
St. Louis University Alumni
State Hospital Association
State Nurses' Association
State Society of X-Ray Technicians

Source: Sister Di Donato, "A History of the Educational Work of the Presentation
Sisters," 142–43. Table edited slightly.

plementation the innovation proved to be a model program in many
ways. All four of the first faculty members whom Sister Dunphy
selected—Sister Caron, Sister Hoffman, Sister Anne Rita Johnson,
and one laywoman—held master's degrees, well above average qualification. At its completion, the school incorporated not only the

TABLE 16. FACULTY OF PRESENTATION SCHOOL OF NURSING, ABERDEEN, 1964–65

Priscilla Allen, R.N., B.S.N., Instructor, Medical-Surgical Nursing. B.S.N., Augustana College, Sioux Falls.

Ruth Anderson, R.N., Instructor, Nursing of Children. Diploma, Lutheran Hospital School of Nursing, Moline, Ill; additional study, Lakeland College, Sheboygan, Wis., Augustana College, Rock Island, Ill.

Margerey Arbogast, R.N., B.A., Assistant Director. Diploma, St. Mary's School of Nursing, Pierre, S. D.; B.A., Yankton College, Yankton, S. D.; additional study, University of South Dakota, Vermillion; University of Colorado, Boulder; Louisiana State University, Baton Rouge; Northern State College, Aberdeen, S. D.

Reverend Robert Beck, B.A., Instructor, Religion, Marriage Preparation, and Medical Ethics. St. Paul's Seminary, St. Paul, Minn.

Sister M. Richard Caron, R.N., B.S.N., M.S.N., Instructor, Psychology, Nursing Fundamentals. Diploma, St. Luke's Hospital School of Nursing, Aberdeen, S. D.; B.S.N.Ed., St. Louis University; M.S.N., Catholic University of America, Washington, D.C.

Sister M. Cecily, R.S.M., R.N., M.S.N., Director of Nursing Education. Diploma, Mercy Hospital, Denver; B.S.N., College of St. Mary, Omaha; M.S.N., Catholic University of America, Washington, D.C.

Sister M. Conception Doyle, R.N., B.S., M.S.N., Director, Freshmen Nursing Program; Instructor, Christian Social Living. Diploma, St. Elizabeth's Hospital School of Nursing, Chicago; B.S., College of St. Catherine, St. Paul, Minn.; M.S.N.Ed., Catholic University of America, Washington, D.C.

Sister M. Alicia Dunphy, B.S., M.Sc. in Ed., Instructor, Religion. Marygrove College, Detroit; Northern State Teacher's College, Aberdeen, S. D.; St. Louis University.

Mrs. Steve Jewett, R.N., Clinical Instructor. Diploma, Mercy Hospital, Des Moines.

Sister M. Anne Rita Johnson, R.N., B.S.N., M.S.N., Instructor, Medical-Surgical Nursing. Diploma, Presentation School of Nursing, Aberdeen, S. D.; additional study, Northern State College, Aberdeen; B.S.N., Marquette University, Milwaukee; M.S.N., St. Louis University.

Sally Johnson, R.N., Assistant Instructor, Medical-Surgical Nursing. Diploma, Presentation School of Nursing, Mitchell, S. D.; additional study, Northern State College, Aberdeen, S. D.

(continued)

resources of Presentation College, but also those of St. Luke's Hospital, Mother Joseph Manor, and the American Health Care Center. In 1966, the Presentations applied to the Department of Health, Education, and Welfare for funds to build a separate teaching center. Securing the money, they completed the structure in 1969.[51]

TABLE 16. FACULTY OF PRESENTATION SCHOOL OF NURSING *(continued)*

Bernard Kenny, M.D., Psychiatrist. M.D., Creighton University, Omaha, and Nebraska Psychiatric Institute, Omaha.

Eldora King, R.N., M.S., Director of Nursing. B.S., New York University, New York City; M.S. in Psychiatric Nursing, Boston University, Boston.

Sister M. Jane Frances Lamm, B.S., M.S., Instructor, Science, Home Economics. South Dakota State College, Brookings; College of St. Benedict, St. Cloud, Minn.; St. Louis University; Catholic University of America, Washington, D.C.

J. D. Mahoney, M.D., Professor of Psychiatry. M.D., University of Pittsburg; F.A.C.P. Head, Department of Psychiatry, Creighton University, Omaha; Associate Medical Director, St. Bernard's Hospital, Council Bluffs, Ia.

Sister M. Claudia McNamara, R.N., B.S.N., M.S.N., Instructor, Anatomy-Physiology. Diploma, McKennan Hospital School of Nursing, Sioux Falls, S. D.; B.S.N., Creighton University, Omaha; M.S.N., Marquette University, Milwaukee.

Sister Marie Patrice Moriarty, B.A., Instructor, English. College of St. Catherine, St. Paul, Minn., and Northern State Teachers College, Aberdeen, S. D.

Sister M. Bernard Quinn, R.N., B.S.N.Ed., M.S.N., Director. Diploma, St. Joseph's School of Nursing, Mitchell, S. D.; B.S.N.Ed., College of St. Theresa, Winona, Minn.; M.S.N., Catholic University of America, Washington, D.C.

H. Rassekh, M.D., Psychiatrist. M.D., University of Geneva, Switzerland. Nebraska Psychiatric Institute, Omaha.

Mrs. Annette Rathert, R.N., Clinical Instructor. Diploma, Sacred Heart School of Nursing, Yankton, S. D.; additional study at Yankton College.

Sister M. Gonzaga Silvis, B.S. in Ed., M.S., Instructor, Chemistry. B.S., Northern State Teacher's College, Aberdeen, S. D.; M.S., St. Louis University.

Sister M. Alma Staudenraus, B.S., Instructor, Diet Therapy. B.S., College of St. Catherine, St. Paul, Minn; Internship, St. Louis University Hospitals.

Mrs. Michael Vazzano, R.N., Clinical Instructor. Diploma, St. Catherine's Hospital, Omaha.

Source: Sister Di Donato, "A History of the Educational Work of the Presentation Sisters," 175–77. Table edited slightly.

Reflecting problems typical of a new program, the first graduates performed poorly on the state boards. Apparently one doctor blamed the curriculum in particular for their failure; yet Sister Hoffman persisted, and soon an average of almost 91 percent of the graduates passed the state examinations on their first attempt.[52]

The Presentations' ever-present philosophical mission, the

TABLE 17. PRESENTATION SCHOOL OF NURSING, 1963–65

Goals

1. To assist students in acquiring professional skills, knowledge, and attitudes on a Christian basis as will qualify them for the following positions:
   a. general duty staff nursing
   b. private duty nursing
   c. military nursing
   d. limited areas of psychiatric staff nursing
   e. nursing in doctors' offices or clinics
2. To help students develop their personal abilities
3. To encourage students to develop their physical, intellectual, and spiritual qualities
4. To encourage students to accept their responsibilities as members of a special group
5. To encourage students to seek truth
6. To assist students in evaluating their immediate educational growth as well as other activities of life in the light of the existence of God and the ultimate goal of man—eternal life with God in Heaven

Curriculum

*Anatomy	*Microbiology
*General chemistry	*English composition
*Christian social living	*Introduction to sociology
*General psychology	*Fundamentals of the Catholic faith
*Catholic life and worship	*Nutrition
Nursing fundamentals I and II	Medical-surgical nursing
Psychiatric nursing	Maternity nursing
Nursing of children	Professional nursing
Marriage preparation	Religion I, II, III
Medical ethics	History and trends of professional nursing

Source: Sister Di Donato, "A History of the Educational Work of the Presentation Sisters," 78–79. Table edited slightly.

*Courses taught at Presentation College

blending of both humanistic and scientific concerns, were inscribed in the six stated aims of the associate degree program: "To foster genuine respect and concern for the uniqueness and dignity of each individual; . . . to practice utilizing scientific principles from the bio-psycho-social sciences; . . . to guide the student in the art of interpersonal relationships; . . . to prepare a safe practitioner who utilizes the nursing process to meet the needs of clients in health and illness in varied structured settings; . . . to develop an awareness of the moral, ethical, and legal responsibilities involved in client care[; and] . . . to emphasize the importance of continuous personal growth and self-direction."[53]

Guided by these goals, the curriculum underwent many smaller changes from 1965 to 1984. Faculty committees studied requirements and tailored credits from seventy-four to sixty-nine and then back again to seventy-one hours. Nevertheless, offerings always included courses in theoretical and clinical nursing, liberal arts, philosophy, ethics, and religion. Students were also involved in prenatal education, community health, and preventive health care programs that would earn for the college much praise from Aberdeen's townspeople.[54]

Most certainly the students' and secular nurses' opinions of the Presentations' nursing program varied from person to person. Those who feared the stigma of being too domestically oriented were critical of the holistic approach which, as one nun put it, demanded a "selflessness" from Presentation students. Yet others whose professional perspective struck a balance between humanism and technical knowledge applauded the Presentations' efforts. Certainly, nuns such as Presentation Sisters from Fargo, whom the Aberdeen Presentations trained, identified with the South Dakota sisters' ideals. Moreover, Joan Kippes, director of nursing services at St. Joseph in 1978, praised the Presentations' professionalism, noting that over the years the nuns had become more sympathetic to lay nurses' drives for increased pay, better benefits, and improved working conditions. Through their educational programs, hospitals, and other health care agencies, the Presentations had achieved a power that often excelled that acquired by strongly union-oriented nurses because the nuns exercised policymaking roles throughout the health care field.[55]

During the 1970s and 80s, Presentation College faculty took advantage of their positions as empowered faculty members. Through a consortium with Northern State College, members gained experience developing courses, and in 1975, the nursing faculty began planning an extension program with the community of Eagle Butte, on the Cheyenne River Reservation in western South Dakota. The sisters also developed an innovative Learning Experience Guide in nursing, which provided individualized instruction and thereby placed more responsibility for advancement on the learners than initially had existed. In addition an American Health Care Center in Aberdeen served a number of townspeople and rural citizens and embodied yet another alternative training-ground for the experiential component of the Presentations' nursing course of study. By the mid-1980s, Presentation College nurse-educators recorded that there were fourteen faculty members in the associate degree program, all of whom held bachelor's degrees in nursing, and three of whom held master's degrees. Faculty-student ratios were approximately one to eight for freshmen and one to twelve for sophomores.[56]

In summary, by the 1980s, the Presentations' involvement in health care education had resulted in the development of modern, well-run operations, advanced beyond the first half of the twentieth century when apprenticeship overshadowed academic training. Conflicts similar to those throughout the national nursing scene had aggravated what Presentations and national accrediting organizations recognized as problems: Administrators had needed the cheap labor of nursing students to keep open even a nonprofit hospital, and some Presentation nurses had feared that they could not become more scientific without abandoning the emotional, nurturing side of practicing their occupation. Yet, unlike many other nursing leaders throughout the country, the Presentations who favored professionalization used their order's traditional belief in women's special talent for soothing and healing to rationalize the need for higher education for nurse educators and administrators. In accepting men into their programs, they proved that these values could be imparted to—and then practiced by—men. Nuns such as Sister Hoffman focused on the sisters' commonly held goal of serving to rally support for the professionalization of the nurses' training program at McKennan. Moreover, the associate degree program at Presentation College was an inspired compromise dedicated to fulfilling both the craft and the science of nursing. Although in the process the Presentations' training programs became segmented, with the LPN course of study including less academic and collegiate study than does the associate degree curriculum, the fact remains that at least some Presentation nurses have professionalized not by rejecting the traditional nineteenth-century woman's ideology of separate spheres but by using it to expand their intellectual horizons. As a supplement to Presentation nurses' strength, they have received outside support from federal and state governments and from the countless people whom they have served on the northern Great Plains.[57]

NOTES

1. Mother Viator Burns to Reverend William O. Brady, July 9, 1948, Presentation Archives, Presentation Heights, Aberdeen, S. D.

2. *Diamond Jubilee Book* (Aberdeen, S. D.: Sisters of the Presentation of the Blessed Virgin Mary, 1961), 36.

3. Mary Ewens, O.P., *The Role of the Nun in Nineteenth-Century America: Variations on the International Theme* (New York : Arno Press, 1971, repr., Salem, N.H.: Ayer Publishers, 1984), 25, 42, 49, 102–3.

4. Vern L. Bullough and Bonnie Bullough, *The Emergence of Modern Nursing* (Toronto: Macmillan, 1969), 99–101.

5. Florence Nightingale, quoted in Elizabeth M. Jamieson, Mary F. Sewall, and Eleanor B. Suhrie, *Trends in Nursing History: Their Social, International and Ethical Relationships* (Philadelphia: W. B. Saunders, 1966), 194.

6. Merle Curti, "Clara Barton," in *Notable American Women; 1607–1950: A Biographical Dictionary*, vol. 1, ed. Edward T. James (Cambridge, Mass.: Belknap Press, 1971), 103–8; James Hennesey, *American Catholics: A History of the Roman Catholic Community in the United States* (New York: Oxford University Press, 1981), 155.

7. Jamieson, *Trends in Nursing History*, 223–25; Ewens, *The Role of the Nun in Nineteenth-Century America*, 265–74.

8. Jamieson, *Trends in Nursing History*, 257–59; Janet Wilson James, "Lavinia Lloyd Dock," in *Notable American Women: The Modern Period, a Biographical Dictionary*, ed. Barbara Sicherman and Carol Hurd Green (Cambridge, Mass.: Belknap Press, 1980), 195–98; Eliot Freidson, *Profession of Medicine: A Study of the Sociology of Applied Knowledge* (New York: Dodd, Mead, 1973), 66; Bullough and Bullough, *The Emergence of Modern Nursing*, 149–50. For a reference to the "secular nun," see Richard Quantz, "The Complex Visions of Female Teachers and the Failure of Unionization in the 1930s" (unpub. paper, authors' possession).

9. Barbara Melosh, *"The Physician's Hand": Work Culture and Conflict in American Nursing* (Philadelphia: Temple University Press, 1982), 39, 59–67, 70–72, 125–42; Ronald G. Corwin, "The Professional Employee: A Study of Conflict in Nursing Roles," *The American Journal of Sociology* 66 (May 1961): 604–15; Jo Ann Ashley, *Hospitals, Paternalism, and the Role of the Nurse* (New York: Teachers College Press, 1976), 98–102.

10. Ashley, *Hospitals, Paternalism, and the Role of the Nurse*, 6, 14; Melosh, *"The Physician's Hand,"* 32, 167; Ashley, *Hospitals, Paternalism, and the Role of the Nurse*, 21.

11. Bullough and Bullough, *The Emergence of Modern Nursing*, 170.

12. Ashley, *Hospitals, Paternalism, and the Role of the Nurse*, 10–11; Melosh, "The Physician's Hand," 37–67.

13. Melosh, "The Physician's Hand," 46–47; Margie Peterson, "The Bachelor Prepared Nurse and the American Nurses' Association: A Dilemma of Unity" (unpub. paper, authors' posession); Ashley, *Hospitals, Paternalism, and the Role of the Nurse*, 96, 126.

14. *Dakota Wesleyan University, 1985–1987 Catalog* (Mitchell: Dakota Wesleyan University, 1985), 124; James Cass and Max Birbaum, eds., *Comparative Guide to Two-Year Colleges and Career Programs*, "South Dakota," (New York: Harper and Row, 1976), 299–302; D. Parnell and J. W. Peltason, eds., *American Community, Technical, and Junior Colleges* (New York: American Council on American Education Community, Technical and Junior Colleges, 1984), 647; communications between Sylvia Starr and South Dakota Nursing Program Officials, Oct. 1, 1986.

15. Communications between Sylvia Starr and South Dakota Nursing Program Officials, Oct. 1, 1986; *South Dakota State University Catalog 1984–85* (Brookings: South Dakota State University, 1984), 140.

16. Sister Conception Doyle, "History of Aberdeen Presentation School of Nursing," Presentation Archives; *Diamond Jubilee Book*, 32; Melosh, "The Physician's Hand," 36–39; *St. Joe Happenings* (May 1976); Dolores Harrington, *A Woman's Will . . . A Sister's Way* (Sioux Falls, S.D.: McKennan Hospital, 1961), 59–60.

17. Sister M. Cabrini Di Donato, "A History of the Educational Work of the Presentation Sisters of Aberdeen, South Dakota" (master's thesis, Northern State College, 1966), 60–61.

18. Sister Di Donato, "A History of the Educational Work of the Presentation Sisters," 62.

19. Sister Doyle, "History of Aberdeen Presentation School of Nursing"; Harrington, *A Woman's Will*, 59; "McKennan Historical Data," Jubilee Data, Presentation Archives; Jamieson et al., *Trends in Nursing History*, 268.

20. Jamieson et al., *Trends in Nursing History*, 268., interview with Sister Bonaventure Hoffman, Aug. 6, 1976, South Dakota Oral History Center, Vermillion.

21. Interview with Veronica Goebel, July 26, 1978, South Dakota Oral History Center.

22. Sister Doyle, "History of Aberdeen Presentation School of Nursing."

23. Sister Di Donato, "A History of the Educational Work of the Presentation Sisters," 64–66.

24. Sister Bonaventure Hoffman, "Manuscript," Presentation Archives.

25. Ibid.

26. Ibid.

27. Interview with Sister Bonaventure Hoffman, Aug. 6, 1976.

28. Sister Lelia Beresford, "Review of the History of St. Joseph Hos-

221

pital," Office, St. Joseph Hospital, Mitchell, S. D.; interview with Sister M. Lelia Beresford, Aug. 11, 1976, South Dakota Oral History Center.

29. Harrington, *A Woman's Will*, 35–37; interview with Sister Richard Caron, June 19, 1978, South Dakota Oral History Center; Sister Doyle, "History of Aberdeen Presentation School of Nursing"; "Jubilee Data"; Jamieson et al., *Nursing History*, 293–95; *U. S. Statutes at Large, 78th Congress, 1st Session*, vol. 55, pt. 2 (Washington, D. C., U. S. Government Printing Office, 1942), 484. For dates on organizational foundings, see *Encyclopedia of Associations*, ed. Katherine Gruder (Detroit: Gale Research, 1987).

30. Sister Hoffman, "Manuscript."

31. Ibid.; *Presentation Nurse*, Nov. 1942; interview with Sister Richard Caron; Sister Doyle, "History of Aberdeen Presentation School of Nursing"; Sister Di Donato, "A History of the Educational Work of the Presentation Sisters," 68–69.

32. Interview with Sister Richard Caron; Sister Hoffman, "Manuscript"; *Presentation Nurse*, March 1944, June 1946; Sister Doyle, "History of Aberdeen Presentation School of Nursing"; "McKennan School of Nursing Tables," Jubilee Data.

33. Interview with Sister Richard Caron; *Presentation Nurse*, Nov. 1946, June 1946; Sister Doyle, "History of Aberdeen Presentation School of Nursing."

34. "McKennan School of Nursing Tables"; Sister Hoffman, "Manuscript"; interview with Sister Richard Caron.

35. Interview with Sister Richard Caron; interview with Sister Bonaventure Hoffman, June 20, 1978, South Dakota Oral History Center; Sister Di Donato, "A History of the Educational Work of the Presentation Sisters," 70.

36. *Presentation Nurse*, March 1944, Fall 1947; Sister Doyle, "History of Aberdeen Presentation School of Nursing"; "Jubilee Data"; interview with Sister Bonaventure Hoffman, Aug. 6, 1976.

37. "Brief History of South Dakota League for Nursing," Presentation Archives; Jamieson et al., *Nursing History*, 327–36; "Unique Role of National League for Nursing," Presentation Archives.

38. Sister Doyle, "History of Aberdeen Presentation School of Nursing."

39. Sister Di Donato, "A History of the Educational Work of the Presentation Sisters," 77.

40. Ibid., 75.

41. Sister Hoffman, "Manuscript."

42. Ibid.; "St. Joseph Questionnaire," Jubilee Data; *Sioux Falls Argus – Leader*, Jan. 4, 1959; "McKennan Historical Data," Jubilee Data; "McKennan School of Nursing Tables," exhibit 2, Heritage Room, McKennan Hospital, Sioux Falls, S. D.; interview with Sister Bonaventure Hoffman, June 20, Aug. 6, 1978; interview with Mrs. Frances Gresby, July 12, 1978, South Dakota Oral History Center; *Diamond Jubilee Book*, 35;

communication between Sylvia Starr and Norbert Goergen, Oct. 1, 1986; Sister Di Donato, "A History of the Educational Work of the Presentation Sisters," 83–84.

43. Interview with Sister Bonventure Hoffman, Aug. 6, 1976; *Presentation Nurse*, Nov. 1942; Harrington, *A Woman's Will*, 37, 61.

44. Interview with Sister Richard Caron.

45. Sister Hoffman, "Manuscript."

46. Ibid.; Interview with Sister Bonaventure Hoffman, June 20, 1978.

47. Sister Hoffman, "Manuscript."

48. Interview with Sister Anna Marie Weinreis, August 10, 1976, South Dakota Oral History Center.

49. Interview with Sister Bonaventure Hoffman, Aug. 6, 1976; Sister Bonaventure Hoffman, "Associate Degree Nursing Program, a Ten Year Report," Presentation Archives; Sister Hoffman, "Manuscript."

50. Sister Hoffman, "Manuscript."

51. Interview with Sister Bonaventure Hoffman, Aug. 6, 1976; Sister Hoffman, "Manuscript" and "Associate Degree Nursing Program."

52. Interview with Sister Bonaventure Hoffman, Aug. 6, 1976.

53. Sister Hoffman, "Manuscript."

54. Ibid.; interview with Sister Bonaventure Hoffman, Aug. 6, 1976; *Presentation College Catalog* (Aberdeen, S. D.: Presentation College, 1984), 38.

55. Interview with Mrs. Joan Kippes, June 5, 1978; interview with Sister Bonaventure Hoffman, Aug. 6, 1976; interview with Sister Jane Francis, June 20, 1978, South Dakota Oral History Center. For a source on nurses entering administrative positions, see Freidson, *Profession of Medicine*, 66.

56. Interview with Sister Bonaventure Hoffman, Aug. 6, 1976; "Presentation College Catalogue Supplement," in *Presentation College Catalog*; Hoffman, "Associate Degree Program."

57. A portion of this chapter is included in Susan Peterson "Adapting to Fill a Need: Presentation Health Care, 1901–1961," *South Dakota History* 17 (Summer 1987).

9. The Evolving Presentation Sister: A Reconstruction of the Old

☐

Beginning with Nano Nagle, the Presentation Order has looked outward, seeking to serve whenever and wherever it has been needed. In so doing, many of the South Dakota sisters have resembled other women religious throughout the world while transforming a mission that was separate from and unequal to that of men into one that is still separate but at last more nearly equal. It is difficult to pinpoint an exact date for this occurrence. Certainly during the post-Vatican II era change was evident, although for decades previous women religious had assumed numerous professional responsibilities in predominately male fields such as hospital administration, and for centuries previous they had turned their other trespasses into rites of passage. Philosophical evolution had not unfolded without strife, and even today some members of the South Dakota Presentation community identify with women in other American congregations who still adhere to the old ways.

The loosening of Presentation nuns' organizational structure since Vatican II has catalyzed the twentieth-century changes in ideology that ironically have portrayed both a liberalization and a renewal of the old ideological tenets. Attempting to remain ever ready to practice her ideals, Nano Nagle had tried to avoid institutionalization, perceiving it as an impediment to her work. Nagle's one-woman crusade to educate the Irish poor eventually wore down her resolve, and in 1776 she formed the Society of the Charitable Instruction of the Sacred Heart of Jesus, which after her death became the Presentation Sisters. Although Nagle's immediate scions accepted enclosure, those in South Dakota and other American regions set aside the rule during the nineteenth century. Thus, from the time of their coming to Aberdeen in 1886, the South Dakota sisters have struggled to design an organizational structure loose enough to allow for professional innovations but defined enough to provide security for its members and conformity to accepted Church beliefs concerning women's natural roles. Although the South Dakota Presentations eliminated enclosure during the early years of their settlement, as their environment gradually became more stable during the early twentieth century they increased the amount of structure in their personal lives, creating a trend that the sisters would not, or perhaps could not, reverse until the late 1950s. Although professionalization within the Presentation apostolates had existed despite, or even because of, the order's confining structure, by mid-century the majority of professional nuns came to believe that as brides of Christ they deserved enhanced power over their lives and their careers.

The Catholic Church had greatly encouraged the closed, efficient convent system. As one historian wrote, "an increasing emphasis on centralism . . . characterized Church affairs after the Vatican Council of 1870."[1] Although in 1900 Pope Leo XIII issued *Conditae a Christo*, which officially recognized nuns with simple rather than solemn vows, a year later *Normae* stated that such congregations must practice "partial cloister," reserving a section of any convent for the members' use only. The Vatican also insisted that no sister could travel alone outside the compound walls.[2]

Similar mandates designed to protect female culpability were issued for American Catholic laywomen. For example, Cardinal James Gibbons, one of the country's most influential churchmen, wrote in 1905 that "the wife is the source of the family. If the fountain is not pure, the stream is sure to be foul and muddy."[3] Nor was the Church particularly supportive of Catholic women involving themselves in social movements before and during the Progressive Era. Even so, some of them did join women of other faiths to crusade actively for prohibition and suffrage or against child labor. Rose Hawthorne Lathrop was a noted example. In a speech given at the 1893 Chicago National Catholic Congress, she attempted to align others with moral causes, intoning, "Oh, woman, the hour has struck when you are to arise and defend your rights, your abilities for competition with men in intellectual and professional endurance, the hour when you are to prove that purity and generosity are for the nation as well as for the home . . . ."[4] Acting on her own words, but within the female sphere, Lathrop five years later became Mother

Mary Alphonsa and founded the Dominican Congregation of Saint Rose of Lima, an order devoted to health care.[5]

The expectation remained for married women to stay home. Even though in 1899 Notre Dame of Maryland (founded fifty-one years earlier) began granting academic degrees to females, Trinity College for Women (which opened a year after Notre Dame) continued to exist only "to insure that . . . students increased in womanliness, gentility, sweet voice, feminine piety, and fear of God."[6] Perpetuating the idea that women should remain within their own social and religious domain, Catholic proscriptive literature for years did not support radical changes in the domestic domain. As late as 1955, Pope Pius XII decreed that "Be she married or single, woman's function is seen clearly defined in the lineaments of her sex, in its propensities and special powers. She works side by side with man, but she works in her own way and according to her natural bent. Now a woman's function, a woman's way, a woman's natural bent is motherhood. Every woman is called to be a mother, mother in the physical sense, or mother in a sense more spiritual and more exalted, yet real nonetheless."[7]

Thus, particularly during this century's first half, the Church's insistence on protecting women from the vicissitudes of the world pressed the South Dakota Presentations and other nuns all over the world into a convent life that resembled a total institution. Another motivation for this occurrence was a secular trend: organizational theorists were touting the efficacy of centralization, a watchword of what Alvin Toffler calls the Second Wave (the modern industrial age). Not surprisingly, such a system gave participants a sense of security because each sister knew exactly what was expected of her.[8] According to their constitution, the nuns were to "without hesitation, comply with the orders of the Superior, . . . and should she happen to reprimand them undeservedly, they are not to murmur, nor complain, but with a submissive mind and pious affection receive her rebukes striving to justify them in their own minds, in order the more perfectly to obey with all the powers and strength of their souls."[9] Moreover, requirements for specific amounts of daily prayer and contemplation directed and focused her spiritual and professional life. Theoretically, these long hours spent in performance of religious and professionally related duties would help solidify the community's bonds through participants' collective struggle.[10]

In the constitutions of 1920 and 1946, a powerful Marian ideology was reaffirmed, although the assertion of the sisters' separate and as yet unequal religious, social, and hence professional roles still surfaced as it had in "The Rules and Constitutions of the Sisters of the Congregation of the Charitable Instruction" of 1793. In both the 1920 and 1946 constitutions, Mary's image was upheld as the nuns' ideal. She was called the " 'Queen of Heaven' . . . [who] . . . is, under God, [our] . . . principal Patroness and Protectress. [We] shall have, individually, unlimited confidence in her; have recourse in all [our] . . . difficulties and spiritual necessities, and by the imitation of her virtues [we] . . . shall study to please her, and to render [ourselves] . . . worthy of her maternal protection."[11] Mary's compelling presence, in both constitutions, reflected the popular conception of Eve's legacy, the danger of vitiation that lay within each woman. In the 1946 document, the nuns therefore instructed themselves "not [to] fix their eyes upon them [men], nor in the least degree show themselves familiar in speech or in any other way, however devout and religious these men may seem."[12]

Despite the limitations, each constitution carefully explained that while the sisters should appreciate Christ's suffering and death for all of humankind, they should exercise restraint in their penitent activities. The 1920 treatise reads, "The Sisters of this Religious Congregation being by their Institute almost constantly employed in the arduous and laborious functions of instructing children, and other works of charity, shall be obliged to fast and abstain only on the days commanded by the Church, and on the eve of the Immaculate Conception, Nativity, Presentation, and Purification of our Blessed Lady."[13]

The 1946 document elaborated further the importance of professional preparation, stating that "The duty of teaching imposes upon the Sisters the obligation to prepare themselves carefully and exactly. . . . According to their abilities, [they] shall have academic and professional preparation so that [they] . . . may be adequately qualified to discharge their duties in the various fields of education. . . . Sisters assigned to the care of the sick shall [also] have special and careful preparation for their duties. . . ."[14]

Along with the drive toward professionalization, by the 1920s and 30s postulant and novice training had become an increasingly structured experience compared to the less routinized frontier life.

In 1920, the minimum age for a postulant was set at sixteen, but the age of profession remained set at twenty-one years of age.[15] Resembling the original constitution, the constitutions of 1920 and 1946 both contained admonitions concerning woman's special propensity for error. In the first, the mistress of novices was instructed to help her charges "root out, as much as possible, those pettish and childish humors, which, especially in the female sex weaken the spirit, and render it vapid and languid. . . ."[16] Moreover, twenty-six years later the mistress was still told to help the novices "restrain any manifestation of weakness, especially those which in women tend to make them soft or without spirit. . . ."[17]

First-year candidates submitted to such strictures as silence periods, censored correspondence, no visits to their families, and no financial allowance. They were required to ask permission for such minor activities as using the telephone. By the second year, the novices wore habits with white veils. Vocational training then supplemented their study of religious life, after the mother superior decided whether each young woman would become a teacher, a nurse, or a domestic worker in the motherhouse. During the third year, the novices continued scriptural and spiritual study in preparation for temporary vows. Their novice mistress taught aspirants how to observe the community's rules and customs and to appreciate their historical involvement in the service professions. The mistress also helped the candidates overcome homesickness, accept authority, and understand the depth of their promise to God.[18] Leading daily exercises of prayer and work, she stressed the value of obedience, through which "a religious soul is intimately united to God . . . ."[19] Finally, the mistress tested the prospective sister's aptitude for religious life, her dedication, and her self-discipline. Sometimes informal initiation of candidates took the form of mild hazing, typical in many organizations. One nun recounted that older sisters made up stories about younger ones, purporting they had been seen in town behaving in a nonpious or unladylike fashion. It is unknown how the novices were to respond when confronted with these accusations, but no doubt they were contrived to emphasize just who was in charge of the convent social structure. If a neophyte questioned the calling and decided not to join the community, authorities explained this to the remainder of the sisters as a sign of God's will, rather than as a fault in the young woman's character. After profession, those who left the order were, according to one nun, spirited off in the night.[20]

Increasing traditionalism in the novitiate paralleled the waning of feminism in the United States after 1930. Although the nuns' own social system was quite closed, postulants and novices were born and reared within the world outside the order and could very easily have been influenced by popular social trends. In any event, domestic familial customs by mid-century had become prevalent within the Presentation community. Unlike their predecessors, those nuns who then took the veil were dressed in white brides' dresses symbolizing their holy marriage and submission to Christ, the bridegroom. In short, external symbols and restrictions in the training of novices received a great deal of emphasis.[21]

After becoming a full-fledged sister, the new nun joined companions who strictly observed schedules concerning work, classes, and domestic chores without questioning tradition's value. During the 1920s, nuns could listen to the radio, and, later in the 1950s, they could also watch television, both at specified times. In general, life was very regimented. Prayer and observance of silence always formed the basis of religious life, but during the more structured eras the women were all expected to attend early morning chapel services held before Mass and at other specific times throughout the day. The strictly defined behavior, which included restrictions on recreational reading material, supposedly insured that if a sister were constantly occupied she would naturally stay on the spiritual track. Couched within such an environment, a woman's sense of power and personal fulfillment came from belonging to a community, having a calling, and surrendering all else to God. Eager for a change, Sister Judith O'Brien rejoiced when bedtime restrictions were lifted during the late 1960s. She had found it almost impossible to find time to complete professional preparations for her job as an instructor at Presentation College.[22]

Even so, the gradual shift toward consolidation and syncronization, beginning within the international Presentation Order late in the nineteenth century, had produced some beneficial results because it strengthened the nuns' world-wide external support system. For example, in 1877, the Presentation convent in South Cork sent an appeal to celebrate the centenary dated from Nagle's profession one hundred years earlier.[23]

The South Dakota congregation moved cautiously toward national and international amalgamation tendencies. Resembling some other superiors across the country, Mother McCarthy dissolved early isolationist sentiment and pushed for modernization by making an application for the South Dakota community to become a pontifical congregation. The change would move the women from the bishop's control to the pope's direct jurisdiction, placing them within a more central, hierarchical Church structure and giving them heightened status. Beginning in 1932, Mother McCarthy wrote Church officials and other convents, particularly the California Presentation Sisters, inquiring about correct procedures. The investigations informed her how best to fulfill her objective and, in 1946, Pope Pius XII gave final approval to the nuns' revised constitution. In addition to the statements on professionalization, one major alteration was the method of electing community leaders so that the sisters elected and sent delegates to their periodic general chapters to vote for the major superior and council members. A product of the ever-growing enthusiasm for modernization and efficiency within the American culture throughout much of the twentieth century, the Presentation's delegate system nevertheless suppressed individual expression among the women, a change to which many nuns strenuously objected.[24]

Keeping in particularly close contact with the San Francisco Presentation motherhouse, Mother McCarthy and Bishop Brady offered refuge in 1942 to Mother M. Carthagh and her entire congregation in case of a Japanese attack on the United States by way of the California coast. Mother McCarthy even reaped unexpected benefits from these gestures when during the mid-1950s the chief executive enjoyed a six-month stay with the San Francisco group during the intervals between her periodic hospitalization there for a corneal transplant. Also on good terms with the Benedictines of Yankton under Mother M. Jerome Schmitt and the Benedictines at Sturgis under Mother M. Lucia, Mother McCarthy served as an intermediary between them and a promoter of religious building projects, Neil J. Gleason of Milwaukee.[25]

Especially among Presentations themselves, such unity was essential to surviving and prospering over the next years, times of change and modernization within American society and the Catholic Church. Although the feminist movement had yet to resurface in mainstream American thought, advances in education and health care demanded added professionalization by religious.[26] To plan a unified response to social change, a Presentation organization, later known as the Presentation North American Conference, was inaugurated at a historic place, Notre Dame University in Indiana. The sisters attending the organization's first meeting in 1952 "resolved to gather bi-annually for the purpose of unity and support . . . ."[27] Mother superiors and novice mistresses comprised the conference's first participants. At the 1955 gathering in San Francisco, Mother Viator Burns was elected president, and in 1957, the meeting convened at Presentation Heights in Aberdeen. A sign of these changing times, during the 1950s the South Dakota order decided to use other Presentation houses throughout the United States as models, resolving to recite the Short Breviary in English rather than in Latin, thereby enhancing each woman's understanding of the material while allowing the nuns more time for professional duties. Invigorated by such changes, the South Dakota Presentations continued to increase numerically, even into the 1960s.[28]

Meanwhile, Presentations in other countries such as Australia met during the 1950s to discuss the benefits of amalgamation. Although each Australian order retained its autonomy, in 1957, six Australian congregations formed the Australian Society.[29] Speaking broadly of the society, of the North American Conference, and of various associations within Ireland, Presentation historian Sister M. Raphael Consedine noted that "they widened the Sisters' perspectives on both international affairs and apostolic challenges." Moreover, she pointed out, "sociologists recognize that the solidarity of any group is strengthened when there is a high degree of collaboration towards a common goal. . . ."[30] Thus the professionalization benefits of modernization seemed to have outweighed the drawbacks.

Not only overseas, but also throughout the United States, the structure and consistency of an increasingly bureaucratized Church attracted growing numbers of people. From 1912 to 1963, the Catholic population in America almost tripled, from 15,015,569 to 43,851,538, while entry into religious orders, primarily women's groups, climbed consistently throughout the century. In 1954, the tally was 158,069 women and 8,752 men in all orders, and by the mid-1960s, these figures had risen to 181,421 and 12,539, respectively.[31]

Despite the apparent strength of the Church in America, a few European critics of Catholicism would eventually win an audience in the United States. The challenges came during and after World War II from both laypersons and parishioners disillusioned by the Church's historic tolerance of tyrannical governments such as Mussolini's fascist state, with its failure to confront the evils of imperialism, and with its unwillingness to respect human rights. A host of European authors including Pere de Lubac and Henri Chenu revealed that the Church's ruling hierarchy seemed willing to oppress any of its members, including low-ranking nuns, when doing so preserved the institution's status quo or advanced its goals.[32]

By mid-century, Catholic Church members in America were beginning to realize that a highly formalized existence, based at least in part on the alleged propensity for female moral decline, was hampering the apostolic life of many nuns. In addition, it seemed that the Church's goal of staffing schools in the United States in order to meet the rising demands of parishioners and to combat the increased secularization of society had also retarded some sisters' professionalization efforts (chapters 1 and 2). In 1948, leading sister-educators throughout the United States established a Teacher Education department within the Catholic Education Association. The purpose of this new agency was to insist that all apostolic nuns obtain higher educational credentials equal to if not higher than their secular counterparts.[33]

Joining the professionalization crusade in 1950, Pope Pius XII encouraged apostolic religious to redesign their modes of attire to better suit health requirements and the practicing of their skills.[34] Meeting in 1951, the First International Convention of Teaching Sisters reiterated the theme. Soon the Sister Formation Movement was born, and during the 1950s and 60s in the United States it became "a nationwide campaign to make sisters more saintly, skilled . . . mature and . . . efficient. . . ."[35] Professionalization therefore was to occur in conjunction with a reassertion of the nuns' traditional call to uplift their clients morally.

Explaining more clearly that nuns' professional ideology should still be associated with a historic but refurbished ideology of separate spheres, Pius XII proclaimed in the apostolic constitution, *Munificentissomus Deus*, that nuns were the daughters of Mary, Mother of God, "the new Eve . . . subject to the new Adam [but] . . . most intimately associated with him in the struggle against the infernal foe."[36] Similarly, nine years later, Presentation historian T. J. Walsh praised all the sisters who had followed the example of Angela Merici: "St. Angela Merici, first and greatest of the modern educators, understood that a woman's life is a life of the affections which must be harmonised and used in the highest way for personal and social betterment. Only when the Ursuline educator accepts the duties of spiritual motherhood does she find the most sacred of womanly experiences a channel of spiritual perfection and thus is fitted to train girls for the functional responsibility of home and family . . . . There is joy in [this] willing work, honour to manual labour and service of God in such humble tasks. And domestic contentment is the prelude to social regeneration."[37]

Like so many sisters throughout the United States, during the 1950s and 1960s the South Dakota Presentations set out to rekindle for themselves the ideological fervor of those first apostolic women of whom Walsh spoke. As a result, they made pragmatic modifications in dress and sleeve length, veil design, and fabric choice, especially for the sister-nurses, whose gowns had been a nuisance for years. In response to the Vatican II Ecumenical Council, the Presentations also initiated a self-study in 1967. This historic council that had met under Pope John XXIII from 1962 to 1963 and under Pope Paul VI from 1963 to 1965 made its dramatic mark on the Presentations and on all other religious communities throughout the world.[38]

The council's final product consisted of sixteen documents that pertained to all aspects of religious life. Two in particular would have an impact on women in the Church: *Perfectae Caritatis* (Decree on the Appropriate Renewal of the Religious Life) and *Gaudium et Spes* (Pastoral Constitution on the Church in the Modern World). The former encouraged congregations to examine their spiritual life and their systems of government, methods of training new candidates, and directions of apostolic activities. Orders then could receive permission to experiment with innovations. Pontifical groups submitted proposed changes to the Holy See for final approval, then they revised their constitutions.[39] The authority to make changes that enabled groups to better serve God as well as their clients was given only when orders proved that they had followed the Vatican II guideline of rediscovering the "sources of all Christian life and . . . the original inspiration behind a given community."[40]

In so stating, the Vatican II Council seemed clear that women religious were to retain their ideology of separate spheres, but in *The Church in the Modern World* the council made some confusing statements about the status of woman's proper place. Defending downtrodden women throughout the world, it claimed that females must not be "denied the right and freedom to choose a husband, to embrace a state of life, or to acquire an education or cultural benefits equal to those recognized for men." Yet the council summarily retracted any suggestion of relaxing traditional gender roles, proclaiming that "children, especially the younger among them, need the care of their mother at home."[41]

Subsequent papal assertions reaffirmed that the Church intended to continue recognizing the efficacy of distinct male and female spheres. In 1966, Pope Paul VI explained, "For us woman is a vision of virginal purity, which restores the most lofty affective and moral feelings of the human heart."[42] To make certain that women religious appropriately reflected this image, bishops all over the world were instructed to observe "renewal" in their dioceses— the 1960s' and 1970s' experimentation following the end of Vatican II. Bishops were to provide all religious with the appropriate amounts of either encouragement or restraint, while orders democratized their organizational structure and charted new professional paths. His Excellency Lambert Hoch, Bishop of Sioux Falls, commented that he saw himself as a shepherd with a crook, which he used to prod his reluctant charges and to restrain the more radical of his flock.[43]

This latter job would be a problem for many bishops throughout the country. A number of women religious hoped that the Vatican II edicts would justify their separate but equal professional opportunities within the Church's structure, and they began demanding that right. It seemed, however, that many male Church officials persisted in viewing their destiny as one of leadership, and women's as one of assistance. For example, despite his commitment to moderation, Bishop Hoch still enjoyed reminiscing with the older South Dakota Presentation nuns, recalling how much better the older days had been.[44]

Proving to be a force against such reactions, some of the more liberal American nuns eventually reorganized their communities. The Church did not recognize them, although members of the new communes worked for any number of social welfare causes and often took vows. Sister Lillanna Kopp, the founder of one such group located in Portland, Oregon, stated in 1972 that it was essential to eliminate "the bureaucratic, authoritarian [male dominated] structures that have driven American nuns out of traditional religious orders by the tens of thousands since the Vatican Council closed in 1965."[45] Sister Anita Caspary, a member of another "defector" group in Los Angeles, concurred. She observed that the nuns' rebellion had been precipitated not only by Vatican II, but also by the nuns' own personal experiences performing difficult professional jobs and then not being recognized as being equally as competent as males. Not unlike nineteenth-century Protestant Elizabeth Cady Stanton and other twentieth-century religious feminists, these nuns sensed the irreconcilable irony within the ideology of women's separate sphere: Church males and anyone else can use and have used the moral-mother prototype of Mary to demand sacrifices and hard work from nuns; yet at the same time, officials have used the corrupt stereotype of Eve to bar women from priestly leadership roles within the Church.[46] So charged Sister Albertus Magnus McGrath in her article "Women as the 'Niggers' of the Church."[47] Thus some rebellious nuns joined the feminists of the 1960s and 70s, abandoning the separate female ideology and arguing for a more androgynous religious mandate leading to professionalization and social reform.[48]

Other liberal nuns embraced a moderate interpretation of feminism that would not become popular within the broader American culture until the late 1970s and 80s. Also claiming inspiration from Vatican II, they attempted to reconcile the paradoxes of traditional ideology by emphasizing the value of woman's separate domain that was equal to or better than man's social and religious station. As if having resolved schizophrenia caused by gender roles, South Dakota Sister Remily changed her saintly but masculine first name from Laurence to Elizabeth. Such changes of namesakes were not uncommon in the post-Vatican II years, as religious became more conscious of their personal callings and identities. In such assertion, some nuns have been able to construct Church-approved philosophies that have loosened the structures of their communities, incorporating a balance between the concept of personhood and an ideology of separate spheres. New statements of principle often eliminated direct pledges of poverty, chastity, and obedience, as did that of the Kentucky-based Sisters of Loretto. Their leader, Sister Luke Tobin, was the only American nun to observe the all-male Vatican II Council in action, and her order was the first in America to strike the balance that she believed the council had mandated. The Sisters of Loretto received permission to allow each nun the personal construction of her vows as long as each retained the essence of tradition.[49] For example, Sister Tobin explained, "Poverty should mean detachment, not dependence. Obedience should be to the needs of people and the community, not just to superiors."[50] Similarly, South Dakota Presentation Sister Cabrini Di Donato reinterpreted an old shibboleth in 1966. In the preface of her thesis on the order's educational work, Sister Di Donato reasoned: "Due to their spirit of humility, [the Presentations] . . . have done little to publicize their work. They considered their efforts, labors, and accomplishments as a matter between themselves and God. They took literally the words of His Son, 'But when thou dost alms, let not thy left hand know what the right hand doth.' . . . Though beautiful and laudable, their motive of self-abnegation has deprived the later members of the Community and the citizens of South Dakota of . . . historical knowledge and . . . edification. . . ."[51]

Other feminist nuns remaining within the Church also perceived the ancient vows as stifling to women and to religious in general, and they believed that centralization of the Church heirarchy had facilitated this oppression. During the 1960s and 70s, scholars conducted research to determine the degree to which sisters had been made into automatons and concluded that nuns were more authoritarian than other women in comparable professional positions such as teaching.[52] Consequently, a new ideology began taking shape within a few renewed orders, promising to bring about a "decentralization of [Church power] but a centralization of coordination and communication, pluralism, and unity" among and within each religious community.[53]

The communities that moved without conflict toward these resolves were the exception. Challenges that the more iconoclastic nuns made evoked turmoil within many orders that housed conservatives, as well as those women who were open to change. As a result, many nuns left orders not only to escape formalism, but also to protest the dismantling of routine and custom. During the 1960s and 1970s, some orders subdivided, and fourteen times more women said farewell to their sisters than did men to their brothers, reducing the total number of nuns from 181,421 in 1965 to 120,000 in 1978.[54]

Although the South Dakota Presentations did not escape the external and internal turmoil of renewal, their resolutions to all sorts of personal and professional conflicts rested within a redefined but preserved ideology of separate spheres. Whereas the younger and middle-aged women usually comprised the moderate-to-liberal group, the older women, whose entire lives had been spent within a relatively closed system, tended to hold the more conservative view. For them, peace and tranquility came from an acceptance of their classic female role, manifested through a constant striving to sacrifice and atone, rather than from a discovery of themselves. Many were wary of a self-confrontation for which their externally controlled surroundings had never prepared them.[55] Consequently, the South Dakota conservatives were, as one nun put it, "terribly terribly bitter" about the attack on their way of life.[56] These women had sympathetic colleagues all over the country for whom change was painful. In 1970, one such nun recorded her reaction to an encounter group experience: "My ideas about myself haven't changed. In fact I guess that maybe they have gotton worse in that as a result of this group I feel more than ever that I'm different, that I don't really belong, that I'm not a group person. I mean I'm, I guess I'm kind of an isolated person. I have chosen to be a psychological and emotional zero. And yet I guess I don't like that choice, but I'm stuck with it because I chose it, and I don't know, I haven't the stuff to change that decision. I guess."[57]

In favor of change were the more liberal nuns who held that woman's special calling justified not only jobs in administration, but also a host of other ministerial positions formerly thought to be for men only. Although similar Presentation views dramatically altered the international Presentation Order, eventually moderates among the South Dakota congregation and within other American orders as well moved communities beyond conflict and toward consensus. Scores of books, articles, and dissertations written by nuns during the 1960s and 1970s held that not feminism but an ideology of separate spheres was powerful enough to argue for nuns' ever-advancing professional roles, securing Church sanction at the same time. In 1966, Minnesota Sister Mary Margaret Irene Healy reported that the nun student teacher about to complete a baccalaureate degree in education was much more secure, self-confident, and well adjusted than her secular counterparts. Life in the sisterhoods, Sister Healy concluded, had provided the religious teachers with meaning and stability, a commodity that during the 1960s and 1970s seemed to be in short supply.[58] Echoing a similar theme a decade later, another Catholic author wrote that in "an age of the uncommitted" the religious conclave has offered a welcome alternative in which ideological purpose has led to high levels of creativity.[59]

As South Dakota Presentation liberals and moderates had hoped, the new atmosphere greatly expanded their professional options. Writing in far-away Belgium, Cardinal Leon Suenens implored nuns to professionalize with increased vigor; his plea was particularly moving to many of the northern Great Plains nuns. Consequently, Mother Myron Martin, who took office in 1964, employed the most democratic leadership style of any superior before her. During her administration, the popular vote was restored, and she approved many nuns' innovative professional aspirations.[60] Sister Kay O'Neil explained how she evolved into one such position. Early in the 1970s, a Dominican nun named Sister Marie Walter Flood instructed an institute for women and men religious involved in the ministry, and Sister O'Neil attended. Although early in her religious life, Sister O'Neil felt empty, at the institute she resolved to become a campus minister, a move that changed her life. "I'm a good person, and I couldn't have said that five years ago," she stated in 1976.[61] The freedom to interpret Nagle's directives for herself gave Sister O'Neil confidence and pride. Explaining that the strictness of the total institution had made it difficult for her colleagues to internalize the timeworn values, Sister Marie Patrice Moriarty maintained that a nun could develop her own feeling of worth and be responsible for disciplining herself at the same time. Making an example of prayer, she elaborated, "we . . . [used to do] things out of habit and regulation. . . . [Now], I may choose my time to pray, . . . but the responsibility is on me to live out what I have promised [to do]."[62]

No matter how independent any of the South Dakota Presentations became, the Marian ideology continued to bond each to the other. As Sister Lynn Marie Welbig put it, "it's part of our being, it's part of who . . . [we] are. . . ."[63] Summing up how the new community structure accommodated and reinforced the renewed philosophical ideals, Sister JoAnn Sturzl explained that each woman finds herself and her place within the group, and this strengthens the system. If some leave because they cannot accomplish the dual task, Sister Helen Freimuth added, that is fine because the ones who do remain are strong and secure, bound as much by ideology as by convent rules.[64]

One of the more specific South Dakota Presentation controversies, which preceded this welcomed consensus, concerned habit alterations. In the 1960s, conservative sisters continued to wear the old garb, while their more liberal colleagues donned secular clothing, placing a ring on the left hand as the only religious symbol. Most Presentations wore modified veils and street-length dresses of basic colors and styles. They and their parishioners (especially Native Americans) believed that nuns should be identified by some sort of uniform, and thus the headgear was a symbol for many Presentations.[65]

Finding security in uniformity, the older sisters were troubled by the diversity. Wearing street clothes, they argued, would lead to an increase in materialism because their fellow sisters would become preoccupied with fashion. Conversely, other nuns saw the habit as an obstacle in dealing with lay people, a mask behind which they had hidden for years. Although, to this day there is still debate over the degree of equality between and appropriate intersection of the traditional male and female worlds, the habit issue was settled by allowing each nun to continue wearing the clothes of her choice. In 1976, Sister Sturzl revealed the relatively moderate position of the South Dakota Presentations, pointing out that during her yearly attendance at a national meeting of superiors, "I'm always struck by the fact that dress . . . [is] no issue there and most of us women are dressed in . . . [street clothes]."[66]

The same two factions were in conflict over governmental dilemmas. In reorganizing the community, the Presentations held a Chapter of Affairs meeting in 1968, at which experimentation was approved in such areas as election of the superior general, a title that replaced the old term, *mother superior*. Although they decided to retain the delegate system in selecting council members, the more liberal sisters wanted to allow direct election of their superior (as they had done before becoming a pontifical order in 1946). The Vatican refused to allow the innovation, so the Presentations continued to use representatives to select the superior general. Some of the sisters resented forfeiting the chance for a direct voice in selecting their leader, but they bowed to the decision of Rome.[67]

The General Council contained four members who served four-year terms and were elected by chapter delegates. The councilors shared responsibility with the superior for health, education, finances, membership admittance, and dismissal. The superior and council became the corporate board of the community and its institutions. Election for the council and superior took place every four years after the 1968 Chapter of Affairs meeting when representative delegates met to examine the community's religious life and to decide on future directions. The General Chapter worked on revisions to the constitutions in 1968, 1970, 1972, and 1980 and sent the results to a canonical lawyer for review before final submission to the pope for approval. In 1968, the popular vote was restored; in 1980, the group changed the title of superior general to that of president, evidence that the women's attitude toward their own community's government was evolving as professionally as it had toward their apostolic missions.[68]

These more recent documents represented enlightened visions of woman's separate ideological mission. For example, the 1980 Constitution made no reference to the female's natural bent toward moral depravity, while the charge of obedience was to be directed toward ideals rather than people. "Consecrated by the Father in obedience, we commit ourselves, in community, to listen and respond to God's word in our lives," it read. The de-emphasis on restrictions to protect the sisters from sin paralleled an emphasis on Nagle's positive apostolic mission: "Nano Nagle, our foundress, lived and worked with those who were sick, poor and deprived. She responded with love to both the young and the old. Her hours of prayer led to her hours of ministry, in which she showed God's love in action." In this and other similar statements, the life of a woman was retained as the Presentation ideal, and yet it seemed to have a transcendent quality that eluded the stain of Eve and endowed all who modeled it with the right to enter any and all professions that represented some aspect of Nagle's ministerial mission.[69]

During the 1960s and 70s, another change occurred within the system of preparing novices for communal life. Not only had the renewal era witnessed defections to the South Dakota Presentations, but it had also witnessed a decrease in the number of young laywomen who sought admission into the sisterhood. For example, Sister Helen Freimuth confessed that if the Peace Corps or VISTA had been available when she joined, she might not have become a nun but a volunteer instead. After much discussion, the sisters attempted to make the novitiate more viable. They changed the title novice mistress to director of formation, after the name of their initiation program. For at least six months during their first phase, new candidates, called associates, lived on the grounds near, but apart from, the larger Presentation community. The candidates received spiritual direction and attended workshops on religious life. In the next stage they experienced a year of integration, in which they lived with the Presentations (according to the norms of the Church), studied the traditions and constitutions of the congregation, and underwent more intensive spiritual direction. In the third step, the order supplemented temporary commitment, community living, and spiritual direction with workshops, sessions before renewal of temporary and final vows, and supervision of the associates' program in their chosen profession.[70]

The entire process was designed to foster the Presentation ideology, a belief that involved, according to Sister Freimuth, a commitment to living and dying among the oppressed and to dedicating one's personal life to the religious community. The director of formation encouraged traits of compassion, gentleness, justice, zeal, detachment, humility, and simplicity; she stressed devotion to the Sacred Heart, the Passion, the Eucharist, and the Blessed Sacrament, all elements found in Mary, Our Lady of the Presentation. Finally, Sister Freimuth explained, the process nurtured asceticism through evangelical counsels, prayer, penance, and the daily practice of the associate's ministry.[71]

Alterations in the formation of a candidate into a full-fledged member exemplified the Presentations' reconciliation of individualism with uniformity and ideological singularity. The new program guided the associates toward vows at their own speed, sometimes taking up to ten years. Once candidates decided they were ready, the supervisor evaluated them in three areas: relationships with clients, co-workers, and supervisors; bonds with community members and peers; and personal development. Greater emphasis than in the past was placed on self-knowledge and introspection and on the development of independent sisters. The trend evolved partially because the Presentation leadership believed that only an order of nuns that stressed self-motivation would attract new candidates, especially when these women had to do without the camaraderie of relatively large initiation classes. In 1984, only three women were in formation, and they were at varying levels, a condition that offered little peer support.[72]

Before the 1970s, the order had also organized its financial structure by catagorizing its property into seven corporations, six viable and one inactive. The former included the four hospitals, Presentation College, and the motherhouse; the latter, the Presentation Children's Home, remained on the books because it was still named in wills by benefactors and used for needy children. The women devised new methods for handling their personal finances. The sisters budgeted amounts every spring for each group after tallying the cost of rent, food, transportation, medical insurance, and personal allowances. Sisters received $20 a month to pay for clothing, cleaning, stationery, entertainment, and personal telephone calls. Retirement benefits included a pension program and Social Security provisions. The pension plan allowed nuns past the age of seventy to receive $100 a month in 1968, and this amount was increased in following years. Under Social Security, the federal government designated the order as an employer and figured the amounts paid in accordance to living costs. Retired sisters lived at Presentation Heights or, if infirm or in need of medical attention, at Lourdes infirmary.[73]

During the 1970s, these aged nuns could look back over an era of change. The South Dakota Presentations, like other sisters throughout the country and the world, had tried to make the best of an iconoclastic age. Deriving benefits from their sisterhood's diminished size, those who remained claim that "when you live in a smaller community you are much more aware of other people; you rub shoulders with them and have your corners knocked off by them. I think this is a very healthy change and makes for a holier quality of life altogether, and it does not get away from the ideal of obedience . . . because everyone is here for a mission."[74]

The shrinking band of South Dakota Presentations continued to find comfort within an international Presentation network. Beginning in 1971, the North Dakota congregation began sponsoring an international newsletter, *Oak Leaves*. The South Dakota group contributed news to the publication which was printed for ten years. Its purpose was "to strengthen communication between Presentation Sisters and to further Nano Nagle's ideals."[75] Even after *Oak Leaves* went out of print, the South Dakota Presentations continued to seek ways to establish ideological oneness with other women who professed to follow Nagle's example. Participating in the international effort to envigorate their order's ideals, President Sister Collins and Vice-President Sister Del Rey Thieman traveled to Melbourne, Australia, in January of 1984 to be part of an international assembly of 350 Presentation Sisters representing every continent. The goal of the assembly was "To foster greater unity among [and between] our congregations, to talk about the various ways that we minister in all parts of the world, and to explore the future of religious life as Presentation Sisters." A sign of the strengthened affiliation, Sister Margaret Cafferty, president of the San Francisco Presentations, was the keynote speaker during a special celebration that preceded the South Dakota Presentations' 1984 Chapter of Affairs Meeting in Aberdeen.[76]

By 1985, the number of women in the South Dakota Presentation order had fallen off from 360 in 1958 to 232 in 1985, but these were professionals who accepted each other's individuality and no longer did things out of habit and regulation.[77] In the final analysis, Presentations all over the world achieved this feat because they commonly and individually experienced their powerful ideological roots. The South Dakota sisters maintained that in so doing "together . . . we live . . . the evangelical counsels and share in the Lord's mission of alleviating oppression and promoting human dignity in His people through prayer and service."[78] Presentations all over the world shared these sentiments. Commenting on the recent apostolic work of widespread Presentations—in San Francisco; St. John's, Newfoundland; Birmingham, Alabama; and Leeds, Australia—Sister Consedine wrote that these "Sisters have responded to the social evil of child abuse, establishing centers for temporary care of children at risk, or taking part in child care programmes sponsored by diocesan or civic authorities . . . [The] words, 'A Presentation religious must be a mother to the poor, destitute, afflicted little ones' are still being heard."[79]

In so stating, the Presentations, like most other nuns, have manifested their vision of feminism, which by the 1980s was becoming popular with mainstream secular feminists in the United States. A new, woman-centered separatism arose that criticized earlier feminists who had attempted to prove female worth by making women fit male stereotypical roles.[80] Although nuns and other women have defended each other's separate but equal social and professional worth, nuns remain women married to God. They therefore in some sense symbolize the Church as a passive, subordinate body, waiting for the "Bridegroom" Jesus to infuse them with the spirit of the Almighty.[81] Yet many of them are also empowered by their legacy. As Sister Cecilia Wilms of Spokane, Washington, wrote:

> I am woman. . .
> Called by the Lord
> To be for many people. . .
> Creative space
> Nurturing womb
> Channel of God's loving mercy
> And so reveal to them
> The woman face of God.[82]

Thus despite challenges to the traditional Marian ideology and the *"sororal community"* which has perpetuated it, the South Dakota Presentations and countless other religious continue to provide a professional environment "where problems and insights are shared and where work is done together."[83] Such a milieu attracted an increasing number of women into religious life, from 120,000 in 1978 to 126,517 by 1980.[84]

Even so, current papal support for nuns' separate-but-equal religious doctrine and for their ever-expanding professional activities is questionable. Pope John Paul II has promoted a more conservative interpretation of the nuns' charge, explaining to a group of religious in 1981 that "As daughters of the Church . . . you are called to a generous and loving adherence to the authentic *magisterium* [teaching authority] of the Church, which is a solid guarantee of the fruitfulness of all your apostolates and an indispensable condition for the proper interpretation of the 'signs of the times.' " Moreover, flowing from this same ideological source, the pontiff continued to argue that other Catholic women should remain in the home as wives and mothers, decreeing that "it will redound to the credit of society to make it possible for a mother—without inhibiting her freedom, without psychological or practical discrimination, and without penalizing her as compared with other women—to devote herself to taking care of her children and educating them in accordance with their needs, which vary with age. Having to abandon these tasks in order to take up paid work outside the home is wrong from the point of view of the good of the family when it contradicts or hinders these primary goals of the mission of a mother."[85]

In part to discuss these matters, John Paul II called for an extraordinary international synod of bishops that began in the winter of 1986. Here the pope and other Church patriarchs were to examine Vatican II pronouncements and assess whether or not they have been addressed appropriately. Relating specifically to religious, the pope insisted that some form of physical community should be maintained with all members, and that they should wear a distinguishing dress. The South Dakota Presentations should be vigilant because many of their activities have taken them outside the motherhouse to live and work. Moreover, the community that they have created (flexible enough to foster internalization of values but rigid enough to discourage disagreement on fundamental Marian ideology) represents an ever-delicate balance that could be upset at any time.[86] On the one hand, the ironies of Eve's and Mary's antithetical influence, sisters might conclude, are irreconcilable. On the other hand, Vatican officials may even challenge the propriety of the separate but equal doctrine that rationalizes women's roles as priests and ministers. Consequently, the South Dakota Presentations' most recent statement on women's social rights and duties is understandably cautious and vague: "to educate ourselves on the attitude toward women as well as the role of women in the Church and Society."[87] Meanwhile, the South Dakota Presentations worked diligently, hoping the pope would sanction what each woman had long discovered to be her own spiritual and professional place.

NOTES

1. M. Raphael Consedine, P.V.B.M., *Listening Journey: A Study of the Spirit and Ideals of Nano Nagle and the Presentation Sisters* (Victoria, Australia: Congregation of the Presentations of the Blessed Virgin Mary, 1983), 321. For a reference to Christian churches' reaction to modernization,

see Robert H. Wiebe, *The Search for Order, 1877–1920* (New York: Hill and Wang, 1967), 44.

2. Mary Ewens, O. P. *The Role of the Nun in the Nineteenth Century: Variations on the International Theme* (New York: Arno Press, 1971, repr., Salem, N.H.: Ayer Publishers, 1984), 254–56.

3. Cardinal James Gibbons, "Pure Womanhood," *Cosmopolitan* 39 (Sept. 1905): 559.

4. Rose Hawthorne Lathrop, quoted in James Hennesey, S. J., *American Catholics: A History of the Roman Catholic Community in the United States* (New York: Oxford University Press, 1981), 191.

5. Sister Marie Carolyn Klinkhamer, O. P., "Mother Mary Alphonsa Lathrop," in *Notable American Women: A Biographical Dictionary*, vol. 2, ed. Edward T. James (Cambridge, Mass.: Belknap Press, 1971), 372–74. For other examples of Catholic women actively involved in social service, see Janet Wilson James, "An Overview," in *Women in American Religion*, ed. Janet Wilson James (Pittsburgh: University of Pennsylvania Press, 1980), 15–16.

6. James J. Kenneally, "Eve, Mary, and the Historians: American Catholicism and Women," in James, *Women in American Religion*, 199; also see Hennessey, *American Catholics*, 187.

7. Pope Pius XII, quoted in T. J. Walsh, *Nano Nagle and the Presentation Sisters* (Dublin: M. H. Gill and Son, 1959), 316.

8. Alvin Toffler, *The Third Wave* (New York: William Morrow, 1980).

9. *Constitutions of the Presentation Sisters of the Blessed Virgin Mary* (Sioux Falls, S.D.: Diocese of Sioux Falls, 1920), 27–28.

10. Erving Goffman, *Asylums: Essays on the Social Situation of Mental Patients and Other Inmates* (Hawthorne, N.Y.: Aldine Publishing, 1961), 1–124.

11. *Constitutions of the Presentation Sisters*, 55, 58–59.

12. *Constitutions of the Congregation of the Sisters of the Presentation of the Blessed Virgin Mary* (Aberdeen, S.D.: Sisters of the Presentation of the Blessed Virgin Mary, 1946), 45.

13. *Constitutions of the Presentation Sisters*, 37.

14. *Constitutions of the Congregation of the Sisters of the Presentation*, 86–87, 89.

15. *Constitutions of the Presentation Sisters*, 14.

16. Ibid., 81.

17. *Constitutions of the Congregation of the Sisters of the Presentation*, 144.

18. Interview with Sister Helen Freimuth, Aug. 5, 1976, South Dakota Oral History Center, Vermillion; interview with Sister JoAnn Sturzl, Aug. 5, 1976, South Dakota Oral History Center; interview with Sister Mary Eleanor Joyce, Aug. 12, 1976, South Dakota Oral History Center; "Brochure on the Founding of the Presentation Sisters," Presentation Archives, Presentation Heights, Aberdeen, S.D.

19. *Constitutions of the Congregation of the Sisters of the Presentation,* 145.

20. Interview with Sister Anna Marie Weinreis, Aug. 10, 1976, South Dakota Oral History Center; interview with Sister Judith O'Brien, June 19, 1978, South Dakota Oral History Center; interview with Sister Grace Farrell, June 19, 1978, South Dakota Oral History Center; "Brochure on the Founding of the Presentation Sisters."

21. Interview with Sister Helen Freimuth; interview with Sister JoAnn Sturzl; interview with Sister Mary Eleanor Joyce; interview with Sister Grace Farrell; interview with Sister M. Sylvester Auth, Aug. 9, 1976, South Dakota Oral History Center; interview with Sister Lynn Marie Welbig, Aug. 10, 1976, South Dakota Oral History Center.

22. Interview with Sister Lynn Marie Welbig; interview with Sister Judith O'Brien; Goffman, *Asylums,* 1–124; interview with Sister JoAnn Sturzl; interview with Sister Anna Marie Weinreis.

23. Consedine, *Listening Journey,* 310.

24. "Summary Data," Presentation Archives; interview with Sister JoAnn Sturzl.

25. Mother M. Carthagh to Rev. Mother M. Raphael, Dec. 30, 1941, Presentation Archives; Bishop William Brady to Mother M. Raphael, Jan. 6, 1942, Presentation Archives; Neil J. Gleason to Mother M. Raphael, Superior, Jan. 30, 1946, Presentation Archives.

26. Interview with Sister Judith O'Brien.

27. Sister Pauline Quinn, "Biographies of Major Superiors, Section IX: Mother Viator Burns, 1946–1958," Presentation Archives.

28. Sister Quinn, "Mother Viator Burns"; see chapter 4 for documentation on the Presentation Order's growth.

29. Consedine, *Listening Journey,* 330.

30. Ibid., 331, 352.

31. Hennessey, *American Catholics,* 286–87.

32. Sister Marie Augusta Neal and Sister N. D. de Namur, "A Theoretical Analysis of Renewal in Religious Orders in the U. S. A.," *Social Compass* 18 (1971): 7–25.

33. Sister Elizabeth Kolmer, A. S. C., "Catholic Women Religious and Women's History: A Survey of the Literature," in *Women in American Religion,* ed. James, 127–40. For an example of one progressive call for nuns' increased professionalization, see Leon Joseph Cardinal Suenens, *The Nun in the World: Religious and the Apostolate* (London: Burns and Oates, 1962).

34. Robert A. Broenen, "Sister Formation," in *Convent Life: Roman Catholic Religious Orders for Women in North America,* ed. Joan M. Lexau (New York: Dial Press, 1964), 188–96.

35. Broenen, "Sister Formation," 188–89.

36. William Johnston, *Christian Mysticism Today* (New York: Harper and Row, 1984), 192.

37. Walsh, *Nano Nagle and the Presentation Sisters,* 318–19.

38. "Chapter Decisions," 1968, Presentation Archives; Walter M. Abbott, S. J., ed., *The Documents of Vatican II* (New York: Guild Press, 1966), xx–xxi.

39. Abbott, *Documents of Vatican II*, 199–308, 466–82; interview with Sister JoAnn Sturzl; Sister Joyce Meyer, "Notes from Classes Given to Professed Sisters and Sisters in Formation," Presentation Archives.

40. *Decree on the Appropriate Renewal of the Religious Life*, in *The Documents of Vatican II*, ed. Abbott, 468.

41. *Pastoral Constitution on the Church in the Modern World*, in Ibid, 228, 257.

42. Pope Paul VI, quoted in Ann Elizabeth Kelly, "Catholic Women in Campus Ministry: An Emerging Ministry for Women in the Catholic Church" (Ph.D. diss., Boston University, 1975), 16.

43. Sister Meyer, "Notes from Classes"; interview with Bishop Lambert Hoch, June 28, 1978, South Dakota Oral History Center.

44. Interview with Bishop Lambert Hoch.

45. "The New Nuns," *Time* 99 (March 20, 1972): 63–64.

46. "The New Nuns," 64; Sister Marie Augusta Neal, S.N.D. and Sister Miriam St. John Clasby, S. N. D., "Priests' Attitudes Toward Women," in *Women in Modern Life*, ed. William C. Bier, S. J. (New York: Fordham University Press, 1968), 55 – 77. For a Catholic laywoman's critique of the Eve stereotype, see Sidney Cornelia Callahan, *The Illusion of Eve: Modern Woman's Quest for Identity* (New York: Sheed and Ward, 1965).

47. Sister Albertus Magnus McGrath, "Women as the 'Niggers' of the Church," *The Critic* 30 (Sept.-Oct. 1971): 24–33.

48. For a description of feminism during these years, see Hester Eisenstein, *Contemporary Feminist Thought* (Boston: G.K. Hall, 1983), 3–4, 58–68.

49. Eisenstein, *Contemporary Feminist Thought*, 136–45; Sister M. Cabrini Di Donato, "A History of the Educational Work of the Presentation Sisters of Aberdeen, South Dakota" (master's thesis, Northern State College, 1966), 136; "The New Nuns"; Sister Alicia Dunphy to Courtney Ann Vaughn-Roberson, Dec. 30, 1986.

50. Sister Luke Tobin, quoted in "The New Nuns," 64.

51. Sister Di Donato, "A History of the Educational Work of the Presentation Sisters," iii-iv.

52. Statements by the Sisters of the Immaculate Heart of Mary, Los Angeles, "The Sisters Join the Movement," in *Women's Liberation and the Church: The New Demand for Freedom in the Life of the Christian Church*, ed. Sarah Bentley Doely (New York: Association Press, 1970), 70–76; Lautrine Anne Luft, "Degree of Authoritarianism of Teaching Sisters and Lay Teachers in Catholic Schools" (Ph.D. diss., University of Wisconsin, 1971).

53. Loretta Koley Jancoski, "Religion and Commitment: A Psychohistorical Study of Creative Women in Catholic Religous Communities" (Ph.D. diss., University of Chicago, 1976), 260.

54. Hennesey, *American Catholics*, 329; "The New Nuns," 63–64;

"Women: Second-Class Citizens?" *Time* 125 (Feb. 4, 1985): 62–63. Also see Lucinda San Giovanni, *Ex-Nuns: A Study of Emergent Role Passage* (Norwood, N.J.: Ablex Publishing, 1978).

55. Interview with Sister JoAnn Sturzl; interview with Sister Martha Raleigh, Aug. 10, 1976, South Dakota Oral History Center; interview with Sister Helen Freimuth, Aug. 5, 1976, South Dakota Oral History Center.

56. Interview with Sister Anna Marie Weinreis.

57. Anonymous nun, quoted in Monica Marie Schmidt, "Effects of Group Interaction on the Self-Perceptions of Women in Religious Life" (Ph.D. diss., University of Illinois, 1970), 103. Similar interviews conducted with older, retired teachers and nurses also reveal a longing for the more structured world. For some sources, see Courtney Ann Vaughn-Roberson, "Having a Purpose in Life: Western Women Teachers in the Twentieth Century," *Great Plains Quarterly* 5 (Spring 1985): 107–24 and "Sometimes Independent but Never Equal—Women Teachers, 1900–1950: The Oklahoma Example," *Pacific Historical Review* 53 (Feb. 1984): 39–58.

58. Interview with Sister Bonaventure Hoffman, Aug. 6, 1976, South Dakota Oral History Center; Consedine, *Listening Journey*, 379; Sister Mary Margaret Irene Healy, B.V.M., "Assessment of Academic Apptitude, Personality Characteristics, and Religious Orientation of Catholic Sister-Teacher-Trainees" (Ph.D. diss., University of Minnesota, 1966).

59. Jancoski, "Religion and Commitment," ii.

60. Sister Di Donato, "A History of the Educational Work of the Presentation Sisters," 132; Suenens, *The Nun in the World;* Sister Pauline Quinn, "Biographies of Major Superiors, Section XI: Mother Myron Martin, 1964–1974," Presentation Archives.

61. Interview with Sister Kay O'Neil, Aug. 9, 1976, South Dakota Oral History Center.

62. Interview with Sister Marie Patrice Moriarty, Aug. 12, 1976, South Dakota Oral History Center.

63. Interview with Sister Lynn Marie Welbig.

64. Interview with Sister JoAnn Sturzl; interview with Sister Helen Freimuth.

65. Interview with Sister Helen Freimuth; interview with Sister JoAnn Sturzl; interview with Sister Martha Raleigh; interview with Sister Helen Nemmers, Aug. 10, 1976, South Dakota Oral History Center; interview with Keith Fitzpatrick, June 5, 1978, South Dakota Oral History Center.

66. Interview with Sister Helen Freimuth; interview with Sister JoAnn Sturzl.

67. Ibid.

68. Interview with Sister Mary Stephen Davis, Aug. 7, 1976, South Dakota Oral History Center; interview with Sister Colman Coakley, Aug. 7, 1976, South Dakota Oral History Center; interview with Sister JoAnn Sturzl; interview with Sister Marie Patrice Moriarty; Sister Quinn, "Mother Myron Martin"; "Draft of the Constitution of the Presentation Sisters, Passed by the 1980 Chapter," Presentation Archives.

69. "Draft of the Constitution." For an example, see interview with Sister Judith O'Brien.

70. Interview with Sister Edla Billing, July 12, 1978, South Dakota Oral History Center; interview with Sister Helen Freimuth; interview with Mother Myron Martin, Aug. 12, 1976, South Dakota Oral History Center; Sister Meyer, "Notes from Classes."

71. Sister Meyer, "Notes from Classes"; interview with Sister Helen Freimuth; interview with Deana Butler, June 20, 1978, South Dakota Oral History Center.

72. Interview with Deana Butler; Sister Meyer, "Notes from Classes."

73. Interview with Sister JoAnn Sturzl; "Chapter Decisions," 1968; interview with Sister Mary Stephen Davis.

74. Anonymous sister, quoted in Sara Maitland, *A Map of the New Country, Women and Christianity* (London: Routledge and Klegan Paul, 1983), 72.

75. Consedine, *Listening Journey*, 357.

76. Sister Mary Denis Collins, quoted in Sister Pauline Quinn, "Biographies of Major Superiors, Section XIII: Sister Mary Denis Collins, 1982–," Presentation Archives

77. Sister Pauline Quinn, "Biographies of Major Superiors, Section X: Mother Carmelita McCullough, 1958–1964," Presentation Archives; Sister Alicia Dunphy to Courtney Ann Vaughn-Roberson, June 27, 1985.

78. "Draft of the Constitution of the Presentation Sisters."

79. Consedine, *Listening Journey*, 379.

80. Eisenstein, *Contemporary Feminist Thought*, 105–6, 136–45.

81. Sister Elaine Marie Prevallet, S. L., "The Meaning of Virginity," in *The New Nuns*, ed. Sister M. Charles Borromeo, C. S. C. (New York: New American Library, 1967), 34.

82. Sister Cecilia Wilms, quoted in Maitland, *A Map of the New Country*, 70.

83. Sister Mary Shanahan, S. H. J., quoted in Ibid., 77.

84. "Women: Second-Class Citizens?", 62; Hennessey, *American Catholics*, 329.

85. Pope John Paul II, quoted in Peter Hebblethwaite, "The Popes and Politics: Shifting Patterns in 'Catholic Social Doctrine,' " *Daedalus: Journal of the American Academy of Arts and Sciences* 111 (Winter 1982): 95, 97.

86. "Discord in the Church"; "Taming the Liberation Theologians," and "Women: Second-Class Citizens?" *Time* 125 (Feb. 4, 1985): 50–55, 56, 59, 62–63; interview with Sister Martha Raleigh; interview with Sister Helen Freimuth. This institutional dilemma is discussed in Aaron Wildavsky, "Church, Capitalism, and Democracy," *The New York Times Book Review Digest* 89 (Dec. 9, 1984): 14–15.

87. "The 1984 Chapter of Affairs Meeting Resolutions," Presentation Archives; Sister Alicia Dunphy to Courtney Ann Vaughn-Roberson, March 11, 1985.

10. Renewal in Action: The Extended Apostolate, 1965–85

□

Beginning in 1969, soon after Vatican II adjourned, the South Dakota Presentations expanded their interpretation of Nano Nagle's dream by offering sisters many new professional opportunities. By then, northern Great Plains farmers and small-town dwellers had evolved from poor settlers into middle-class Americans, and in the process many Presentations had lost the feeling that they were serving the downtrodden. By mid-century, nuns who were between forty and fifty years old had come of age within a highly restricted community system and during a time of social retrenchment. American feminism virtually died after suffrage was won in 1920, and the ensuing three decades brought little hope of its resurrection. Simultaneously, the South Dakota Presentation community became increasingly rigid and domestically focused. Consequently, by the 1950s, the middle-aged Presentations in many different congregations particularly longed for new professional opportunities to serve.[1] Between 1946 and 1966, the international order founded more than 160 new missions, producing an expansion, as one nun wrote, "which brought its own anxieties . . . [and] its own rewards."[2] Winning additional support from Vatican II edicts and the American social milieu of the 1960s and 1970s, a number of South Dakota Presentations continued to find meaningful professional outlets, developing careers that survive well into the 1980s.

During the 1960s, a new generation of Democrats inspired by President John Kennedy waged war on injustice and prejudice, asking a somewhat complacent citizenry to provide each person with the opportunity for a healthy and productive life. The civil rights movement and the appearance of numerous federal programs, a part of

President Lyndon Johnson's Great Society, incited women religious to be part of this era. Priests and nuns joined lay people in freedom rides and voter-registration drives, and they brought back to their communities a reawakened interest in the fight against discrimination. Sisters studying for advanced degrees came into contact with movements on various university campuses, and many of the women expressed the desire to work with disadvantaged blacks instead of returning to their motherhouses.[3]

The federal government provided other, more indirect incentives for the Presentations' and other American nuns' evolving apostolic interests. In the public sector some new programs, curricular changes, and modernized facilities made possible through the national Elementary and Secondary Education Act of 1965, contributed to a crisis for parochial schools because Catholic parents witnessed a comparatively minimal growth in these Church-sponsored institutions. In the public schools the increased use of audio-visual equipment, new counseling services, and sophisticated athletic departments forced Catholic educators to upgrade their offerings, but parishes found financing such efforts a great burden. At the same time on the northern Great Plains, as elsewhere, the number of sisters available to staff Catholic schools began to decline, and it became necessary to hire lay teachers at much higher salaries than the nuns had received. This contributed even more to rising expenses, and many eastern South Dakota parishes faced the possibility of closing their schools.[4]

In the health care arena, the Presentations were confronted with accelerating costs, as well as with complex government regulations that had to be followed if the order were to receive federal funds. The diminishing number of sisters put added pressure on Presentation administrators to hire laypeople. As some sisters realized that their modern duties differed little from those of lay personnel, they yearned to relive their forebears' experiences as Christian community-builders in new frontier settings. Thus some South Dakota sisters became part of an international Presentation apostolic movement into such fields as parish ministry, prison visiting, hospital and industrial chaplaincy, counseling, and social welfare work.[5]

Many of these Presentations applied for and received permission to expand their ministry options, although as they left the motherhouse the order's authorities cautioned the nuns not to lose track of their essential ideological base. In 1969 Sister M. Noel Kuntz was one of the first to apply, taking a job as midwife among the Navajo Indians of New Mexico. Other sisters presented proposals to the superior general and the general council. If approved, they left either in small groups or alone; their selections varied. A few left South Dakota to teach or nurse in other regions, a move which, some Presentations argued, deprived their institutions and agencies of valuable professionals; however, the opportunity to go elsewhere provided a number of nuns with opportunities previously closed to them, such as ministering in large parishes, on college campuses, or on Indian reservations. Nuns also returned to college, pursuing advanced degrees in professional fields such as social work, a new area of expertise for the Presentations. Sister Carol Quinn joined adult-education efforts in a black ghetto in Chicago, and Sister Consuela Covarrubias went to teach in a bilingual school in Milwaukee. In response to a request from Rome that American religious communities send 10 percent of their membership into Latin America, the order also helped establish and staff two hospitals and missions in Mexico.[6]

The Presentations' general conflicting attitudes toward the extended apostolate followed the same lines as did the controversy over habits. The more conservative, usually the older, Presentations were wary that the nuns who lived primarily within the secular world would lose their commitment to Presentation goals. Identifying with her own more traditional Presentation reference group, one nun commented in regard to the extended apostolate that "nobody likes it."[7] Because some of the younger sisters seemed to disregard this sentiment and continued to work in far-away places, many of these older nuns feared the professional changes that occurred.[8] Their persistent traditionalism upheld a separate and unequal depiction of the nun's appropriate professional role. They perceived one "correct" role for the nun, that as a woman she should remain in the professional areas where the physical and spiritual shelter of a convent would be close by. "If God had wanted women to be priests He would have called some. . . . I think His own mother would have been one," explained Sister Sylvester Auth.[9]

On the other hand, often after having experienced a secular higher education, some of the younger and more middle-aged women came to believe that a woman's proper place was more a product of social thought than of divine intervention, and that even Nano Nagle's eighteenth-century legacy justified the nuns' entry into the domains formerly thought to be male. Consequently, some Presentations, like other nuns throughout the United States, chose the ministry for their special work and convinced their colleagues to tolerate the choice. Presentations who supported this giant step argued that it represented an extension of education or health care and that it perfectly addressed Nagle's charge to assist the destitute. More specifically, they insisted that ministering, teaching, and healing in Mexico, in a Chicago ghetto, and on Indian reservations exemplified the essence of their order's ideological intent. Thus, at the same time that this rather unique philosophical argument called on tradition to defend women's right and responsibility to nurture and serve God's children, it capitalized on the more modern feminist ideals of male and female equality. In borrowing both from time-honored and contemporary beliefs, the new nuns maintained that women had unique sensibilities that equipped them for special duties, equally important to those typically performed by men; but when "called," the nun's professional purview could justifiably intersect with that long thought to be male.[10]

Moderates feared that the variant visions of Marian ideology threatened to erode their sisterhood, the very mechanism by which their ideals were maintained.[11] Although positive to some extent about a nun's ability to internalize her community's values, nuns such as Sister Lynn Marie Welbig held that those women working and living alone for extended periods of time risked losing their own sense of purpose and contributed little to the community. For example, as a coordinator and supervisor for all the Presentations' educational projects, Sister Welbig sometimes felt that certain sisters became somewhat estranged from the order's central purpose.[12]

Because superiors or presidents were unwilling to call these pioneers back home, the extended apostolate persisted. In 1976, Sister Myron Martin, a former superior and then a mission coordinator, noted there were a total of twenty-six nuns working in the United States whose professional commitments were in areas other than teaching or nursing, while nineteen Presentations lived and worked alone or with one other sister. Although some of the nuns' professional extension work lay in the health care and education fields, many sisters' remote locations from the motherhouse, the solitary nature of their work, or the nature of their positions made them trailblazers.[13]

Augmenting the work of Sister Quinn, several other Presentations had diversified the education apostolate by the mid-1970s. Sister M. Consolata Grace became a music instructor at the Chancy Music Company in Celton, California; Sister Mary Pius Gutoski became a public school primary teacher in Flint, Michigan; Sister Darlene Gutenkauf taught with Franciscan nuns in a LeMars, Iowa, high school; and Sister Diane Copps was the only Presentation stationed at St. Mary's in Aberdeen, South Dakota. Other nuns who held educational policymaking and administrative roles were Sister Rose Anne Melmer, a principal at Nativity of Mary's School in Bloomington, Minnesota; Sister Kathleen Bierne, a curriculum coordinator in the Sioux Falls Diocesan Office of Education; and Sister Louise Erne, a parish coordinator of religious education in South Dakota.[14]

At the same time, other Presentation nuns were involved in higher education: seven sisters were pursuing either baccalaureate or graduate degrees. Practicing the skills they had learned through an advanced higher education, Sisters Karen Watembach and another Presentation nun conducted research with the Crow at an Indian reservation in Lodge Grass, Montana. Nuns stationed at Sioux Falls were Sister Francene Evans, who (chapter 6) taught at Sioux Falls College; Sister Karen La Follette, who was a Sacred Heart Parish social worker; and Sister Genevieve Gill, who was with Catholic social services.[15]

Well-educated health care specialists taught and administered programs in their areas, as well. Practicing nursing were Sister M. Bernadette Farrell in Orangeburg, South Carolina, and Sister Lucy Callaghan in Vicksburg, Mississippi. Sister M. Marcia Scheele was a nurse educator located at St. Mary's College in O'Fallon, Missouri. She lived with Sister M. Bernard Quinn, who chaired the department of nursing at that institution. Other health care administrators included Sister M. Theodora Paul, activities director at a Chamberlain, South Dakota, community hospital; Sister M. Vincent Fuller, executive secretary for the South Dakota Board of Nursing in Sioux Falls; and Sister Mary Schneider, a health-planning curriculum consultant in Sioux Falls.[16]

Sister DePazzi Zimprich was actively involved in extended health care. Trained as a nurse, she supplemented her bachelor of science degree in nursing with study in pediatrics before applying to the South Dakota Presentation Order and the Indian Health Service for a job as a community health officer on the Cheyenne River Indian Reservation in the western part of the state. After Sister Zimprich was approved, she moved into federal government housing in the town of Eagle Butte on the reservation, although she visited the motherhouse monthly. In her new role, Sister Zimprich oversaw the maternal child care division of the community health department in the Indian Health Service. Her duties required her to administer physical examinations to newborn babies before their discharge from the hospital and to monitor preventive medicine programs for all the reservation's youngsters up to age five. Her case load reached approximately 750 children, for whom she made annual assessments of their physical, behavioral, psychological, and social needs. She worked closely with tribal and federal health programs and with education programs such as Head Start.[17]

Presentations with ministerial professions represented the most radical departure from the classic school teacher role because the ministers performed many duties that parish priests had previously handled alone. Involved in some sort of ministry during the seventies and eighties were Sister Virginia McCall of St. Lambert parish at Sioux Falls and Sister Edla Billing, a member of a ministry team at Circle, Montana. Parish visitors offering spiritual support to others included Sister Virginia Calmus of Christ the King at Sioux Falls and Sister Gabriella Crowley at Mobridge, South Dakota.[18]

South Dakota Presentation Sister Sheila Schnell also made a ministerial career for herself. She had earned a bachelor's degree and a master of arts in theology and had always pondered how best to serve God's people. When a friend heard of a position in Moline, Illinois, as the director of adult enrichment and family life for the three parishes there, she informed Sister Schnell, who then applied for the job. After the community in Aberdeen approved her proposal, Sister Schnell moved to Illinois and began directing adult experiences in faith development. She concentrated on prayer guidance and Bible study, as well as on organizing retreats for singles, senior citizens, widows, and divorced parents. In cooperation with the Catholic Board of Education and a lay advisory committee, she planned programs in liturgy study and parish renewal. She lived in a duplex with another Presentation nun; their guiding principle was simplicity in furnishings and food, as they shared prayer and supported each other in their stewardships. Because her job required only a ten-month contract, Sister Schnell spent two summer months at the Aberdeen convent. Reflecting great personal satisfaction with her work, in 1979 the nun commented that for the first time professionally and spiritually she was in the right place, or at least headed in the right direction; in 1985 there she remained.[19]

Sister Katherine O'Neil held similar posts. As a student enrolled in a women's studies course at Southwest Minnesota State University in Marshall, Minnesota, Sister O'Neil had learned that in early Christian history deaconesses had assisted bishops, and that until the High Middle Ages some abbesses continued to function within the Church hierarchy. Inspired by these early contributions, after earning her bachelor's degree in library science and a master's in psychology and counseling, Sister O'Neil applied for and secured a position in the campus ministry office at Southwest Minnesota State University in Marshall. Sister O'Neil felt some resistance as a nun in a priestly role, but she was excited to be involved in a national movement in which more and more sisters took up youth-related endeavors. Sister O'Neil worked in teams with Protestant pastors, although she spent more than a third of her time in personal consultation with college students. She also devoted much of her schedule to workshop preparation, and with students she planned Masses that were more meaningful to them than those celebrated in local parishes. She also coordinated an outreach program to involve people from the city of Marshall with the Campus Ministry followers.[20]

Whenever possible, Sister O'Neil and her Presentation co-worker, Sister Michelle Meyers, visited the Aberdeen motherhouse even though Sister O'Neil believed that her own strong commitment and her companion's support were enough to sustain her. In 1979, Sister O'Neil left Marshall to organize another pastoral project in Hutchinson, Minnesota, where through St. Cloud State University she was administering and teaching women's studies by 1985, including assertiveness training and acquisition of social skills.[21]

By 1985, the Presentations' ministerial outreach activities had become widespread—primarily throughout South Dakota, Montana, and Minnesota; to a lesser extent, in twenty other states; and in two

TABLE 18. TYPES OF EXTENDED MINISTRIES, 1985

Education

Directors of religious education in parishes
College campus ministry
Teaching in schools and colleges other than those run by Presentations
Chicago education program for dropouts
Work with Hispanic programs
Workshops on personal development and sexism
Facilitators for discussion groups

Health Care

Pastoral care in health care institutions other than those run by
  Presentations
Nursing education and care in institutions not run by Presentations
Regional mental health centers
Community health service director in South Dakota
Executive secretary of South Dakota State Board of Nursing
Chemical dependency centers
Indian health on reservations

Social Service

Diocesan Catholic charities
With divorced, single, and separated
Women's Resource Center
Work with the poor in urban areas

Parish Work

Team ministry

(continued)

foreign countries, Mexico and Zambia. Most of the nuns' positions
continued in some way to represent the educational and health care
fields, but the diverse application of these traditional areas was impressive.[22] A list of these activities is recorded in Table 18.

Perhaps the most dramatic example of the Presentations' commitment to the extended apostolate was their decision to participate
in Latin American mission activity. Spanish Dominicans had Chris-
tianized the Chiapas area of Mexico centuries before, creating a
longlasting emotional bond between them and the Indian natives
who compose approximately 26 percent of Mexico's 48,000,000 total
population. Dominican fathers from San Francisco had first envi-

TABLE 18. TYPES OF EXTENDED MINISTRIES, 1985 *(continued)*

Consultants

Nutrition in area hospitals and nursing homes
Early childhood in diocesan offices of education
Cencoad—Manpower, regional
Medical records

Spiritual Direction and Retreats

Directing short and long retreats
Shalom and other ecumenical experiences
Prayer groups
Bible studies

Foreign Missions

Medical missions in Mexico
Catechetical mission in Mexico
Teaching in government school and work in spiritual formation in
    Zambia, Africa

Miscellaneous

Day care centers
Foster grandparent program
Summer volunteer work such as immigrants, Appalachia, religious
    instruction, inner city

Source: Sister Alicia Dunphy to Courtney Ann Vaughn-Roberson, March 11, 1985.

sioned the Presentations' venture, sending three priests to Mexico
in January 1963. Here they met with local physicians and drew up
plans for a central hospital in the mountains of southern Chiapas.
The task, it was decided, must be broken down into stages, the first
of which was the construction of a dispensary. The Dominicans
requested help from volunteers within religious life and in the secular world. They contacted the Presentations of San Francisco, who
then asked for sisters from other motherhouses throughout the National Presentation Federation. The first sister-emissary from Aberdeen was a registered surgical nurse, Sister Elizabeth Remily, who
had been working at St. Joseph Hospital in Mitchell. Before leaving
for Chiapas, she joined three sisters from the San Francisco foundation for language training and orientation. Sister Janice Mengenhauser and Marilyn Meninga, a Presbyterian lay volunteer, would

later join the team. Once again reflecting the traditional family, South Dakota Presentation Sister Marguerita Beaner served as the housekeeper for a time. She, however, eventually returned to South Dakota to receive nurse's training. The Dominicans also asked for aid from the Sonora County, California, Medical Sociey, which in November 1963 sent six doctors to Chiapas to study the health of the people who lived there. They discovered that life expectancy fell below forty years of age, that undernourishment was widespread, and that ignorance of hygiene and new agricultural methods was common.[23] Before the sisters arrived, the Dominicans had already begun their medical program in the mountain town of Ocosingo. Pat Arca, a lay volunteer and registered nurse, trained infirmary staff to work with villagers and began dispensaries in the province's outlying areas. Arca had few diagnostic instruments and could treat only symptoms. Most of the ailments she encountered dealt with malnutrition and parasites. Although she had a large supply of drugs donated by Catholics from the United States and adequate equipment for minor emergencies, Arca desperately needed medical personnel and more sophisticated instruments for basic laboratory work. A government hospital in Ocosingo had provided little succor for Indian villagers because a prejudiced staff preferred to work with non-Indian *Latinos* (members of Spanish rather than Indian descent). The government hospital contained no facilities for bed patients and, because of clogged pipes, often had no running water. In addition, the physician would see Indian patients between ten o'clock and twelve o'clock only. Thus there existed a great need for an improved medical facility in the region.[24]

Meanwhile, the Presentation sisters from San Francisco and Aberdeen began their training period. They spent two months at the Summer Institute of Linguistics at the University of Washington, studying with Dr. Benjamin Elson. The nuns concentrated on information that would help them communicate in the Tzeltal dialect, the most widely spoken Indian tongue in Chiapas. Then in August 1965, they traveled to Cuernavaca, Mexico, to do intensive work at the Intercultural Formation Center. They participated in workshops and retreats until January 1966, when they left for Ocosingo. Sister Remily was to operate the dispensary there, while the others—Sisters Mary Reginald and Mary Raymond—would serve as teachers in catechetics and adult education. They had combined cultural, linguistic, and religious study during their orientation period, hoping that adjustment to the environment could be speedy and painless.[25]

The surroundings, however, continually challenged their emotional and spiritual strength. The Presentations and their associates continually attempted, for example, never to contradict the native medicine men who exercised power in the local communities. Moreover the local "doctors' " own vulnerability to public criticism was a constant reminder to the nuns of their possible fate. Once a witch doctor (as the super-naturalistic healers are sometimes called) incurred the wrath of a family who sneaked into his home and, as Sister Remily recounted, "sliced his head off with a machete and shot [his daughter] . . . five times in the back." The marauders took the father's head because, they believed, as long as it remained joined with the body, the man's spirit would still be alive. The next day the daughter was brought to the Presentations, and although she survived, her emotional state was severely impaired.[26]

The California and South Dakota Presentations endured privations similar to those that their missionary sisters experienced in other locations all over the world. Presentation nuns from the Kaoma district of Zambia, Africa, from South India, and from Pakistan, wrote letters to motherhouses, summarized by historian M. Raphael Consedine: "For the new missionary, or for a seasoned missionary going to a different area, there are first the problems of survival. Under humorous phrases, letters hide the physical and emotional difficulties of adjustment. The missionaries soon learn what they have to face: heat, cold, humidity, torrential rains, journeys on roads which make nonsense of the speed of modern transport." There was always an ever-present loneliness and isolation. "No mail came through, and we thought you had forgotten us," one missionary nun wrote, representing many.[27]

After her first month at Ocosingo, Sister Remily also wrote to her sisters in Aberdeen. Describing her surroundings, she explained that the town was located in a valley between high mountains, and only one road, a dirt trail from Comitan, was always passable. Others were open only during the dry season that extended from February to July. Most people traveled by foot, a few by horseback. The sisters treated Indians who lived in villages containing from one or two hundred people, scattered throughout the mountains, the closest settlement being an hour away by horse. The climate was cold and damp during the rainy season, and the Indians had no heat in their homes. Constructed of bamboo and mud with grass roofs and earthen floors, these one-room structures had neither windows nor chimneys, and family members all lived, ate, and slept in the same room. In an early communication, Sister Remily commented that she and her fellow missionaries had no immediate plans for building a school or a hospital. They would concentrate instead on teaching nutrition, agriculture, sanitation, and catechetical classes.[28]

Thus, the sisters began a program of schooling Indian infirmary workers to help them in educating the villagers. They chose capable men to come in from their colonies for two-day courses in learning how to take care of the sick. After the training period, the Indians returned to the mission for monthly meetings. The learners received instruction in basic sanitation and disease prevention, as well as in detection and simple teatment of ailments. One sister commented that the students were primarily uneducated, but they possessed intelligence, were well versed in jungle life, and were eager for knowledge. Most of them spoke Tzeltal and a smattering of Spanish, so the North Americans occasionally encountered communication difficulties as they instructed the men about simple cleanliness and the need for protein in their diets.[29]

In 1967, a combination of events led to the construction of a hospital at Altamirano, a settlement even more isolated than Ocosingo. Cenami, an Indian organization in Mexico, received a donation from a group of German Catholic bishops to finance construction, and the Indians in the area contributed land for the project. They began work on a four-bed structure, which would house an examination area, surgery rooms, and laboratory facilities. The building was made of materials from the local surroundings, and the villagers at Altamirano joined in working to complete the facility. Using two brick-making machines, the laborers carted materials, laid bricks, and made door and window frames. In July 1968, Sisters Remily and Mengenhauser, who had by now become part of the project, moved into the newly completed headquarters, Hospital San Carlos. They received aid from Dr. Marcos Antonio Castillo, a recent medical graduate who was appointed resident physician. The sisters and "Dr. Tony," as they fondly referred to him, bore the heavy load of setting up the hospital, teaching infirmary staff, and running the pharmacy. They gained assistance from local people who helped in the office, made repairs, maintained electrical equipment, laundered, and cooked. Sister Remily commented in a letter to the motherhouse that working with the villagers was slow but, with patience, it was sure.[30]

Once the hospital was completed the sisters received visitors who offered their services for short periods of time. Three plastic surgeons from Stanford University operated on cleft-palate victims, and a dentist from Seattle performed extractions and taught classes in tooth decay prevention. The Mexican government sent several student social service doctors to study with Castillo and the sisters because the governor of Chiapas had visited the health center and had been impressed with it. Even Bishop Lambert Hoch visited in 1970. At that time he offered to donate a a four-wheel-drive vehicle for the hospital's use, so the nuns made plans to return to South Dakota in order to drive it back to the mission. Added to these efforts were those of a group of young volunteers from a parish in Sioux Falls, who during a two-week visit scrubbed and painted hospital rooms, dug ditches for a new central water system, and tore down an old building to make room for a patient-family hostel. Those who helped out were not always Catholic. On a visit to the United States, Sister Remily told Marilyn Meninga, a young female laboratory technician who had graduated from the McKennan program and was working in that hospital, about the Mexican venture. Although Meninga was a Presbyterian, the Minnesota native became so enthusiastic about helping out that she returned to Mexico with Sister Remily and stayed for two years.[31]

Dr. William Delaney II, who, like his father, had worked with the Presentation Sisters at St. Joseph Hospital in Mitchell, made four visits, thereby creating a family tradition of sacrificial service. Together he and other physicians who worked with the Presentations embodied the selfless professional commitment to care similar to the nun's ideology. Formerly Dr. Delaney had performed surgery with Sister Remily, who convinced him to make the initial trip. On his first sojourn, the physician was frustrated to discover that he could do little, although he returned three more times, extending each visit to a two-week tour. His duties included teaching surgical techniques to Dr. Castillo and performing skin grafts and other surgeries himself. After returning to South Dakota for the last time, Delaney described his experience in an interview. The medical facility, he observed, was a well-constructed, one-story Mexican-style structure containing a dispensary, major and minor surgery rooms, two examination spaces, a laboratory, an x-ray area, and an intensive-care unit. Although the Presentations' goal was to turn the facility over to Indian and Hispanic religious, professionals, and other staff members, they emphasized some traditional values in preparing the community for this role. Resembling ideals that the international Presentation order had taught since the eighteenth century, a focus on industry and responsibility was evident in the facility's operational procedures. Entire families sometimes stayed at the hospital if one of their members was ill, but they received no charity, Delaney recalled. If they had no money, patients and family members paid for care by barter or by performing tasks around the hospital grounds. Expenses for those treated totaled approximately 80 cents a day, including room and board for the patient, as well as shelter for those accompanying the sick. Although physical examinations were free, patients paid for all medications that they used.[32]

The Presentations tried many approaches to educating the Indians about maintaining good health. They set up an experimental garden in which they grew lettuce, radishes, peanuts, potatoes, and soybeans, in hopes of persuading the villagers to add more vegetables to their diets. They tried to raise chickens, hogs, and goats to provide more protein, and the nuns paid for Indian assistance so that the latter could buy the animals. Together, natives and sisters worked at the hospital, cutting fence posts, growing feed, and doing other chores. The women also began a cooperative milk program with surrounding inhabitants, gave the children medication for worms, and showed the mothers how to mix powdered milk, which was donated in part by a Mexican company and otherwise paid for by contributions from pupils in South Dakota Presentation parochial schools. The milk powder was distributed monthly. To test their progress, Presentation nurses weighed the Latin American youngsters and recorded the results. After six months, they found that some of the children had gained as much as ten kilograms (twenty-two pounds). Others, however, became ill from the milk because of lactose sensitivity, and their mothers discontinued feeding it to the children. Thus, the project had mixed results, as did most of their other experiments. Sister Remily stated that trying to persuade people to change, even for their own improved health, was often difficult when it opposed generations of custom.[33]

During their stay at Hospital San Carlos, the Presentations experienced frustrations involving visa troubles and travel difficulties. The nuns were required to have their tourist cards renewed every six months, which they accomplished by traveling to Guatemala for a few days to have their passports stamped and their medical records checked. On one such trip in 1969, they forgot their medical certificates and were chagrined to find that they must pay a small bribe of five pesos (less than a dollar) to the customs officials in order to reenter the country. The itinerary they followed was to fly from Altamirano to Comitán and then to take the bus to the border.[34]

Other difficulties arose when Sister Mengenhauser returned to South Dakota to drive the four-wheel-drive vehicle that Bishop Hoch had donated back to Altamirano. She filled the truck with medical supplies and drove to El Paso. There, Mexican authorities delayed her because she had no permit to bring the equipment into Mexico. After several days they allowed her to cross, but other problems arose because the vehicle was loaded too heavily, and the excessive weight led to engine trouble. On the last leg of the excursion the roads became impassable, so Sister Mengenhauser had to abandon the vehicle in Tuxtla, fly to Comitán, and obtain a driver to help bring her cargo over the swollen rivers and muddy trails. Each time they crossed a body of water they first unloaded their cargo and then packed it again on the other side. Finally, with help from passersby, Sister Mengenhauser drove the much abused vehicle into Ocosingo and then on to Altamirano.[35]

Problems in the daily operation of the hospital plagued the sisters. Getting supplies into Altamirano was usually a gamble, and poor mail service often led to delays. This problem grew even worse until police discovered that a local mail carrier was stealing parcels. After postal inspectors removed him from his position, workers in the process of cleaning out the thief's office found several boxes of books, letters, and sample drugs that six months earlier had been sent to the sisters. During the dry season, water shortages also caused difficulties, and Sister Remily remembered one instance in 1972 in which the hospital did not have even enough water for the nurses to use in pulling a young girl's decayed tooth. Dry weather also caused fires in the jungle, and smoke became such a hazard that planes often had to be grounded to avoid accidents in the haze.[36]

Despite obstacles, clinic records showed that the mission filled a growing need, and that the staff made continual improvements. In 1967 alone, they vaccinated more than 500 children for such diseases as diphtheria, tetanus, whooping cough, smallpox, tuberculosis, and polio with serum donated by the Mexican government. By 1969, the number had increased to more than two thousand children from twenty-seven villages in the area. From March 1969 to March 1970, the Presentations admitted approximately five thousand people for treatment of tuberculosis, meningitis, diarrhea, tumors, malnutrition, impetigo, and pneumonia. In the next year the census grew to more than six thousand, and by 1975 the nurses counted seven thousand patients a year. Doctors took full advantage of a dental unit completed in 1970, which aided the physicians who extracted, filled, and repaired teeth. In 1971, a road built to connect Altamirano with Ocosingo helped speed communications and provided a clear route under which electrical cables could be buried. Up to that time a generator had supplied the hospital.[37]

By 1975, the Presentations at Altamirano began negotiating to transfer their operation to a group of Mexican Sisters of Charity. The Presentations' original goal of establishing the hospital had been achieved, and they welcomed their comrades, who first began to arrive in 1976. Sister Remily exemplified the persistence and yet the moderation of the Presentation order: unlike other Catholics working in Central and South America, she and her comrades did not practice liberation theology, a Marxist-inspired philosophy portraying Christ's message as a justification for revolution against oppressive institutions. Mirroring official papal thought, the Presentations were aware of Marxism's potential threat to the Church, which was itself an institution capable of abusing human freedom in the name of perpetuating itself.[38] Sister Remily later explained, "either you started a revolution . . . [to] overthrow the whole thing or else you worked within the system, . . . try[ing] in some way to change . . . it."[39] Consequently, empowering people to meet their basic needs had been the nuns' priority.

This was one reason the Presentations required that every patient pay for health care services, and that all persons, rich or poor, wait their turns in line. The progressive, not radical, Presentation philosophy had encouraged all races of Mexicans to work together, a goal toward which the sisters hoped their clients would continue to strive.[40] Confident that their efforts would continue to bear fruit after their departure, Sister Remily wrote, "our work has been accomplished. The idea of a mission is to help the local people to [achieve] . . . independence and decrease dependence on foreigners. The seed has been planted, and through the help of many, many people at home, that seed has been watered for twelve years."[41]

Although this respect for cultural differences had not been a mark of international Presentation mission work throughout the nineteenth and early twentieth centuries, by the 1970s, Presentations all over the world shared Sister Remily's beliefs. In 1983, another Presentation missionary wrote that she and her sisters "work to promote the Christian and human values of the multi-cultural ideal. Through language and cultural programmes, and through the promotion of liturgy which expresses cultural diversity, they seek to instill a sense of self-worth in migrant children and adults. . . ."[42]

For the South Dakota Presentations, however, the multicultural mission did not expressly intend to liberate the Indian women from their second-class gender status, although it did not glorify the sufferer. Personally, Sister Remily was appalled at the Indian women's role as mere "beasts of burden," but the nuns tried not to dwell on the injustice of it. Moreover, rather than meditating on Nano Nagle's pain or on the Christ symbolized by a "bloody crucifix" hanging in agony on some church wall, Sister Remily and the other nuns taught women, men, and children that figures such as Nagle and Christ offered models of dignity and self-respect that lay within all persons. "We were Presentations," Sister Remily reminisced, "and they'll never forget us for that."[43] In such statements, Sister Remily and her companions seemed to diverge somewhat from their international order's tendency to teach or glorify self-denial that had begun with Nagle. Continuing the tradition, Sister Mary Maura McCarthy wrote to her sisters in Dubuque, Iowa, from her congregation's Bolivian mission:

> I remember some ten years ago leaving the States filled with resurrection zeal, believing that Christ is risen—we have already won, so why sweat? And time after time in Bolivian churches I would watch an old woman or perhaps a young man come into a church or chapel, make a beeline for the

crucifix or for Christ laid out in the tomb. And I would shudder. As the years went on and I became wiser, I realized how very essential the suffering and crucified Christ is to a Bolivian who faces death at median age forty-seven, or who has perhaps lost three babies before she is twenty-five, or who may be shot tonight for standing up for his rights this morning. It is I who needed to learn how Christ continues to suffer in His body, the poor.[44]

After remaining with their own Latin American neighbors in an advisory capacity for eight months, the South Dakota and California Presentations left the hospital in 1976, but promised to continue collecting money and supplies for the effort. After the Sisters of Charity had been at Altamirano for more than a year, Sister Remily encountered an American couple who had taken their sick child there. The travelers praised the quality of care, which remained as high as it had been when the Presentations were in control.[45]

Happy that her travail had been rewarded, Sister Remily sought to be part of another similar project. In 1979, she began investigating the possibility of opening another hospital in Mexico. That year Sister Remily and South Dakota Presentation Sister Kathleen Zimmer joined Sister Joanna Anita Bruno of the San Francisco motherhouse on a 5,700-mile journey in search of a new mission sight. Leaving Sioux Falls after consulting with Bishops Dudley and Hoch, they began their excursion on August 30 of that year. They stopped to see the San Francisco Presentations and to commune with Sister Thaddea Kelly and with South Dakota Sisters Patrice Marie Moriarty and JoAnn Sturzl, who were attending a national conference of Presentation superiors. In Mexico City they recontacted Dr. Castillo and convinced him to work with them once again. After considering several options, they finally decided to locate with the Holy Ghost Fathers at the San Luis Potosi mission, rejecting alternative villages such as Amuzgos because the Amuzgos Indians sometimes assassinated missionaries. In July of 1981, the nuns established their living quarters at San Antonio, a small township about the size of their last homesight, Altamirano, Chiapas.[46]

The area was already equipped with a clinic, so Sister Remily and the others went right to work. "Medically our fame grows . . .," she soon recorded. Assisting their efforts Dr. Castillo agreed to help the nuns set up legal arrangements with the Mexican government and to serve as medical director of their health care program. Again he proved very helpful both as a skilled surgeon and as a liaison with Mexican officials. Once while Castillo was at San Antonio, the elders of the town, the president, and the federal commission on health called a meeting that Castillo attended. There he told his fellow citizens "how fortunate they were" that Presentations had chosen their community.[47]

The nuns were performing what seemed to be miracles. Late one evening in June of 1980 a man knocked at their door, blurting out, "Hurry, Madre, there is a child dying in a house next to mine." Sisters Zimmer, Bruno, and Remily rushed after him and upon arriving at the home found several hysterical people. The family and friends were helpless to save a three-year-old child, who was choking on a thick "posol" (probably a hominy dish called *pozole*), however Sister Zimmer performed a Heimlich maneuver to remove the obstruction and saved the child's life.[48]

Whereas the progress was slowed by a people bound to "customs, superstitions and such," at other times the nuns had to restrain the natives' over-eagerness to modernize. "They are [unknowingly] injecting medicines," wrote Sister Remily. "Everyone loves to learn to inject, just in case!! I have seen some of their needles and syringes; we would not use them for a dying cow."[49] To comfort and encourage the nuns through the first uplifting and yet frustrating year, Sister Mary Denis, the South Dakota Presentation president, paid them a visit, and, as Sister Remily recalled, "helped us find meaning in our meager living arrangements."[50]

Reinforced, the nuns continued to move along in their progressive but accepting way, initiating a hospital building program in 1981. By 1984, with the facility completed, the nuns began to prepare to turn the project over to the people for whom it was built. Not only had several local women expressed an interest in becoming nuns, but the Presentations had also located a permanent doctor for the mission, Dr. Salvador Escobedo. Juan Reyes, a man who had undergone surgery in South Dakota Presentation hospital, walked over the mountains each morning to take x-rays. Sister Zimmer had trained a young man and woman as lab assistants. Two other natives managed the record and census office, while the mission hospital employed a Huastecan woman as a translator for the Nahuatl language.[51]

By 1985, the nuns had extended their services beyond offering religious and medical attention. Not unlike nineteenth-century Irish Presentation teachers, they had helped educate and employ several teen-age Huastecan girls, finding jobs for four of the youngsters working for families in Mexico City. In return the girls received the opportunity to complete their high school education. As Sister Zimmer observed, "They will be able to send money home to help their families and hopefully learn some skills that will help them break out of the cycle of poverty, . . . [offering] limited food, no school, [and] no chance to reach beyond the boundaries of the mud hut."[52]

In January of 1985, the Presentations were still in San Antonio calling on their charismatic ability to convince physicians and lay people to give selflessly of their time and expertise, serving anywhere from twenty to eighty-five patients per day. Two dentists, Paul J. Leon and Daniel A. Harvey, came from Aberdeen that year. In addition four laypersons from the United States who had visited the mission two years previously returned to donate their time and industry. Robert and Dorothy Sutherland from Michigan and Hank and Jo Baker from Virginia spent two weeks working at the mission. Operating from within their own separate-but-equal gender roles, the women sewed and mended hospital sheets while the men repaired malfunctions in the hospital's plumbing and electrical wiring. Religious joined the trail of visitors that year. Sister Myron Martin, still mission coordinator, and Sister Denis both spent time with their colleagues. On another occasion Bishop Dudley of Sioux Falls visited for a second time. He participated in a special feast day celebration of the Holy Ghost Fathers, in which a Huastecan choir sang the liturgy. "It was a great occasion for the people to have a Bishop come," Sister Remily recounted.[53]

Looking back on what, for Sister Remily and the South Dakota Presentations, were twenty years of joys and strife working within the extended apostolate, several observations can be made. By predicating their professional growth on the belief that as religious women their call was to nurture and instruct, the Presentations prevented conflict over the various interpretations of the Marian ideal from eroding community life at the motherhouse or at other Presentation outposts throughout the world. Moreover, they marshalled both internal and external support for professional expansion within traditional fields and involvement in some that were totally new. Besides performing as principals or as elementary and secondary teachers, sisters instructed in colleges other than their own, worked in parish and community adult education programs, and organized diversified instructional activities. In the medical apostolate, the nurses practiced in homes for the aged, organized pastoral care departments for the hospitalized and their families, and trained allied health personnel. In many respects, following a somewhat modernized image of Nano Nagle served them well.

NOTES

1. Interview with Mother Myron Martin, Aug. 12, 1976, South Dakota Oral History Center, Vermillion.

2. M. Raphael Consedine, P.B.V.M., *Listening Journey: A Study of the Spirit and Ideals of Nano Nagle and the Presentation Sisters* (Victoria, Australia: Congregation of the Presentation of the Blessed Virgin Mary, 1983), 333.

3. H. Warren Button and Eugene F. Provenz, Jr., *History of Education and Culture in America* (Englewood Cliffs, N.J.: Prentice-Hall, 1983), 300–15; Eric F. Goldman, *Crucial Decade and After: America, 1945–1960* (New York: Vintage Books, 1956), 341–46; interview with Bishop Lambert Hoch, June 28, 1978, South Dakota Oral History Center; interview with Mother Myron Martin; Thomas T. McAvoy C.S.C., *A History of the Catholic Church in the United States* (Notre Dame: University of Notre Dame Press, 1970), 464–68.

4. Interview with Sister Mary Eleanor Joyce, Aug. 12, 1976, South Dakota Oral History Center; interview with Sister Helen Freimuth, Aug. 5, 1976, South Dakota Oral History Center; John D. Pulliam, *History of Education in America* (Columbus, Ohio: Charles E. Merrill, 1976), 125.

5. Interview with David Rykhus, June 2, 1978, South Dakota Oral History Center; interview with Keith Fitzpatrick, June 5, 1978, South Dakota Oral History Center; interview with David Patton, June 26, 1978, South Dakota Oral History Center; interview with Sister Colman Coakley, Aug. 7, 1976, South Dakota Oral History Center; Consedine, *Listening Journey*, 374.

6. Interview with Sister Lynn Marie Welbig, Aug. 10, 1976, South Dakota Oral History Center; interview with Sister Mary Eleanor Joyce; "Chapter Decisions," 1968, Presentation Archives, Presentation Heights, Aberdeen, S. D.; Sister Alicia Dunphy to Courtney Ann Vaughn-Roberson, March 11, 1985; interview with Sister Pam Donelan by Susan Peterson, April 17, 1985.

7. Interview with Sister M. Eucharia Kelly, Aug. 12, 1976, South Dakota Oral History Center.

8. Interview with Sister Anna Marie Weinreis, Aug. 10, 1976, South Dakota Oral History Center.

9. Interview with Sister Sylvester Auth, Aug. 9, 1976, South Dakota Oral History Center.

10. Interview with Sister Kay O'Neil, Aug. 9, 1976, South Dakota Oral History Center; Ann Elizabeth Kelly, "Catholic Women in Campus Ministry: An Emerging Ministry for Women in the Catholic Church" (Ph.D. diss., Boston University Graduate School, 1975), 9–10, 21–22; interview with Sister Mary Eleanor Joyce; interview with Mother Myron Martin; Sister Sheila Schnell to Susan Peterson, Feb. 4, 1979; interview with Sister Pam Donelan.

11. Interview with Sister Marie Patrice Moriarty, Aug. 12, 1976, South Dakota Oral History Center.

12. Interview with Sister Lynn Marie Welbig.

13. Interview with Sister Myron Martin.

14. Ibid.

15. Ibid.

16. Ibid.

17. Sister Mary DePazzi to Susan Peterson, Feb. 9, 1979.

18. Interview with Sister Myron Martin.

19. Sister Sheila Schnell to Susan Peterson, Feb. 4, 1979.

20. Interview with Sister Kay O'Neil.

21. Ibid.; Sister Pam Donelan to Courtney Ann Vaughn-Roberson, June 1985.

22. "Apostolate Statistical Sheet," 1985, Presentation Archives.

23. *Los Companeros*, vol. 1, no. 4 (n.d.); *Dominicans on Mission*, vol. 1, no. 1 (n.d.), vol. 1, no. 8, (n.d.); interview with Sister Elizabeth Remily, Sept. 5, 1976, June 1, 1978, South Dakota Oral History Center; *Presentation Chronicle*, Feb. 1965; interview with Sister Myron Martin; Consedine, *Listening Journey*, 381.

24. *Presentation Chronicle*, Feb. 1965; *Los Companeros*, vol. 1, no. 4.

25. "Mexican Mission File," Presentation Archives; *Presentation Chronicle*, Feb. 1965; *Los Companeros*, vol. 1, no. 4; interview with Sister Elizabeth Remily, June 1, 1978.

26. Interview with Sister Elizabeth Remily, Sept. 5, 1976.

27. Consedine, *Listening Journey*, 386; anynomous Presentation nun, quoted in Ibid., 386.

28. Sister Elizabeth Remily to the Sisters, Feb. 1966, Presentation Archives.

29. Karen Moore to the Sisters, Sept. 1, 1969, Presentation Archives; Sister Toni Marie to the Sisters, May 1, 1969, Presentation Archives.

30. *Dominicans on Mission*, vol. 3, no. 3 (n.d.); *Los Companeros*, July 1967, vol. 9, no. 7, (n.d.); Sister Elizabeth Remily to the Sisters, Feb. 15, 1967, Nov. 28, 1969, Presentation Archives.

31. Sister Elizabeth Remily to the Sisters, Nov. 16, 1960, April 1971, Presentation Archives; Karen Moore to the Sisters, Feb. 8, 1970, Presentation

Archives; Sister Margarita to the Sisters, Aug. 1972, Presentation Archives; interview with Sister Elizabeth Remily, Sept. 5, 1976.

32. Interview with William A. Delaney, June 6, 1978, South Dakota Oral History Center; Sister Elizabeth Remily to the Sisters, April 1971, Presentation Archives.

33. *Los Companeros*, Aug., Sept., Oct., 1967; Sister Elizabeth Remily to the Sisters, Nov. 1966, Sept. 6, 1971, Presentation Archives; interview with William A. Delaney; interview with Sister Elizabeth Remily, June 1, 1978.

34. Sister Elizabeth Remily to the Sisters, Oct. 1966, Nov. 28, 1969, Presentation Archives; Sister Janice Mengenhauser to the Sisters, July 15, 1971, Presentation Archives.

35. Sister Janice Mengenhauser to the Sisters; Sister Elizabeth Remily to the Sisters, Nov. 28, 1969.

36. Sister Anita Bruno to the Sisters, May 1971, Presentation Archives; Sister Kathleen to the Sisters, June 1972, Presentation Archives.

37. Sister Janice Mengenhauser to the Sisters, Sept. 29, 1969, Presentation Archives; "Mexican Mission File"; Sister Elizabeth Remily to the Sisters, Sept. 1975, Presentation Archives; Sister Anrita Bruno to the Sisters, Oct. 6, 1970, Presentation Archives.

38. Sister Elizabeth Remily to the Sisters, Sept. 1975, Presentation Archives; Aaron Wildavsky, "Church Capitalism, and Democracy," *The New York Times Book Review Digest* 89 (Dec. 9, 1984): 14–15; William H. Howick, *Philosophies of Education* (Danville, Ill.: Interstate Printers and Publishers, 1980), 129–34; Peter Hebblethwaite, "The Popes and Politics: Shifting Patterns in 'Catholic Social Doctrine,' " *Daedalus: Journal of the Academy of Arts and Sciences*, 111 (Winter 1982): 85–99.

39. Interview with Sister Elizabeth Remily, Sept. 5, 1976.

40. Interview with Sister Elizabeth Remily, June 1, 1978.

41. Sister Elizabeth Remily to the Sisters, Sept. 1975.

42. Anynomous Presentation nun, quoted in Consedine, *Listening Journey*, 376.

43. Interview with Sister Elizabeth Remily, Sept. 5, 1976.

44. Consedine, *Listening Journey*, 392.

45. Sister Elizabeth Remily to the Sisters, Sept. 1975, Aug. 1976, Jan. 1977, July 1977, Presentation Archives; interview with Sister Elizabeth Remily, June 1, 1978; interview with Sister Pam Donelan by Susan Peterson.

46. Sister Joanna (Anita) Bruno, Sister Elizabeth Remily, and Sister Kathleen Zimmer to Friends, Oct. 1979, Presentation Archives.

47. Sister Elizabeth Remily to Communities and Friends, June 1980, Presentation Archives.

48. Anonymous man, quoted in Sister Elizabeth Remily to Communities and Friends.

49. Ibid.

50. Sister Elizabeth Remily, P.B.V.M. to Friends, Jan. 1985, Presentation Archives.

51. Sister Elizabeth Remily to Friends, Oct. 1981, Nov.-Dec. 1984, Presentation Archives.

52. Sister Kathleen Bierne, P.B.V.M. to Sisters, Families, Friends, July 1985, Presentation Archives.

53. Sister Elizabeth Remily to Friends, Jan. 1985, Presentation Archives.

11. Conclusion

□

Unsuspecting of all that the Presentation Sisters' worldly future held, Nano Nagle did know one thing: she must use her own education to bring to the Irish poor a rudimentary academic knowledge, an appreciation for the nobility of woman, and a chance for spiritual redemption. Nor did Nagle's successors foresee in Dakota Territory that their mission of educating youth for a literate, moral, and spiritual life would later provide a rationale for the professionalization of their order. Nevertheless, in following Nagle's example of giving clients the best of Christian womanhood, during the twentieth century many of the South Dakota Presentations strove for professional recognition in the fields of which they were a part. In the process, they underwent changes, maintained their solidarity despite periodic conflict, and won the trust of their clients and the public. Because even the most liberal continued to profess what was by modern standards a traditional women's creed while providing vital professional services at the same time, their male church supervisors could not help granting them support.

For the American Presentations, as for other orders throughout the United States, gaining and retaining social power meant making themselves an integral part of their surroundings. Consequently, the Irish nuns who came to Dakota Territory in the late nineteenth century underwent several adjustments. Besides enduring the harsh winds, severe winters, and blistering summers, which stood in marked contrast to the mild weather of their homeland, the sisters were faced with establishing their own frontier ministries; however, Sioux Indian pupils were largely unavailable, some white settlers were quite indifferent to them, and financial support was scarce. At this point the Presentations could have returned to Ireland, but instead they decided to serve those receptive local Anglo-American and European Catholic settlers, who in the Presentations' view were in need of guidance and instruction.

Financial and physical hard times continued after the Presentation community split in 1892, and the South Dakota sisters' continued trials proved that white parishoners' enthusiasm for education could be as mercurial as that of the Indians. This realization led to another important accommodation, the elimination of the enclosure rule. The Presentations and Church officials were convinced that to serve the Catholic and non-Catholic population the nuns must be able to travel outside their convent walls, obtaining school funds and maintaining constant contact with the families whose children they taught. The prohibition was lifted, and Pope Pius XII gave final dispensation when the Presentations became a pontifical order in 1946.

Further Presentation efforts to answer neighbors' needs led to the development of yet another apostolate when a diphtheria epidemic raged in 1900. No adequate health care facility existed, so the nuns rushed in to fill the void by providing apprentice-based nursing care and temporary shelter. Their success at founding and running St. Luke's Hospital, which opened a year after the medical emergency, led to requests from three other cities for similar operations. Despite those who would discourage the nuns from entering the professional world of medicine and despite the primacy of the education apostolate in the international Presentation Order, the South Dakota sisters obtained the necessary approval to support hospital administration and nursing as new ministries.

To serve the same ideological end, throughout the community's history some sisters have made housework their vocation, thereby relieving the other nuns to become educated and to devote themselves wholeheartedly to their work. The freedom to be professionally singleminded afforded certain Presentations the same advantages that traditionally married professional men have always had: a supportive family and a dutiful housekeeper. Yet no matter how much some Presentations may have taken on typically male social roles, they have continued to defend their right to practice certain professions and strive for self-improvement in the terms of their order's Marian philosophical source.

Dated, then, but modern, many professionally minded Presentations kept in touch throughout the twentieth century with national education and health care developments, each professional nun seeking to become more and more highly proficient in her given field. In the process, most have not only professionalized, but also become important persons in the social settings of which they became a part. The parish schools in which the nuns taught not only served students' and parents' needs, but also provided an alternative to public education, stressing more of the liberal arts tradition than has generally been offered in common school curricula, while adding the dimension of religious instruction. With the creation of the Diocesan Office of Education, the Presentations took advantage of the potential for educational policymaking and, despite the shrinking numbers of sister-teachers in recent years, have continued to advise bishops concerning future educational needs.

The Presentations also made noteworthy contributions as college instructors and administrators. At Notre Dame Junior College, they enabled more than a thousand students to gain the beginnings of higher education at a time when four-year colleges in South Dakota were too expensive for, or inaccessible to, many rural people. Then with the founding of Presentation College in 1951, the nuns finally owned and controlled a higher educational facility that offered students the opportunity to grow spiritually, intellectually, and physically within any number of certificate, associate degree, or university-parallel programs. In addition, the college provided an accessible stepping stone toward the academic preparation of Presentation teachers, nurses, administrators, and counselors.

Through medical care the sisters' impact was dynamic. Not at all confined to a Catholic population, Presentation hospitals and schools of nursing served people from all walks of life. In fact, many non-Catholics have preferred the Presentation hospitals over other denominational or public facilities because of the personal attention paid patients and their families. Moreover, while tending to the business obligations of their institutions—developing financial programs, organizing construction plans, coordinating nursing education, participating in the Cadet Nurse Corps during World War II, competing for federal grants, running pastoral care programs, and founding Presentation Health Services, Incorporated—the nuns have provided a continually relevant administrative career option for women, once thought to be strictly for men.

The eventual triumph of Presentation nursing educators in their bid for academic policymaking was an important national contribution to the professionalization of a stereotypically female occupation. Presentation nurse-educators have also influenced many students and doctors to combine a dedication to nurture and care with an emphasis on science and academics. Perhaps some scholars are correct that no matter how much formal education nurses obtain, their occupation's academic body of knowledge will always comprise a less sophisticated piece of the physicians' more expansive scientific realm;[1] however, by owning and operating their own hospitals and requiring physicians and other employees to accept the nuns' own philosophical orientation, the Presentation Sisters have contributed significantly to women's respect and authority in the health care field.

Thus, when given the opportunity many Presentations seemed willing to circumvent the preeminence of humility when only assertiveness could get the job done. Even the early-day teachers, through the voice of their reverend mother, sometimes hesitated to accept male clerics' requests to staff schools when the teacher-trainees were not yet adequately prepared. As the political divisions of the turbulent chapter meetings in the later years revealed, some of the older women did disapprove of their fellow sisters' moves into traditional male roles such as the ministry or their establishment of single or perhaps dual resident dwellings; yet because their basic woman-centered ideology was maintained, the conservatives did allow these changes to take place, and the sisterhood survived. Thus, by maintaining its basic philosophical intent, the South Dakota Presentation community and other orders of nuns liberalized tradition. It evolved to buttress the expansion of the nuns' occupational options and the professionalization of their career fields, leading to the sisters' increased higher education, autonomy, and identification with nationally accepted professional goals.

Governing these changes for the South Dakota Presentations, a legislative body known as a chapter was the highest community authority. Between chapters the reverend mother and her council implemented the chapter decrees. Through the decades of the early twentieth century up until mid-century, increasingly, the manner of government was authoritarian, especially after the sisters lost the direct election of superiors in 1946. After Vatican II, the leadership group relied much more on consultation with the sisters, who regained the popular vote in 1968. The present title for the major superior is president, replacing superior general and reflecting a shift in the style of government.

Similar trends were evident in the lives and work of various Presentation leaders. Initially Teresa Mulally was unable to budge her Dublin community away from the strict practice of enclosure and other cloister stipulations such as prayer scheduling. In Dakota Territory, Mother Joseph Butler initially attempted to maintain the enclosure rule, which, as the eighteenth- and even twentieth-century constitutions revealed, was rooted in a negative social and religious depiction of woman's moral frailty; however, eventually Mother Butler acquiesced to the order's more spiritual ideal to serve, a value that helped the nuns transcend pejorative depictions of female weaknesses. Mother Butler did, however, protect her nuns from outside influences, even from the infiltration of other Presentations. Even so, the policy of mirroring Nagle's persistent expansion of services was set. Each new superior's tenure evidenced an increased willingness to assert womankind's positive contributions and to insist on the nuns' right to acquire expert knowledge and to use it in helping those in need.

From the time of Mother Aloysius Forrest, the leaders sent prospective professionals to colleges other than Northern at Aberdeen, although the superiors were always careful to preserve the benefits of sisterhood in the lives of those who left the motherhouse. Innovations such as Mother Carmelita McCullough's House of Studies and other smaller-scale living arrangements helped insure that the drive to professionalize would not be tainted by the increasingly self-centered philosophical approach that revisionist scholars have discovered, for example, in physicians. Presentation superiors and presidents could only hope and pray, however, for those sisters whose jobs took them far away from Aberdeen, and for whom no living companion could be found, that the power to keep the ideals alive would reside within each solitary nun. The result has been many strong-minded nuns who have managed to maintain their ideals.

Thus, the more modern South Dakota Presentation chief executives have helped perpetuate the separate-but-equal ideal. The extended apostolate has been a case in point. Retaining Nagle's apostolic model, various South Dakota Presentations argued for new apostolic choices and for the academic preparation necessary to enter a given field. In so doing, women such as Sister Elizabeth Remily captured the full force of their own and their community's potential. Involved not just in managing an entire health care unit in a culture once foreign to her, Sister Remily also emphasized the importance of caring in conjunction with or as a motivation for using her expert skills. Like other apostolic nuns, she continued the early twentieth-century Presentation policy, which kept alive the intent of the long-standing definition of professionalism; for, theoretically, it stressed the importance of ethics and service as much as the attainment of academic qualifications and autonomy.[2]

Recently, professional women from the secular world have also challenged male and female colleagues to value morality, nurturing, and caring as highly as the prototypical male proclivity for precision and objectivity. Educator and author Florence Howe has called on women employed within the traditional female occupations to create positive portrayals of those who "teach children,—[or] serve the sick, the troubled, and the needy . . . ."[3] Philosopher Jane Roland Martin, too, has suggested that educators include values from the female realm within their definition of the truly learned person who, in her view, must be both caring and just. Similarly, psychologist Carol Gilligan has challenged moral development experts to eradicate their male-normed paradigms. Finally, diverse representatives of feminist thought from Mary Daly to Betty Freidan have tended in recent years to validate rather than devalue the traditional female experience, although other feminist observers fear that such a celebration of women's distinctive potential could perpetuate the separate and forever unequal women's ghetto.[4]

Evidenced by this debate, the key to nuns' and other traditionally motivated womens' professional success is forever tenuous. Internally the South Dakota Presentations and other nuns must retain basic agreement on their essential mission so that their sisterhoods will survive and their professionalization efforts will continue. Particularly since Vatican II, throughout the United States and the world apostolic nuns have struggled to appropriately define their distinctly female charge. It seems that they are almost shadowed by Eve; although Mary atones for Eve's wrongdoing, Mary has not eliminated the Church's memory of the world's first woman and her original sin. Even so, recent South Dakota Presentation Constitutions attempt to do this through their thoroughly positive portrayal of the sisters' mission, with no hint of the stain of Eve.[5]

Secular but traditional professional women, along with new separatist feminists, must also deal with potential ironies within the history of their own domestic ideology, which during the nineteenth and much of the twentieth centuries rationalized primarily single women's entry into career fields such as teaching, nursing, and social work. It remains to be seen whether post-World-War II married women can continue to rely on a domestic belief system (the core of which contends that married woman's first responsibility is to her husband and children) to defend their professional activities. Even if nuns and other like-minded women are successful in perpetuating their separate female ideals, apparent in the holistic professional ethos emerging in today's society, another ultimate irony could act itself out. If successful, the new attitude could infiltrate the academic training and practice of typical male professional fields, eliminating external discrimination toward women, which paradoxically has mobilized their solidarity. Thus the need and climate for the distinctively female professional contribution would cease to exist.[6] A new professional prototype which for Christians is "no longer [of] . . . Men or women. . . but. . . one in Jesus Christ" could therefore, jeopardize the nuns' rationale for living together and operating under a separate religious ideological umbrella.[7]

The future of apostolic religious women's external environmental support system also is questionable. International Christianity is splitting apart on the issue of separate spheres. For example, the General Council of the United Church of Canada recently adopted new female images of God announcing that male domination should be abolished.[8] Yet Pope John Paul II seems to be in favor of retaining elements of woman's classic social and religious roles. As of this writing, however, it remains to be seen whether his leadership will reinstate the separate but unequal or perpetuate the separate-but-equal philosophy, necessary to rationalize many apostolic nuns' professional goals. Should the Catholic Church continue to promote its current conservative stance, defections from or the dissolution of many sisterhoods could follow; while those who remain and accept censure might abandon hope for increasing or even maintaining the professional expertise necessary to meet ever-changing demands of clients. South Dakota Presentation Sister Kay O'Neil concurred with other observers that until clergy, parishioners, and religious resolve major ideological differences the Church will not thrive.[9] Also aware of the uncertainty that the Presentations and other women religious face, another South Dakota Presentation wrote: "Now what can be said for the future? Will the visible and invisible links forged in the past continue to bind us to God, to one another, and to our apostolate? Will the spirit to meet the challenges to make the sacrifices be our guide in the future as it has been in the past?"[10] Only time will tell.

NOTES

1. Eliot Freidson, *Profession of Medicine: A Study of the Sociology of Applied Knowledge* (New York: Dodd, Mead, 1973), 51, 53.

2. Some authors suggest that nursing, social work, and to a lesser degree teaching have higher professional rank than do many other career fields because the former have maintained a strong service ideal. For an example, see Richard H. Hall, "Professionalization and Bureaucratization," *American Sociological Review* 33 (Feb. 1968): 97. Other authors support the utility of nursing's traditional service ideal. For a source, see Everett C. Hughes, Helen MacGill Hughes, and Irwin Deutscher, *Twenty Thousand Nurses Tell Their Story* (Philadelphia: J. B. Lippincott, 1958), 272–73.

3. Florence Howe, "Women and the Power to Change," in *Women and the Power to Change*, ed. Florence Howe (Berkeley: Carnegie Commission on Higher Education, 1975), 167.

4. Jane Roland Martin, "The Ideal of the Educated Person," *Educational Theory* 31 (Spring 1981): 97–110; "Excluding Women from the Educational Realm," *Harvard Educational Review* 52 (May 1982): 133–48; and *Reclaiming a Conversation: The Ideal of the Educated Woman* (New Haven: Yale University Press, 1985); Carol Gilligan, *In a Different Voice: Psychological Theory and Women's Development* (Cambridge: Harvard University Press, 1982). Works identifying successful female professionals who possess an integrated personality are Patricia N. Feulner, *Women in the Professions: A Social-Psychological Study* (Palo Alto: R. and E. Research, 1979) and Hester Eisenstein, *Contemporary Feminist Thought* (Boston: G. K. Hall, 1983). Compare Betty Friedan, *The Feminine Mystique* (New York: Dell Publishing, 1963) with the more recent work by Friedan, *The Second Stage* (New York: Summit Books, 1981).

5. For instructive discussions of the legacies of Eve and Mary, see Sidney Cornelia Callahan, *The Illusion of Eve: Modern Woman's Quest for Identity* (New York: Sheed and Ward, 1965); James Kenneally, "Eve, Mary, and the

Historians: American Catholicism and Women," in *Women in American Religion,* ed. Janet Wilson James (Philadelphia: University of Pennsylvania Press, 1976), 191–206.

6. Mark B. Ginsburg, "Teacher Education and Class and Gender Relations: A Critical Socio-Historical Analysis," presented at the American Educational Studies Association, Pittsburgh, Oct./Nov. 1986.

7. St. Paul, quoted in Galatians 3:28 in *The Way* (Wheaton, Ill.: Tyndale House Publishers), 1014.

8. *The Globe and Mail,* Aug. 18, 1986, A3.

9. Interview with Sister Kay O'Neil, Aug. 9, 1976, South Dakota Oral History Center, Vermillion.

10. Sister M. Martha, "Brief History of the Presentation Community in Aberdeen, 1886–1972," Presentation Archives, Presentation Heights, Aberdeen, S.D.

Appendix A

Presentation Congregations Throughout the World
(with dates of first foundations)

One Autonomous Group in Canada

St. John's, Newfoundland	1833

Eight Autonomous Groups in U.S.A.

California	1854
Newburgh, New York	1874
Dubuque, Iowa	1875
North Dakota	1880
Watervliet, New York	1881
Staten Island, New York	1884
Fitchburg, Massachusetts	1886
South Dakota	1886

Six Autonomous Groups in Australia
Forming the Society of Australia
Congregations of the P.B.V.M.

Tasmania	1866
Victoria	1873
Wagga Wagga, New South Wales	1874
Lismore, New South Wales	1886
Western Australia	1891
Queensland	1900

Two Autonomous Groups in Ireland

Dublin	1793
North Presentation, Cork	1799

The Union

Ireland	1775
England	1836
India	1842
Pakistan	1895

Zimbabwe	1949
New Zealand	1950
U.S.A.	1955
Scotland	1970
Zambia	1971
Chile	1981

Source: M. Raphael Consedine, P.B.V.M., *Listening Journey: A Study of the Spirit and Ideals of Nano Nagle and the Presentation Sisters* (Victoria, Australia: Congregation of the Presentation of the Blessed Virgin Mary, 1983), 405.

Appendix B

Presentation College:
Reporting the Finances for the Year 1963–64

Educational and General:

Student Fees:	Tuition-regular sessions	$ 41,561.00	
	Laboratory and incidental	9,096.00	
All student fees			$ 50,657.00
Endowment Income: Contributed services—total		$ 135,196.00	
Less: Contributed services allocated to student aid		2,493.00	
Endowment income unrestricted			$ 132,703.00
Gifts and Grants:	Unrestricted	$ 26,308.00	
	Restricted	1,300.00	
			$ 27,608.00
Organized activities relating to educational departments			0
Other sources			0
All educational and general income			$ 210,968.00

Auxiliary Enterprises:

Residence halls	$ 25,749.00	
Food services	66,877.00	
Bookstore	6,896.00	
Laundry	17,330.00	
Other auxiliary enterprises	133.00	
		$ 116,985.00

Student Aid:

Grants and gifts for student aid	$ 3,500.00	
Contributed services allocated to student aid	2,493.00	
All student aid		$ 5,993.00

Higher Educational Operations:

Summer school	$ 2,811.00	
Workshops	1,780.00	
All other educational operations		$ 4,591.00

All income	$ 338,537.00

GENERAL FUNDS EXPENDITURES
FOR YEAR ENDED MAY 31, 1964

Educational and General:
General Administration:

President's office	$ 8,002.00	
Dean of studies	6,545.00	
Business office	5,670.00	
All general administration		$ 20,217.00

Student Services:

Dean of women	$ 3,260.00	
Registrar	5,492.00	
Student counselors	4,300.00	
Placement office	500.00	
Campus positions	500.00	
Health services	500.00	
Chapel	2,289.00	
All student services		16,841.00

Public Services and Information:

Publicity and public relations office	$ 2,741.00	
Alumnae office	300.00	
All public services and information		$ 3,041.00
General institutional expenditures		8,917.00
Instruction expenditures		75,486.00
Library		8,002.00
Operation and maintenance of plant		67,174.00
All educational and general		$ 199,678.00

Auxiliary Enterprises:

Residence halls	$ 35,968.00	
Food services	62,248.00	
Bookstore	6,783.00	
Laundry	17,008.00	
Other auxiliary enterprises	35.00	
All auxiliary enterprises		$ 122,042.00

Student Aid:
Scholarships and grants applied	$	5,993.00		
All student aid			$	5,993.00

Higher Educational Operations:
Summer school	$	2,720.00		
Workshops		2,420.00		
All other educational operations			$	5,140.00

All expenditures	$	332,853.00

BALANCE SHEET
MAY 31, 1964

ASSETS

General Fund Assets:
Imprest cash funds	$	300.00		
Cash in bank		12,748.00		
Student accounts receivable (net)		4,565.00		
Inventories		2,440.00		
Total general funds assets			$	20,053.00

Loan Fund Assets:
Cash in bank	$	2,642.00		
Loans to students		3,940.00		
Total loan funds assets			$	6,582.00

Plant Funds Assets:
Land	$	32,463.00		
Buildings		1,638,205.00		
Furniture and equipment		197,240.00		
Total plant funds assets			$1,867,908.00	

Scholarships and Permanent Funds Assets:
Savings account-scholarship fund	$	2,084.00		
Total scholarship and permanent funds assets			$	2,084.00

Currency Funds Assets:
Cash in bank	$	580.00		
Temporary investments		2,000.00		
Total			$	2,580.00

Total Assets—All Funds	$1,899,207.00	

LIABILITIES AND FUNDS BALANCES

General Funds Liabilities:
Accounts payable $ 900.00

General funds balance   19,153.00

Total general funds liabilities and
funds balance $ 20,053.00

Loans Funds Liabilities:
Loans or accounts payable $ 0

Loan funds balance   6,582.00

Total loan funds liabilities and loan
funds balance $ 6,582.00

Plant Funds Liabilities and Reserves:
Mortgages payable (college share) $ 455,128.00
Reserve for depreciation   255,425.00
                                        $ 710,553.00

Plant funds balance   1,157,355.00
Total plant funds liabilities, reserves,
and funds balance $1,867,908.00

Scholarship and Permanent Funds
Balance: $ 2,084.00
Total scholarship and permanent
funds liabilities and funds balance $ 2,084.00

Currency Funds Liabilities:
Deposits held for student
organizations $ 2,580.00

Currency funds balance   0

Total agency funds liabilities $ 2,580.00

Total Liabilities, Reserves and Funds
Balances—All Funds $1,899,207.00

Source: Sister M. Cabrini Di Donato, "A History of the Educational Work of the
Presentation Sisters of Aberdeen, South Dakota," unpublished master's thesis, Northern State College, 1966, 180–83.

Bibliography

PRIMARY SOURCES

I. Dissertations and Theses

Danylewycez, Marta Helen. "Taking the Veil in Montreal, 1840–1920: An Alternative to Motherhood and Spinsterhood," Ph.D. diss., The University of Toronto, 1982.

Di Donato, Sister M. Cabrini. "A History of the Educational Work of the Presentation Sisters of Aberdeen, South Dakota," master's thesis, Northern State College, 1966.

Fallon, Sister Mary Leo Clement. "Early New England Nuns," Ph.D. diss., Boston College, 1936.

Frances, Sister Catharine, S. S. J. "The Convent School of French Origin in the United States, 1727 to 1843," Ph.D. diss., University of Pennsylvania, 1936.

Galvin, James Michael. "Secularizing Trends in Roman Catholic Colleges and Universities, 1960–1970," Ed.D. diss., Indiana University, 1971.

Healy, Sister Mary Margaret Irene, B. V. M. "Assessment of Academic Aptitude, Personality Characteristics, and Religious Orientation of Catholic Sister-Teacher-Trainees," Ph.D. diss., University of Minnesota, 1966.

Jancoski, Loretta Koley. "Religion and Commitment: A Psycho-historical Study of Creative Women in Catholic Religious Communities," Ph.D. diss., University of Chicago, 1976.

Kelley, Ann Elizabeth. "Catholic Women in Campus Ministry: An Emerging Ministry for Women in the Catholic Church," Ph.D. diss., Boston University Graduate School, 1975.

Luft, Lautrine Anne. "Degree of Authoritarianism of Teaching Sisters and Lay Teachers in Catholic Schools," Ph.D. diss., University of Wisconsin, 1971.

Moriarty, Sister Marie Patrice, P.B.V.M. "A Feasibility Study of Adopting a Program of Interdisciplinary General Education for a Two-Year College Curriculum at Presentation College," Ed.D. diss., Laurence University, 1972.

Schmidt, Monica Marie. "Effects of Group Interaction on the Self-Perceptions of Women in Religious Life," Ph.D. diss., University of Illinois, 1970.

291

Schuler, Paul Julian. "The Relation of American Catholics to the Foundations and Early Pratices of Progressive Education in the United States, 1892–1917," Ph.D. diss., Notre Dame University, 1970.

Thompson, Sister Mary St. George, B.V.M. "A Study of the Socialization Process During a Sister Formation Program," Ph.D. diss., University of Chicago, 1963.

II. Documents (from sources other than Presentation Archives)

Beresford, Sister Lelia. "Review of the History of St. Joseph Hospital," Office, St. Joseph Hospital, Mitchell, S.D.

Bicentennial Edition: Historical Statistics of the United States Colonial Times to 1970, Washington, D.C.: U.S. Department of Commerce, Bureau of Census, 1975.

Census of the Population and Housing, South Dakota, Washington, D.C.: U.S. Government Printing Office, 1981.

Census of the Population, Characteristics of the Population, South Dakota, vol. I, pt. 43, 1960, Washington, D.C.: U.S. Government Printing Office, 1961.

Census of the Population South Dakota, 1910, Washington, D.C.: U.S. Government Printing Office, 1913.

Dakota Wesleyan University, 1985–1987 Catalog, Mitchell: Dakota Wesleyan University, 1985.

"Department of Pastoral Care," Holy Rosary Hospital, Miles City, Mont.

Diamond Jubilee Book, Aberdeen, S.D.: Sisters of the Presentation of the Blessed Virgin Mary, 1961.

Digest of Education Statistics, 1983–1984, Washington, D.C.: U.S. Department of Education, 1984.

"Draft for CPE Accreditation," Holy Rosary Hospital, Miles City, Mont.

"Files of Newspaper Clippings," 1952–60, Heritage Room, McKennan Hospital, Sioux Falls, S.D.

"Long Range Plan," St. Luke's Hospital, Aberdeen S.D.

"McKennan School of Nursing Tables," Exhibit II, Heritage Room, McKennan Hospital, Sioux Falls, S.D.

Minimum Standards for Accreditation of K–12 School Systems in the State of South Dakota, Bulletin 99-A, Pierre: State of South Dakota Department of Public Instruction, 1973.

Minimum Standards for Accreditation of K–12 School Systems for the State of South Dakota, Bulletin 99, Pierre: State of South Dakota Department of Public Instruction, 1970.

Official Yearbook of Sacred Heart Catholic Church, Aberdeen, S.D.: Sacred Heart Catholic Church, 1901–2.

Presentation School of Nursing Bulletin, 1960–62, Aberdeen, S.D.: The Presentation Sisters, 1962.

Sacred Heart Catholic Church Official Yearbook, Aberdeen, S.D.: Sacred Heart Catholic Church, 1902.

Bibliography

Secondary School Standards: Policies, Minimum Standards, Regulations for Accreditation of Secondary Schools, Bulletin No. 21-C, Pierre: State of South Dakota Department of Public Instruction, 1960.
South Dakota University Catalog 1984–1985, Brookings: Dakota State University, 1984.
"The Will of Helen McKennan," Heritage Room, McKennan Hospital, Sioux Falls, S.D.
United States Code Congressional Service, 81st Congress, 1st Session, Washington, D.C.: West Publishing and Edward Thompson, 1949.
U. S. Statutes at Large, 78th Congress, 1st Session, vol. 55, pt. 2, Washington, D.C.: U. S. Government Printing Office, 1942.
U. S. Statutes at Large, 81st Congress, 1949, vol. 63, pt. 1, Washington, D.C.: U.S. Government Printing Office, 1950.

III. Documents in the Presentation Archives, Aberdeen, S.D.

CONSTITUTIONS
"The Rules and Constitutions of the Sisters of the Congregation of the Charitable Instruction," 1793. A copy of this document is in M. Raphael Consedine, P.B.V.M. *Listening Journey: A Study of the Spiritual Ideals of Nano Nagle and the Presentation Sisters* (Victoria, Australia: The Congregation of the Presentation of the Blessed Virgin Mary, 1983) found in the Presentation Archives.
Constitutions of the Congregation of the Presentation of the Blessed Virgin Mary (Aberdeen, S.D.: The Sisters of the Presentation of the Blessed Virgin Mary, 1946).
Constitutions of the Presentation Sisters of the Blessed Virgin Mary (Sioux Falls, S.D.: Diocese of Sioux Falls, 1920).
"Draft of the Constitution of the Presentation Sisters, Passed by the 1980 Chapter."

INTERVIEWS
Mrs. Aldea Coultier by Sister De Sales, Nov. 18, 1957.

JUBILEE MATERIALS
"McKennan Historical Data."
"McKennan Manuscript."
"McKennan School of Nursing Tables."
"St. Joseph Manuscript."
"St. Joseph Questionnaire."
"St. Luke's Manuscript."
"Holy Rosary Manuscript."
"Jubilee Data."

LETTERS
William J. Bauder to Mother Viator Burns, July 25, 1950.
Sister Kathleen Bierne, P.B.V.M. to Sisters, Families, Friends, July, 1985.

Bishop William O. Brady to Mother M. Raphael, Jan. 6, 1942.

Sister Anita Bruno to the Sisters, Oct. 6, 1970; May 1971.

Sister Joanna (Anita) Bruno, Sister Elizabeth Remily, and Sister Kathleen Zimmer to Friends, Oct. 1979.

Mother Viator Burns to Most Reverend and Dear Bishop William O. Brady, Jan. 23, 1948.

Mother Viator Burns to Most Reverend William O. Brady, Oct. 23, 1947; Jan. 23, 1948; July 9, 1948; April 26, 1952.

Mother M. Carthagh to Rev. Mother M. Raphael, Dec. 30, 1941.

Bishop William J. Condon to Mother M. Viator Burns, July 25, 1950.

Sister Stephen Davis to Sister Alicia Dunphy, March 24, 1986.

E. S. de Courcy to Mother Raphael McCarthy, Oct. 2, 1943; Feb. 9, 1945; Feb. 19, 1945; March 12, 1945; March 13, 1945; March 19, 1945.

Neil J. Gleason to Mother M. Raphael, Superior, Jan. 30, 1946.

Sister Agnes Gonzaga to Mother Raphael McCarthy, March 20, 1945.

Sister Kathleen to the Sisters, June 1972.

Sister Margarita to the Sisters, Aug. 1972.

Sister Toni Marie to the Sisters, May 1, 1969.

Mother M. Raphael McCarthy to T. J. Manning, July 19, 1943.

Mother Raphael McCarthy to the Sisters, Sept. 10, 1941.

Mother Raphael McCarthy to Rev. J. J. O'Neil, July 19, 1943.

Mother Raphael McCarthy to Rev. E. S. de Courcy, Oct. 5, 1943; March 16, 1945.

Mother Raphael McCarthy to Most Reverend William J. Condon, D.D., Jan. 15, 1946.

Mother M. Raphael McCarthy to Senator Karl Mundt, Dec. 3, 1951.

Sister Frances Menahan to Mother Joseph Butler, no date.

Sister Janice Mengenhauser to the Sisters, Sept. 29, 1969; July 15, 1971.

Karen Moore to the Sisters, Sept. 1, 1969; Feb. 8, 1978.

Sister Elizabeth Remily to Communities and Friends, June 1980.

Sister Elizabeth Remily, P.B.V.M. to Friends, Oct. 1981; Nov.-Dec. 1984; Jan. 1985.

Sister Elizabeth Remily to the Sisters, Feb. 1966; Oct. 1966; Nov. 1966; Feb. 15, 1967; Nov. 18, 1969; Nov. 28, 1969; Nov. 16, 1970; April 1971; Sept. 6, 1971; Sept. 1973; Sept., 1975; Aug. 1976; Jan. 1977; July 1977.

Sister JoAnn Sturzl to the Most Reverend Paul O. Dudley D. C., Feb. 21, 1979.

MANUSCRIPTS AND RECORDS

"1984 Chapter of Affairs Meeting Resolutions."

Aberdeen American News Scrapbook.

"Anoka Contract Agreement," March 1945.

"Apostolate Statistical Sheet."

"Brief History of South Dakota League of Nursing."

"Brochure on the Founding of the Presentation Sisters."

Butler, Mother Joseph. "Annals," 1912.

———. "State of South Dakota, County of Brown."

"Chapter of Affairs Meeting," 1968.

"Chapter Decisions," 1968.

Doyle, Sister Conception. "History of Aberdeen Presentation School of Nursing."

"Draft of the Constitution of the Presentation Sisters, Passed by the 1980 Chapter."

Dunphy, Sister Alicia. "Summary Data for Encyclopedia Dictionary of Canonical States of Perfection," 1968.

"File on Mother Raphael McCarthy."

"Final Report of the Executive Committee."

Gerald, Sister M. "Areas of the Hospital Apostolate."

Hoffman, Sister Bonaventure. "Associate Degree Nursing Program, a Ten-Year Report."

———. "Manuscript."

Martha, Sister M. "Brief History of the Presentation Community in Aberdeen, 1886–1976."

McCarthy, Mother Raphael. "History of the Orphanage."

"Mexican Mission File."

Meyer, Sister Joyce. "Notes from Classes Given to Professed Sisters and Sisters in Formation."

"*Miles City Star* Scrapbook."

"Missions."

"News Release on Mother Joseph Manor."

"Notre Dame Academy Historical Data."

"Preparation of Religious Elementary Teachers, Report of Activity of Religious Communities of Women."

"Presentation Annals."

Presentation College Catalog, vol. 21, Aberdeen, S.D.: Presentation College, 1984.

Quinn, Sister Pauline, "Biographies of Major Superiors"

"Section I: Introduction."

"Section II: Prologue, Teresa Mulally."

"Section III: Mother John Hughes, 1886–1892."

"Section IV: Mother Aloysius Chriswell, 1892–1894."

"Section V: Mother Joseph Butler, 1894–1915."

"Section VI: Mother Aloysious Forrest, 1915–1921, 1927–1932."

"Section VII: Mother Agatha Collins, 1921–1927."

"Section VIII: Mother Raphael McCarthy, 1932–1946."

"Section IX: Mother Viator Burns, 1946–1958."

"Section X: Mother Carmelita McCullough, 1958–1964."

"Section XI: Mother Myron Martin, 1964–1974."

"Section XII: Sister JoAnn Sturzl, 1974–1982."

"Section XIII: Sister Mary Denis Collins, 1982–."

"Report of Activity of Religious Communities of Women in the Preparation of Religious Elementary Teachers."

"Report of Parochial Schools Taught by the Presentation Sisters of the Blessed Virgin Mary, 1949–50."
"Sister Marie Toni File."
"Sisters of the Presentation of the Blessed Virgin Mary Chapter Decisions."
"Statistics: Total Education Program."
"St. Luke's Hospital Long Range Plan."
"Summary of Criteria."
"Teaching Contract between Mother M. Raphael and Msgr. J.M. Brady," 1943.
"Teaching Contract, State of South Dakota, County of Brown," 1914.
"Unique Role of National League for Nursing."

IV. Interviews

South Dakota Oral History Center, The University of South Dakota, Vermillion conducted by Herbert T. Hoover and Susan Peterson. Some transcripts are available.

Atkinson, Douglas, July 12, 1978; Auth, Sister Sylvester, Aug. 9, 1976; Beresford, Sister Lelia M, Aug. 11, 1976; Billing, Sister Edla, July 12, 1978; Butler, Deanna, June 20, 22, 1978; Cadlo, Joe, July 13, 1978; Caron, Sister Richard, June 19, 1978; Casey, Sister Fanahan, June 20, 1978; Clarke, Sister Francelle, Aug. 13, 1976; Coakley, Sister Colman, Aug. 7, 1976; Coss, Sister Rita, Aug. 13, 1976; Davis, Sister Mary Stephen, Aug. 7, 1976; Delahoyde, Monsignor Louis, July 19, 1978; Delaney, Dr. William A. June 6, 1978; Dempsey, Sister Anthony, June 27, 1978; Dunn, Sister Frances Mary, Aug. 5, 1976; Dunphy, Sister Alicia, Aug. 6, 1976; Farrell, Sister Grace, June 19, 1978; Fitzpatrick, Keith, June 5, 1978; Francis, Sister Jane, June 20, 1978; Freimuth, Sister Helen, Aug. 5, 1976; Goebel, Veronica, July 26, 1978; Gresby, Frances, July 12, 1978; Harrington, Albert, June 14, 1978; Heinemann, Dan, July 16, 1978; Hoch, Bishop Lambert, June 28, 1978; Hoffman, Sister Bonaventure, Aug. 6, 1976, June 20, and June 26, 1978; Joyce, Sister Mary Eleanor, Aug. 12, 1976; Kelly, Sister Eucharia, Aug. 12, 1976; Kippes, Joan, June 5, 1978; Lucas, Sister Edward, Aug. 6, 1976; McCall, Sister Eleanor, June 22, 1978; McCardle, Robert, July 29, 1978; Martin, Mother Myron, Aug. 12, 1976; Moriarty, Sister Marie Patrice, Aug. 12, 1976; Morris, Henry, June 30, 1978; Nemmers, Sister Helen, Aug. 10, 1976; O'Brien, Sister Judith, June 19, 21, 1978; Ogden, Sister Veronica, Aug. 13, 1976; O'Neil, Sister Kay, Aug. 9, 1976; Patton, David, June 26, 1978; Peterson, Winnefred, July 29, 1978; Pierret, Sister Madonna, July 13, 1978; Raleigh, Sister Martha, Aug. 10, 1976; Remily, Sister Elizabeth, June 1, 1978, Sept. 5, 1976; Rykhus, David, June 2, 1978; Steinman, Sister Alexius, June 21, 1978; Sturzl, Sister JoAnn, Aug. 5, 1976; Talbot, Sister Irene, June 7, 1978; Weinreis, Sister Anna Marie, Aug. 10, 1976; Welbig, Sister Lynn Marie, Aug. 10, 1976.

V. Letters and Oral Communications (from Sources other than Presentation Archives)

Communication between Sylvia Starr and Wyland J. Borth, State Superintendent's Office, Aug. 25, 1986, in the authors' possession.

Communication between Sylvia Starr and Sister Colman Coakley, Oct. 1, 1986 in the authors' possession.

Communication between Susan Peterson and Sister Pam Donelan, April 17, 1985.

Communication between Sylvia Starr and Norbert Goergen, Oct. 1, 1986, in the authors' possession.

Communication between Sylvia Starr and South Dakota Nursing Program Officials, Oct. 1, 1986, in the authors' possession.

Communication between Sylvia Starr and Rex Swanson, Oct. 20, 1986.

Communication between Sylvia Starr and a St. Luke's representative, Oct. 1, 1986, in the authors' possession.

Bishop William O. Brady to Mother Viator Burns, Jan. 20, 1948, Office of the Catholic Chancery Records, Diocese of Sioux Falls, S.D.

Bishop William O. Brady to Reverend and Dear Sister Superior Viator Burns, Jan. 20, 1948, Office of the Catholic Chancery Records, Diocese of Sioux Falls, Sioux Falls, S.D.

Bishop William O. Brady to Sister Superior Viator Burns, Feb. 2, 1948, Office of the Catholic Chancery Records, Diocese of Sioux Falls.

William O. Brady to the Venerable Sisters, Dec. 13, 1947.

Sister Mary DePazzi to Susan Peterson, Feb. 9, 1979.

Sister Pam Donelan to Courtney Ann Vaughn-Roberson, June 20, 1985.

Sister Alicia Dunphy to the authors, Jan. 6, 1981; March 22, 1985; April 26, 1985; Fall 1985; Dec. 4, 1985; Feb. 14, 1986; Aug. 11, 1986.

Sister Alicia Dunphy to Courtney Ann Vaughn-Roberson, Fall 1985; March 11, 1985; June 27, 1986; July 28, 1986; Aug. 11, 1986; Oct. 30, 1986; Nov. 24, 1986; Dec. 30, 1986.

Sister Monica Parkinson to Mrs. Maxine Horman, Office, St. Joseph Hospital, Mitchell, S.D.

Sister Sheila Schnell to Susan Peterson, Feb. 4, 1979.

VI. Newspapers and Newsletters

Aberdeen American News; Anoka Union; Bishop's Bulletin; Daily Republic; Dakota Catholic; Dominicans on Mission; The Globe and Mail; Los Companeros; Outline; Presentation Chronicle; Presentation Nurse; Presentation School of Nursing Bulletin; Sioux City Journal; Sioux Falls Argus Leader; St. Joe Happenings.

VII. Papers

Bulger, Paul G. "Education as a Profession," Washington, D.C.: ERIC Clearinghouse on Teacher Education, 1972.

Forsyth, Patrick B. "The Professions and the Predominant Gender Hypothesis," presented at the American Educational Research Association meeting, Montreal, April 1983.

Ginsburg, Mark B. "Teacher Education and Class and Gender Relations: A Critical Socio-Historical Analysis," presented at the American Educational Studies Association meeting, Pittsburgh, Oct. 1986.

Griswold, Robert L. "Domesticity and Western Women," unpublished manuscript, authors' possession.

Lowenthal, Al, and Robert Nielsen. "Unionism and Professionalism: Sibling?" Washington, D.C.: American Federation of Teachers, 1977.

Martin, Jane Roland. "Seeing What Is Missing from Education Theory and Practice Through the Study of Women," presented at the American Educational Research Association meeting, Montreal, April 1983.

Packard, John S. "The Universitization of Nursing Education," presented at the American Educational Studies Association meeting, Pittsburgh, Oct. 1986.

Peterson, Margie. "The Bachelor Prepared Nurse and the American Nurses' Association: A Dilemma of Unity," unpublished paper, authors' possession.

Quantz, Richard. "The Complex Visions of Female Teachers and the Failure of Unionization in the 1930s," unpublished paper, authors' possession.

Renner, Marguerite. "Teachers' Motivations in the Debate to Find the Perfect Teacher: Competing Ideologies in Late Nineteenth-Century American Schools," presented at the Western Social Science meeting, Fort Worth, April 1985.

SECONDARY SOURCES

I. Articles and Book Chapters

Agre, Gene P. and Barbara Finkelstein. "Feminism and School Reform: The Last Fifteen Years," *Teachers College Record* 80 (Dec. 1978): 307–15.

Allmendinger, David F., Jr. "Mount Holyoke Students Encounter the Need for Life-Planning, 1847–1850," *History of Education Quarterly* 19 (Spring 1979): 27–46.

Atkin, J. Myron. "Who Will Teach in High School," *Daedalus: Journal of the American Academy of Arts and Sciences* 110 (Summer 1981): 91–104.

Ause, Marshall. "Shared Services, Trend for the Future," *All of Us* 9 (Sept. 1980):2.

Bardwick, Judith M., and Elizabeth Douvan. "Ambivalence: The Socialization of Women," in *Readings on the Psychology of Women*, ed. Judith M. Bardwick, New York: Harper and Row, 1972, 52–58.

Bernard, Richard M., and Maris A. Vinovskis. "The Female School Teacher in Ante-Bellum Massachusetts," *Journal of Social History* 10 (Spring 1977): 332–45.

Bland, Sister Joan, S. N. D. "Sister Julie McGroarty," in *Notable American Women: A Biographical Dictionary,* ed. Edward T. James, Cambridge, Mass.: Belknap Press, 1971, 466–68.

Blauvelt, Martha Tomhave. "Women and Revivalism," in *Women and Religion in America,* vol. 1, *The Nineteenth Century,* ed. Rosemary Radford Ruether and Rosemary Skinner Keller, New York: Harper and Row, 1981, 1–45.

Broenen, Robert A. "Sister Formation," in *Convent Life: Roman Catholic Religious Orders for Women in North America,* ed. Joan M. Lexau, New York: Dial Press, 1964, 188–96.

Bunkle, Phillida. "Sentimental Womanhood and Domestic Education, 1830–1870," *History of Education Quarterly* 14 (Spring 1974): 13–30.

Burnstyn, Joan N. "Historical Perspectives on Women in Educational Leadership," in *Women in Educational Leadership,* ed. Sari Knopp Bicklen and Marilyn B. Brannigan, Lexington, Mass.: D.C. Heath, 1980, 65–77.

Clark, Burton R. "The 'Cooling-Out' Function in Higher Education," *American Journal of Sociology* 65 (May 1960): 569–76.

Cogan, Morris L. "Toward a Definition of Profession," *The Harvard Educational Review* 23 (Jan./Dec. 1953): 33–50.

Coleman, James. "Public Schools, Private Schools, and the Public Interest," *The Public Interest* 64 (Summer 1981): 19–30.

Conway, Jill. "Perspectives on the History of Women's Education in the United States," *History of Education Quarterly* 14 (Spring 1974): 1–12.

Cook, Blanche Wiesen. "Female Support Networks and Political Activism: Lillian Wald, Crystal Eastman, Emma Goldman," in *A Heritage of Her Own: Toward a New Social History of American Women,* ed. Nancy F. Cott and Elizabeth Pleck, New York: Simon and Schuster, 1979, 413–14.

Corwin, Ronald G. "The Professional Employee: A Study of Conflict in Nursing Roles," *The American Journal of Sociology* 66 (May 1961): 604–15.

Cott, Nancy F. "Young Women in the Second Great Awakening," *Feminist Studies* 3 (Fall 1975): 15–29.

Cross, K. Patricia. "The Woman Student," in *Women in Higher Education,* ed. W. Todd Furniss and Patricia Albjerg Graham, Washington, D. C.: American Council on Education, 1974, 29–71.

Curti, Merle. "Clara Barton," in *Notable American Women: 1607–1950: A Biographical Dictionary,* vol. 1, ed. Edward T. James, Cambridge, Mass.: Belknap Press, 1971, 103–8.

Daly, Mary. "Theology After the Demise of God the Father: A Call for the Castration of Sexist Religion," in *Sexist Religion and Women in the Church,* ed. Alice L. Hageman, New York: Association Press, 1974, 125–42.

Davis, Natalie Zemon. "Gender and Genre: Women as Historical Writers,

1400–1820," in *Beyond Their Sex: Learned Women of the European Past,* ed. Patricia H. Labalme, New York: New York University Press, 153–82.

Deweese, Charles W. "Deaconesses in Baptist History: A Preliminary Study," *Baptist History and Heritage* 12 (Jan. 1977): 52–57.

"Discord in the Church," *Time* 125 (Feb. 4, 1985): 50–55.

Dougherty, Mary Agnes. "The Methodist Deaconess: A Case of Religious Feminism," *Methodist History* 21 (Jan. 1983): 90–98.

Dunn, Mary Maples. "Saints and Sisters, Congregational and Quaker Women in the Early Colonial Period," in *Women in American Religion,* ed. Janet Wilson James, Philadelphia: University of Pennsylvania Press, 1976, 27–46.

Ellis, John Tracy. "American Catholics and the Intellectual Life," *Thought: Fordham University Quarterly* 30 (Autumn 1955): 351–88.

Engel, Gloria V. "The Effect of Bureaucracy on the Professional Authority of Physicians," *Journal of Health and Social Behavior* 10 (March 1969): 30–41.

Ewens, Mary, O. P. "The Leadership of Nuns in Immigrant Catholicism," in *Women and Religion,* 101–49.

Ferrante, Joan M. "The Education of Women in the Middle Ages in Theory, Fact, and Fantasy," in *Beyond Their Sex: Learned Women of the European Past,* ed. Patricia H. Labalme, New York: New York University Press, 1980, 9–42.

Filene, Peter G. "An Obituary for the Progressive Movement," *American Quarterly* 22 (Spring 1970): 20–34.

Fraser, Dorothy Bass. "The Feminine Mystique: 1890–1910," *Union Seminary Quarterly Review* 27 (Summer 1972): 225–39.

Freedman, Estelle. "Separatism as Strategy: Female Institution Building and American Feminism, 1870–1930," *Feminist Studies* 5 (Fall 1979): 518–19.

Garrison, Dee. "The Tender Technicians: The Feminization of Public Librarianship, 1876–1905," *Journal of Social History* 6 (Winter 1972–73): 131–59.

Gibbons, Cardinal James. "Pure Womanhood," *Cosmopolitan* 39 (Sept. 1905): 559–61.

Gifford, Carolyn De Swarte. "Women in Social Reform Movements," in *Women and Religion in America,* 294–340.

Goode, William J. "Community within a Community: The Professions," *American Sociological Review* 22 (Feb. 1957): 194–200.

———. "The Protection of the Inept," *American Sociological Review* 32 (Feb. 1967): 5–19.

Goodwin, Gregory L. "The Nature and the Nurture of the Community College Movement," *Community College Frontiers* 4 (Spring 1976): 5–13.

Greenwood, Ernest. "Attributes of a Profession," *Social Work* 2 (July 1957): 45–55.

Bibliography

Groneman, Carol. "Working-Class Immigrant Women in Mid-Ninteenth-Century New York: The Irish Woman's Experience," *Journal of Urban History* 4 (May 1978): 255–73.

Hall, Richard H. "Professionalization and Bureaucratization," *American Sociological Review* 33 (Feb. 1968): 92–104.

Hebblethwaite, Peter. "The Popes and Politics: Shifting Patterns in 'Catholic Social Doctrine,' " *Daedalus: Journal of the American Academy of Arts and Sciences* 111 (Winter 1982): 85–99.

Horner, Matina. "Feminity and Successful Achievement: A Basic Inconsistency," in *Feminine Personality and Conflict*, ed. Judith M. Bardwick, et al., Belmont, Calif.: Brooks-Cole Publishing, 1970, 45–74.

Howe, Florence. "Women and the Power to Change," in *Women and the Power To Change*, ed. Florence Howe, Berkeley: Carnegie Commission on Higher Education, 1975, 127–69.

James, Janet Wilson. "An Overview," in *Women in American Religion*, 11–17.

———. "Lavinia Lloyd Dock," in *Notable American Women: The Modern Period, a Biographical Dictionary*, ed. Barbara Sicherman and Carol Hurd Green, Cambridge, Mass.: Belknap Press, 1980, 195–98.

Jameson, Elizabeth. "Imperfect Unions: Class and Gender in Cripple Creek, 1894–1904," in *Class, Sex, and the Woman Workers*, ed. Milton Cantor and Bruce Laurie, Westport, Conn.: Greenwood Press, 1977, 166–202.

Jarvis, Peter. "A Profession in Progress: A Theoretical Model for the Ministry," *The Sociological Review* 24 (May 1976): 351–64.

Jennings, Mary Kay. "Lake County Woman Suffrage Campaign in 1890," *South Dakota History* 5 (Fall 1975): 390–409.

Jones, Jacqueline. "Women Who Were More than Men: Sex and Status in Freedmen's Teaching," *History of Education Quarterly* 19 (Spring 1979): 47–60.

K., Gabriel Gyarmati. "The Doctrine of the Professions: Basis of a Power Structure," *International Social Science Journal* 27 (Winter 1975): 649–54.

Keller, Rosemary Skinner. "Lay Women in the Protestant Tradition," in *Women and Religion in America*, 242–93.

Kelley, Mary. "At War with Herself: Harriet Beecher Stowe as Woman in Conflict within the Home," in *Woman's Being, Woman's Place: Female Identity and Vocations in American History*, ed. Mary Kelley, Boston: G. K. Hall, 1979, 201–15.

Kenneally, James J. "Eve, Mary, and the Historians: American Catholicism and Women," in *Women in American Religion*, 191–206.

Klegon, Douglas. "The Society of Professions: An Emerging Perspective," *Sociology of Work and Occupations* 5 (Aug. 1978): 259–83.

Klinkhamer, Sister Marie Carolyn, O. P. "Mother Mary Alphonsa Lathrop," in *Notable American Women: A Biographical Dictionary*, vol. 2, 1971, 372–74.

Koehler, Lyle. "The Case of the American Jezebels: Anne Hutchison and

Female Agitation During the Years of Antinomian Turmoil, 1636–1640,"
in *Our American Sisters: Women in American Life and Thought*, ed.
Jean F. Friedman and William G. Shade, Lexington, Mass.: D. C. Heath,
1982, 17–40.

Kolmer, Sister Elizabeth, A. S. C. "Catholic Women Religious and Women's
History: A Survey of the Literature," in *American Quarterly* 30 (Winter
1978): 639–51.

Lavrin, Asunción. "Women in Convents: Their Economic and Social Role
in Colonial Mexico," in *Liberating Women's History: Theoretical and
Critical Essays*, ed. Berenice A. Carroll, Urbana: University of Illinois
Press, 1976, 250–77.

Leggatt, T. "Teaching as a Profession," *Professions and Professionalization*,
ed. J. A. Jackson, London: Cambridge University Press, 1970, 155–77.

Litwack, E. "Models of Bureaucracy which Permit Conflict," *American
Journal of Sociology* 67 (1961): 177–84.

Lougee, Carolyn C. " 'Noblesse,' Domesticity, and Social Reform: The Education of Girls by Fenelon and Saint-Cyr," *History of Education Quarterly* 14 (Spring 1974): 87–113.

Loveland, Anne C. "Domesticity and Religion in the Antebellum Period:
The Career of Phoebe Palmer," *The Historian* 39 (May 1977): 455–71.

Luebke, Frederick C. "Ethnic Group Settlement on the Great Plains," *The
Western Historical Quarterly* 8 (Oct. 1977): 405–30.

Lutz, Alma "Elizabeth Cady Stanton," in *Notable American Women*, vol.
3, 1971, 342–47.

Martin, Jane Roland. "Excluding Women from the Educational Realm,"
Harvard Educational Review 52 (May 1982): 133–48.

———. "The Ideal of the Educated Person," *Educational Theory* 31 (Spring
1981): 97–110.

McCluskey, Rev. Neil G., S. J. "Cathoic Schools after Vatican II," in *Trends
and Issues in Catholic Education*, ed. Russell Shaw and Richard J.
Hurley, New York: Citation Press, 1969, 335–47.

McDonald, Lucile. "Mother Joseph," in *The Women Who Made the West*,
ed. Western Writers of America, Garden City, N.Y.: Doubleday, 1980,
120–29.

McGrath, Sister Albertus Magnus. "Women as the 'Niggers' of the Church,"
The Critic 30 (Sept.-Oct. 1971): 24–33.

McNamara, Jo Ann. "A New Song: Celibate Women in the First Three
Christian Centuries," *Women and History* 6/7 (Summer/Fall 1983): 1–
154.

Melder, Keith E. "Mask of Oppression: The Female Seminary Movement
in the United States," *New York History* 55 (July 1974): 261–79.

———. "Woman's High Calling: The Teaching Profession in America, 1830–
1860," *American Studies* 13 (Fall (1972): 19–47.

Meyer, B. "Sister Formation Movement," *New Catholic Encyclopedia*, vol.
13, New York: McGraw-Hill, 1967, 261–62.

Montagna, Paul D. "Professionalization and Bureaucratization in Large

Professional Organizations," *American Journal of Sociology* 74 (Sept. 1968): 138–45.

Moran, Gerald F. "Sisters in Christ: Women and the Church in Seventeenth-Century New England," in *Women in American Religion*, 47–65.

Morrissey, Elizabeth, and David F. Gillespie. "Technology and the Conflict of Professionals in Bureaucratic Organizations," *The Sociological Quarterly* 16 (Summer 1975): 319–22.

Neal, Sister Marie Augusta, and Sister N. D. de Namur. "A Theoretical Analysis of Renewal in Religious Orders in the U. S. A.," *Social Compass* 18 (1971): 7–25.

Neal, Sister Marie Augusta, S.N.D., and Sister Miriam St. John Clasby, S.N.D. "Priests' Attitides Toward Women," in *Women in Modern Life*, ed. William C. Bier, New York: Fordham University Press, 1968, 55–77.

"The New Nuns," *Time* 99 (March 20, 1972): 63–64.

Norlin, Dennis A. "The Suffrage Movement and South Dakota Churches: Radicals and the Status Quo, 1890," *South Dakota History* 14 (Winter 1984): 308–34.

Orzack, Louis H. "Work as a 'Central Life Interest' of Professionals," *Social Problems* 7 (Fall 1959): 125–32.

Palmieri, Patricia A. "Here Was Fellowship: A Social Portrait of Academic Women at Wellesley College, 1895–1920," *History of Education Quarterly* 23 (Summer 1983): 195–214.

Parsons, Talcott. "Implications of the Study," in *The Climate of Book Selection: Social Influences on School and Public Libraries*, ed. J. Periam Danton, Berkeley: University of California School of Librarianship, 1959, 77–96.

Perrucci, Robert. "Engineering Professional Servant of Power," *American Behavioral Scientist* 14 (March/April 1971): 492–506.

Peterson, Susan. "Adapting to Fill a Need: Presentation Health Care, 1901–1961," *South Dakota History* 17 (Summer 1987).

———. "A Widening Horizon: Catholic Sisterhoods on the Nothern Plains, 1874–1910, *Great Plains Quarterly* 5 (Spring 1985): 125–32.

———. "Challenges to the Stereotypes: The Adaptation of the Sisters of St. Francis to South Dakota Missions, 1885–1910," *Upper Midwest History* 84 (1984): 1–9.

———. "Doing 'Women's' Work: The Grey Nuns of Fort Totten Indian Reservation, 1874–1900," *North Dakota History* 52 (Spring 1985): 18–25.

———. "Holy Women and Housekeepers: Women Teachers on South Dakota Reservations, 1885–1910," *South Dakota History* 13 (Fall 1983): 245–60.

———. "Religious Communities of Women in the West: The Presentation Sisters' Adaptation to the Northern Plains Frontier," *Journal of the West* 21 (April 1982): 65–70.

Prevallet, Sister Elaine Marie. "The Meaning of Virginity," in *The New*

Nuns, ed. Sister M. Charles Borromeo, C.S.C., South Bend, Ind.: New American Library, 1967, 31–37.

Richter, Thomas. "Sister Catherine Mallon's Journal: Part 1," *New Mexico Historical Review* 52 (Spring 1977): 135–55.

———. "Sister Catherine Mallon's Journal: Part 2," *New Mexico Historical Review* 52 (Summer 1977): 237–50.

Riley, Glenda. "Farm Women's Roles in the Agricultural Develpment of South Dakota," *South Dakota History* 13 (Spring-Summer 1983): 83–121.

Riley, Glenda Gates. "Origins for the Argument for Improved Female Education," *History of Education Quarterly* 9 (Winter 1969): 455–70.

———. "The Subtle Subversion: Changes in the Traditionalist Image of the American Woman," *The Historian* 32 (Feb. 1970): 210–27.

Ritzer, George. "Professionalization, Bureaucratization, and Rationalization: The Views of Max Weber," *Social Forces* 53 (June 1975): 627–34.

"Rome Sends a Strong Message," *Time* 128 (Sept. 1, 1986): 65.

Rosen, George. "The Hospital: Historical Sociology of a Community Institution," in *The Hospital in Modern Society,* ed. Eliot Freidson, New York: Free Press, 1963, 10–36.

Rothman, Robert A. "Deprofessionalization: The Case of Law in America," *Work and Occupations* 11 (May 1984): 183–206.

Rouillard, P. "Marian Feasts," in *New Catholic Encyclopedia,* vol. 9, 210–12.

Ruether, Rosemary Radford. "Women in Utopian Movements," in *Women and Religion in America,* 46–100.

Ryan, Mary P. "A Woman's Awakening: Evangelical Religion and the Families of Utica, New York, 1800–1840," in *Women in American Religion,* 89–110.

Scott, Anne Firor. "The Ever Widening Circle: The Diffusion of Feminist Values from the Troy Female Seminary, 1822–1872," *History of Education Quarterly* 19 (Spring 1979): 3–25.

Scott, W. Richard. "Professionals in Organizations—Areas of Conflict," in *Professionalizaton,* ed. Howard M. Vollmer and Donald L. Mills, Englewood Cliffs, N.J.: Prentice-Hall, 1966, 265–75.

Sexton, Patricia Cayo. "Schools Are Emasculating Our Boys," in *And Jill Came Tumbling After: Sexism in American Education,* ed. Judith Stacey, Susan Béreaud, and Joan Daniels, New York: Dell Publishing, 1974, 139–41.

Simpson, Richard L., and Ida Harper Simpson. "Women and Bureaucracy in the Semi-Professions," in *The Semi-Professions and their Organization,* ed. Amitai Etzioni, New York: Free Press, 1969, 196–265.

Smith-Rosenberg, Carroll. "The Female World of Love and Ritual: Relations Between Women in Nineteenth-Century America," in *A Heritage of Her Own,* 311–42.

Smylie, James H. "*The Woman's Bible:* And the Spiritual Crisis," *Soundings* 59 (Fall 1976): 305–28.

Bibliography

Sorensen, James E., and Thomas L. Sorensen. "The Conflict of Professionals in Bureaucratic Organizations," *Administrative Science Quarterly* 19 (March 1974): 98–106.

"Taming the Liberation Theologians," *Time* 125 (Feb. 4, 1985): 56, 59.

Theodora, Sister Mary, C.S.M. "The Foundation of the Sisterhood of St. Mary," *Historical Magazine of the Protestant Episcopal Church* (March 1945): 38–52.

Thorpe, Cleata B. "Education in South Dakota, 1861–1961," in *South Dakota Historical Collections* 36 (1972): 209–591.

Turbin, Carole. "And We Are Nothing but Women: Irish Working Women in Troy," in *Women in America: A History*, ed. Carol Ruth Berkin and Mary Beth Norton, Boston: Houghton Mifflin, 1979, 202–22.

Turner, Frederick Jackson. "Statement of the Frontier Thesis: Later Explanations and Developments," in *The Frontier Thesis: Valid Interpretation of American History?* ed. Ray Allen Billington, New York: Holt, Rinehart, and Winston, 1966, 9–30.

Udy, Stanley H., Jr. "Administrative Rationality, Social Setting, and Organizational Development," *American Journal of Sociology* 68 (Nov. 1962): 299–308.

———. "Technical and Institutional Factors in Production Organizations: A Preliminary Model," *American Journal of Sociology* 67 (Nov. 1961): 247–54.

Ulrich, Laurel Thatcher. "Vertuous Women Found: New England Ministerial Literature, 1668–1735," in *Women in American Religion*, 67–88.

Urban, Wayne J. "Organized Teachers and Educational Reform During the Progressive Era, 1890–1920," *History of Education Quarterly* 16 (Spring 1976): 35–52.

Vatican II. "*Gaudium et Spes* (Pastoral Constitution on the Church in the Modern World)," in *The Documents of Vatican II*, ed. Waller M. Abbott, New York: Guild Press, 1966, 199–308.

———. "*Perfectae Caritatis* (Decree on the Appropriate Renewal of the Religious Life)," in Ibid., 466–82.

Vaughn-Roberson, Courtney Ann. "Having a Purpose in Life: Western Women Teachers in the Twentieth Century," *Great Plains Quarterly* 5 (Spring 1985): 107–24.

———. "Sometimes Independent but Never Equal—Women Teachers, 1900–1950: The Oklahoma Example," *Pacific Historical Review* 53 (Feb. 1984): 39–58.

Webster, Janice Reiff. "Domestication and Americanization, Scandinavian Women in Seattle 1888 to 1900," *Journal of Urban History* 4 (May 1978): 275–89.

Wein, Roberta. "Women's Colleges and Domesticity, 1875–1918," *History of Education Quarterly* 14 (Spring 1974): 31–48.

Wildavsky, Aaron. "Church, Capitalism, and Democracy," *The New York Times Book Review Digest* 89 (Dec. 9, 1984): 14–15.

Wilensky, Harold L. "The Professionalization of Everyone?" *The American Journal of Sociology* 70 (Sept. 1964): 137–58.

Williams, Mother M. "Mother Mary Aloysia Hardey," in *Notable America Women*, vol. 2, 1971, 130–32.

Williams, T. J. "The Beginnings of American Sisterhoods," *Historical Magazine of the Protestant Episcopal Church* (Dec. 1947): 363–68.

"Women: Second-Class Citizens?" *Time* 125 (Feb. 4, 1985): 62, 63.

Zikmund, Barbara Brown. "The Struggle for the Right to Preach," in *Women and Religion in America*, 193–243.

II. Books

Abbott, Walter M., ed. *The Documents of Vatican II*, New York: Guild Press, 1966.

Anson, Peter F. *The Call of the Cloister: Religious Communities and Kindred Bodies in the Anglican Communion*, London: S.P.C.K., 1955.

A School Sister of Notre Dame. *Mother Caroline and the School Sisters of Notre Dame*, vols. 1 and 2, St. Louis: Woodward and Tiernan, 1928.

Ashley, Jo Ann. *Hospitals, Paternalism, and the Role of the Nurse*, New York: Teachers College Press, 1976.

A Sister of the Precious Blood. *Not with Silver or Gold: A History of the Sisters of the Congregation of the Precious Blood, Salem Heights, Dayton, Ohio: 1834–1944*, Dayton: Sisters of the Precious Blood, 1945.

Bailey, Thomas A., and David M. Kennedy, eds. *The American Spirit: United States History as Seen by Contemporaries*, vol. 2, Lexington, Mass.: D.C. Heath, 1984.

Bardwick, Judith M., ed. *Readings on the Psychology of Women*, New York: Harper and Row, 1972.

Bell, Daniel. *The Reforming of General Education*, New York: Columbia University Press, 1966.

Berkin, Carol Ruth, and Mary Beth Norton. *Women of America: A History*, Boston: Houghton Mifflin, 1979.

Bicklen, Sari Knopp, and Marilyn B. Brannigan, eds. *Women in Educational Leadership*, Lexington, Mass.: D.C. Heath, 1980.

Bier, William C. S. J., ed. *Woman in Modern Life*, New York: Fordham University Press, 1968.

Billington, Ray Allen, ed. *The Frontier Thesis: Valid Interpretation of American History?* New York: Holt, Rinehart, and Winston, 1966.

Blair, Karen J. *The Clubwoman as Feminist: True Womanhood Redefined, 1868- 1914*, New York: Holmes and Meier, 1980.

Bledstein, Burton J. *The Culture of Professionalism: The Middle Class and Development of Higher Education in America*, New York: W. W. Norton, 1976.

Blouet, Brian W., and Frederick C. Luebke, eds. *The Great Plains: Environment and Culture*, Lincoln: University of Nebraska Press, 1979.

Bibliography

Borgia, Sister M. Francis, O.S.F. *He Sent Two: The Story of the Beginning of the School Sisters of St. Francis*, Milwaukee: Bruce Publishing, 1965.

Borromeo, Sister M. Charles, C. S. C., ed. *The New Nuns*, South Bend, Ind.: New American Library, 1967.

Brubacher, John S., and Willis Rudy. *Higher Education in Transition: A History of American Colleges and Universities, 1636–1976*, New York: Harper and Row, 1958.

Buetow, Harold A. *Of Singular Benefit: The Story of Catholic Education in the United States*, London: Macmillan, 1970.

Bullough, Vern L., and Bonnie Bullough. *The Emergence of Modern Nursing*, Toronto: Macmillan, 1969.

Burton, Katherine. *Bells on Two Rivers: The History of the Sisters of the Visitation of Rock Island, Illinois*, Milwaukee: Bruce Publishing, 1965.

Button, H. Warren, and Eugene F. Provenzo, Jr. *History of Education and Culture in America*, Englewood Cliffs, N.J.: Prentice-Hall, 1983.

Callan, Louise, R.S.C.J. *Phillipine Duchesne: Frontier Missionary of the Sacred Heart: 1769–1852*, Westminster, Md.: Newman Press, 1957.

———. *The Society of the Sacred Heart in North America*, vols. 1 and 2, New York: Longmans, Green, 1937.

Callahan, Sidney Cornelia. *The Illusion of Eve: Modern Woman's Quest for Identity*, New York: Sheed and Ward, 1965.

Calvert, M. *The Mechanical Engineer in America, 1830–1910: Professional Cultures in Conflict*, Baltimore, Md.: Johns Hopkins University Press, 1957.

Cantor, Milton, and Bruce Laurie, eds. *Class, Sex, and the Woman Worker*, Westport, Conn.: Greenwood Press, 1977.

Carroll, Berenice, ed. *Liberating Women's History*, Urbana: University of Illinois Press, 1976.

Cass, James, and Max Birbaum, eds. *Comparative Guide to Two-Year Colleges and Career Programs*, New York: Harper and Row, 1976.

Concepta, Sister Maria, C.S.C. *The Making of a Sister-Teacher*, Notre Dame, Ind.: University of Notre Dame Press, 1965.

Consedine, M. Raphael, P. B. V. M. *Listening Journey: A Study of the Spirit and Ideals of Nano Nagle and the Presentation Sisters*, Victoria, Australia: Congregation of the Presentation of the Blessed Virgin Mary, 1983.

Corwin, Ronald G. *Militant Professionalism: A Study of Organizational Conflict in High Schools*, New York: Appleton-Century Crofts, 1970.

Cott, Nancy F. *The Bonds of Womanhood: Woman's Sphere in New England, 1780- 1835*, New Haven: Yale University Press, 1977.

Curti, Merle. *The Social Ideas of American Educators*, Totowa, N.J.: Littlefield, Adams, 1978.

Danton, J. Periam, ed. *The Climate of Book Selection: Social Influences on School and Public Libraries*, Berkeley: University of California School of Librarianship, 1959.

Degler, Carl N. *At Odds: Women and the Family in America from the Revolution to the Present,* New York: Oxford University Press, 1980.

de Tocqueville, Alexis. *Democracy in America,* New York: Alfred A. Knopf, 1945.

Doely, Sara Bentley, ed. *Women's Liberation and the Church: The New Demand for Freedom in the Life of the Christian Church,* New York: Association Press, 1970.

Douglas, Ann. *The Feminization of American Culture,* New York: Alfred A. Knopf, 1978.

Duratschek, Sister M. Claudia, O.S.B. *The Beginnings of Catholicism in South Dakota,* Washington, D.C.: Catholic University of America Press, 1943.

Eckenstein, Lina. *Woman under Monasticism,* New York: Russell and Russell, 1963.

Eisenstein, Hester. *Contemporary Feminist Thought,* Boston: G. K. Hall, 1983.

Ellis, John Tracy. *American Catholicism,* Chicago: University of Chicago Press, 1955.

Elson, Ruth Miller. *Guardians of Tradition: American Schoolbooks of the Nineteenth Century,* Lincoln: University of Nebraska Press, 1964.

Epstein, Barbara Leslie. *The Politics of Domesticity, Women, Evangelism, and Temperance in Nineteenth-Century America,* Middletown, Conn.: Wesleyan University Press, 1981.

Epstein, Cynthia Fuchs. *Woman's Place: Options and Limits in Professional Careers,* Berkeley: University of California Press, 1970.

Etzioni, Amitai, ed. *The Semi-Professions and Their Organization,* New York: Free Press, 1969.

Ewens, Mary, O. P. *The Role of the Nun in Nineteenth-Century America: Variations on the International Theme,* New York: Arno Press, 1976, repr. Salem, N.H.: Ayer Publishers, 1984.

Fallows, Marjorie R. *Irish Americans: Identity and Assimilation,* Englewood Cliffs, N.J.: Prentice-Hall, 1979.

Faragher, John Mack. *Women and Men on the Overland Trail,* New Haven: Yale University Press, 1979.

Feulner, Patricia N. *Women in the Professions: A Social-Psychological Study,* Palo Alto, Calif.: R. and E. Research Associates, 1979.

Fiorenza, Elisabeth Schüssler. *Bread Not Stone: The Challenge of Feminist Biblical Interpretation,* Boston: Beacon Press, 1984.

Fleckenstein, Karl, and Leon Heinz. *Joseph Cardinal Suenens: Open the Frontiers: Conversations with Cardinal Suenens,* New York: Seabury Press, 1981.

Foner, Philip S., and Sally M. Miller, eds. *Kate Richards O'Hare: Selected Writings and Speeches,* Baton Rouge: Louisiana State University Press, 1982.

Freidan, Betty. *The Feminine Mystique,* New York: Dell Publishing, 1963.
———. *The Second Stage,* New York: Summit Books, 1981.

Bibliography

Freidson, Eliot. *Profession of Medicine: A Study of the Sociology of Applied Knowledge,* New York: Dodd, Mead, 1973.

, ed. *The Hospital in Modern Society,* New York: Free Press, 1963.

Friedman, Jean F., and William G. Shade, eds. *Our American Sisters: Women in American Life and Thought,* Lexington, Mass.: D.C. Heath, 1982.

Fromm, Erich. *Escape from Freedom,* New York: Holt, Rinehart and Winston, 1984.

Furniss, W. Todd, and Patricia Albjerg Graham, eds. *Women in Higher Education,* Washington, D.C.: American Council on Education, 1974.

Gilligan, Carol. *In a Different Voice: Psychological Theory and Women's Development,* Cambridge: Harvard University Press, 1982.

Gilmore, Sister Julia, S. C. L. *We Came North: Centennial Story of the Sisters of Charity of Leavenworth,* St. Meinrad, Ind.: Abbey Press, 1961.

Giroux, Henry A. *Ideology, Culture, and the Process of Schooling,* Philadelphia: Temple University Press, 1981.

Goffman, Erving. *Asylums: Essays on the Social Situation of Mental Patients and Other Inmates,* Hawthorne, N.Y.: Aldine Publishing, 1961.

Goldman, Eric F. *Crucial Decade—and After: America, 1945–1960,* New York: Vintage Books, 1956.

Goldman, Marion S. *Gold Diggers and Silver Miners: Prostitution and Social Life on the Comstock Lode,* Ann Arbor: University of Michigan Press, 1981.

Greeley, Andrew M. *From Backwater to Mainstream: A Profile of Catholic Higher Education,* New York: McGraw-Hill Book, 1969.

Griswold, Robert L. *Family and Divorce in California, 1850–1890: Victorian Illusions and Everyday Realities,* Albany: State University of New York Press, 1982.

Gruder, Katherine. *Encyclopedia of Associations,* Detroit: Gale Research, 1987.

Haberman, Martin, and T. M. Stinnett. *Teacher Education and the New Profession of Teaching,* Berkeley: McCutchan Publishing, 1974.

Haberstein, Robert, and Edwin A. Christ. *Professionalizer, Traditionizer, Utilizer: An Interpretive Study of the Work of the General Duty Nurse in Non-Metropolitan Central Missouri General Hospitals,* Columbia: University of Missouri, 1963.

Hageman, Alice L, ed. *Sexist Religion and Women in the Church,* New York: Association Press, 1974.

Harrington, Dolores. *A Woman's Will . . . A Sister's Way, the McKennan Hospital Story, 1911–1961,* Sioux Falls: McKennan Hospital, 1961.

Harris, Barbara J. *Beyond Her Sphere: Women and the Professions in American History,* Westport, Conn.: Greenwood Press, 1978.

Haskell, Thomas L. *The Emergence of Professional Social Science: The American Social Science Association and the Nineteenth-Century Crisis of Authority,* Urbana: University of Illinois Press, 1976.

Hayden, Mary, and George A. Moonan. *A Short History of the Irish People: From the Earliest Times to 1920,* New York: Longmans, Green, 1922.

Hennesey, James, S. J. *American Catholics: A History of the Roman Catholic Community in the United States*, New York: Oxford University Press, 1981.

Hoffman, Nancy. *Woman's "True" Profession: Voices from the History of Teaching*, Old Westbury, N.Y.: Feminist Press, 1981.

Howe, Florence. *Women and the Power to Change*, Berkeley: Carnegie Commission on Higher Education, 1975.

Howick, William H. *Philosophies of Education*, Danville, Ill.: The Interstate Printers and Publishers, 1980.

Hoy, Wayne K., and Cecil G. Miskel. *Educational Administration: Theory, Research, and Practice*, New York: Random House, 1982.

Hughes, Everett C., Helen MacGill Hughes, and Irwin Deutscher. *Twenty Thousand Nurses Tell Their Own Story*, Philadephia: J. B. Lippincott, 1958.

Hurley, Sister Helen Angela. *On Good Ground: The Story of the Sisters of St. Joseph in St. Paul*, Minneapolis: University of Minnesota Press, 1951.

Jackson, J. A., ed. *Professions and Professionalization*, London: Cambridge University Press, 1970.

James, Edward T., ed. *Notable American Women: A Biographical Dictionary*, vols. 1, 2, and 3, Cambridge, Mass.: The Belknap Press, 1971.

James, Janet Wilson., ed. *Women in American Religion*, Philadelphia: University of Pennsylvania Press, 1980.

Jameson, Anna Brownell Murphy. *Sisters of Charity, Catholic and Protestant*, London: Longman, Brown, Green & Longmans, 1855.

Jamieson, Elizabeth, Mary F. Sewall, and Eleanor B. Suhrie. *Trends in Nursing History: Their Social, International, and Ethical Relationships*, Philadelphia: W. B. Saunders, 1966.

Jean, Sister Patricia, S.L. *Only One Heart: The Story of a Pioneer Nun in America*, Garden City, N.Y.: Doubleday, 1963.

Jeffrey, Julie Roy. *Frontier Women: The Trans-Mississippi West, 1840–1880*, New York: Hill and Wang, 1979.

Johnston, S. M. *Builders by the Sea*, Jericho, N.Y.: Exposition Press, 1971.

Johnston, William. *Christian Mysticism Today*, New York: Harper and Row, 1984.

Kaufman, Polly Welts. *Women Teachers on the Frontier*, New Haven: Yale University Press, 1984.

Kelley, Mary, ed. *Woman's Being, Woman's Place: Female Identity and Vocations in American History*, Boston: G. K. Hall, 1979.

Kerber, Linda. *Women of the Republic: Intellect and Ideology in Revolutionary America*, Chapel Hill: University of North Carolina Press, 1980.

Larson, Magali Sarfatt. *The Rise of Professionalism: A Sociological Analysis*, Berkeley: University of California Press, 1977.

Lehman, Andrea, ed. *Peterson's Guide to Two-Year Colleges*, Princeton, N.J.: Peterson's Guides, 1985.

———. *Peterson's Guide to Four-Year Colleges*, Princeton, N.J.: Peterson's Guides, 1985.

Lemlech, Johanna, and Merle B. Marks. *The American Teacher: 1776–1976*, Bloomington, Ind.: Phi Delta Kappa Educational Foundation, 1976.

Lexan, Joan M. *Convent Life: Roman Catholic Religious Orders for Women in North America*, New York: Dial Press, 1964.

Lortie, Dan. *Schoolteacher: A Sociological Study* , Chicago: University of Chicago Press, 1955.

Ludlow, John Malcolm. *Woman's Work in the Church: Historical Notes on Deaconesses and Sisterhoods*, London: Alexander Strahan, 1866, repr., Washington, D.C.: Zenger Publishing, 1978.

Luebke, Frederick C. and Brian W. Blouet, eds. *The Great Plains: Environment and Culture*, Lincoln: University of Nebraska Press, 1979.

Maitland, Sara. *A Map of the New Country: Women and Christianity*, London: Routledge and Kegan Paul, 1983.

Martin, Jane Roland. *Reclaiming a Conversation: The Ideal of the Educated Woman*, New Haven: Yale University Press, 1985.

Mathews, Donald G. *Religion in the Old South*, Chicago: University of Chicago Press, 1977.

McAvoy, Thomas, T., C.S.C. *A History of the Catholic Church in the United States*, Notre Dame: University of Notre Dame Press, 1970.

———. *The Great Crisis in American Catholic History*, Chicago: Henry Regnery, 1957.

McCann, Sister Mary Agnes. *The History of Mother Seton's Daughters: The Sisters of Charity of Cincinnati, Ohio: 1809–1917*, vols. 1, 2, and 3, New York: Longmans, Green, 1917.

McDonald, Sister M. Grace, O. S. B. *With Lamps Burning*, Saint Joseph, Minn.: Saint Benedict's Priory Press, 1957.

McEntee, Sister Mary Veronica, R. S. M. *The Sisters of Mercy of Harrisburg: 1869–1939*, Philadelphia: Dolphin Press, 1939.

McGill, Anna Blanche. *The Sisters of Charity of Nazareth Kentucky*, New York: Encyclopedia Press, 1917.

Melosh, Barbara. *"The Physician's Hand": Work Culture and Conflict in American Nursing*, Philadelphia: Temple University Press, 1982.

Melville, Annabelle M. *Elizabeth Bayley Seton: 1774–1821*, New York: Charles Scribner's Sons, 1951.

Mohr, James C. *Abortion in America: The Origins and Evolution of National Policy* Oxford: Oxford University Press, 1978.

Monroe, Charles R. *Profile of the Community College*, San Francisco: Jossey-Bass, 1977.

Myers, Sandra L. *Westering Women and the Frontier Experience, 1800–1915*, Albuquerque: University of New Mexico Press, 1982.

New Catholic Encyclopedia, New York: McGraw-Hill Book, 1967.

Newcomb, Covelle. *Running Waters*, New York: Dodd, Mead, 1947.

Newman, Cardinal John Henry. *On the Scope and Nature of University Education*, London: J.M. Dent and Sons, 1915.

Norton, Mary Beth. *Liberty's Daughters: The Revolutionary Experience of American Women, 1750–1800*, Boston: Little, Brown, 1980.

311

O'Callaghan, Sister Rosaria. *Flame of Love,* Milwaukee: Bruce Press, 1960.

O'Neill, William L. *Coming Apart: An Informal History of America in the 1960s,* New York: Quadrangle, 1971.

Parnell, D., and J. W. Peltason, eds. *American Community, Technical and Junior Colleges,* New York: Macmillan Publishing, 1984.

Pearson, Jim B., and Edgar Fuller, eds. *Education in the States: Nationwide Development Since 1900,* Washington, D.C.: National Education Association of the United States, 1969.

Power, Eileen. *Medieval Women,* London: Cambridge University Press, 1975.

Pratte, Richard. *Ideology and Education,* New York: David McKay, 1977.

Pulliam, John D. *History of Education in America,* Columbus, Ohio: Charles E. Merrill Publishing, 1976.

Quinn, Bernard, et al., eds. *Churches and Church Membership in the United States, 1980: An Enumeration by Region, State and County Based on Data Reported by 111 Church Bodies,* Atlanta: Glenmary Research Center, 1982.

Ritzer, George. *Man and His Work: Conflict and Change,* New York: Appleton-Century-Crofts, 1972.

Rosenberg, Rosalind. *Beyond Separate Spheres: The Intellectual Roots of Modern Feminism,* New Haven: Yale University Press, 1982.

Rossiter, Margaret. *Women Scientists in America: Struggles and Strategies to 1940,* Baltimore: Johns Hopkins University Press, 1982.

Rudy, Willis. *Higher Education in Transition: A History of American Colleges and Universities, 1936–1976,* New York: Harper and Row, 1976.

Ruether, Rosemary Radford. *Womanguides: Readings Toward a Feminist Theology,* Boston: Beacon Press, 1985.

Ruether, Rosemary Radford, and Rosemary Skinner Keller. eds. *Women and Religion in America,* vol. 1, *The Nineteenth Century, a Documentary History,* New York: Harper and Row, 1981.

Ryan, Mary P. *Cradle of the Middle Class: The Family in Oneida County, New York, 1780–1865,* New York: Cambridge University Press, 1981.

Sandler, Martin W., Edwin C. Rozwenc, and Edward C. Martin. *The People Make a Nation,* vol. 1, Boston: Allyn and Bacon, 1971.

San Giovanni, Lucinda. *Ex-Nuns: A Study of Emergent Role Passage,* Norwood, N.J.: Ablex Publishing, 1978.

Schell, Herbert. *History of South Dakota,* Lincoln: University of Nebraska Press, 1961.

Schlissel, Lillian. *Women's Diaries of the Westward Journey,* New York: Schocken Books, 1982.

Schultz, Harold J. *History of England,* New York: Barnes and Noble, 1968.

Segale, Sister Blandina. *At the End of the Santa Fe Trail,* Milwaukee: Bruce Publishing, 1948.

Shannon, James P. *Catholic Colonization on the Western Frontier,* New Haven: Yale University Press, 1957.

Shaughnessy, Gerald. *Has the Immigrant Kept the Faith? A Study of Im-*

migration and the Catholic Growth in the United States, 1790–1922, New York: Macmillan, 1925.

Sicherman, Barbara, and Carol Hurd Green, eds. *Notable Amerian Women: The Modern Period, A Biographical Dictionary,* Cambridge, Mass.: Belknap Press, 1980.

Sklar, Kathryn Kish. *Catharine Beecher: A Study in American Domesticity,* New Haven: Yale University Press, 1973.

Smigel, Erwin O. *Wall Street Lawyer: Professional Organization Man!* New York: Free Press, 1964.

Sochen, June. *Movers and Shakers: American Women Thinkers and Activities 1900- 1970,* New York: Quandrangle/New York Times Book, 1973.

Stacey, Judith, Susan Béreaud, and Joan Daniels, eds. *And Jill Came Tumbling After: Sexism in American Education,* New York: Dell Publishing, 1974.

Stanton, Elizabeth Cady. *The Woman's Bible: Parts I and II,* New York: European Publishing, 1895, repr., New York: Arno Press, 1972.

Stock, Phyllis. *Better than Rubies: A History of Women's Education,* New York: Putnam, 1978.

Strasser, Susan. *Never Done: A History of American Housework,* New York: Pantheon Books, 1982.

Suenens, Cardinal Leon Joseph. *The Nun in the World: Religious and the Apostolate,* London: Burns and Oates, 1962.

Syasz, Margaret Cornell. *Education and the American Indian: The Road to Self- Determination Since 1928,* Albuquerque: University of New Mexico Press, 1974.

Toffler, Alvin. *The Second Wave,* New York: William Morrow, 1980.

The Official Catholic Directory, 1986, New York: P. J. Kenedy and Sons, 1986.

The Poor Clares of Reparation and Adoration. *Religious Communities in the American Episcopal Church and in the Anglican Church of Canada,* West Park, N.Y.: Holy Cross Press, 1956.

The Way: The Living Bible, Wheaton, Ill.: Tyndale House Publishers, 1972.

Thomas, Sister Evangeline M. *Footprints on the Frontier: A History of the Sisters of Saint Joseph: Concordia Kansas,* Westminster, Md.: Newman Press, 1948.

Tyack, David B. *The One Best System: A History of American Urban Education,* Cambridge, Mass.: Harvard University Press, 1974.

———, ed. *Turning Points in American Educational History,* New York: John Wiley and Sons, 1967.

Tyack, David B., and Elisabeth Hansot. *Managers of Virtue: Public School Leadership in America, 1820–1980,* New York: Basic Books, 1982.

Urban, Wayne J. *Why Teachers Organized,* Detroit: Wayne State University Press, 1982.

Vollmer, Howard M., and Donald L. Mills, eds. *Professionalization,* Englewood Cliffs, N.J.: Prentice-Hall, 1966.

Walsh, James J. *Mother Alphonsa: Rose Hawthorne Lathrop*, New York: Macmillan, 1930.

Walsh, Sister Marie De Lourdes. *The Sisters of Charity of New York: 1809–1959*, vols. 1 and 2, New York: Fordham University Press, 1960.

Walsh, T. J. *Nano Nagle and the Presentation Sisters*, Dublin: M. H. Hill and Son, 1959.

Welter, Barbara. *Dimity Convictions: The American Woman in the Nineteenth Century*, Athens: Ohio University Press, 1976.

The Western Writers of America, eds. *The Women Who Made the West*, Garden City, N.Y.: Doubleday, 1980.

Whyte, William Foote. *The Organization Man*, Garden City, N.Y.: Doubleday, 1957.

Wiebe, Robert H. *The Search for Order, 1877–1920*, New York: Hill and Wang, 1967.

III. Films

Guillford, Andrew, and Randall Teeunen. "Country School Legacy: Humanities on the Frontier" (film funded by Mountain Plains Library Association and the National Endowment for the Humanities and owned by the Plains and Peaks Regional Library System, Colorado Springs, Colo., 1981).

Glossary

Apostolate(s): The avocational mission(s) of a religious order.

Beguine sisterhoods: Cadres of religious women who began organizing in the twelfth century to perform acts of charity. Initially they were described as extra regulars because they occupied a position midway between monastic and lay status.

Breviary: A collection of Psalms, hymns, and prayers. It is an abbreviation of many other books combined into one, referred to as the Divine Office, which is said in religious communities.

Canon Law: Church law.

Cardinal protector: A cardinal whose special responsibility is to represent and attend to the interest of a particular religious institute or pious association.

Confraternity of Christian Doctrine: The Catholic Church's official association of the faithful devoted to the work of religious education.

Corporal penance: Physical suffering endured to show repentance for sin.

Enclosure/unenclosure: The practice of retaining a place (cloister) which no person but a religious may enter and (in totally enclosed orders) from which no member of a given order may depart.

Holy See: A term designating Rome as the bishopric of the pope.

Juniorate directress (mistress): The supervisor and mentor of postulants and novices.

Latin Breviary: The Breviary written in Latin.

Lauds: The first of the seven canonical hours of the Day Office of the Breviary, originally said after Matins. It is an office of praise.

Lay sisters: A term defining women religious who are principally committed to performing the domestic duties of a monastery.

Little Office of the Blessed Virgin Mary: An abridged version of the Common Office of the Blessed Virgin in the Divine Office, used on feasts of Our Lady.

315

Matins: The Night Office of the Breviary, originally said in the middle of the night.

Ministerial professions: Roles (with the exception of the giving of sacraments) that until the latter part of the twentieth century were reserved for priests.

Motherhouse: The headquarters of a community organized with branch houses.

Novice: A person who has been received into the novitiate (by being clothed with the habit) as a candidate for full membership in a religious community.

Parish minister: One who by virtue of her/his office has the care of souls within the precincts of her/his parish.

Plenary council: Comprised of archbishops and bishops of a country or region and presided over by a legate of the Holy See. The council determines matters to be discussed and ratifies decrees.

Pontifical congregation: A congregation of religious whose constitution has been approved by the pope and whose ultimate governance derives from the pope.

Postulant: A person who has been received into the postulancy as a candidate for the habit of a religious community.

Provincial Church council: A consultative and deliberative assembly of bishops and certain other prelates and clerics, convoked in each ecclesiastical province at least every twenty years to discuss and make decrees about pertinent Church matters in a given territory.

Short Breviary: An abridgement of the Breviary that consists of Morning Prayer and Evening Prayer.

Simple vows: Those professed with no reservations; however, a community may dispense them for due cause.

Sisterhood: A title used to designate the member of a community of religious women. Sisters usually dwell in communities, are bound by vows, and are devoted to spiritual and charitable work.

Solemn vows: Those that exist when a community withdraws the right to dispense vows.

Teacherages: Communal living quarters for teachers who work especially in rural areas of the United States. They have been slowly phased out during the mid-twentieth century.

Vows: Promises deliberately made to God and publicly received and recognized by the Church. Nuns usually make religious vows of poverty, chastity and obedience. Religious vows may, under certain circumstances, be declared invalid, commuted, or dispensed.

Sources: *The New Catholic Dictionary* (New York: Van Rees Press, 1929); *The New Catholic Encyclopedia*, vol. 4 (New York: McGraw Hill Book, 1967); The Poor Clares of Reparation and Adoration, *Religious Communities in the American Episcopal Church and in the Anglican Church of Canada* (West Park, N.Y.: Holy Cross Press, 1956).

Index

and nursing degree, 200; and Saint Joseph's Hospital, 212
Daly, Mary, 16, 280
Daly, Sister M. Columbia, 98
Daly, Sister M. Winifred, 102
Daughters of Charity, 5, 11
Davis, Sister Mary Stephen, 87, 183–84
Deaconesses, 257
Deadwood, Dakota Territory, 62
Decree on the Appropriate Renewal of the Religious Life, 233
de Courcy, Father E.S., 107
Delaney, Dr. William A., 171
Delaney, Dr. William II, 263–64
de Lubac, Pere, 232
Dempsey, Sister Anthony, 122, 146
Denis, Sister Mary, 269, 270
Deragisch, Father Joseph, 101
Dewey, John, 81
Di Donato, Sister M. Cabrini, 102, 144, 153, 167, 236
Diphtheria, 15; epidemic of 1900, 164, 165, 276
Dix, Dorothea, 197
Dock, Lavinia Lloyd, 198
Doctors, SDS hospital administrators and, 212–13
Dominican Congregation of Saint Rose of Lima, 226
Dominicans, 258–60
Dominican Sisters, 125, 126, 128
Donnelly, Father Arthur, 59
Dorn, Sister Adrienne, 122
Dougherty, Mary Agnes, 14
Douglas, Ann, 13
Doyle, Sister M. Conception, 208, 209
Dualism, 16
Dudley, Bishop Paul V., 135, 268, 270
Dunn, Sister Frances Mary, 153, 154
Dunphy, Sister Alicia, 147, 152, 213, 214
Duratschek, Sister M. Claudia, 146

Eagen, Father Eugene, 101
Eagle Butte, S.D., 218, 256
Earling, Mrs. (Saint Luke's Hospital administrator), 202
Ecumenical Council, Vatican II, 233–34, 236

Ecumenicism, 17
Educational Association of the Sisters of Mercy, 15
Eisenman, Father Sylvester, 84, 85
Elementary and Secondary Education Act of 1965, 252
Elisabeth of Schnau, Saint, 3
Elson, Dr. Benjamin, 260
Emmitsburg Daughters of Charity, 197
Emmitsburg Sisters of Charity, 9, 11, 14, 197; foundation of, 9
Enclosure, 5, 7, 10, 35, 62, 66, 224, 279; imposed on all religious, 4; SDS permanently dispensed from rule of, 53, 71, 276; SP and, 8; Ursulines and, 5, 7. *See also Apostolicae Sedes*; Council of Trent
Episcopalians. *See* American Episcopal Church
Erne, Sister M. Louise, 125, 255
Escobedo, Dr. Salvador, 269
Evans, Sister Francene, 153, 255
Evans, Sister M. Ruth Ann, 125
Eve, 35, 227, 233, 235, 240, 245, 280–81
Even, Sister M. Robert, 125
Ewens, Mary, 7, 8

Faith and Freedom Series (Sister M. Marguerite), 81
Fargo, Dakota Territory, 63–64, 67
Farrell, Sister Grace, 93, 99, 134
Farrell, Sister Jeanne Marie, 107–8, 124
Farrell, Sister M. Bernadette, 255
Fascism, 232
Feminism, 15–16, 251; nuns and, 15, 235–38; SDS and, 243–44
Fenelon, Cardinal Francois, 34
Fiorenza, Elizabeth Schussler, 17
Fitzgerald, Sister M. Borgia, 98
Fitzgerald, Sister M. Brendan, 106, 107
Fitzgerald, Sister M. Clement, 144
Fitzpatrick, Keith, 134
Flame of Love (O'Callaghan), 124
Fleming, Bishop Michael Anthony, 39
Flexner Report, 199
Flood, Sister Marie Walter, 238
Foffe, Father Chrysostom, 46
Ford Foundation, 179

327

cans, 125; as fund-raisers, 66, 104–5; and German POWs, 177; and government regulatory agencies, 182–83; during Great Depression, 97, 100; habits of, 124, 233, 239, 253; and Holy Rosary Hospital, 172–73; in health care, 164–90, 256, 258–70; and health care apostolate, 164–90; and hospices, 189; and hospital administration, 18, 164–90, 252, 255, 276, 277; hospital nursing schools administered by, 201–20 (see also Presentation Central School of Nursing); and international sisterhood, 243 (see also Sisters of the Presentation of the Blessed Virgin Mary); as journeyman teachers/administrators, 90–98, 100–2, 106–8, 111, 124–27, 129, 132; and Learning Experience Guide, 218–19; and liberation theology, 266; and McKennan Hospital, 174–76; male nurses in hospitals administered by, 209–10, 219; in Mexico, 253, 258–70; ministry of, 189, 252, 254, 256–59, 278; mission activity of, 85 (see also SDS, in Mexico; SDS, among Native Americans); among Native Americans, 253, 254, 255, 256; in New World, 8–9, 11; in 1960s, 120–38; and North Dakota counterparts, 243; and North Dakota faction's separation, 69; and Notre Dame Junior College, 141, 143–48; as nurses, 15, 255, 277; and nurses' training, 141, 144, 148, 151, 176–77, 196–220, 276–78; and orphans, 103–4; and pastoral care, 189, 254, 256-59, 278; as pontifical congregation, 230, 276; and Presentation College, 141, 143–44, 147–60; and Presentation North American Conference, 231; and prison visitation, 252; professional affiliations of, 130, 213, 214; and professionalization, 77–112, 225, 230–31, 275–80; and progressive education, 80–81, 85; as public relations experts, 183–84; as public school teachers, 95; and pursuit of higher education, 102, 109–11, 123; qualifi-

cations for joining, 241–42; relaxation activities of, 99; and "renewal," 18, 237; retirement arrangements of, 242; and Saint Luke's Hospital, 165–69, 170–72; and Saint Mary's Academy, 96–98; and schools of Mitchell, S.D., 90–94; and social work, 252, 253, 255; teaching philosophy of, 77–78, 110–11; today, 19, 251–71; in twentieth century, 88–112; in Washington, D.C., area, 124; in Zambia. *See also* Dakota Sisters of the Presentation of the Blessed Virgin Mary; Irish Sisters of the Presentation of the Blessed Virgin Mary; Sisters of the Presentation of the Blessed Virgin Mary; South Dakota

South Dakota State Board of Nursing Examiners, 202, 203
South Dakota State College, 58, 146; and nursing degree, 201
South Dakota State University, 143
South Dakota Teachers Association, 58
South Indian Congregation, 12
Spalding, Bishop John Lancaster, 9, 56, 67, 78
Stanton, Elizabeth Cady, 16, 235
Staudenraus, Sister M. Eunice, 101
Stein, Dale, 190
Steinman, Sister M. Alexius, 93, 100
Stephan, Father James, 63, 64
Sterilization, 185–86; at Saint Vincent's Hospital, 186
Stock, Minnie Farlin, 63
Stoltz, Sister M. Loretta, 124
Stowe, Harriet Beecher, 13
Strong, Rev. Josiah, 40
Stumpff, Sister M. Annette, 126
Sturzl, Mary, 135
Sturzl, Sister Joseph Ann (JoAnn), 120, 135–36, 188, 190, 239, 268
Suenens, Leon Joseph Cardinal, 80, 238
Suffrage, women's, 56–57
Suffragists, 57
Sullivan, Sister M. Cecelia, 95, 98
Sullivan, Sister M. Mildred, 101
Supreme Court, U.S.; rulings of relative to Church, 81
Sutherland, Dorothy, 270

SUSAN CAROL PETERSON is an assistant professor of history at the University of North Dakota in Grand Forks. She has a Ph.D. in history from Oklahoma State University and is the author of numerous articles and essays on the roles that nuns, women teachers, and missionaries played in Western history.

COURTNEY ANN VAUGHN-ROBERSON earned her undergraduate degree from the University of Kansas and her graduate degrees from Oklahoma State University. She has published articles in journals such as *History of Higher Education Annual, Pacific Historical Review, Great Plains Quarterly,* and *Issues in Education.* She and Susan Peterson are at work on a study of women and men in teaching and nursing in the American West.